Buddha Is Hiding

CALIFORNIA SERIES IN PUBLIC ANTHROPOLOGY

The California Series in Public Anthropology emphasizes the anthropologist's role as an engaged intellectual. It continues anthropology's commitment to being an ethnographic witness, to describing, in human terms, how life is lived beyond the borders of many readers' experiences. But it also adds a commitment, through ethnography, to reframing the terms of public debate—transforming received, accepted understandings of social issues with new insights, new framings.

Series Editor: Robert Borofsky (Hawaii Pacific University)

Contributing Editors: Philippe Bourgois (UC San Francisco),
Paul Farmer (Partners in Health), Rayna Rapp (New York University),
and Nancy Scheper-Hughes (UC Berkeley)

University of California Press Editor: Naomi Schneider

Buddha Is Hiding

Refugees, Citizenship, the New America

Aihwa Ong

UNIVERSITY OF CALIFORNIA PRESS

Berkeley   Los Angeles   London

University of California Press
Berkeley and Los Angeles, California

University of California Press, Ltd.
London, England

Library of Congress Cataloging-in-Publication Data

Ong, Aihwa.
    Buddha is hiding : refugees, citizenship, the new America /
Aihwa Ong.
        p.   cm.—(California series in public anthropology ; 5)
    Includes bibliographical references and index.
    ISBN 0-520-22998-3 (cloth : alk. paper)—ISBN 0-520-23824-9
    (pbk. : alk. paper)
    1. Cambodian Americans—California—Oakland—Social
conditions.   2. Cambodian Americans—California—Oakland—
Ethnic identity.   3. Cambodian Americans—Civil rights—
California—Oakland.   4. Refugees—California—Oakland—
Social conditions.   5. Refugees—Civil rights—California—
Oakland.   6. Citizenship—Social aspects—United States—Case
studies.   7. Oakland (Calif.)—Social conditions.   8. Oakland
(Calif.)—Ethnic relations.   I. Title.   II. Series.
F869.02B83   2003
305.895'93079466—dc21   2003001857

Manufactured in the United States of America

13   12   11   10   09   08   07   06   05   04
10   9   8   7   6   5   4   3

The paper used in this publication is both acid-free and totally
chlorine-free (TCF). It meets the minimum requirements of
ANSI/NISO Z39.48–1992 (R 1997) (*Permanence of Paper*).

For Bob

CONTENTS

ILLUSTRATIONS

ACKNOWLEDGMENTS

Two small grants from the University of California—a research fellowship from the office of the president of the University of California, and a Gender Institute fund—helped launch this study on Southeast Asian refugees.

A Rockefeller Foundation Gender Roles Program grant made possible more sustained fieldwork in the early 1990s. In the course of writing this book on and off over the past ten years, I have benefited from the support and advice of many individuals. I am indebted to Brackette F. Williams, friend and interlocutor, who read many drafts of the book. Her advice and references on the history of race in America were especially penetrating and useful. From a different direction, discussions with Pheng Cheah helped orient my own argument on the changing meaning and basis of citizenship. I am grateful to Judy Ledgerwood for her comments on Cambodian history and culture, and to Kathryn Poethig and Lindsay French for sharing their insights on the experiences of Cambodian refugees. Earlier versions of some chapters were read by Lawrence Cohen, Donna Goldstein, and Anna Tsing. Finally, I must mention the enthusiastic support of Robert Borofsky, the series editor of Public Anthropology, and Naomi Schneider of the University of California Press. I of course bear full responsibility for errors of judgment and interpretation.

As always, my husband, Robert R. Ng, fourth-generation American, has been a wonderful supporter—a technical wizard, giver of music and humor, and partner in life's adventures. Our children, Pamela and Benjamin, have made possible our living life in full.

A.O.
Berkeley, May 2002

PROLOGUE

In the fall of 1970, I left Malaysia and arrived as a college freshman in New York City. I was immediately swept up in the antiwar movement. President Nixon had just begun his "secret" bombing of Cambodia. Joining crowds of angry students marching down Broadway, I participated in the takeover of the East Asian Institute building on the Columbia University campus. As I stood there confronting policemen in riot gear, I thought about what Southeast Asia meant to the United States. Were Southeast Asians simply an anonymous mass of people in black pajamas? Southeast Asia was a far-off place where America was conducting a savage war, supposedly against communism. American lives were being lost, and so were those of countless Vietnamese, Cambodians, Laotians, and others.

This rite of passage into American society was to shape my attitude about U.S. citizenship. As a foreign student, I was at a disadvantage, ineligible for most loans, fellowships, and jobs. My sister, a naturalized American, could have sponsored me for a green card, but the bombing of Cambodia, symptomatic of a wider disregard for my part of the world, made American citizenship a difficult moral issue for me.

.   .   .

More than a decade later, when I moved to the San Francisco Bay Area, I encountered refugees fresh from Indochina. As a new mother, I was grappling again with the meanings of citizenship. My son's birth engendered a new struggle with the moral implications of becoming a naturalized citizen. Becoming American is bigger than merely acquiring a new legal status, or the right to vote in the United States. We are told that "Citizenship is one of the greatest privileges the United States confers upon alien-born residents," but becoming "naturalized" entails an inexplicable loss in exchange for a kind of dubious freedom, and an even more complicated sense of self for someone already multicultural and transnational in practice. Out of curiosity about what becoming American might mean for others, I dropped in on citizenship classes in Oakland's Chinatown. Old women, more gamely than the old men they outnumbered, struggled with English along with memorizing the various branches of the government, the names of past presidents and important officials in California, and absorbing a grandiose view of freedom and its limitless possibilities. The would-be citizens were preparing for what was probably the most important test in their lives, because acquiring American citizenship meant the right to send for sons, daughters, grandchildren, and siblings still in the home country. Sitting in the class, I wondered whether becoming citizens as a consequence of an American war might be a rather different experience for refugees from Southeast Asia.

In the past few decades, perhaps since the end of the Vietnam (or Indochina) War, the patriotic language used to analyze citizenship has given way to more specific concerns about the government of an ever-changing population. How can citizenship be explored when it is lived in an age not of heroic sacrifices, but of pragmatic considerations about productivity and profits? How have the inroads of American neoliberalism transformed this practical notion of citizenship? In *Flexible Citizenship,* I suggest that new affluent Asian immigrants—relocating their families and wealth to North America, while pursuing business interests in Asia—represent a new kind of disembedded citizenship.[1] This is a parallel study of the "other Asians"— Southeast Asian war refugees—who flowed in at roughly the same time, and it will focus on the practices that embed these newcomers in specific contexts of subject-making. For disadvantaged newcomers, citizenship is not a matter of acquiring multiple passports or identifying business opportunities, real estate deals, or top universities in global cities, but rather a matter of figuring out the rules for coping, navigating, and surviving the streets and other public spaces of the American city. These immigrants are subjected, in a much more persistent way than are the privileged ones, to the variety of human technologies that conspire, not entirely successfully, to make them particular kinds of ethnic minorities, laboring subjects, and moral beings.

The research on which this study is based began as a series of forays into Southeast Asian communities in the mid 1980s. From spring 1988 until fall 1989, I conducted sustained research among Cambodian refugees in Oakland and San Francisco. At that time, there were approximately fifteen thousand Cambodians in the San Francisco Bay Area.[2] Not having been trained as an anthropologist of Cambodia, and lacking prior connections to the community, I depended heavily on the help, goodwill, and skills of three Khmer-speaking assistants at different points of the research. I am most grateful to Katharya Um, then a graduate student in political science and now an associate professor of ethnic studies at the University of California at Berkeley. My other assistants were Maelady Kim, a health worker and translator at the Children's Hospital in Oakland, and Vannari Om, an outreach worker. Ms. Kim and Ms. Om put me in contact with most of the research subjects, accompanying me on household visits and patiently translating the interviews. Ms. Um also assisted in some visits, but she mainly helped by transcribing tapes of interviews, rendering the Khmer into precise English. I am grateful for the help given by these three, for there would have been no study without their sympathetic interest, contacts, and excellent service as mediators.

The study population was divided into three parts: Cambodian families in two low-income housing projects in Oakland, a self-help group in a poor neighborhood in San Francisco, and other informants who had moved out of the inner city and were engaged in middle-class occupations. Altogether, I surveyed sixty households to ascertain family composition, education, household budget, and social networks. I gathered life histories of twenty women, from their lives in Cambodia to their experiences in California.

I relied on Cambodians in Oakland and San Francisco to tell me their stories of flight and adjusting to a new life in America. The majority of Cambodians I met in the Bay Area originally came from small towns and villages all over Cambodia and had fled to the Thai border in the northwest after the Vietnamese invasion in January 1979. Some came from Cambodian communities in South Vietnam, and a handful were survivors of the 1975 forced trek from Phnom Penh. After the Vietnamese invasion of 1979 dispersed the Khmer Rouge forces, many refugees eventually arrived in Khao-I-Dang (KID), the official United Nations holding center for Cambodians just inside the Thai border.[3]

Many of the Cambodians I interviewed had rural or small-town origins, and only a few had been educated beyond grade school. Some had been middle-class professionals such as teachers, soldiers, and monks, and a few were Sino-Cambodians from the urban merchant class. Professionals and ethnic Chinese were often singled out for execution by the Khmer Rouge, who had a rabid hatred of intellectuals and so-called capitalist traders. Because the survivors of these upheavals were predominantly female, most of my subjects were middle-aged or older women. I met and conversed with women mainly in their homes; approximately one-third of the families I got to know were headed by widows or divorcees.[4]

I also met and interviewed refugee workers, service providers, nurses, bureaucrats, priests, and others in the wider society with whom Cambodian refugees come into daily contact. During the same period, I also conducted research among affluent Chinese immigrants; some of my findings are discussed in the final chapter, which situates the Cambodian experiences within the larger context of new Asian immigrants in California.

The research was conducted intermittently, while juggling work and family obligations, and without actually leaving home for extended periods of time, as conventional fieldwork requires. Instead, the terrain of my fieldwork in the larger sense is also the space of my current home and country. In this kind of "commuter fieldwork,"[5] I spent much time figuring out the logistics of research, and I came to focus mainly on informants who could be reached by commuter trains and by car trips that did not take more than three hours each way. I also made special trips to Merced and Sacramento to visit Southeast Asian refugees, including the Mien and the Hmong, who have settled in California's Central Valley.

I relied more on interviews and less on participation than I would have liked, but I did visit people's homes, service offices, and clinics; attended weddings; and went to church with Cambodian informants. Contemporary anthropology is characterized (I hope!) by respect for people's privacy, and one would not expect to be intruding into people's lives and observing them outside of carefully defined schedules. I spent weekends and the summer months pursuing remaining questions. I had marvelous access to Cambodian Americans, especially to women who, despite their past ordeals and hard present lives, were warm and gracious in welcoming my intrusions. Once they learned I was not part of any state agency, many (primarily middle-aged and older women) were eager to talk about their families, losses, and current difficulties in the United States. On many occasions I and my research assistants, sitting on floor mats, spent hours listening to tales of brutality, large and small, and crying along with the refugees. They wanted their stories told, in the words of a Cambodian woman, "so that Americans know how we suffer." She meant not only their experiences during the war years, but also the difficulties encountered in the process of becoming American.

Beyond the mass-media images of sudden death syndrome, bride kidnaps, street gangs, and now soul loss, Southeast Asian refugees are among the most invisible groups in the North American consciousness.[6] For some reason, these images—mainly associated with the Hmongs—have become the markers of Southeast Asian Americans (a term that is in itself problematic). Here, I consider how Cambodian refugees came to interpret, embrace, and critique in different contexts of everyday life what they perceived being an American kind of person to be all about. There is a widespread sense that the experiences with the Pol Pot regime, flight from Cambodia, and learning to live in America have put into abeyance Khmer-Buddhist values of compassion and reciprocity, as well as continuities with the past. As a Cambodian monk living in a Californian farming community expressed it, "Buddha appears to be in hiding" for many survivors and their children. The Pol Pot regime overturned the Buddhist world in Cambodia. In the United States, the exigencies of coping and getting through life have conspired to keep Buddha from reappearing fully in the lives of Cambodian Americans. At the center of it all is a shift of ethical regimes as these refugees are compelled to construct and contest a new sense of self in different domains of American life.

I study the idea of citizenship not only in the idiom of rights articulated in the legal context, but also in the context of the ways in which a set of common (in this case American) values concerning family, health, social welfare, gender relations, and work and entrepreneurialism are elaborated in everyday lives. These values are part of the biopoliticization of American life, wherein the individual is the bearer of sovereignty. I thus focus on everyday processes of being-made and self-making in various domains of administration, welfare, church, and working life. Taking citizenship as a social process of mediated production of values concerning freedom, autonomy, and security, I explore the interconnected everyday issues involved in shaping poor immigrants' ideas about what being American might mean, and how newcomers may be also active participants within institutional constraints and possibilities. In official and public domains—refugee camps, the welfare state, the court system, community hospitals, local churches, and civic organizations—refugees become subjects of norms, rules, and systems, but they also modify practices and agendas while nimbly deflecting control and interjecting critique.

Obviously, there are many areas of these immigrants' lives in which they do not deal with service agents or with key institutions of American society, and other kinds of self-formation occur outside of those institutional webs of power relations. My goal is not to give a rounded ethnographic portrayal of Cambodian refugees in the final decades of the twentieth century. Rather, I consider their encounters with the welfare state, the community hospital, the courthouse, the church, and the marketplace as everyday processes of making and self-making that have roots in the experiences of earlier generations of urban migrants, especially African Americans. To become "good enough" citizens, newcomers must negotiate among different forms of regulation, and be taught a new way of being cared for and of caring for themselves in their new world.

What key cultural values, codes, and rules are internalized and contested in the process of learning to belong? This process is influenced by polarizing concepts of whitening and blackening that are traceable to the process of differentiation that took place between European settlers and Native Americans, and has subsequently been deployed flexibly in later formations of ethnic-group models, including interactions with African Americans and Asian immigrants. Bipolarism also works to create distinctions within racial categories, so that stratifications have emerged within the diverse populations of Asian ancestry, separating those new Asian Americans who get to become white from those who do not.

Thus while this book is focused on the daily experiences of Cambodian refugees, it is also a rumination on the wider implications of American citizenship for the poor, and on the country's shifting sense of who are deserving and undeserving citizen-subjects. Today, Asia is the leading source of immigrants to the United States, and new arrivals continue to face the legacy of orientalism that developed from American domination of Asia during the past hundred years. Especially at the petty-official level, as well as in public life, poor Asian newcomers in particular experience a continuity of policy and practice that promotes "ethnic cleansing," in the sense of removing the features of immigrants' supposedly primitive cultures that are socially determined to be undesirable. Institutional policies of assimilation, ethnic reformation, and erasure are variously taken up by social workers, nurses, the police, church workers, and teachers, who make available the opportunity to enact what count as American values—personal autonomy, self-centeredness, greed, and materialism—in a land of many possibilities. Although Cambodian refugees come from a historical and cultural trajectory that is radically different from those of other Americans, there are remarkable continuities and similarities with the experiences of stigmatization and regulation experienced by generations of poor African Americans and immigrants from Latin America as well as those from Asia.

At the same time, the interpretations and strategies of refugee-clients who experienced and acted on these policies reveal similarities among inner-city minorities in their forms of adaptation and critique. Cambodian refugees adopted some of the available materials and alternative views of family and life, but they also declined others. There is an interesting continuum of practices between children of earlier Asian immigrants, who broker relations and discipline the poor Asian newcomers, and the Cambodian refugees' strategies of negotiation, evasion, and struggle. First, to what extent do the processes of citizenship-making succeed in changing or removing the supposedly undesirable characteristics of Cambodian cultural ways, and to what extent do they fail? What kinds of moral quandaries do these new immigrants feel, and how are their experiences different from those of state agents, or from those of the children of earlier generations of immigrants, who are themselves struggling with a similar set of practical and moral issues relating to ethnicity formation and livelihood? Second, in what ways do Cambodian cultural values modify or deflect the agendas of social programs? How do Southeast Asian refugees respond differently from the new Asian business immigrants to lessons in self-government and economic instrumentality? Such questions destabilize homogenizing notions about the Asian American community and even the so-called underclass. They suggest that globalization has given rise to a new kind of Asian *homo economicus* alongside the exploited Asian worker—the ethical poles of a citizenship topography produced by transnational assemblages of capitalism.

.   .   .

In the fall of 1987, on a rainy afternoon, I was called to take my citizenship test in an office of the Immigration and Naturalization Services in San Francisco. My examiner happened to be Vietnamese American, perhaps a newly minted official, whose English was still rough and uncertain. When my name was called, I stepped up to his desk, but before I could prop my umbrella against the chair and remove my damp raincoat, he barked at me to stand straight and raise my right hand. He curbed his contempt when he read the line that indicated my profession, a professor. Then, with some chagrin, he led me through a perfunctory review of questions about the president, Congress, and the Bill of Rights. Perhaps, I thought to myself, I had been right to have deferred this process for seventeen years (and, ironically, had done so fundamentally as a protest against the Vietnam War). My husband is a fourth-generation Chinese American (California native), after all, but it was not until I became a mother that I decided, with some qualms, to commit myself to my children's future. I could not decide whether the curt, military treatment was a routine part of the dominating process one must experience in order to be considered eligible, especially for the nonwhite foreigner. Nor could I disentangle this ritual humiliation from the official's instant judgment about my social standing, my "race," my gender, and my body. His job was after all about policing the national body and subordinating the deviant other who may attempt to gain entry. Two years later, pregnant and holding the hand of my three-year-old son, I attended a swearing-in ceremony at the Greek Theater on the Berkeley campus. The excited crowds, stirring speeches, blaring music, bursts of laughter, and balloons bobbing in the blue sky could not quite eclipse the memory of that day in the INS office. After that, I suppose, I couldn't not write this book, as a testament to the existentialist paradox of citizenship.

Introduction

Government and Citizenship

When I moved from Massachusetts to California in the early 1980s, at a time in which the American public saw Asian Americans as people largely of Chinese, Japanese, or Korean ancestry, I was struck by the range of peoples from the Asia Pacific who lived here. Geopolitical conflicts and economic globalization made the 1980s an especially turbulent era for global population flows, as rising tides of immigrants from Latin America and Asia flocked to urbanized countries. In the San Francisco Bay Area, *people of color* took on new dimensions of meaning and entangled possibilities. Taiwanese computer programmers and Indian engineers were becoming the norm in the computer companies that had already begun to change aspects of the global economy. But what struck me even more forcibly were the Mayan Indians, still wrapped in their colorful clothes, working in English gardens, and the sarong-clad and turban-wearing Laotians shopping at the neighborhood market. Amid the orchards and fields of California's Central Valley, where Mexican farmworkers predominated, Southeast Asian refugees tended pockets of onions and herbs. Gujeratis from India had begun to control the motel business, Asian-operated restaurants were hiring Hispanic busboys, and electronics factories were becoming dependent on Bengali and Vietnamese workers.

As someone who came from Southeast Asia, I tend to consider the Vietnam War as the actual and symbolic starting point for the reshaping of America as a Pacific nation. The withdrawal of U.S. troops from mainland Southeast Asia was in a sense the beginning of the end of the cold war. Streams of war refugees from the region escaped over land and sea, many perishing along the way. Those who survived were ultimately sent, by way of border camps, to Australia, Western Europe, and the United States. Wars in Sri Lanka, Afghanistan, Ethiopia, and Central America sent more waves of refugees to the same destinations. The flow of Asian newcomers to the American West Coast and the Southwest was exceeded only by the influx of Central American refugees and migrant workers.[1] Coincidentally, the electronics revolution in California intensified demands for Asian capital and expertise.

The eighties thus witnessed diverse streams of Asian immigrants—war refugees and business managers, technology workers and investors, mountain people and university graduates. Asian Americans now represent more than 11 percent of the population in California. The San Francisco Bay Area is home to more than a million Asian Americans.[2] Newspapers have pointed to the increasing number of wealthy and skilled immigrants from Taiwan, China, India, and South Korea who constitute an upwardly mobile or upper-class fraction of Asian Americans. The media also cover those "other Asians"—Cambodians, Laotians, and Mien—not so much identified with their high-tech expertise as with their "high fertility rates."[3] This book focuses on those other Asians.

CITIZENSHIP VIA EXCLUSION, SUCCESSION, AND DIFFERENCE

For some time now, American citizenship has been a subject of intense debate. Scholars have moved inevitably beyond a narrow focus on citizenship as a set of legal rights—either you have it or you don't—to a consideration of group membership that includes a variety of citizens and noncitizens. There are citizens (native and naturalized), and there are holders of green cards and legal refugees who will probably eventually apply for naturalization. Then there is a growing category of holders of temporary visas—skilled workers on H-1B visas, students, and contract migrant laborers. Finally, there are illegal residents, foreigners without papers who nevertheless live and work as part of U.S. society. Great waves of migrations from Latin America and Asia, the mobility of business travelers and students, and the ever-growing number of individuals with dual citizenship add up to a society of astonishing flux and diversity. The substance—the marrow, the soul, and the ethics—of American citizenship is in a prolonged crisis. As the model of adherence to a single cultural nationality wanes, a steady "desacralization" of state membership takes place.[4] Concomitantly, there has been a shift in the focus of discussions about citizenship from concerns with political practice based on shared civic rights and responsibilities to an insistence on the protection of minority rights. Prominent liberal political theorists argue that liberalism needs to protect minorities as a matter of both justice and self-interest.[5]

But the current debate about multiculturalism cannot ignore the persistence of problematic, partial concepts of American citizenship that have been a source of struggle for earlier generations of American immigrants. Alexis de Tocqueville, whose point of view has influenced generations of thinkers, explored the contradiction between the grand visions and practices of democracy, on the one hand, and the threat posed by the "tyranny of the majority" to the rights and freedoms of minorities on the other.[6] Max Weber worried about the effects of Puritanism and rationalized capitalism (which, he argued, found its highest expression in America) on the poor and on social altruism.[7] Concerns about majority rule and discrimination against the poor are basic themes in this tradition, and there is also an array of studies on the effects of racial exclusion, class inequality, and gender discrimination on equal access to social status, jobs, political representation, and human dignity. Reginald Horsman argues that the formation of the concept of an Anglo-Saxon race was historically the central impetus to the nation's emergence, and that national myths about American exceptionalism—progress, prosperity, and freedom—cannot be disentangled from exclusions and marginalizations based on race.[8] In *American Citizenship,* Judith Shklar remarks, "The tension between an acknowledged ideology of equal political rights and a deep and common desire to exclude and reject large groups of human beings from citizenship has marked every stage of history of American democracy."[9] The extensive scholarship on exclusions based on race, class, and gender has defined and configured contemporary thinking about the deep inequalities at the heart of American democracy. Historians have studied how the racial logic that originated in the exclusion of Native Americans was used to marginalize generations of African Americans and came to shape their race and class positions on a grid of citizenship.[10] Similarly, feminists have argued that poor women have long been excluded from social citizenship because of unequal treatment under the law, and even by the inadequate protection afforded by the modern welfare state.[11]

For minorities and immigrants, the meaning of achieving citizenship has long rested on a set of expectations that scholars refer to as ethnic succession. More a structure of beliefs than an empirical reality, ethnic succession is a set of expectations that in a just and moral world, ethnic minorities will attain entry to the mainstream of American society through gains achieved in successive generations. According to this concept, the legacy of having been exploited and the desire that future generations be able to build on their achievements, especially in defending the meaning of free labor, are what encouraged earlier workers to lay claim to communal or ethnic identification. Both African American and first and second generations of immigrants were forced to work in dangerous and poorly paid jobs in growing cities and industrial settings. Their periodic protests and eventual union organization changed the quality and conditions of work in these locales.[12] Having made important contributions across generations, and thus being owed a moral debt by society, minorities and ethnic immigrants believed that they had earned the right to become full citizens.[13] The model of ethnic succession holds that as the moral capital of suffering and contribution is built up from generation to generation, each minority or immigrant group should be absorbed into a higher social rank. As members of that group also improve materially in class terms, they should become equal citizens with mainstream whites.[14] The idealism associated with ethnic succession thus celebrates the promise of American citizenship, while also critiquing the failure of society to meet that egalitarian democratic vision. Achieving citizenship is an unending process of struggle against undemocratic exclusions based on ethnicity and race, with the assumption that the social status of a particular minority group will improve over time with cumulative increases in experiences of adversity and material gains, and will in turn lift up the individuals belonging to that group.

The recent book *Immigrant America* by Alejandro Portes and Ruben G. Rumbaut is a prime example of applying this model, of exclusion gradually yielding to acceptance, to the rate of naturalization and political incorporation of various types of immigrant groups. According to Portes and Rumbaut, the moral project of citizenship is threatened by the very groups who once were immigrants: "The political debate about immigration in the United States has always been marked by vigorous calls for restriction. The most ardent advocates of this policy are often children of immigrants who wear their second-generation patriotism outwardly and aggressively. This position forgets that it was the labor and efforts of immigrants—often the parents and grandparents of today's restrictionists—that made much of the prosperity of the nation possible."[15] The anti-immigrant ideological position seeks to deny ethnic succession to later waves of immigrants, foreign-born people who could otherwise claim to deserve citizenship for the same reason, the suffering of earlier generations. The periodic "nativist movements" against allowing certain categories of foreign-born individuals to qualify for ethnic-succession opportunities have motivated the formation of panethnic coalitions based on broader demographic characteristics of class, labor, and lifestyle orientation.[16]

In recent decades, then, the denial of the symbolics of suffering to certain groups has shifted minority struggles away from assimilation and toward an insistence on cultural difference, and the full inclusion of difference in our notion of American citizenship. For instance, in the late 1980s, the very visible politicized street theater of gay activism demanded public acceptance of difference in sexual orientation as a moral right. In an increasingly open and multicultural America constantly replenished by immigrants, the view of America as a single cultural nation—white Anglo-Saxon, (Judeo-)Christian, and heterosexual—could no longer be sustained. Inspired as well by African American civil rights struggles since the 1960s, gay proponents of what has been called "the politics of recognition" demanded public acknowledgment of cultural diversity. Building on the notion that contribution earns worthy citizenship, one early tactic was that of closeted gay individuals "coming out"; the intention was to expose to society examples of "worthy" persons who had suffered as a result of social discrimination, bias, and ignorance of their complex role in society. The gay rights movement also stressed the middle-class notions of self-realization and accomplishment as criteria for inclusion in the full benefits of citizenship. Charles Taylor's seminal essay argues that equal rights are realized only when there is mutual respect for cultural difference, putting into practice the promise of liberalism for nurturing the modern, authentic self.[17]

A parallel battle for inclusion is being waged by low-skilled and poor newcomers whose cultural differences do not quite fit middle-class forms or norms. In California, activist Chicano scholar-advocates such as Renato Rosaldo define cultural citizenship as "the right to be different" (in terms of race, ethnicity, or native language) with respect to the norms of the dominant national community, without compromising one's right to belong, in the sense of participating in the nation-state's democratic processes. The enduring exclusions of the color line often deny full citizenship to Latinos and other peoples of color. From the point of view of subordinate communities, cultural citizenship offers the possibility of legitimizing demands made in the struggle to enfranchise themselves. These demands can range from legal, political, and economic issues to "matters of human dignity, well-being, and respect."[18] Rosaldo and others point to the political and economic constraints underpinning claims to cultural citizenship. For instance, laws controlling the "normal" timing and use of public spaces conform to middle-class norms but undermine the civil rights of immigrant workers who cannot avail themselves of the public spaces in the same way because of work-schedule constraints and noise-level concerns. There is a sense that dominant norms discriminate against the cultural difference of new immigrants, whose cultural expressions are at variance with those norms and with middle-class sensibilities. Indeed, middle-class Americans seek to maintain their comfort level by encoding white–black oppositions in behavioral and discursive strategies that draw lines against those perceived to be culturally deviant.[19] These semiconscious codes are exquisitely clear to newcomers and are part of the everyday experience of minorities and immigrants as they learn to negotiate rules of belonging that are taken for granted by the mainstream.

These lines of inquiry—exclusion on the basis of race, culture, and class; ethnic-succession beliefs that shape the minoritization process; and the valorization of cultural difference among minority groups—have dominated recent studies of American citizenship. Given that analytical categories of culture have been insufficiently problematized, claims about the cultural difference of minorities seem to suggest that "culture" has remained the same despite experiences of dislocation, generational fractures, and upward mobility over time in the American nation. Furthermore, calls by minority groups for a unilateral claim of cultural citizenship seem informed by the view that cultural difference is only a bottom-up construction, and somehow

ɔf regulation from above. That naïveté can end up supporting domi-
ideologies that rank individuals on the basis of culture, race, and ethnicity, thereby facilitating the cultural or ethno-racial inscription of individual
achievements and failures. While the prevailing pluralist discourse accepts
"difference" as an object of analysis, I argue that "culture" (or "race," "ethnicity," or "gender") is not the automatic or even the most important analytical domain in which to understand how citizenship is constituted. Rather,
what matters is to identify the various domains in which these preexisting
racial, ethnic, gender, and cultural forms are problematized, and become
absorbed and recast by social technologies of government that define the
modern subject.

In this book, I examine the technologies of government—that is, the policies, programs, codes, and practices (unbounded by the concept of culture)
that attempt to instill in citizen-subjects particular values (self-reliance, freedom, individualism, calculation, or flexibility) in a variety of domains. What
is at stake is the definition of the modern *anthropos* or human being by rational forms and techniques that converge in an identifiable problem-space.
My questions include: What are the effects of everyday techniques of government in various settings—Pol Pot's labor camps, refugee sanctuaries, the
American welfare state, community hospitals, and so on? What preformed
racial and cultural categories are mobilized and deployed, and how are they
encoded and recast in the service of producing normative values and behaviors among target populations? What are the counterstrategies and ethical
reflections of citizen-subjects who evade, subvert, or criticize such rationalities (i.e., instrumental actions or reasonings) and practices of regulation?
Finally, what are the effects of neoliberal borderless rationality in transforming the symbol and substance of American citizenship?

At a broad level, I have followed Cambodian refugees in their transitions
through different modalities of government—the Buddhist absolutism of
modern Cambodia, the policing state of the Khmer Rouge, the mediating
world of refugee camps, and the advanced liberal democracy of the United
States. Each context calls for a different modality of what it means to be
human and of how life is valued and classified in relation to political calculations about labor, ethics, and the economy. I examine the practical problems of government in each domain in turn (welfare state, community hospital, court system, and so on), following Cambodian Americans as they make
their way through the institutional contexts that teach them the values and
technical competence expected in America. I investigate how human technologies regarding ethics, the body, race, religion, gender, and labor converge and function in constituting particular categories of citizen-subjects.
I identify as well the everyday practices of subjects who are acted upon and
who act on their own behalf in pursuing values and assets that may contra-
dict the ones assigned to them by the prevailing norms. For the refugees in

this study, the tension between the American stress on individualism, pragmatism, and materialism on the one hand, and the Khmer-Buddhist ethos of compassionate hierarchy, collectivism, and otherworldliness on the other, is a central dynamic in the ethical project of becoming citizens.

American notions of the ideal citizen are linked to the concept of the bourgeois individual—an observation made by Max Weber[20]—and these notions are embedded in a variety of official programs and unofficial practices that participate in governing subjects. Michel Foucault's work on the social technologies of governmentality—which he defines as "the conduct of conduct"—provides an analytical basis for examining the everyday techniques of being-made and of self-making in a variety of regulatory environments.[21] He argues that advanced liberal societies tend to depend on regulation rather than discipline; they rely on human-science policy and techniques to "govern through freedom," thereby inducing citizen-subjects to become self-motivated, self-reliant, and entrepreneurial.[22] For Cambodian immigrants, as it was for earlier generations of American urban migrants, the transition from a religion-inflected ethos of hierarchy and dependency to an ethics of individualistic striving and wealth making is a profoundly unsettling experience, and one they are ambivalent about. A study of the human technologies of citizen-making thus reveals the religious and ethical underpinnings of political calculations about bodies and humanity, and shows how the processes of freedom often depend on means of subjection. My intention is to bring into focus the ambiguities and the ambivalence about losses and gains that suffuse the practices whereby individuals both produce and shape their lives as particular kinds of American citizens.

FROM CHAIN OF BEING TO THE GOVERNMENT OF LIFE

Concepts of political identity from the earliest times have almost all been based on religious continuums of greater or less moral privilege or worthiness. In feudal Europe, the great chain of being linked the lowliest serf, through his lord, to the king, who embodied the supreme Christian power.[23] In the Middle Ages, the institutions of the state were closely identified with religious values and structures. In premodern China, a Confucian ethics-regulated society was presided over by a Son of Heaven (the emperor) who might lose the mandate of heaven if the multitude of his subjects, perceiving that he had lost his virtue, instigated rebellion.[24] In premodern mainland Southeast Asia, the Theravada-Buddhist law of karma defined the social tiers of king, aristocrats, the monastic order (sangha), and peasants. The spiritual hierarchy was based on different rates of embodiment of religious merit; the king by definition had accumulated the most meritorious acts in previous lives.[25] Thus, in many parts of the premodern world, religious beliefs and practices determined political schemes of enchained beings.

The modern period signaled a reworking of such religiously based no-tions of political subjection, as the rise of the secular state incorporated many of the key legal and political features of Christian ethics. A new concept of individualism based on natural law came to stress the interiorization of this-worldly freedom by self-sufficient and individual men of reason.[26] In a model of popular sovereignty, every member of civil society was held to be an equal partner, sharing the same universal rights in the political state.[27] Of course, such rights were illusory for many because the practical application of lib-erty was to hold private property, thus excluding those who did not own commodities (including, for some, ownership of themselves). Marx observed that the modern state gave rise to "an independent and egoistic individual" in isolated pursuit of economic self-interest.[28] The property-owning bour-geois individual *(burgher)* became conflated with the "civil society" *(burger-liche Gesellschaft)* model of a citizen capable of rational-consensual agree-ment.[29] Marx claims that the threshold of humanity is set at property ownership. Because of this conflation of property ownership and rational subjectivity, the bourgeois individual became the modern ethical figure of citizenship—ethical in the sense of enacting the accepted social norms of meaningful conduct in a civil society.[30]

The liberal, free-market subject as the model of citizenship thus presup-poses a form of economic action that, Weber famously argues, is underwritten by Protestant religious ethics.[31] The link between the ideal or model citizen and the bourgeois individual / homo economicus bolsters the connection between the bourgeois individual and Protestant ethics, a now-unconscious association that is made operational by governmentality and its various agen-cies. I argue, therefore, that the American idea of the free subject (the in-dividual of liberalism) is in fact the product of governmentality and its hid-den religious and cultural presuppositions. This study focuses on the tension between this individualistic ethics as it is exercised through modern biopo-litical techniques (discussed further below), on the one hand, and the cul-tural and religious ethics (Buddhism, American feminism, and so on) of the new immigrants being examined, on the other.

Michel Foucault identifies "bio-power" as the central concern of the mod-ern liberal state in the fostering of life, growth, and care of the population. The biopolitical rationality makes strategic use of bodies of knowledge that invest bodies and populations with properties that make them amenable to various technologies of control.[32] This power over life is exercised with the purpose of producing subjects who are healthy and productive, goals that redound to the security and strength of the state. But the state itself has no essence: "the state is nothing more than the mobile effect of a multiple regime of governmentality."[33] Studying the government of a population thus entails a study of the diverse techniques arising from multiple sources that act on the body, the mind, and the will, dedicated to making individuals, families, and collectivities "governable."[34] A repertoire of techniques of power, informed by the human sciences, comes to constitute "the social," defining categories of sexual deviants, criminals, and troublesome workers, in opposition to what is thereby considered "normal" society. Such social norms define which category of subjects is more or less valued as citizens of the nation.

In Foucault's terms, this exercise of government, "a rationalization that obeys—and this is its specificity—the internal rule of maximum economy," is called liberalism. The United States is the most liberal society in this regard, because its government starts not from the reason of the state itself, but from the existence of society, and its self-limiting measure of "governing too much."[35] And in this country, biopolitical calculations intertwine deeply with neoliberal considerations to extend the logic of the market. Economistic methods and calculations infiltrate areas of social life not primarily economic, regulating behavior to maximize activities that are profitable and marginalize those that are not. Especially since the 1970s, the norms of good citizenship in advanced liberal democracies have shifted from an emphasis on duties and obligations to the nation to a stress on becoming autonomous, responsible choice-making subjects who can serve the nation best by becoming "entrepreneurs of the self."[36] Extensive inroads by market-driven logic have shaped family and welfare policy, refugee and immigration politics, public law, penal law, health politics, and church practice. The most worthy citizen is a flexible homo economicus. In our age of globalization, the figure of entrepreneurial prowess is increasingly multiracial, multicultural, and transnational.[37] As immigration has expanded the diversity of subjects who can be assigned to American ethno-racial categories, the rationality of such racial classification increasingly intersects with the logic of the mobile homo economicus.

Sovereign power in this country is diffused through a network of welfare offices, vocational training schools, hospitals, and the workplace, where bureaucrats and their minions mobilize a variety of knowledge that can be used to shape the conduct of subjects, in order to maximize certain capabilities and minimize certain risks. Professionals and bureaucrats endeavor in a multiplicity of ways to instill appropriate norms of self-reliance and autonomy that will "empower" individuals, thus making the unsuccessful into good citizen-subjects. Every day, celebrations of market freedom and progress, with their underlying assumptions about the relative moral worthiness of different categories of subjects, influence and shape social practices and the possibilities of citizenship. These social technologies can be conceptualized as a mode not of ruling through oppression, but of "governing through the freedom and aspirations of subjects rather than in spite of them."[38]

There is no uniformity in the effects of these multiple regimes of control that would enable one to say that a single totalizing form of citizenship is thereby produced. It is perhaps much more useful to talk about the "concrete assemblages"[39] produced by converging rationalities that function in connection with other assemblages, and about what effects such divergent mixes have on the citizenship forms in different social milieus. Biopolitics, racial schemes, democratic values, feminist principles, and ethics intersect in the specific assemblages of refugee camp, welfare program, nonprofit organization, courthouse, marketplace, and church. These assemblages integrate people and functions through modes of surveillance, regulation, punishment, and reward. For poor people and at-risk newcomers, these administrative, economic, and social realms are where bureaucrats and service workers guide and act upon their conduct, seeking to avert so-called personal failures and to achieve desirable qualities in their subjects such as health, employability, wealth, and social integration. As I argue later, such problematizing modes of government, geared simultaneously toward the normalizing and the empowering of citizens, are regularly critiqued, deflected, manipulated, and transformed by newcomers as they learn to become self-governing subjects in ways not fully intended by the programs.[40] Sovereignty in America is sustained by negotiating the diverse micropolitics of being governed and learning the techniques of self-government in various social milieus traversed by multiple flows of rationality.

WORTHY CITIZENS: RACIAL BIPOLARISM AND GENDER DIFFERENTIATION

The interpenetration of the disparate forms that come to shape conduct results in social integration being realized through the differentiation of citizen-subjects. Besides neoliberal biopolitical considerations, two other major classificatory logics—racial bipolarism and engendering discourses—interpenetrate to shape unequal and differentiated types of belonging for minority populations. Judith Shklar has stated that "[f]rom the first the most radical claims for freedom and political equality were played out in counterpoint to chattel slavery, the consequences of which still haunt us. The equality of political rights, which is the first mark of American citizenship, was proclaimed in the accepted presence of its absolute denial. Its second mark, the overt rejection of hereditary privileges, was no easier to achieve in practice, and for the same reason. Slavery is an inherited condition."[41] Racial logic has always lain like a serpent in the sacred ideal of American citizenship.

Indeed, from its inception, the American nation was imagined as an implicitly racial and class formation, one governed by an Anglo-Saxon hegemony that projected white race and class interests as universal for the entire nation.[42] The concept of the American nation as a specific, racially homogeneous identity has been and continues to be the measure by which all potential citizens are situated as either integral or marginal to the nation. In their theory of racial formation in the United States, Michael Omi and

Howard Winant insist that race is a key "organizing principle" of social action, both at the "macro level" of economics, politics, and ideological practices and at the "micro level" of individual action.[43] Historically, the intertwining of race and economic performance has shaped the ways in which different immigrant groups have attained status and dignity, within a national ideology that projects worthy citizens as inherently white.

The tendency to frame ideas about immigrants in terms of a bipolar racial order has persisted, and newcomers are located along the continuum from black to white. It is obvious that these racial categories are fundamentally about degrees of undeserving or deserving citizenship. Such relative positioning in the national moral order is not state policy, but rather part of the political unconscious that variously informs official action and public perception. As Brackette Williams has pointed out, there is a black–white continuum of status and dignity, and the relative positioning of a (sub)ethnic group determines its perceived moral claim to certain areas of privilege and advantage, as well as conditioning fear of threats to these prerogatives from subordinated races.[44] These processes of relative positioning, group status competition, and group status envy result in cultures becoming race-based traditions.

Racial bipolarism has historically been part of a classificatory system for differentiating among successive waves of immigrants, who were assigned different stations along the path toward whiteness. Historical studies show that by the late nineteenth century, citizens originating from England, the Netherlands, and to a lesser extent Scotland and Italy had forged financial and kinship networks within and beyond the United States. The consolidation of this white American elite with transnational connections has been celebrated in novels by Henry James and Edith Wharton, among others. At the same time, there was a structure of expectations (in the idealized construct of ethnic succession) for how things ought to work out in a just and moral world of citizenship acquisition for less-fortunate immigrants such as Poles, Italians, Germans, and Slavs, referred to by the derogatory term PIGS (as opposed to WASPs, the originary-raced components). The succession model was about constructing a racial identity that transcended the component nationalities of the immigrants to become, ideally, generic white.

One legacy of white–black relations under slavery and Emancipation aimed at legitimizing the social order as a natural order was the use of "the Negro" as a "contrast conception" or "counter-race."[45] The free working man came to embody republican citizenship, and any immigrant who failed to gain independent livelihood was in danger of sinking to the status of wage slave, the antithesis of the independent citizen. In the nineteenth century, this logic of racial classification situated poor Irish immigrants on the East Coast and "Negroized" Chinese immigrants on the West Coast close to the black end of the continuum, because their working conditions were similar to those of unfree black labor.[46] Later non-Christian European immigrants such as Jews did not until the mid-twentieth century ascend to white status through the euphemized process of ethnic succession.[47] More recently, certain segments of African American, Spanish-speaking, and Asian immigrants have become whitened.

The racializing processes that define worthy and unworthy citizens have infused the government of poverty, especially the classification and regulation of new immigrants and migrants to the cities. The ideology of the work ethic, historically developed in contradistinction to slavery, denied full social citizenship to those who did not independently attain material citizenship, namely, the unemployed and the welfare-dependent. Of course, the effects of implicit racial and cultural ranking do not exhaust all of the conditions that go into processes of subjectification—or processes by which citizens are made and induced to be self-making. Neoliberal ideas about human capital have somewhat complicated the links between concepts of race and deserving citizenship.

The interweaving of ideologies of racial difference with liberal conceptions of citizenship entered a new phase after World War II, when debates about who belonged came to be framed in business-economic terms of balancing the provision of security against the productivity of citizens. Economistic calculation, statistics, and categorization based on time expenditure and self-discipline gave rise to the assessment of citizens as human capital, weighing those who could pull themselves up by the bootstraps against those who were economically dependent.[48] The grounding of postwar citizenship in a human-capital model put pressure on minority groups to perform economically and contributed to the stigmatization of those who make claims on the welfare state. Ideological discourses contrasting the contributions to the nation of different races often conflated race and class, as for example in the polarizing contrast between the "underclass" and the "model minority," two key categories for thinking about minoritization in postwar America.[49] The framing of racial difference in terms of differential economic contribution and performance constructed long-term residents and newcomers as the contrasting embodiments of what Williams calls "ethnicized citizenship."[50]

Increasingly, citizenship is defined as the civic duty of the individual to reduce his or her burden on society, and instead to build up his or her own human capital—in other words, to "be an entrepreneur of her/himself."[51] Indeed, by the 1960s, liberal economics came to evaluate nonwhite groups explicitly according to their claims on, or independence of, the state. Minorities who scale the pinnacles of society often have to justify themselves in such entrepreneurial terms. An apt example was the 1991 nomination of Clarence Thomas to the Supreme Court of the United States, a move widely viewed as a token appointment of an African American to the powerful white-dominated institution. In his confirmation hearings, Judge Thomas painted himself as a deserving citizen who struggled out of a hardscrabble past by pulling himself "up by [his] bootstraps." The can-do attitude is an inscription of ideal masculine citizenship; its legitimating power was perhaps sufficient to overcome the ugly stain of sexual harassment that plagued the judge's confirmation hearings. To those who see a fundamental dynamic of exclusion along racial lines, the Thomas case is an aberrant one, the exception that proves the rule that has stacked the odds against the excluded racial minority.

The assigning of racializing labels—model minority, refugee, underclass, welfare mother—is part of the racial classificatory process that, modulated by human capital calculations, continues to engender ethnicized subjectivity. Stereotypical ethno-racial figures—of effete or aberrant forms of masculinity, for example—were first fashioned for Native Americans, then passed on to African Americans during slavery. After Emancipation, a strategic patterning that linked race and gender was the basis for building otherness, welfare identity, and structures of oppression.[52] Most particularly, strategies of control that relied on educational transformations were intended to cleanse a minoritized culture of its "primitive" features. As part of this strategy, African American males, when they were not suspected of being rapists or lynched, were beseeched to toss off the shackles of structural boyhood that had been inculcated by means of majority reference and behavioral expectation.[53] These negative racialized gender elements were extended and refined, so that today, stereotypical images of blackness are associated with deviant masculinity, lack of the work ethic, and welfare dependency. While much scholarship on gender and the body has focused on patriarchy (and desire), or has sought to embed the meaning of gender subjectivity within the body, my approach considers the way technologies of control intersect with racializing schemes that serve to blacken and stigmatize minority bodies associated with welfare. Biopolitical decisions about welfare clients, low-skilled workers, good parents, and ethnic models are influenced by historically branded black images of weakness, indolence, and primitivity. As part of the political unconscious, such thinking influences the conduct of social experts and social workers who seek to regulate the behavior of minoritized populations considered less civilized than society at large. The surveillance of poor women designated at-risk—surveillance of their inner bodies, their sexual conduct, their performance as mothers—is inseparable from engendering reforms more in keeping with neoliberal, even feminist sensibilities.

Women's bodies become the site, and the female gender the form, in a biopolitics of citizenship. For instance, administrative practices directed at Cambodian refugees were often animated by the goal of cleansing the perceived elements of "Asian patriarchy" or primitivity. Social workers considered refugee women and children to be less tarnished by this racializing stigma, and thus more desirable citizen-subjects. While refugee men were marginalized, refugee women became at once more dependent on systems of female clientship and subject to lessons in personal autonomy. The biopolitics of welfarism, combined with feminist defense of the poor Asian woman, created whitening processes such as marrying a white man that allowed the war refugee to achieve the status of a "postcrisis" subject and a good enough citizen. It seems that social interventions and regulations are producing for minority populations a feminine sociality that has elements of a contractualist connection with the wider society, while ethnic male sociality remains intracommunity and disempowered.

Ethno-racial stereotypes operate as branding mechanisms directed at citizen-subjects considered to be at risk, who are measured according to the economic calculus. The bipolar racializing scheme is a social regulatory scheme that situates such at-risk subjects along the continuum of more or less likely to succeed. They become racialized not simply because of their perceived skin color, and ethnicized not simply because of claims of a particular ancestral culture, but because they have been assessed as belonging to a category and inscribed with a radical indeterminacy in the game of becoming self-motivated, self-propelling, and freedom-loving American citizens. At the same time, a wider cultural discourse, by primitivizing some minority groups, categorizes these subjects as different from other Asian American groups, such as ethnic Chinese, whose assumed Confucian values are depicted in dominant bourgeois discourse as the most recent incarnation of neoliberal enterprise values. Cultural discourses converge with the rationality of the market, conflating the moral value of liberal egoism with one's command over capital. The neoliberal discourse that increasingly defines citizenship in economic terms, by insisting that citizenship is the civic duty of individuals to reduce their burden on society and to build up their human capital,[54] becomes a vital supplement to the classic liberal rights-based definition of citizenship. As we shall see, racial classificatory logic has placed poor Asian immigrants such as Cambodian refugees at the black pole: they are identified with inner-city African Americans and set off clearly not only from whites, but also from other Asian groups such as Vietnamese and Chinese Americans. Indeed, there is a continuum of ideas about human capital, cultural primitivism, and compassionate domination, and of practices based on these ideas, that are directed at newer Asian immigrants, both rich and poor, who are subjected to parallel processes of minoritization in this era of expanding transpacific frontiers of capitalism.

TECHNIQUES FOR SUBJECT-MAKING AND SELF-MAKING

The history of the "care" and the "techniques" of the self would thus be a way of doing the history of subjectivity; no longer, however, through the divisions between the mad and the nonmad, the sick and nonsick, delinquents and nondelinquents . . . ;

but, rather, through the putting in place, and transformations in our culture, of "re-lations with oneself," with their technical armature and their knowledge effects. And in this way one could take up the question of governmentality from a different an-gle: the government of the self by oneself in its articulation with relations with others (such as one finds in pedagogy, behavior counseling, spiritual direction, the pre-scription of models for living, and so on).
    MICHEL FOUCAULT, *Ethics: Subjectivity and Truth*

Everyday citizenship in America is viewed in this study in terms of the effects of multiple rationalities (biopolitical, class, ethno-racial, gender) that directly and indirectly prescribe techniques for living for independent subjects who learn to govern themselves. Instead of considering citizenship solely in terms of the state's power to give or deny citizenship, I look at social policies and practices beyond the state that in myriad mundane ways suggest, define, and direct adherence to democratic, racial, and market norms of belonging.[55] I examine citizenship not in terms of legal status or according to a possessive criterion (legal citizens versus noncitizens), but rather in terms of what Foucault calls an "analytics of power" that plays a role in shaping people's attitudes, behavior, and aspirations in regard to belonging to a modern liberal society.[56] This diffusion model of power locates its dynamism in the pervasive, mutable system of relations and interactions among individuals, focusing on the effects an actor has on the action of others in realizing a successful goal. Such a notion of power problematizes the connection between the rationality and the action, the command and the effect; and, in this study, the connection between aspirations to democratic citizenship and the internalization of these norms as self-government.

    "Governmentality" thus involves two entangled processes of subjectification:[57] one is "subjected to someone else by control and dependence, and tied to one's own identity by a conscience of self-knowledge";[58] but because no relationship of power is all-encompassing, "[e]very power relation implies at least *in potentia,* a strategy of struggle."[59] A strategy of power elicits a counterstrategy, so that interactions among power relations produce processes of ongoing adjustment, negotiation, and conflict.

    Such an analytics of power allows me to make intelligible the power relations involved in the shaping of subjects as refugees and as citizens at two levels. First, a concern with the historically contingent relation between knowledge and power allows me to trace the genealogy of those categories in American refugee policy, racial and orientalist rankings, poverty law, and the welfare state that continue to shape contemporary ideas about ethnicity that are central to the transformation of Cambodian refugees into American citizens. Second, examining micropractices of control suggests how the specific technologies of governmentality—grids of knowledge/power, mechanisms of surveillance, hierarchical categories—are involved in the everyday molding of modern subjects into citizens.[60] How do such dividing practices operate—in refugee camps, welfare offices, community hospitals—and how do their effects determine who is to be punished or rewarded, marginalized or supported, disliked or loved by immigration officers, social workers, and members of civil society? But in order to trace the shifting genealogy of morals in the overlapping spaces of refugee and citizen, we need to study not only the social technologies that inform its framing and deployment, but also the interpretations and strategies of the refugees and citizen-subjects that define the contours of citizenship.

It is in the space of encounter and enmeshment—in the practices directed at newcomers, and the mutual daily interactions that ensue—that the meaning and exercise of citizenship happen. By focusing on successive encounters between Cambodian refugees and particular authorities, I hope to make intelligible the multiple processes and forms that are the concrete reality of becoming American. Poor refugees and immigrants are subjected to a series of determining codifications and administrative rulings that govern how they should be assessed and treated, and how they should think of themselves and their actions. These processes of being subjected, by objectifying modes of knowledge/power, and of self-making, in struggling against imposed knowledges and practices, are central to my understanding of citizenship as a sociocultural process of "subject-ification." The effects of technologies of governing—as relayed through social programs and experts seeking to shape one's subjectivity—can be rejected, modified, or transformed by individuals who somehow do not entirely come to imagine, to act, or to be enabled in quite the ways envisioned in the plans and projects of authorities. Thus while governing technologies are involved in the making of citizens by subjecting them to given rationalities, norms, and practices, individuals also play a part in their own subjectification or self-making.[61] Ambivalence is an unavoidable product of the process.

The individual local authorities and mediators in such micropolitics are professionals—doctors, teachers, social workers, church workers, probation officers—who translate the problematics of government into everyday operations. Nikolas Rose calls these "experts of subjectivity"—or professionals "who transfigure existentialist questions . . . and the meaning of suffering into technical problems about the most effective ways of managing malfunction and improving 'quality of life.'"[62] Their job, in other words, is to teach clients to be subjective beings who develop new ways of thinking about the self, acting upon the self, and making choices that help them to strive for personal fulfillment in this life. Paul Rabinow has identified such professionals as "middling modernizers," the experts who deploy knowledge/power in service of the mundane chores of producing and instilling the ubiquitous and invisible norms and forms of modern society.[63] Bruno Latour identifies a relay of power dynamics when a successful command "results from the actions of a chain of agents each of whom 'translates' it in accordance with his/ her own projects."[64] Service agents are in a position in which they not only broker relations but also translate dominant discourses into micro-practices that allocate, classify, categorize, and formalize categories of the human—refugee, patient, welfare recipient, raced subject, feminist, middle-class parent, American teenager, or flexible worker—and then try to mold their subjects into exemplars of the desirable categories. Far from being the product of any overarching program, citizenship is the cumulative effect of a multiplicity of bureaucratic figures who are concerned with the practicalities of democracy, daily figuring out ways to produce subjects who can be induced, nudged, and empowered to become self-sufficient and goal-oriented citizens.

Because of their multiple, diffused, and open-ended nature, normalizing practices never have a totalitarian effect, as some readings of Foucault's work might suggest. Indeed, Foucault has argued that regulatory programs "never work out as planned," not only because different strategies may be opposed, but because subjects interpret and act in ways that undo systems of classification (cultural, ethnic, moral), refuse different kinds of objectives (involving needs, desires, behavior), and thwart rules of surveillance and punishment.[65] There is a continual give-and-take in the power relations between the agent and the subject in a panoply of institutional contexts. The gaze of the expert or the state agent is never as comprehensive anywhere, including clinics and prisons.[66] The individual is never totally objectified or rationalized by state agencies and civic associations, nor can the individual totally escape the power effects of their regulatory schemes. But Foucault too rarely tells us how subjects resist the schemes of control, or how their tactics and outcomes are culturally creative, and frequently surprising. By exploring the day-to-day experiences of Cambodian refugees in the context of Foucault's power–resistance axis, I demonstrate how liberal governance in its everyday form entails a certain violent subjection in the process of becoming free, so to speak.

THE CAMBODIAN TRANSITION

During the European colonialization of countries such as Cambodia, modern values of citizenship such as notions of liberty, equality, and fraternity were neglected. Instead, the rationalization of colonialism focused on assembling selected cultural artifacts in museums to produce an iconography of a national culture under European tutelage.[67] This manufacturing of an imagined moral community of the modern nation gave new life to religion-based concepts of political subjection in postcolonial countries. In colonial Cambodia, for example, the French installed Prince Norodom Sihanouk as king, thus placing him in a line of continuity with past rulers. The French glorification of the Angkor Wat legacy also bolstered Sihanouk's position as an absolutist ruler of his Buddhist subjects.[68] And the transformation from a religion-based notion of political subjection to one based on laws, from a community- and religion-oriented ethos to individualistic values, remains partial in many parts of the formerly colonized world.

In 1975, the war-traumatized Cambodian state was turned upside down again when the Khmer Rouge forces led by Pol Pot (also called Saloth Sar) engaged in a willful experiment to create an instant agrarian utopia. In Pol Pot time, the moral subject was no longer the Buddhist king or monk, or even the Western-educated professional, but the "revolutionary" figure, someone who through sheer physical exertion and primitive tools could conquer the jungle and build a self-sustaining peasant paradise. The kinds of citizen-subjects most valorized in advanced liberal countries—the educated, professionals, artists, religious leaders, capitalists—were hunted down and killed by village functionaries and teenage soldiers who availed themselves of the absolute power vested in the mysterious Angkar ("the Organization"— the Khmer Rouge). In this misguided, Marxist-inspired attempt at state formation, urbanites, skilled workers, teachers, and artists were considered enemies of the state, while peasants in their home villages were considered the true citizens. Life reduced to raw labor power was the basis for strengthening the state.

In their transition from Pol Pot's utopian communism to the advanced liberalism of the United States, Cambodian refugees moved from a regime of power over death to a regime of power over life, from a state that governed by eliminating knowledge to one that promotes the self-knowing subject, from a system based on absolute control to one that governs through freedom, from a society that enforced initiative for collective survival to one that celebrates individualistic self-cultivation. My point is not so much to set up a stark contrast in political sovereignty, but rather to stress the radical disjunction between different styles of reasoning in these two modalities for the governing of population. Cambodian refugees in the United States encountered what were to them novel kinds of social regulation, and pressures to perform as knowing subjects who are "free" to refuse or accept rules, "free" to govern themselves.[69]

.   .   .

Part I begins in the nightmare world of the Pol Pot time (1975–1979). There are many political accounts of the war, but my focus is on the memories of some Cambodian war survivors living in Oakland, California. My intention is to grasp their experiences of different ways of being human—in rural Cambodia, the violent agrarian utopia of the Khmer Rouge, and the world of refugee camps. In chapter 1, refugees remember a Buddhist-Khmer culture based on political and ritual subordination tempered by the Khmer-Buddhist emphasis on compassion, kindness, and mutuality. The Pol Pot regime radically desacralized society and overturned all aspects of social life, including family and gender relations. Chapter 2 follows war survivors to border camps, where they encountered Western modes for defining, saving, and governing refugees. Encounters with aid agencies and immigration authorities shaped understandings about the superiority of Americans as first-class citizens and about the importance of patronage systems in gaining access to resources.

Part II explores the everyday strategies and techniques of citizen-making by following Cambodian refugees through various institutions in Northern California. A plethora of social services—refugee agencies; the community hospital; the welfare office and related agencies; law enforcement, the court system, and the prison—constituted the newcomers as particular kinds of clients who in turn devised microstrategies for gaining access to resources. Within these assemblages of power, many refugee experiences were analogous to those of African American urban migrants, including imposed labels of stigmatization—underclass, welfare mother, shiftless men—that shaped the process of ethno-racialization. Chapter 3 describes the political scene that met Cambodian refugees when they arrived in the long-imagined Land of the Free. It sketches the broader picture of American refugee policies, as well as changes in the ethical figure of refugees that occurred in the era of Reaganomics. Heated debates regarding race, poverty, employment, and the underclass influenced the treatment of Southeast Asian refugees as racialized, disciplinable subjects bound for low-wage, flexible labor markets.

Chapter 4 deals with refugee medicine as a disciplinary scheme for producing not only good patients, but also good citizens. Refugee patients were skillful at both subverting and compelling the medical gaze, and at interpreting the medical categories in the light of their own religious beliefs about health, the body, and care of the family. Medical practitioners, like the refugee patients, were themselves caught up in the same webs of power, which involved complex negotiations, contestations, and subterfuge.

Chapter 5 moves the scene to the welfare office, where an assemblage of policies and strategies shaped the relations between local authorities and refugee-clients. Welfare agents were often motivated by what one may call a form of ethnic cleansing, or the ridding of supposed primitiveness in cultural others in order to transform them into productive workers, in a process of pseudohomogenization. It is widely assumed that welfare assistance and payments will allow impoverished citizens to survive, but the implicit goal is to allow them to devise strategies that will convince them that their class position is temporary, and that debased social rank can be undone by material goods and achievements. In this setting, Khmer-Buddhist notions of family dependency and unity clashed with what Cambodians came to understand as American values, and engendered ambivalence about techniques in caring for the self.

Chapter 6 pursues the effects of the racial and gender fracturing further, by focusing on what I call refugee love, an attitude and set of practices that can be traced to plantation owners' paternalism toward slaves, the compassionate domination modeled by Christianity, and the "benevolent assimilation" of Pacific conquest. These practices, often found in feminism-inspired social workers, were aimed at saving refugee women and their children from Asian patriarchy. But the strategies were partially undermined by the motivations of the Cambodians themselves, by what they perceived and adopted as part of their understanding of what counts as American values. While refugee women did indeed try to free themselves from some aspects of a domestic patriarchy, they adopted some of what was proffered and rejected the rest.

Chapter 7 considers some social interventions into the family, particularly attempts to remake parent–child relations. Social workers sought to reform and remove the "primitive" aspects of Cambodian practices and substitute a model of negotiative interactions between parents and children. Lawyers, psychiatrists, and the police tried to impress upon parents the right of teenagers to personal freedom. These experts sought to undermine the moral authority of Cambodian parents while claiming that they were assisting refugees in adapting to an American ideal of middle-class parenting.

Part III moves beyond state-linked institutions to consider emerging notions of individual identity—the authentic self, the risk-taking subject—in two areas of the public sphere, the church and the marketplace. Chapter 8 deals with the loss of Buddhism and the search for a spiritual compass in the Church of Jesus Christ of Latter-Day Saints. Among the young Cambodian converts, Mormonism provided the means to create some kind of combined religion and to serve eschatological needs. It was also a path to higher education, and to assimilation into white middle-class society. American churches came to provide moral discipline and community in exchange for an ambivalent salvation in which the inward search for the self was inseparable from racial subordination.

Chapter 9 discusses the risk-taking ventures of Cambodians who shaped their own sense of belonging by starting businesses at the bottom, both family-run and gang-operated. Street gangs were a form of self-enterprise; like Cambodian-operated doughnut shops, they were the vehicles for mobilizing resources and shaping a sense of the enterprising self who could be effective in America. While these kinds of small-scale entrepreneurial activities have rich precedents in earlier immigrant communities, they are now overshadowed by the efforts of new Asian immigrants who deploy capital and extensive connections.

Part IV situates the subject-making of poor immigrants within the dramatic high-tech revolution in California. Wealthy and skilled Asian immigrants are welcome for their capacity to undertake high levels of risk-taking in the Silicon Valley and beyond. The stark contrast between the positioning of Southeast Asian refugees and that of the new Asian professionals is a dramatic illustration of how globalizing forces are producing new forms of American citizenship. The employment of unprotected migrant workers combined with managerial strategies that exploit the ambiguity of borders etch new latitudes of citizenship that reach beyond the United States. The conclusion asks: What are the structural continuities or discontinuities in the meaning and substance of American citizenship?

PART I

In Pol Pot Time

In less than half a century, Cambodian men and women were asked to alter and exert themselves to fit the interests of their leaders or the ephemeral concerns of other states. . . . Over the years, as ordinary Cambodians were forced to cope with these demands, with traumatic economic and social changes, and with intensifying, often random violence, they were also expected to raise their families, produce crops for sale and export, become wiser with age, and provide cannon fodder for one regime after another. They were seen as servants (in Khmer, neaq bonmrao, *"those who are commanded") of those in power.*

DAVID P. CHANDLER, *The Tragedy of Cambodian History*

Chapter 1

Land of No More Hope

When the Vietnamese invaded, she was alone, wandering around looking for her family. It wasn't until in the camps that she met up with them. Her father and an older sibling had died. Only her mother and a sister were left. But then, once they had found each other, they didn't get along, so she went and stayed with a Vietnamese man in another part of the camp. She's what we call "a person with no pillar of support," a person with no direction, like a lotus leaf just drifting aimlessly, floating like a weed, in the middle of the river. Wherever she ended up, she just stayed there, and if she did not end up anywhere, she just floated on.

In Khmer Buddhism, the pillar or column of support *(preah kamlaong)* refers to the parents, who should be revered as near-deities.[1] The speaker above—I'll call him Yann[2]—is a Cambodian teacher who met this woman who had lost everything in a Thai refugee camp; he married her and they later moved to Oakland with their two daughters. They lived in a housing complex that held a lively community of Cambodian refugees. The one-bedroom apartment was dark, the curtains drawn against the California sunshine and the kids playing in the yard outside. When I visited, his wife, an invalid, was lying on a cot, intermittently moaning in her nightmares. She required around-the-clock care. Yann was kept very busy, but his daughters, barely out of their childhood, helped with the household chores and the care of their mother.

In Yann's story, his wife came to stand for all women who were swept up in the vortex of war "in Pol Pot time," a term Cambodians used to refer to the years of Khmer Rouge revolution (1975–1979).[3] Cambodians speak of Pol Pot time as a period of social reversals: the rural ruled the urban, the uneducated ruled the educated, and (sometimes) children ruled their parents. Often separated from their fathers, brothers, and husbands, women were at the mercy of warfare, starvation, and constant fear, while struggling to protect children and aged relatives. Some had been through so many traumas that they were set adrift like lotus leaves floating in the stream. Many more survived with their bodies and minds undamaged but scarred and found unexpected resilience, rooted in their desire to live and to protect their children. Families were fragmented by war, mass relocation, labor camps, torture, death, and exile. Conventional Khmer-Buddhist notions of family obligation, gender roles, and personal propriety were scattered to the winds as displaced urban dwellers struggled to survive in the harsh labor camps of Democratic Kampuchea (DK), and later found refuge in the world of Thai border camps.

During those times, Cambodians experienced multiple displacements, encounters with authorities who wielded absolute power over their lives and death, and the kind of terror and hardship that transformed their identity as men and women, their sense of who they were as human beings. These refugees were to experience even more transformations in their lives in the United States.

When I began my research in the mid 1980s, there were approximately fifteen thousand Cambodian refugees living in the San Francisco Bay Area, and the majority were crowded into rundown sections of Oakland and San Francisco. Families were packed into shabby public-housing apartment buildings, radically different from the verdant village homes many were forced to abandon years before. In one Oakland complex, people avoided the long, dark hallways reeking of urine after dark; in the evenings, people swore, they heard gunshots. The jangling and clanging caused by people going in and out of the iron apartment doors contributed to the prisonlike atmosphere that pervaded the entire complex. Loud sounds tended to set the older refugees shaking, as they flashed back to some war trauma. The old, infirm, and shell-shocked seldom ventured beyond their doors for fear of becoming disoriented or of being mugged. Their fears were not entirely imaginary: just before my research began, a small child playing in the courtyard had been accidentally run over by a truck, and street predators quickly identified these newcomers as easy marks. In many households, surviving family members and their friends had managed to patch together a family of sorts, clinging to one another and counting on welfare checks to help them navigate the storm-tossed world of inner-city America.

REFUGEE STUDIES AND THE CONCEPT OF THE HUMAN

In recent years, there has been a flood of reporting about refugees from wars, natural disasters, and economic crises—the upheavals they endured, the statistics, the humanitarian efforts, the threats to the nation-state and to peace, and the personal stories. We've been told that tens of millions of the world's population are now classifiable as refugees. There has also been a proliferation of other kinds of materials about refugees from around the world—exhibitions, brochures of relief organizations, movies, and the like—detailing wrenching stories of terror and anguish suffered in war. These stories are used by organizations to seek funds for their programs addressing poverty, starvation, and human-rights violations. And the academic community has linked refugee issues to the nation-state, considering how the displacements of large populations have affected the ways nation-states imagine themselves as discrete geopolitical entities and how modern statecraft regulates refugees in order to exclude them from territorial citizenship.[4] An ethnographic analysis of the actual experiences of refugees will show, however, that not all refugees are defined as being outside the norms of the (intended) host countries; the question becomes how, in each political situation, refugees are differentially categorized and assessed as being more or less assimilable into national norms of moral belonging and citizenship.

Giorgio Agamben notes that "by breaking the continuity between man and citizen, *nativity and nationality*," refugees "put the originary fiction of modern sovereignty in crisis" because the refugee is truly the "man of no rights" who exposes "the fiction of the citizen."[5] For instance, in the 1930s, the Westphalian concept of national sovereignty based on the birth–nation link was severely challenged by laws that denationalized masses of marked citizens under the Third Reich.[6] Such laws privileging a certain race (German blood and culture) over other citizens introduced "the principle according to which citizenship was something of which one had to prove oneself worthy and which could therefore always be called into question."[7] And "the rights of man" were repeatedly violated as the sheer humanity of refugees was often not sufficient in itself for them to receive political asylum abroad. Even when accepted by a host country, refugees of ethno-racial and cultural backgrounds different from those of the dominant majority were subjected to questions about their worthiness as new citizens. Despite the lip service paid to the principles of human rights, modern political sovereignty is based on the power to exclude or kill what Agamben calls "bare life," in order to constitute the foundation of the nation-state and define the status of citizenship in biopolitical terms. This ambiguity in the concept of citizenship cannot be revealed by a study of formal laws or by relying on a notion of citizenship as something that is simply possessed (like a passport), but rather through an ethnographic investigation of the political reasonings and practices that assess groups differently and assign them different fates.

Scholarly interest in refugees, especially those from Southeast Asia, has focused on gathering firsthand accounts as a way to detect the varying conditions and progress of the conflicts they are fleeing, and to write a complex history of the present.[8] Research conducted among Southeast Asian immigrants in the United States has been used as a way to give voice to refugees and to express the needs of the community in exile.[9] There is also a growing body of eloquent memoirs told by Cambodian survivors themselves.[10] Anthropological writings on refugees tend to examine how the refugee experience disrupts traditional cultural practices, and how traditions are continued and transformed abroad.[11]

My intention in this study is different: to explore not so much how "culture" develops when transplanted to a new setting, but rather how the modern *anthropos* is reconceptualized in various political situations. I do so by tracing the specific logics that shape different notions of being human in successive contexts of the refugee–citizen continuum. I trace the movement of Cambodian refugees from the modern Cambodian state to the violent state of the Khmer Rouge, then the world of refugee camps, and finally settlement in the United States. Along the way, I consider how administrative rationality and everyday practice informed by that logic shape different notions of what it means to be human in these successive contexts. My analysis is based on the refugees' own perspectives on their ordeals—especially their views on how families, community, and the relations between women and men were irrevocably changed by the war, the flight to safety, and life in refugee camps, and how these experiences affected their adjustments to life in the United States.

A HISTORICAL RUPTURE

The oldest refugees remember French rule (1863–1953), which by making Cambodia a protectorate kept it free of invasions and land grabs by Vietnam and Thailand.[12] Even so, by the beginning of the twentieth century, Cambodia was yoked with Vietnam and Laos in "French Indochina." French-educated Vietnamese—civil servants, entrepreneurs, and urban professionals—came to live in Phnom Penh, along with ethnic Chinese traders from Vietnam and China. Vietnamese fisherfolk spread along the waterways, particularly around the Tonle Sap. The French viewed the Vietnamese as a stronger "race" than the Cambodians, and thereby intensified the age-old enmity between the two groups. After Cambodia gained independence in 1953, Prince Norodom Sihanouk continued to be wary of the pro-American regimes in Thailand and Vietnam, and he sought China's protection in order to maintain Cambodia's autonomy in the widening Indochina conflict. In 1970, the United States began secret aerial bombardments of Vietcong sanctuaries in the Cambodian countryside. Prince Sihanouk was soon overthrown by U.S.-backed General Lon Nol. By the time Congress stopped the bombing campaign in 1973, more than half a million tons of bombs had fallen.[13]

According to David Chandler, the merciless air attacks had two important political results: demonstrating the claim of the Communist Party of Kampuchea (CPK) that the United States was the principal enemy, and inspiring thousands to join an anti-American crusade.

> The bombing destroyed a good deal of the fabric of pre-war Cambodian society and provided the CPK with the psychological ingredients of a violent, vengeful, and unrelenting social revolution. This was to be waged, in their words, by people with "empty hands." The party encouraged class warfare between the "base people," who had been bombed, and the "new people," who had taken refuge from the bombing, and thus had taken sides, in CPK thinking, with the United States.[14]

The number of traumatized and displaced peasants who joined the Khmer Rouge, the armed forces of the CPK headed by Pol Pot, rose.[15] Approximately two million refugees swarmed into Phnom Penh, which was kept afloat by U.S. aid. In April 1975, the Khmer Rouge entered the city and instituted a utopian program for total change. Phnom Penh was emptied of all its inhabitants; they became the "new people" in a vast system of brutal labor camps controlled by the Revolutionary Organization (Angkar Padevat, usually called simply the Angkar). In their attempts to build socialism swiftly, the CPK ended what they called feudal institutions, such as the monarchy, Buddhism, family life, private property, the right of people to move freely, and anything else they deemed an impediment to revolution. By the time of the Vietnamese invasion in 1979, Democratic Kampuchea had lost about one and a half million lives to warfare, starvation, disease, and mass executions.[16] While the leaders of the revolution did not intend to cause losses of such magnitude, they "were confused but unrepentant."[17] For the refugees who finally settled in Oakland, the destruction of old Cambodia began an unraveling and reordering of family life, and of cultural and personal identity, that has not yet ended.

BEFORE POL POT TIME

In their dreams, many refugees return to Cambodia, to a time before the Khmer Rouge. While many are plagued by nightmares of death, destruction, and flight, they also dream of home villages, orchards full of fruit-bearing trees, flourishing rice paddies (see figure 1), and large families. To their way of thinking, this was a time when they were real Cambodians, before the wars of the 1970s, before they became known as Cambodian refugees, before their families and culture were torn asunder and they had to become different kinds of people. They saw their lives as moving through a series of stages: before Pol Pot time, Pol Pot time, America, the future.

Subjecthood and Subjectivity in Pre-1975 Cambodia

Modern Cambodian society after the early twentieth century was based on two intertwined forms of political subjecthood, one shaped by this-worldly patron–client networks, the other by the Buddhist concept of an order of beings in a transcendent infinitude. As the supreme patron, the Buddhist king derived his power from two realms of action: the politics of patronage and protection on the one hand, and the accumulation of charismatic authority on the other.[18] On the worldly level, kingly power was based on accumulating entourages, followers, and chiefs who at the local level deployed peasants, slaves, and mercenaries for corvée, trade, war, and other activities that generated wealth and power.[19] One might envision the state as a great

Figure 1. An idealized image of Cambodia before Pol Pot time on currency outlawed in 1975.

consumerist institution in which rulers and officials "consumed" (lived off) the regions and departments under their control.[20] Society was held together by "a flexible set of dyadic relationships extending downward from the king" in patronage networks that linked the Buddhist monastic order *(sangha),* and the bureaucracy of the capital and major settlements *(kompong)* to smaller villages and minority peoples living at the edges of the kingdom.[21] At each level, patrons offered protection in return for loyalty, and personal relationships, not law, governed the sense of personhood. The majority of Cambodians lived in a rural setting, and village society was informally organized, the family and the *sangha* being the only functional institutions. In order to attain security and other benefits, people without power sought patrons, whether among more powerful kinsmen, local monks, bandit leaders, officials, or itinerant holy men.[22] Political subjecthood was defined by positioning within multitiered networks of patron–client relations (along axes of urban–rural, Khmer–non-Khmer, elite–peasant, male–female) that constituted the primary relationships of the moral economy.[23]

At the same time, the majority of Cambodians were Buddhist, and their deference to a despotic monarch was based on the Buddhist concept of a chain of beings whose moral status was bound to a wheel of rebirth and accumulation of merit in previous lives. The king, having earned his exalted position from merit accumulated in his previous lives, was the upholder of the righteous order informed by the *dharma* (Buddhist teachings). He extended paternalistic protection to the people in return for the obedience of a loyal following. In the modern period, Prince Sihanouk saw himself as part of the tradition of rulers who were the little people's chief protector and chief source of happiness. David Chandler claims, perhaps with little exaggera-

Figure 2. Angkor Wat depicted on an old banknote no longer in circulation.

tion, that "Sihanouk saw Cambodia as a personal possession, a family, or a theatrical troupe. Many of his subjects, particularly older people, agreed to play supporting roles and endowed him with supernatural powers. So did the courtesans who surrounded him."[24] Sihanouk, who was supported by the French authorities, was able to leverage his religious authority to maintain an absolute form of sovereignty through the 1960s.

Under French rule (1863–1953), Cambodia became a protectorate in which kingly authority came to rely more and more on charismatic appeal to the people, especially those marginalized and exploited. In order to justify their tutelary rule in the protectorate, the French amassed historical texts, artifacts, and images to construct the idea of Cambodge, which glorified the Angkor Wat kingdom (ninth to the fifteenth centuries) as the golden age of a civilization that had been in decline ever since. Besides constituting Angkor Wat as the national monument (figure 2), the French introduced the modern notion of the nation based on birth, race, and culture.

They also promulgated the idea of a national religion, linking birth and religious affiliation to construct a national identity based on religion (*sasenaa-jiet*). A cognate notion, *sasenaa-kmae*, added a racial dimension to the concept of a Khmer religion.[25] Gradually, by 1959, this concept of a national Khmer race came to exclude Vietnamese and Chinese residents, who were required to assimilate to Khmer customs, morals, and traditions in order to be eligible for citizenship.[26] By manufacturing Cambodian concepts of national culture and race, and by regulating temple schools and the training of the *sangha,* the French colonizers hoped to control forces for nationalism.

Life in the countryside had only tenuous connections to the capital, but by the middle of the twentieth century, most rural subjects, while ignorant of the finer details of the modern nation, had internalized the idea of Angkor Wat as the national icon, the seat of the Khmer soul. Their understanding of citizenship was shaped by the normalized hierarchy of Khmer and Khmer-Loeu (aboriginal groups) at one end, and of Chinese and Vietnamese residents at the other. Because Cambodia was the weakest country in war-torn mainland Southeast Asia, politicians such as American-supported Lon Nol (who held power from 1970 to 1975) maintained their position by playing on the people's persistent fear of racial genocide (by the Vietnamese) and by labeling all communists as *tmils* (nonbelievers), and thus non-Khmers.[27]

In everyday life, ordinary people continued during these years to be under the direct power of village chiefs, the *sangha,* and, increasingly, the Khmer Rouge. Chandler notes that "In the years 1945–79, some four-fifths of the population were farmers and their families, people who took their low status for granted and thought social change unlikely or impossible. Toward superiors they were deferential. They constructed arrangements with those they perceived as being above them, resented exploitation, and hoped for the best."[28] But because the links between different levels of the political system were tenuous, there was much local autonomy, and villagers were in effect clients of local officials. Weak local institutions and overdependence on patrons or saviors shaped a notion of citizenship based on client subjectivity.[29]

Such vertical relations of patron–clientelism and personal deference were balanced somewhat in the villages by bilateral kinship ties and a Khmer-Buddhist ethos of compassion that shaped male and female roles in kinship and community affairs. Anthropologists believe that societies with bilateral kinship systems tend to attenuate male domination while providing a source of informal power to women. Based on her research in a village outside Phnom Penh about 1960, May Ebihara claims that women formed networks for carrying out ordinary activities, and that parents did not demonstrate a strong bias favoring sons over daughters.[30] Nancy Smith-Hefner links both horizontal and vertical sets of relationships when she argues that the "practical" Buddhism of ordinary Cambodians integrated values of reciprocity and honor into a hierarchical system of old over young, men over women, the *sangha* over the laymen, and the king over the little people.[31] Possibly also, the independence of dispersed peasant holdings, limits on communal activity, and the active role of women in the fields and in trade might have given them a degree of household authority that was not seen among women in urban families, who tended not to work for income.[32]

Refugees Remember

Cambodian refugees in Oakland had conflicting memories about gender arrangements and personal power before Pol Pot time, their recollections colored by their struggles to make new families and experiment with new

---

freedoms in California. Their narratives moved between happy memories of family before the war and reassessments and critiques of those memories in light of current day-to-day efforts to get by in California. Their stories of life before the killing fields were an interesting mix: they commented critically on the Cambodian family ethos and marital relations, but also betrayed nostalgia for male authority, and for the kind of family stability and predictability people associate with the old days. Although male and female informants seemed to agree on the family norms, practices, and morality that existed in Cambodia before 1975, men expressed a more uncompromising view of male authority than women, who remembered a more balanced distribution of gender power in everyday life. The intervening years of struggle to survive as individuals and as families under the Angkar, during the flight, in the refugee camps, and in the United States have all influenced the construction of a contrastingly defined "traditional" Cambodian culture. These stories about the remembered past in turn color their stories about Cambodian adjustment to American society and their struggles with new concepts of gender, the family, and the individual.[33]

In their stories about the time before Pol Pot, male authority appears to have been rather more entrenched than the existence of bilateral kinship ties might imply. Peter Thuy, a former monk who became a social worker and handled many cases of family conflict in the refugee community, wistfully recalled in hindsight that in old Cambodia, "a man enjoyed submissive and unchallenged obedience from his wife." Perhaps unconsciously influenced by a sense that living in America had weakened Asian male authority, refugee men claimed that male power was unchallenged in prewar Cambodia. An elderly man who worked as a *krou khmer* (ritual specialist) asserted,

> When we were in our country, it was as if we were in hell. We did whatever we wished. Even if it was a disagreement over a single word, we would beat each other up. Men would beat up their wives if a meal was not tasty. . . . As you know, these are people from the countryside, used to "trudging and wading through the mud." The men, we had authority over women. Whatever we said, the wives had to obey. Whatever the husband ordered, the wife must obey. The laws set the husband higher than the wife.

The *krou,* who had formal training in Theravada Buddhism, added that Buddhist precepts do not give men the authority to control or beat their wives, but that Cambodians, like ordinary Thais and Laotians (with whom they share the religion), did not properly adhere to Buddhist doctrines.

While the ideal woman was submissive and obedient, rural Cambodian women shared with their counterparts elsewhere in Southeast Asia a reputation for running their households, engaging in trade, and pushing their husbands around. While the actual extent of domestic abuse in prewar Cambodia is unknown, anthropologist Judy Ledgerwood thinks that it was not common: "May [Ebihara] and I lived in a village for a year and never once heard of a man striking his wife (though she once saw a man chased through the village by a woman with a frying pan)."[34] Furthermore, women's preference for matrilocal residence—or living close to the home village of their own family—meant that they could always call on their natal family for support and protection.[35] Because of the strength of women's sisterly networks, the potential for interventions in domestic disputes deterred male abuse at home.[36] Thus, Cambodian men's memories of overwhelming male power at home must be taken with a grain of salt.

In Oakland, Peter confided that the Cambodian husband's need to maintain authority over his wife placed limits on confidences, and thus on conjugal intimacy. For instance, women would not repeat criticisms they made about their husbands behind their backs, and "most men did not tell their wives their problems."[37] Men made many big decisions without consultation, he said. I suspect that as a social worker, Peter had learned about middle-class American norms emphasizing companionable marriages and emotional intimacy, and he might actually have been expressing dissatisfaction about his own marriage. He explained that these Cambodian "restrictions on words and actions" between husband and wife spilled over into sexual relations, and complained that Cambodian norms allowed wives to have sex only in the missionary position. When I mentioned the erotic figures of heavenly angels *(apsara)* sculpted on the walls of Angkor Wat as possible signs of a more lively tradition in Cambodian culture, he shook his head sadly. "There was only one position allowed" women in sex, he insisted; but men had the right to seek sexual variety outside marriage.

He continued that before Pol Pot time, men could have secondary wives, but their first wives had the option of prohibiting it. In many cases, he knew, men who were traveling without their urban families disguised their married status and, if they were posted in the countryside, took another wife. Peasant girls were often tricked this way because of their strong desire to marry rich men or men who drew a regular salary, such as teachers and soldiers. Another Cambodian informant estimated that about three out of ten rich men had secondary wives. These women did not have the same rights as the first wife, who controlled her husband's income and whose children inherited his property. The taking of second wives increased during the years of war, when men were posted to the provinces.

Furthermore, Peter remembered that "a man might have different wives or mistresses, whereas if his wife had a lover, he could go to court and get permission to kill both of them." This statement was erroneous, carelessly uttered in the heat of a subterranean sex war within the refugee community. He probably meant that a man who caught his wife in bed with another man could kill them both in rage and not be charged. When I checked this point with an older woman, she noted that "During the Sihanouk period [1953–1970], we had laws. If you beat your spouse or your children, the police would be called and you'd be arrested." She admitted, however, that this was very rarely done.

Memories like these suggest that Cambodian society, at least for the ordinary folk, both rural and urban, placed a higher value on men than on women. Statements of this kind were always made in the context of Cambodian refugees' awareness that women and men are considered equal in America—a message drummed into them by social workers. The older woman continued,

> Cambodian women were taught to obey their husbands. Before marriage, the mothers would teach daughters what we call a code of conduct for women: how to take care of the husband, not to go out anywhere, that we should have dinner ready by the time he gets home from work.
>
> In our country, men put more value on themselves, so it was up to the women to do all the household chores. All the men did when they got home was bathe, eat dinner, and go to bed. Some husbands, after they got home, they went out for fun while we stayed at home with the children. If a man wanted two or three wives, he could.
>
> As for Cambodian women, after one or two kids, they could not go out and get a job. So they had to depend on their husbands. So, if we used harsh words with them, they had the right to strike us. In Cambodia, men were more valued than women.

At the same time, women were in practice supposed to run the household. Married women were considered virtuous for managing the household budget and environment in such a way as to make the home "peaceful, pleasant, and enjoyable." The wife and mother's virtue was bound up with activities that brought safety, order, and prosperity to her family.[38] This set of ideals was expressed by Mrs. Chann, a middle-aged woman who had been a prosperous trader in the Battambang area. She remembered a rather companionable division of labor in farming families, where men did have some responsibilities:

> Plowing and raking were a man's job. The husband also transplanted the rice seedlings. He would get up at dawn to go to the fields while his wife stayed home and cooked. She would leave to join him only after the food was done. If she had parents to care for the baby, she would go to the fields and transplant rice seedlings. Once she got there, her husband would tie up the cow and eat his lunch. Then he would go and help her. That's if he was a good husband. . . . Sometimes the wife was very strong and she plowed and raked instead of her husband. But men did have greater leeway to enjoy themselves outside the domestic circle.

Mrs. Chann's recollections seem to jibe with anthropologists' findings that men and women were partners in that they shared farmwork and had complementary responsibilities, as in other Southeast Asian agrarian societies. Married women were actively involved in many networks of activities relating to labor exchange and local trade, and they participated actively in public affairs. Mobility restrictions, however, were imposed on unmarried women, who were not supposed to go out alone after dark for fear of losing their virtue.

A conversation with a Mr. Heng confirmed much of what the others had told me:

> In our country, the man had rights. A man could travel far, could stay out at night. If a woman stayed out late, she would be criticized and chastised. A man could go out anytime, and if he came home late and was scolded by his wife, he could always say he was making money for her. . . . But if a woman came home late, she would be accused of having a lover; she had no rights.

In fact, male mobility was linked to the masculine ability to earn a livelihood, as well as to virility and prowess. Male public life was focused on building patron–client relations that gave them access to different sources of economic, social, and political power. Men represented their families in public life and mediated for their wives and children. Nevertheless, women's power at home was substantial.

Mrs. Chann provided some details. She noted that in the villages and small towns, widows or divorced women were pretty independent in running their own households and raising their children. Although women were expected to be faithful to one man for their entire life, divorce was not unknown. A woman's reputation suffered only if she was suspected of adultery or in some other way was the direct cause of the breakup. Upon divorce, conjugal property was divided equally. The husband was entitled to take only the eldest of the children with him, and if he was not interested in doing so, the wife had custody of all the children. Some divorcees returned to their natal families; others raised their children on their own by taking in sewing. In other cases, they might leave their children with relatives or pay a neighbor to look after them.

The authority structure between husband and wife was reinforced by the parents' overwhelming power over children. Informants mentioned that in most households, whether rural or urban, children worked alongside parents of the same sex, helping with household chores or work in the fields and orchards. Families with more than ten children were not uncommon. In most cases, older children took care of younger ones. Children were expected to be respectful and grateful to their parents; they could not "look their parents in the eye, not even after marriage." Parents could also discipline their children as they saw fit. Peter stated baldly that "the father had the right to punish his children, including hanging them up by their hands. The mother had no right to intervene."

Mrs. Chann gave a more benign picture of parent–child relations. She claimed that Cambodian mothers did not believe in beating children, who were equally treasured regardless of sex. At puberty boys joined the temple for a short time (one to three years); there they learned to recite Buddhist prayers and studied Buddhist scripture. Most important, they learned to distinguish between right and wrong and to express gratitude and responsibility toward their parents. As temporary monks, they could amass merits (by doing good deeds): eighteen for their mother and twenty-one for their father. Mrs. Chann was puzzled that after "having suffered through the pain of pregnancy and childbirth" she deserved less gratitude than her husband.[39] Her educated husband, who spoke French and Thai fluently, said that it was because the father made new life possible in the mother: "You need a husband in order to have a child!" Despite her own doubts and her status as a powerful businesswoman, Mrs. Chann accepted the gender hierarchy that held that "the father is the pillar of the household."

But Mrs. Chann soon modified her position, noting that although Cambodian men were frequently "treated like lords in their homes," social status often undercut masculine privilege in a marriage. She was the daughter of a Sino-Cambodian rice miller who owned huge tracts of rice fields. Her mother was a Cambodian woman from a prosperous farming family near Battambang. Cambodian women engaged in petty trade, but large-scale commerce tended to be dominated by Sino-Cambodian families like Mrs. Chann's. Thus they were very well off, but even so they did not belong to the Battambang elite, which was controlled by entrenched families of noble blood. She remarked that in rich families like hers, the parents of the bride could demand a large dowry in gold and silks and that the full wedding expenses be paid by the groom's family, especially if his family had a slightly lower status.

> Sometimes the groom's family might be poor, but if he had an education and one could tell that his character was good, he could be brought into the family and trained in the arts of the higher-status person. And the bride's family would not ask so much dowry. But if the man had asked for the daughter's hand in marriage, he had to pay for everything.

Mrs. Chann was speaking from personal experience, for she was married to a university student in just the manner described. Female power, whether among the peasants or the middle class, was based on the control of household money, some of which was obtained through trade. "Whatever he made, he put in my hand. Among us Cambodians, that's the practice in nine cases out of ten. I have had control of the money since the day I was married."

Mothers played an important role in preparing girls for marriage. In the past, about age seventeen, when "the girl's flesh had blossomed forth," she "entered the shade" and was kept out of sight of men (including her father). During this confinement—which lasted from three months to a year—the girl learned embroidery and weaving. She wore long-sleeved blouses and refrained from eating meat so that her complexion would be beautiful. When she finally left the shade, "it was like a wedding festival," and food was offered to monks. Her suitors were carefully scrutinized for their family background and level of education, and for whether they had been ordained to monkhood. The chosen groom would perform "groom service," coming around to serve the in-laws by carrying water and chopping wood. The practice of entering the shade was confined to girls in well-off families; it instilled in them the retiring and circumspect role they were supposed to play in marriage. By the 1970s, however, such rituals surrounding puberty and marriage had begun to fade under the pressures of urbanization and exposure to Western culture. Nevertheless, careful surveillance of girls continued.[40]

Although the Sino-Cambodians were strict with their daughters, they favored giving girls some education and initiating them into the family business. Mrs. Chann and all her nine siblings went to school. After her marriage, she and her husband opened a dry-goods store that soon grew into a two-building affair. She handled the daily accounts and discussed only the big transactions with her husband. They rented out their inherited orchards and rice paddies to poor peasants. Mrs. Chann was also the family creditor: she amassed houses and distributed them among her seven children when they grew up. Opportunities like these to participate in the family business increased women's economic power and gave them some public stature as traders and creditors.

To summarize, then, in the memories of Cambodian refugees, the elite urban or provincial family was characterized by male control over women and children, a power that included the right to administer physical punishment. Wives were expected to be obedient and deferential to their husbands, and women's power derived mainly from running the household and handling the kitchen budget, as well as occasionally from petty trade. Women in farming families worked in the fields, but by and large the male and female spheres were separate, with women and girls playing important roles at home and in local economic activities. While boys had fewer social constraints than girls, they were also subject to the physical control of their fathers. Male power in the public domain was expressed by representing their families to authorities, by travel, and by seeking outside sexual liaisons (and sometimes multiple wives in different locations). These arrangements were given a legitimizing cast by folk Buddhist beliefs that women had less merit than men. Rural men were subordinated to more powerful men in the patronage networks that ordered the wider Cambodian society.

In Phnom Penh, especially among the middle class (which was dominated by Chinese and Vietnamese) in the 1970s, girls were gradually gaining more freedom to participate in the public sphere. Some women were enrolled in French schools and studying to be doctors and professionals. Through education they gained prestige and employment and could expect more respect from their husbands. But the majority of urban women were housewives or worked in family businesses under the supervision of their male relatives. Within the tiny group of intellectuals, women such as the wives of Pol Pot and his brother-in-arms Heng Samrin received university education in Paris. Thus although gender inequality was not part of Buddhist scriptural teachings, gender relations were deeply inscribed by the tenets of practical Buddhism and political absolutism.

The everyday effects of gender hierarchy in the city and in the countryside were modulated by Khmer-Buddhist values of kindness and compassion. Belief in karma and reincarnation underlay the most basic understandings of moral subjectivity, regardless of gender, age, or station in life. Karma *(kam)* is the notion that actions in one's previous lives and the resulting accumulation of merit *(bon)* determine one's current life situation. One can modify one's fate by accumulating merits through performing good deeds, avoiding vices, praying, offering food and money to monks, and by becoming a monk. By doing good deeds, one can transfer merits to another person, especially a relative; the ethics of practical Buddhism was thus inseparable from the principles of mutuality within the family and sociality in the wider community.[41]

At the same time, Khmer-Buddhist concepts of the ethical subject stress gender differences. Women are viewed as more attached to material things and earthly affairs—as represented by childbirth, cooking, and trading—and thus are potentially less morally worthy, or spiritually subordinated to men as a category. Women enjoyed domestic power as wives and mothers, and they gained moral worth from caring for their families and from embodying the highest ideals of gentleness and compassion. Although married women exercised autonomy in day-to-day affairs, young unmarried women were strictly controlled, for their moral subjectivity was considered more susceptible to corrupt influence. Theravada Buddhism defined the virtuous young woman as someone sexually repressed, vigilantly monitored, and not putting herself in situations in which her virtue might be challenged.[42] Anthropologist Judy Ledgerwood has written extensively about the traditional idea of the perfectly virtuous woman, *srey kruap leak,* who was based on the divine qualities of serenity, gracefulness, and sweetness in action and speech.[43] In the chain of moral beings, men were positioned to be relays of power—from the king to officials to monks to male heads of household. At every level, men acted as moral preceptors and agents of control, especially of young women and children at the bottom.

By 1970, challenges to Buddhism had begun, as Lon Nol, in trying to locate political sovereignty more absolutely in the state, attacked the "thousands of years of absolutism, arbitrariness, and tyranny."[44] The Khmer Rouge, led by the Communist Party of Kampuchea, went further. In 1975, they sought to desacralize the nation altogether and to found a truly modern state that would kill off religion.

POL POT TIME

After their capture of Phnom Penh in April 1975, the Khmer Rouge dramatically marked the beginning of a new political order based on a novel relationship between state and population. Phnom Penh was emptied immediately, and people were driven at gunpoint into the countryside devastated by U.S. bombing, where they were forced to labor to produce food in peasant collectives. Equally traumatic to many Cambodians were the massive desecration and destruction of Buddhist temples, the forced defrocking of virtually the entire *sangha,* and the killing of thousands of monks and members of the Buddhist royal family. Peter Thuy was then a young monk working with U.S. armed forces along the Kampuchea border area.[45] He recalls that before setting up a new village for the displaced urbanites, the Khmer Rouge gathered up people with religious knowledge and forced them to destroy Buddha images in front of the public. Then the monks were killed. Khmer Rouge soldiers—who as communists had been branded nonbelievers—boasted that murder was no sin, and that they would not be punished for their deeds. He explained, "So the people realized that they had better listen to the Angkar. Or you listen to Buddha [and face the consequences]. Now there is no Buddha in Cambodia, the temple was destroyed, and by one [Pol Pot] who had been born from Buddhism."

This destruction of the figure of the sacred, who could be killed with impunity and without punishment, also sounded the death knell for the traditional religion-based culture and was the act that constituted a new political sovereignty. Agamben has argued that the essence of the modern state was in the state of exception, under which the *Homo sacre* "may be killed and yet not sacrificed," the bare life that is at once excluded and yet captured within the political order.[46] As refugees in their own country, ordinary Cambodians realized that under the Khmer Rouge, a new kind of moral being and a new political subject were being forged from the fire of massive desacralization.

To many, Pol Pot time represented a total rupture of the belief in Khmerness as a continuing cycle of Buddhist karma and the accumulation of merit.[47] The Pol Pot time was a period of wildness and great reversal in which the Buddhist world itself was destroyed. In his account of life under the Khmer Rouge, Pin Yathay remembered a prophecy:

Puth was a nineteenth-century sage who prophesied that the country would undergo a total reversal of traditional values, that the houses and the streets would be emptied, that the infidels—*thmils*—would hold absolute power and persecute the priests. But people would be saved if they planted the kapok tree—*kor,* in Cambodian. *Kor* means "mute." The usual interpretation of this enigmatic message was that only the deaf-mutes would be saved during this period of calamity. Remain deaf and mute. Therein, I now realized, lay the means of survival. Pretend to be deaf and dumb! Say nothing, hear nothing, understand nothing![48]

The vast majority of Cambodians had not yet heard of Pol Pot, but they suddenly found themselves controlled by ferocious and well-armed peasant soldiers clad in black uniforms, the members of the shadowy regime called Angkar. Time was reordered, and 1975 became, in the words of outside observers, Year Zero—a start from scratch to be achieved by abolishing currency, evacuating cities, eliminating the elite, and wiping out religion.

The Policing State and Its Population

The Pol Pot regime sought to mobilize raw labor power to build a self-sustaining agrarian utopia (harking back to the glorious past of Cambodge), a state that could protect itself from foreign domination (Vietnamese and American) and turn its back on the knowledge, institutions, and infrastructures of modern society. Foucault has differentiated between two kinds of modern state: the liberal state based on government of the population, and the policing state based on a governmental technology that harnesses the population in service of strengthening the state.[49] The Angkar sought to be a policing state, but the Khmer Rouge never reached a level of organization or efficiency, bungled on a massive scale, killed off enemies of the state at a high rate (more than four hundred thousand), and lost more than a million and a half people to primitive working and living conditions.

Pin Yathay, who was trained as an engineer, gives an on-the-ground view of Khmer Rouge rule. The Angkar transmitted power through a chain of provincial and district leaders, who commanded village chiefs. "In general nothing was written down. The application of the orders, therefore, depended on the interpretation placed on them by each leader, depending on his level of education and on his ability to remember the orders."[50] Yathay's general impression, however, was that there was no established rule. "In the absence of published law, discipline varied at the whim of each village chief."[51] Indeed, many scholars and refugees reported that conditions of brutality varied across districts and provinces. Much of the random violence happened at the local level, as village leaders and individual soldiers delegated to themselves the absolute power of the Angkar.[52]

The goal of Democratic Kampuchea was to strengthen the state by means of cooperative self-sufficiency, using a dual policy of increasing rice production and increasing the population. To the first end, the Khmer Rouge turned the entire country into a series of labor camps and peasant cooperatives. Family members, including teenagers, were dispersed among production teams and cooperatives and placed in single-sex work groups. The old and the very young were also put to work, and even nursing mothers had to leave their babies in order to participate in rice cultivation. People had to work ten to twelve hours a day, with primitive tools, while subsisting on a thin rice gruel.[53]

This relentless labor had a disastrous effect, with many people dying, mainly through the Khmer Rouge's brutality, ineptitude, and neglect. Chandler reports that the northwest, where Battambang is located, was particularly heavily affected by Angkar bungling. Even as rations decreased, there was pressure to produce food surpluses. Thousands of the "new people" were mobilized to clear the jungle. "No Western-style medicines were available, and thousands soon died from malaria, overwork, and malnutrition."[54] For survivors who later escaped to Western countries, slavery and starvation left an indelible imprint.

Yann referred to Democratic Kampuchea as "the land of no more hope." He was a keen observer, a teacher from Svay Rieng near the Vietnamese border, who was displaced by border fights and the U.S. bombing. Like many others, he fled to Phnom Penh, where he lowered himself by becoming a cyclo driver. As the Khmer Rouge came closer to the capital, he fled to Battambang in the northwest, near the Thai border:

> I hid myself among the people from the area. The Khmer Rouge forced us to work. We had to carry stuff, clear the land for farms, plant fruit trees and grow potatoes. They kept taking us off one job and giving us another. They took us out of the orchards and put us to transplanting rice seedlings. They then took us out of rice transplanting and made us build canals, all according to their command. We just let them use us, we just stayed silent. We just asked to be alive. . . . We never had enough to eat. We had to carry soil, but they gave us only gruel. But what could we do? We just had to bear it. We were living under their control. Just bear it, or die by opposing them.

Although early anti-Angkar propaganda claimed that the organization's goal was the "destruction of the family," Michael Vickery argues that evidence shows that Democratic Kampuchea was actually concerned about increasing the population. The dispersal of family members to different work teams was perhaps part of a move to form peasant cooperatives, but the real goal seemed to be to break up kinship networks. In fact, demographic policy seemed to be "to encourage the formation and maintenance of nuclear family units of husband, wife, and children" for reproduction purposes.[55] Village chiefs approved marriages within the same class, and they encouraged sexual relations and having babies. People were forced into marriage for the purpose of producing more babies. Vickery claims that "DK policy was immeasurably stricter than the pre-revolutionary norms [on premarital sex and marriage] it mirrored, and it served to modify, not destroy, the family through transferring parental authority over adults to the state and breaking down the family into nuclear units."[56]

Mrs. Sophat, who was separated from her husband in the march out of Phnom Penh, told me that after she arrived at a labor camp near Battambang, "the Pol Potists" forced her to remarry. Some urban migrants speculated that the Khmer Rouge instituted forced marriage because they were trying to get people to put down roots and raise children, so as to stabilize the new society more quickly. The scarcity of food and widespread illness did not seem to inspire doubts about the wisdom of increasing the population. There were seven couples in Mrs. Sophat's work gang who had not known each other before they were compelled to marry (many later separated):

> They summoned us to get married. I was in the fields; we were transplanting rice. The Pol Potists called a meeting, but they never said anything about marriage. They did not want us to know. When I got there I was given a pair of pants and a red scarf. I was happy because I hadn't had anything to wear. Then we were told to go to the kitchen. There they said, . . . "They've arranged for you to take a husband." My heart sank, but I didn't dare argue for fear of being killed. Such things were not allowed.

Along with other involuntary couples, they were married under raised bayonets. Her second husband was like herself, a new person—someone who had been forcibly relocated to the area. He had been a soldier under Lon Nol but had hidden his identity. His family was a rarity: all of its members survived because each made an escape and they all changed their identities. Together, Mr. and Mrs. Sophat fled in an attempt to avoid starvation, but were finally caught and put into a reeducation camp. They were punished by being made to do heavy work, like digging by hand: "That was worse than being in prison. The men had leg shackles, but not the women; they knew we couldn't escape far." She was in the reeducation camp for three months before her brother obtained her release. The Khmer Rouge had planned to kill him, but changed their minds when he proved useful repairing trucks and other machines. He made up a story that her husband was missing and that she should be allowed to go look for him. Later reunited, she and her second husband finally made it to the border, with her mother and two children from her first marriage.

Reclassifications: Revolutionaries and Enemies

Little has been known about how the Khmer Rouge sought to build a new social order based on a biopolitical differentiation between useful and revolutionary citizens on the one hand, and useless intellectuals and bourgeois traitors of the revolution on the other. An abstract hierarchy of classifications

and rationalities categorized people as country folk or urban exiles, prole-
tarians or educated bourgeois, loyal Cambodians or pro-Western imperialist followers and traitors, adults or children, each with a different value in
the social order. While the communist utopia sought to abolish classes, it developed a polarized scheme of people who were assessed to be useful or not
useful to the state—citizens or enemies. Peasants in their home areas (bases)
were called old people or base citizens *(bracheahuan mouladthan)*.[57] As the true
agrarian subjects, they had the right political status and enjoyed better access to all kinds of resources. Displaced urban dwellers were called the new
people in the countryside, people who were relatively worthless in building
the agrarian utopia. They were collectively considered enemies of the state
(kbot cheat) and were harshly treated.[58] These differences were enforced with
savage and random authority, and being labeled meant the difference between eking out a livelihood and deep exploitation, between the right to live
and being executed. As Ledgerwood and others have observed, most
refugees consider the Pol Pot years as a time in which the social order was
upended. "The most obvious reversal was between 'old' or 'base' people,
people who had lived in the previously liberated areas of the countryside,
and 'new' people who were evacuated from the cities. . . . 'Old' people were
given positions of political, social, and economic superiority over highly educated, formerly wealthy, and powerful urbanites."[59] Thousands of suspect
people were tortured and killed in prison camps.[60] People revealed to have
been educated professionals, ethnic Chinese, or soldiers under the Lon Nol
government were randomly killed. The Khmer Rouge, by contrast, constituted a kind of revolutionary aristocracy.

Mrs. Sophat said of her first husband, from whom she had been separated
in the exodus from Phnom Penh,

> I lost contact with my husband forever. Later, I only received news he had
> died. . . . Even if he had made it safely out to the countryside, my husband would
> not have survived Pol Pot because he looked the type, looked like a person of
> some consequence. They would not have let him live. By his look and demeanor,
> if they had found him, they would have killed him. They wouldn't have kept
> him alive. His entire family died; not even a niece or nephew survived. They
> killed all of them. We didn't dare keep any of his pictures or addresses or any-
> thing. Otherwise, the Khmer Rouge would have killed my entire family. I buried
> his passport at Toul Andet. I didn't dare keep it for fear that it would have cost
> my life and those of his children.

Another refugee in Oakland—Mrs. Lim, a Sino-Cambodian—was a member of the commercial class; her family had been in Phnom Penh for three
generations. She did not grow up speaking Chinese and had very little schooling as a child. Her family was driven to the countryside, where they were
forced to take up farming and given very little to eat in Svay Rieng province:

They took away my younger siblings. That is why I almost went mad. Except for me, my siblings are gone. They killed them off: an older sister, a younger sister, and a younger brother. My older sister with her ten children. My father was murdered too. My mother was almost taken away. For every minor infraction, they'll take you away. If you're light-skinned, they'll say you're Vietnamese. You'll be killed. We could not even let them see us cry. That is why we almost lost our minds.

They killed light-skinned people. Professors, all the professionals, they didn't spare anybody. My brother was a teacher; they took him away. We thought they wouldn't kill teachers. . . . Even a little baby who hasn't done anything to anybody, they were also taken to be killed. If they didn't throw them on a bayonet, then they would smash them against the tree trunk until they died and dropped to the pit below. My nieces and nephews who were only about three months old were also taken to be killed.

Refugee Tony Ngin reported that Sino-Cambodians living in the provinces fared a little better because they could be embedded in peasant society. He noted that the major difference in suffering was between people expelled from Phnom Penh and those who originated from Battambang. Tony's father was a Cantonese businessman who owned grocery stores in Battambang. Like all local residents, they were sent out to the surrounding countryside to work as farmers. Battambang families like his were better able to survive than migrants from Phnom Penh because they could hold on to their belongings and had access to all kinds of local resources: "Most of the migrants from Phnom Penh perished." Later, Tony's father and a brother also succumbed to starvation. Tony, then in his early twenties, agreed that the Khmer Rouge singled out professionals, teachers, and other employees of the former Lon Nol government, but didn't persecute people simply because they were ethnic Chinese, like his family. After the Vietnamese invasion, Tony and the rest of his family walked overnight to the Thai border, and the Khmer Rouge allowed them to pass in exchange for a few U.S. dollars.

Mrs. Tech was the daughter of farmers who lived near Kompong Rouge. She was married to a soldier under the Lon Nol government:

The night the Khmer Rouge took my husband from my arms is still fresh in my mind. Back then we did not tell them anything about being in the civil service and all, just that he was a farmer. I don't know how they knew. They took everyone in our group. There were three persons in the house who worked in the military, including my husband. They came and called all of them away to be beaten to death, but one survived. He was only unconscious and was later able to sneak away. At night, he came back to get his wife. I was unconscious like the dead, so exhausted from work and fear.

After the Vietnamese invasion, Mrs. Tech met up with the survivor, who told her that her husband had been killed that night. By then, she had escaped with her four remaining children to Battambang.

In the labor camps, surviving new people were subjected to daily political education to eliminate their bourgeois attitude and individualist leanings. The goal was to shape the perfect revolutionary who would serve Angkar with total submission. "The Khmer Rouge attitude to those with qualifications was uncompromising: 'To leave them alive contributes nothing. By exterminating them, nothing is lost to the Revolution.' Educated people were simply threats to be eliminated."[61]

Angkar policies also inverted conventional age and sex hierarchies. Angkar's ragged bands of teenage soldiers not only wielded power in the labor camps, but they also sought out enemies of the regime, tortured and killed suspects, arranged forced marriages, and, according to survivors, generally created a daily theater of terror and arbitrary brutality. Children were taught to inform on their parents, and were used in other ways as potential threats to their parents' authority. Ledgerwood mentions that Khmer refugees whom she interviewed said that some women betrayed their husbands by revealing their past or by making false accusations.[62] None of the refugees in Oakland whom I interviewed complained about being explicitly betrayed by children or wives.

Khmer Rouge policies for overturning conventional societal relationships had an extensive impact on gender relations. Some women were forced into marriage and many were raped, and thus were continually exposed to conditions in which they could not protect their virtue. Female informants told of themselves and other women losing male protectors and being forced to struggle on their own to save their surviving children. Their stories suggest that female survivors tried, under the most daunting circumstances, to live up to Khmer-Buddhist ideals of womanhood. Mrs. Tech's story is one of possibly countless examples of a woman's valiant attempt to hold her family together in those war years. In 1979, as the Vietnamese invasion of Democratic Kampuchea brought chaos, an opening was created for many Cambodians to escape to the Thai border:

> I was a single mother with four sick children. I carried all my sick children by turn, running from one place to another to find a place free from the Khmer Rouge, when the Vietnamese occupied my country. I needed to find money to support the children. My hands were full. I took my two older sons who were very sick to the Battambang hospital, where they were admitted. I did not have any money; I had to leave them there.
>
> I escaped to the Thai border, where I set up a little business to make some money. When I arrived, all my energies were almost gone, and the two children who were with me were very sick too. I brought them to the hospital at the border. We were admitted and then sent to Khao-I-Dang hospital by ambulance. We stayed at the hospital for several months. When I felt better, I wanted to go back to Battambang to pick up my two boys. But I didn't know how to do this. I was already in Thailand and had the two younger ones with

me. I did not know what to do. I felt terrible that I could not go back and pick up my children to be reunited with us in Thailand. It had been extremely difficult to escape. I have felt sorry and sick ever since.

In many cases, the loss of a father, husband, or other male protector stripped women and children of any degree of safety, and women had to resort to all kinds of devices—burying evidence of family status, faking their class or ethnicity, submitting to forced marriages, seeking male companions, engaging in smuggling and barter—to escape arbitrary violence and survive deprivation. Unrelenting hunger drove almost everyone to steal food for their children. Some sold bits of jewelry concealed in their sarongs to buy food and medicine that was often ineffective. Many died from lack of medical care, an experience that has made Cambodian refugees extremely concerned about access to medicine. Children were often forcibly separated from their parents, and those temporarily abandoned generally became permanently lost or orphaned.[63] Khmer Buddhist values had to be discarded as profound distrust guided every effort to remain alive.

For its victims, the Pol Pot years shattered any sense of security and trust in social relations, even within the family. The high degree of insecurity, incidence of betrayal, and other reversals attenuated cultural norms. In the midst of life-and-death choices and the extremity of daily survival, people depended on subterfuge, disguise, lying, and silence. Individuals tried to disappear into the local old people among whom they were settled, passively followed orders, and dumbed down their behavior. They became adept at dissimulation and dual consciousness in order to escape unwelcome attention or detection.[64] The very tactics and transgressions required to survive and to hold families together kept women from guarding their virtue. Women who had sexual contacts outside marriage or who had been raped suffered additional moral devaluation; widows and unmarried women were stigmatized as lacking all moral value.[65] Those who survived and reached refugee camps felt that just as there were no more virtuous women, there seemed to be no more Buddhism as well.

The words of poet U Sam Oeur invoke the Buddhist motherland buried by war:

> No places to hide, no skies under which to rest;
> and the moaning of children,
> and the cries of mothers
> out of blazing fire across the land,
> And your bodies, brothers, shielding us
> from the bullets, and your blood
> splashing over our Mother, induce my soul
> to ever worship jasmine and lotus blossoms.[66]

Chapter 2

A Hilton in the Border Zone

On January 7, 1979, the Vietnamese invaded Phnom Penh and deposed the Pol Pot regime. In the months that followed, sporadic fighting and the ensuing chaos pushed more than half a million people toward the Thai border. When the United Nations–sponsored Khao-I-Dang (KID) camp was opened over the border in Thailand at the end of the year, Mrs. Sophat, the woman who had been forced into marriage under Khmer Rouge bayonets, immediately began plotting to escape with as many family members as she could gather. They went to Battambang to look for her first husband's family: "Only two sisters had died." The group (consisting of Mrs. Sophat, her second husband, her mother, and two children from her first marriage) then set out, walking for three days and nights toward the border. They stepped carefully around land mines. Mrs. Sophat was pregnant with her third child. At her new husband's home village, a man gave them two grams of gold and said that they could repay him when they had some money. Her husband then slipped into the New Camp that had risen up on the Kampuchea side of the border across from Khao-I-Dang. He bought rice and other food to trade. When he returned for them, fighting had broken out in the border area, and Vietnamese soldiers kept the family from crossing into Thailand. Together with others who had fled to the area, they decided to make a nighttime run for the border:

> There were about two hundred of us. So we filed out secretly that night without letting the Vietnamese know. We waded in water up to our chest. But I was carrying the little one all the way across. My mother begged, "I can't go on. You all go without me!" but my husband just carried her over. He also lugged a pail of clean water. I had a bag of rice which I clutched along with the baby, and some clothes. At one point, the Vietnamese gave chase. They tried to herd us back . . . we all scattered through the jungle until we ran into the Khmer Rouge. . . .

We pleaded, "We fled from the Vietnamese to look for you, Brothers [*Bong*]. We don't want to live with the Vietnamese." We just said anything to save our lives. Then they searched us, everywhere. They wanted to see if we were concealing gold. . . . They did not kill us, but those who came later, that's when it all began. They'd rape and kill. Whoever could escape, did. Those who couldn't were killed.

Mrs. Sophat's group often could not distinguish between the Thai border patrols (some of whom operated as bandits) and the Khmer Rouge.

It's difficult because they wore the same clothing and they didn't talk. Cambodians and Thais look the same, you know. There was a lot of deception. With banditry in the border area, there were lots of Thais pretending to be Khmers. Mostly the Khmer Rouge donned the para-fatigues in order to blame the killing on the "paras."[1]

They found her second husband's father at the New Camp. Transportation was provided between that camp and Khao-I-Dang, but people were reluctant to avail themselves of it because there were wild rumors that the trucks were really taking people to be dumped at Dangrek, where many refugees had died. Then the camp was attacked again:

Fighting broke out again and we fled. Bullets fell like raindrops. We had no money except what I made selling belongings, and I paid a guide to take us through the jungle. We slept there. The next day, my son almost drowned in the river. When we first got to Khao-I-Dang camp, we had no rations, and so I carried him to the hospital. . . . One night he had diarrhea and became very ill. I had sent my sister-in-law to stay with him for the night. The next day they took him to the morgue. They thought that my son had died. I said he could not have died because he spoke to me before I went to bed. But his eyes were shut, and I thought that he was indeed dead. I was crying. . . . An Indian doctor told me through the interpreter that there was nothing anyone could do. That I must let go. Thinking about his words, I went to fetch my son's clothing. Then I saw his hand move. They had already covered him in plastic. I lifted the sheet and saw my son open his eyes. I ran out and called the doctors, everyone, shouting that my son was alive again. They carried him back to the hospital room. He couldn't walk for three months; his legs were all shriveled up. He was about twelve years old.
   He's grown now and is very handsome. When I look at him, I am reminded of his late father.

Mrs. Sophat recounted this escape story in her crowded Oakland apartment. In several respects, she was not typical of the Cambodian refugees who came to California: she had a middle-class background, had been a trader in the Cambodian-Thai border zone, and managed to save many members of her family. Most of the educated urban Cambodians who survived sought refuge in France, and Cambodians from the old diplomatic elite before Pol Pot went to Washington, D.C. The majority of refugees who arrived in the United States were small-town folk or peasants, mostly from northwestern Cambodia, around Battambang.

The Cambodian refugee situation in many ways challenges our notion of refugees as displaced peoples seeking refuge outside their homeland. Nation-states and the United Nations have specific criteria that define what constitutes refugee-subject status and how refugees are governed; their institutional mechanisms are what transform displaced populations into bona fide refugees, who then become subjects with particular rights, however narrow and arbitrary those rights might be. The experiences of refugees from Southeast Asia show how international realpolitik and global public opinion, shaped by the imagery of the mass media, intersect to produce refugee subjects. On the ground, a plethora of nongovernmental international assistance agencies (called volags, for "voluntary agencies") are actually responsible for reterritorializing the displaced as refugees within camps and, subsequently, help train the refugees in the skills and attitudes they will need to become citizens of particular countries. The border camps, in other words, are sites for the production of particular kinds of refugee subjects.

AT THE INTERSECTION OF REALPOLITIK AND HUMANITARIANISM

In one of the many ironies of the Indochina conflict, it was the Vietnamese invasion of Kampuchea in early 1979 that set Cambodians free from their own despotic regime and established the short-lived People's Republic of Kampuchea (PRK). Ongoing fighting and ambushes by retreating Khmer Rouge soldiers provided the cover for an outflow of Cambodians to the Thai border area. Half-dead refugees walked, stumbled, and crawled out of the jungle toward the camps. They came as straggling bands of families, groups of orphans, Khmer Rouge deserters, and smugglers, preyed upon by both the retreating Khmer Rouge and the Thai soldiers. As Mrs. Sophat's story implies, many died along the way from exhaustion, sickness, hunger, bullets, and land mines.[2]

From the perspective of the Thai government, these people were not genuine refugees, because a new regime had been installed in Phnom Penh. Michael Vickery says, "They were 'displaced persons' on the Cambodian side of the border, and 'illegal immigrants' on the Thai side."[3] Since 1975, the ill-defined Thai-Cambodian border zone had been crisscrossed by smugglers, bandits, and traders; and now they were joined by Cambodian refugees and various forces who had opposed Democratic Kampuchea, collectively referred to as Khmer Serei. In June 1979, Thai soldiers forcibly returned tens of thousands across the border. An international outcry put pressure on Thailand to embrace more humanitarian policies. Convinced that the newly formed PRK was in administrative collapse and that widespread starvation was imminent, the American embassy in Bangkok, along with American and European charities, rushed emergency aid to the border zone.

Humanitarian interventions, Nevzat Soguk has argued, are not merely about resolving a problem; they are also practices of active regimentation that "work principally to recuperate state sovereignty in the face of specific historical challenges."[4] And indeed, it is important to keep this perspective on statecraft in mind when examining the broader theater of political machinations that produced the Cambodian refugee situation. Vickery argues that the Thai and U.S. governments, both implacably opposed to the Vietnam-dominated PRK, sought "to use the refugee situation to influence future political developments within Cambodia."[5] By November, half a million Cambodians were massed along the border, and observers noted that controlling such a huge proportion of Cambodia's reputed four million surviving population might give Bangkok political advantages vis-à-vis the Phnom Penh regime. Vickery, who opposed giving refugee status to noncombatants in this case, maintains that realpolitik, mass-media imagery, and political expediency all converged to produce circumstances that persuaded poor Cambodians to become refugees. The Voice of America began Khmer-language broadcasts about KID as a place for Cambodians to go to "seek freedom," and rumors spread that KID refugees could expect a quick resettlement in countries other than Thailand or Cambodia.[6] The Thai government agreed to open a string of "holding centers" to care for Cambodian refugees who might later wish to return to their homeland or to be resettled abroad. The major border camp was established at Khao-I-Dang, and the United Nations High Commission for Refugees (UNHCR) set up operations.

But political expediencies aside, humanitarian issues were paramount. In 1979, the situation inside Cambodia was dire: there was widespread malnutrition and the threat of starvation. The Vietnamese invasion came as the harvest was being gathered, and retreating Khmer Rouge troops took supplies with them or destroyed the harvest so as to leave nothing for the Vietnamese soldiers. Famished Cambodians ransacked and consumed food stockpiles, eating the grain intended for the next year's crops. As Judy Ledgerwood points out, "The crucial issue is not whether or not there should have been aid sent, or whether the crisis was created, but rather whether the aid should have been sent over the border (which certainly did draw people there) or whether it should have been given to the PRK."[7] As the refugees' stories show, many people living near the border, especially in the Battambang region, escaped Cambodia because there was no food, because the Khmer Rouge forced people to move toward the border, and in some cases because they were still attempting to elude Khmer Rouge control. As the PRK became more established and the food emergency passed, some people went to the border to join the resistance groups or to trade.

THE VOLAG UNIVERSE

OXFAM, UNBRO, ICRDP, UNHCR, UNICEF, WHO, FPP, FHH, WR, COER: these acrimonious acronyms cluster like flies round the wounds of sick nations. The missionary, the priest, and the lady with the lamp have given way to the relief worker and the photojournalist and the television reporter.
MARGARET DRABBLE, *The Gates of Ivory*

More than a decade later, in 1992, British writer Margaret Drabble observed that the border zone was occupied by two sets of displaced populations, who reflected the larger geopolitical fault lines of the Indochina conflict. Along the Thai border were the "camps of the displaced Khmers" on one side, and on the other side, the "camps of the displaced West."[8] Relief workers, mainly from Western countries, provided food, medicine, clothing, blankets, language instruction, and emigration advice to hundreds of thousands of refugees seeking security and eventual repatriation to third countries.[9] There was a strained symbiosis between the refugees and the relief workers. The latter had in a sense escaped the greed and wealth of the West to tend to the dying, the sick, and displaced around the world. This "great army of the faithful disillusioned"[10] found a site where they could demonstrate their capacity for brotherly compassion and sacrifice against the backdrop of a selfish world. Like refugees, they were thus geographically and spiritually displaced from their own sphere and installed in temporary quarters along the border. There was, of course, a significant difference in power between the two displaced populations, for besides saving lives and giving hope, relief workers were also cultural agents socializing refugees to live in the world they themselves had temporarily fled.

A constellation of aid agencies—American Refugee Committee, OXFAM, Médecins sans Frontières, Catholic Charities, and so on—constituted the universe in which Cambodian arrivals were transformed into refugees. Many of the American volags were run by church groups whose main task was to find local sponsors for refugees seeking resettlement abroad. Relief agencies and their workers are an increasingly common form of humanitarian intervention, and they must be recognized as transnational systems of power in their own right. Indeed, once the volags were set up in the Thai border zone, they exerted pressure on the government authorities to expand the area of operations, and to convert what were holding centers into more permanent settlements.[11]

And the power of the volags went beyond their tending to the needs of ever larger bodies of displaced persons. Relief workers, however genuine their humanitarian urgency, are perhaps unavoidably agents of compassionate domination. They introduce specific technologies of governing that orient and shape the everyday behavior of refugees (usually from the less-developed world), transforming them into particular kinds of modern human beings (bound for Western liberal democracies).[12] In the Thai border zone, and in the three refugee processing centers based in Thailand, the Philippines, and Indonesia, refugees were assisted by an international network of relief agencies that began the work of reorganizing their collective survival and their moral sense of who they were to become. Families were reunited, recombined, and newly formed; and relief organizations began the task of physically and socially converting the refugees into "citizens of the world" using public-health campaigns, schools, and even women's organizations.[13]

THE REFUGEE HILTON

Khao-I-Dang was called the Hilton of refugee camps because its huge facilities were designed for permanent settlement—an improvement over more temporary camps, where people were kept as virtual prisoners. Operated by the UNHCR and the Thai army, KID was also prisonlike, encircled by barbed wire and armed military guards. Thai soldiers enriched themselves at the expense of the refugees by raiding, extortion, and participating in the black market. The soldiers terrorized them, raping women and taking children to sell into prostitution. Refugees were vulnerable to military recruiters and thieves, as well as being at the mercy of hunger and boredom. Hiang Ngor, the actor who starred in the film *The Killing Fields,* confirmed that although the camp administrators brought some order and peace during the day, at night many refugees were victimized by the very Thai soldiers who were supposed to protect them. "If we violated any rules, like smuggling liquor, they would beat us. Even if we did not break any rules, they would beat us up also. There were no laws. And we could not demand any justice because we had no rights, no freedom. . . . Sometimes the Thai guards would rape Cambodian girls but they did not dare to do it too blatantly because we were protected by the relief agencies. If any of the troops were guilty, they would be transferred from the area."[14] The rape of female refugees, especially young girls, by Thai soldiers was often mentioned by refugees, but there are no statistics or studies to indicate how extensive the crime was. By the later 1980s, reforms improved safety; other forces were brought in that included female soldiers, and the camp developed "flourishing markets, an adequate water supply, excellent feeding facilities, schools, recreational facilities, and even a local Khmer dance academy."[15]

At KID, Cambodian refugees experienced a whole new set of conflicting power conditions relating to access to food, trade, and patronage. Refugees had to learn quickly the system of camp nomenclature that determined who was entitled to better treatment and more resources. Their chances improved if they could change their status from illegal alien to legal refugee. By 1982, those who had entered illegally and did not have properly registered names and KID numbers were not entitled to food allocations or handouts. Those discovered to be illegal aliens were sent to another camp, which was less stocked with supplies—though Ngor reported that one Khmer Serei official covertly allowed a certain number of non-KID members to remain in each sector of the camp, and provided food rations for them. And food was not supposed to be distributed to male refugees, so that the UNHCR would not be accused of feeding combatants in the war.[16] Thai soldiers who handled food supplies may have resented the fact that their own impoverished people were excluded from receiving a share of the largesse from overseas.

The Hilton sobriquet was perhaps not entirely a joke for the educated urbanites, who had the chance to obtain positions working with the volags. Ngor himself managed to work as a food distributor in the camp. He claimed that by the end of 1979, "most of Cambodia's old middle class and elite showed up in Khao-I-Dang."[17] Many of the middle-class refugees resisted whenever they could the camp's organizational discipline. They engaged in a clandestine trade in the camp's daily rice rations, selling them to the even more impoverished residents of neighboring Thai villages. Others sold sexual favors to obtain a variety of goods from the Thai soldiers. According to Vickery, these "bourgeois refugees" rejected suggestions that they grow vegetables on vacant land.[18] The most subversive activity, in the view of the camp authorities, was "the persistence in black-market dealings with surrounding Thai villages that could have endangered the status of the camp."[19] These unofficial market activities emphasized the "privileged" status of refugees in comparison to Thai peasants, and thus potentially undermined the Thai authorities.

Initially, the UNHCR turned black-market traders over to the Thai guards, whom the refugees considered as brutal as the Khmer Rouge.[20] Indeed, the camp hierarchy and rules were sometimes reminiscent of the Angkar, and people had to resort to the same kinds of personal strategies they had used under the Pol Pot regime to secure their safety and survival. Ngor explained that conditions for the refugees could change radically depending on the abilities of the Red Cross administrator running the camp. In 1982, for example, the administrator could not stand up to the Thai troops, and the situation in the camp deteriorated as their abuse of refugees went unpunished.[21] Refugees seeking food for personal consumption and trade found themselves caught between the sometimes contradictory policies of the Thai army and the UNHCR. The politics of food and the competition for access to other resources were key rituals in camp life that came to shape Cambodians' understanding of power relations within the volag world. The conditions fostered all-too-familiar clientelist practices, but with some differences: now women as well as men could play the game, and the cast of potential patrons was an international one.

The nongovernmental organizations were there not only to improve health and provide security, but also to train people to become the kind of refugees who might qualify for asylum in the West. Indeed, volag agents themselves personified the "superior citizens" Cambodians might want to become. The classifications and practices of these organizations elaborated regulations concerning work, leisure, the use of time, and proper social behavior, with the goal of teaching the minimal skills needed to live in European or American societies. Daily activities central to refugee survival—the distribution of food and the allocation of other resources, including English lessons and medical care—gave form to these structures for ordering social relations. Intended to promote the health and well-being of refugees, volag practices also enforced clear-cut disciplinary and symbolic social differences between the service providers and the refugees, and reinforced the dominance of the former. I suggest that refugees were constituted not merely through legal categories but by everyday encounters and interactions with camp personnel, who shaped the conditions of living in the volag world.

Once their health improved, refugees began to look for ways to supplement the handouts. Barry Levy, an American doctor working at KID, reported,

> Many of the Cambodians at the camp worked long hours in the heat—not merely for the wages of 50 cents a day, but largely out of pride and a desire to contribute to their community. Cambodian construction workers built huts and hospital wards and dug latrines. Cambodian public-health workers gave thousands of immunizations for polio, measles, and other diseases to children who were susceptible to them. Cambodian technicians performed microscopic examinations in the clinical laboratory. Cambodian artisans—including one woman who was almost blind—made bamboo baskets, mugs, and fish traps and sold them at the crafts center.[22]

Jobs, however, were hard to come by, and the majority of the refugees had to contend with poverty, boredom, and low status.

In the early 1980s, a camp trainer put out a notice seeking refugees to be trained as hospital workers. She expected about twenty to forty students, but instead got more than four hundred applicants.[23] French nurses taught classes from memory; the vast majority of the students were men with a range of professional backgrounds from their lives before Pol Pot.[24] Phauly Sang, who was in her twenties when she spent time at KID and had studied as a pharmacist in Phnom Penh, recalled in an interview with me that

> When I was in Khao-I-Dang, they had a job opening in the hospital there. They said, "People need to help people!" I told my camp section leader my profession. I was assigned to work in the lab. My first boss was American; he spoke only English. The second boss and the head of the lab, she was Belgian. She translated for me in French. I worked only a few months, testing blood.

Another woman, who had been a doctor in Phnom Penh, wanted to work with the Americans rather than the French because she wanted to learn English. Ngor, who had been a doctor before the war, appeared to have made the same choice, and while working for the ARC he slowly became reacquainted with healing and American medical techniques, while picking up English.[25] Using such strategies, educated Cambodians became enmeshed in a system of dependency on American and other Western supervisors, and this hierarchy of white patronage improved their opportunities for eventual resettlement in the United States.

Despite the American bombing in the early 1970s and the Vietnamese invasion that allowed them to escape the Khmer Rouge, the Cambodians regarded Americans as their saviors, and America was their preferred destination. One of them told me that America was the richest country in the world; it could make big wars, but it could also provide massive support and freedom from the communists. The Hilton camp was thus the site at which they came to perceive that Americans were the main donors of food and dollars, even though the relief workers actually came from many different countries. Such institutional dependence was among the initial lessons in the meaning of American citizenship.

The Medicalization of Life

At KID, medicine was a major part of the social technology for reconstituting refugee bodies and persons. Cambodians in the camps had just come from a desperate situation in which relatives were dying from lack of medicine. The Khmer Rouge refused to use Western medicine, and cadres sometimes administered bogus medicines to the sick. Now they found themselves in the position of having too much medicine—which paradoxically also incited fears of dying out as a people. Health services in the camp were for many rural Cambodians their first encounter with a good system of health maintenance that included inpatient hospitals and outpatient clinics. Upon arrival, refugees were screened in order to detect the emergency cases of malnutrition, dehydration, and serious disease, especially in children. Seriously ill patients were immediately taken to emergency wards.[26] A medical worker noted that the Hilton camp "experienced the mixed blessing of a glut of medical personnel"; at one point there were more than twenty resettlement agencies involved in some aspect of health care, whereas in a nearby camp there was only a single physician in charge, who also took care of the tens of thousands of Thai peasants in the vicinity.[27]

This plethora of health agencies brought survivors suddenly under various medical regimes that played a role in shaping their identity as refugees. As physicians attended to the health of their bodies, refugees were taught new social needs, norms, and practices that were expected of immigrants bound for the modern West. They were eager for medicine; at the same time, however, there was much resistance to some forms of medical treatment. For instance, their encounters in old Cambodia with French medicine had taught them to expect to receive all medications in the form of injections, and many felt dissatisfied when camp health workers did not give them shots. Refugees encountered Western medics in the camps with great expectations but also ambivalence and anxiety, especially relating to institutional norms of what it meant to be good patients.

One case is particularly illustrative of the complexities of the refugees' encounters with medicine at KID. In 1979, a Thai relief organization introduced a birth-control program, already implemented in nearby villages, to KID. It set as a priority maintaining "the health and well-being of the Cambodian 'illegal aliens' while they were guests of the Thai government."[28] The program had good intentions—building up the refugees' health before they began to produce babies. But when the Thai family-planning medics proposed using DepoProvera injections, even though other contraceptives were available, foreign relief workers at KID objected, since DepoProvera had been medically linked to cancer. They characterized the program as "genocidal," which did not help the refugees develop a trusting relationship with the Thai medical authorities. A Cambodian nurse, who took the shot and suffered side effects from it, explained another reason for the refugees' wariness:

> Problems arose within families: husbands did not want their wives to have injections because they thought that the Thai people would not have sympathy toward Cambodian people; it was feared that they may have wanted to destroy our race, which was already partly massacred.[29]

Furthermore, Thai workers used food, which was both a source of nutrition and a form of currency in the camp, as an inducement to women to participate in the program: they were urged to take a shot of DepoProvera in return for a chicken. According to my informants who spent time at KID, this succeeded in getting many Cambodian women to take the shot. Since chicken was only a weekly treat, the offer was very tempting, despite rumors about the contraceptive's side effects.

Mrs. Yann, mentioned in the previous chapter, was another who started using DepoProvera in the camp, after Mr. Yann found her "struggling along by herself" and married her. He complained that after she received the shot, she got so sick that she almost died; "but I took care of her and she got well again." He restored her health using Cambodian herbs, but they feared that she would not be able to have a baby. Later, an American worker helped them adopt an orphaned baby girl.

In the camp, then, refugees whose recent experience was of a nearly complete absence of medicine had to adjust to a situation in which gaining access to medical intervention required yielding up intimate information about their personal lives. They had strong motivation to conform to the new regimes of medical practice: Western-style medicines such as injections were regarded as a kind of magic bullet for their many ills. This opened the way for the health agencies to play a role in redefining the refugee subject within a field of rational observation with specific expectations of health and body care.[30] In order to get medicines and other good things, they learned the importance of meeting the appropriate criteria and submitting to the new disciplines and norms of the volag technologies.

SCREENING FOR GOOD REFUGEES

For many refugees, the camps were the first places they came under the gaze of foreigners—Western experts and officials. The most nerve-racking encounters were those with officials of the United States Immigration and Naturalization Service (INS), who held the key to their resettlement in America. Between 1983 and 1985, the United States accepted fifty thousand refugees from Cambodia, out of the half million who had fled to the border.[31] INS officers arrived at KID to screen refugees, to determine who deserved to emigrate to the United States and who did not. The criteria, never very clear to the refugees themselves, seem to have been to distinguish bona fide political refugees from others, as well as noncommunists from communists. There is some irony here because while the majority of Cambodians in the camps were people who would have fitted the United Nations' definition of the politically persecuted, some were merely economic refugees seeking a better life in the West. Nevertheless, in practice, INS officers simply assumed that all Cambodians in the camps were political refugees, since they had escaped from a communist country. Their main concern was in not letting any communists slip the net.

Although there was overwhelming evidence that only a tiny percentage of refugees at KID were members of the Khmer Rouge, a "Khmer Rouge screening process" rejected thousands on the unsubstantiated suspicion that they participated in Khmer Rouge brutality or were affiliated with them. Stephen Golub has reported that the most circumstantial evidence, such as working involuntarily under the Angkar authorities or recounting stories that did not fit an assumed pattern of life in Khmer Rouge collective farms, was used to reject applicants.[32] Translation problems and social differences such as the refugees' body language—smiling even under stress, reporting the deaths of relatives with a dispassionate expression—made them Khmer Rouge suspects in the eyes of INS officers. Golub concludes, "The INS tends to perceive Khmer Rouge affiliation where it does not exist."[33] The INS interviewers lacked the cultural and political knowledge to assess the applicants' stories accurately, and their fear of letting communists through affected the fate of many.[34]

The refugees themselves, having excelled at second-guessing the Khmer Rouge in a life-or-death crapshoot, contributed to the miscommunication with the INS. Based on their experience, they treated all officials as all-powerful figures to be feared, placated, and humored, rather than as people to whom one could tell the complex truths about one's situation. Silence, dissembling, and faked life stories—essential to survival under the Angkar—were resorted to in navigating the often confusing questioning by INS bureaucrats. The rules for resettlement often seemed arbitrary; for instance, extended family groups were limited to eight members, but nuclear families were not. Since Cambodian survivors did not conveniently fit into these neat categories of extended and nuclear families, many refugees who had no surviving nuclear family members resorted to strategies like claiming fake kinship relations with departing refugees. Others changed their names and ages in order to fit into something resembling a nuclear family that would be eligible for sponsorship.[35] The upshot of the cross-cultural miscommunication and the strategies of second-guessing was that many refugees, who might have been eligible for resettlement, were denied admission to the United States because their attempts to fit the rigid categories of family units backfired. And despite the INS officials' efforts, many people who had been part of the Khmer Rouge organization actually gained admission.

By their process of identifying the "good Cambodians" who deserved to be resettled, the INS impressed upon the refugees the importance of being properly labeled according to bureaucratic categories defined by the official agencies and volags that were destined to be so crucial to their lives in diaspora. Those who cleared the INS screening were channeled to transit camps where they were subjected to language and cultural orientation classes aimed at transforming them into citizen subjects ready for resettlement in their destination country.

English and Citizenship in the World

English-language classes were an obvious first step toward that goal, and they were very popular. My informants told me that children and adults paid fifteen baht a day for hour-long lessons in the alphabet, basic grammar, and arithmetic. Some children took private lessons at night. A camp official complained that the camp agencies created "unrealistic expectations" among the refugees. "The refugees thus came to believe that if they could learn English their chance for resettlement in the United States was virtually assured. This, in turn, may have contributed to an overall reluctance on the part of the refugees to consider repatriation or resettlement in a country within the Southeast Asia region."[36] Many of the women who were heads of families expressed the desire that their children "grow up in a free country." This wish had in fact been fostered by American relief officials, who seemed to promise so much through their patronage and charity.

Camp organizations tended to take over the socialization of children from their parents. Children came in for special attention as the most vulnerable subjects in the camps, who represented the survival of Cambodians as a group. As a result, refugee adults and children came to be prepared by different agencies for their new needs and norms as potential citizens in the West. The director of an American volag wondered about the "appropriate models for the children in refugee camps." She worried about the effect of sporadic disruptions from fighting and bad weather on support programs— such as schools, women's associations, and public-health campaigns—that were crucial to the preschool years, because they laid "the critical foundation for the good 'citizen[s] of the world' [they have] a right to become. . . . 'World citizen' development cannot continue until the rains start and the fighting stops."[37]

But those young refugees being transformed into citizens of the world were taking in more than lessons on the three R's. In everyday interactions with refugee teachers, they were also imbibing messages about American social hierarchies. Carol A. Mortland suggests that the experiences of the Cambodian refugees in the border camps could be regarded as a rite of passage. She describes them as "the symbolic actions of transition which had been deliberately created by an international community to transform . . . refugees from Southeast Asia into people fitted for incorporation into new societies."[38] The volags' role in "transform[ing] refugees into viable migrants" entailed a system of symbols through which dependency was thoroughly institutionalized.[39]

Conducting research in the Bataan refugee processing center (PRPC) in the Philippines, Mortland observed that hierarchical status systems determined by American criteria—such as ability to speak English, and attitudes about attendance rules, speech, and use of physical space—were central to lessons preparing refugees to become American. "Despite their general air of familiarity, Americans do not deal with refugees except as superiors, teachers, and bosses. . . . When higher status residents wish to emphasize their power, refugees are forced to demonstrate their own humility by physical as well as verbal gesture."[40] Thus the acquisition of English, at a rudimentary level, included lessons in symbolic subordination in the American citizenship and labor markets.

The administrative buildings in the PRPC carried signs that proclaimed,

> Refugee transformation, the primary goal of the PRPC operations, is achieved through a psycho-social recuperative process involving the "critical phases of adaptation, capability building, and disengagement" which result in changing a "displaced person" into an "Individual Well Equipped for Life in His Country of final destination."[41]

The processing logic was to instruct refugees to "speak good English, be employable, be unwilling to accept welfare, and be happy" in America.[42]

A social worker put his finger on the predicament of Cambodian people who ended up in camps: "Most of them are what the world calls 'boat people,' and from the moment they get picked up by Thai police, they lose complete control of their lives. From that moment on, they're forced to live by some-one else's rules. Something is destroyed in the process—the cultural values that may have prevailed before."[43] Not to deny the refugees' capacity to struggle on their own behalf, but they now lived in an alien cultural environment in which they were supposed to acquire basic job skills and learn how to apply for jobs, and how to cope with the crime and racism they were likely to encounter in the United States. In the daily life of the camp, they were already learning the implicit norms of subservience for nonwhites. As the children picked up English more rapidly than their parents, adults began to lose prestige in the children's eyes. Thus—especially for refugees who had been elite members of the old Cambodian society—the experience of social reversal foreshadowed their experiences in the Land of the Free.

Women's Loss of Virtue and Gain of Autonomy

This reversal of the social order reverberated in other ways within the Cambodian refugee community. While many hold that there is pervasive mistrust of refugees, and that the refugee state mitigates gender inequality, the Cambodian situation demonstrates that cultural ideals shape refugee interpretations of trust and that camp politics and survival strategies may upend gender hierarchy as well.[44] Thus—as discussed in the previous chapter—while young and middle-aged Cambodian women came under suspicion as immoral women, their very struggle with daily exigencies of camp life empowered them vis-à-vis men, lingering cultural disapproval notwithstanding.

No longer able to command the respect they had been accustomed to before the Pol Pot time, middle-class Cambodians in the camps also had to contend with the loss of self-respect and of trust between men and women. Women were especially vulnerable to mistrust by the community because of their loss of virtue. The ideal of the perfectly virtuous woman could not be sustained in the war years, when women were often unprotected, violated, and in the company of male strangers. In other words, they violated all gender and kinship norms, though they did so under duress. Marjorie A. Muecke notes that being refugees put Cambodian women at risk for self-mistrust, being unable to uphold the ideal of perfect virtue, and being separated from their children.[45] Indeed, the large number of unprotected young women and widows, and the threat and frequency of rape in the camps, made practically all women immoral in terms of Khmer tradition. Women who had been raped, or compelled to take lovers for self-protection, dealt with their shame by keeping silent, and even denied that they had ever been violated in order to preserve what was left of their status as good women.[46] I met a woman who had been gang-raped who was abandoned by her husband after they arrived as a nuclear family in Oakland. The taint of rape was so intolerable to him that he considered her trash and left her homeless, along with their boy. This woman only mentioned her violation to me because she was desperate and thought that I could intervene on her behalf with a social worker to get her housing. But although all of my other female informants would tell me about torture, killings, and loss of family members, sexual abuse was the one kind of unspeakable experience they would not discuss.

Gender mistrust was further compounded once men and women were re-united in the camps, where everyone was competing for the favor of relief workers. Women seemed to have lost the ideals of serenity and self-restraint, and had begun to act in a self-directed manner, taking the initiative in seek-ing resources from the volags, which appeared to be more sympathetic to female clients than to male ones. There were more adult female than male survivors in the camps, and women had to contend for attention for their families. Unlike men, who could more easily engage in smuggling, trade, and construction work, many women were dependent on handouts, and they came to view any American air worker as a potential benefactor. Life in the camp revolved around getting enough food and daily amenities, and food supplies were given to women rather than men. In order to improve their family's well-being, therefore, women spent a lot of time building pa-tronage relations with relief workers, and put up with disciplining condi-tions and religious classes in exchange for preferential access to goods and services.

For instance, even though the voluntary agencies were not supposed to engage directly in missionary activities, many women found that by attend-ing church services, they could compel different kinds of assistance. Women found church workers most sympathetic about their family circumstances. Mrs. Sophat remembered that "when I was in Khao-I-Dang, I went to church. The church people helped us: they gave us things and clothes. I didn't know which church it was, but it was American. They came to help us in our homes, giving us food and clothing. They brought them to our homes. Sometimes they even gave us money." Her mother added, "They bought food and filled our cabinets. Sometimes they gave us twenty dollars. Every two to three days, they'd give my son, who was at the hospital, some money. They'd exchange the dollars for bahts to give us. They felt sorry for us." The church workers, who were less intimidating than other camp officials, often visited homes and provided much-needed support. From Cambodian women's perspective, it did not matter which church or which denomination assisted them, or the content of its teachings.

The gender fracture in access to volag patronage only widened as time went on, and it produced tensions between Cambodian wives and husbands. The unequal access to food rations induced men to take multiple wives in order to augment their food supplies. Some women retaliated against polygyny by taking lovers of their own—indicating a totally new attitude regarding sex and family loyalty.[47] Gender hostility was especially bad in camps that were controlled by a mix of royalist factions fighting against the PRK government. Many women were left in these camps to raise children alone because men were dead, or ill, or frequently absent while participating in the fighting. These women were under severe stress, and some in their husband's absence took other male protectors, or took to gambling or prostitution to raise money for their children.[48] Thus, on top of the upheavals of the Pol Pot years, camp life dealt severe shocks to the old Cambodian family system and its unquestioned norms of male dominance.

Although the majority of refugees I met arrived in the Bay Area in 1979 and the early 1980s, the effects of refugee camps on their family structure and gender relations were similar to those of refugees who stayed longer in the camps. Male power in the family and male prerogative in general had been destabilized, along with women's dependence on men and unquestioning obedience to their husbands. Between the ascendancy of the Khmer Rouge in 1975 and their arrival in the United States, the disappearance and death of fathers and husbands, women's daily struggle to ensure their own survival and that of their children, and the thousands of children left to fend for themselves had all shattered the traditional family arrangements. While some ideals of the Cambodian family lingered, women discovered that they could take care of themselves and their children, often without a male presence, much less male guidance. At the same time, many men found that they could not protect their families, or even make a living to support them.

THE ARC OF MOTHER'S MILK

The tendency toward women's increased access to Western institutions and decreased dependence on men, though by no means a universal phenomenon, widened the fissure between husbands and wives, adding to confusion over the disruption of gender roles. Forced into the role of sole family caretaker, refugee women were overwhelmingly motivated to learn autonomy in order to ensure the survival of their children. And it seemed that the gap only widened further after relocation to the United States.

Mrs. Sophat's continuing saga in Oakland brought this home to me. Ten years after she had settled into life in California, she continued to think of relatives who were still in the camps. She was living off welfare checks because her husband, who had become an alcoholic, was unemployed. Despite the meagerness of her Aid to Families with Dependent Children (AFDC) check, Mrs. Sophat had not forgotten those left behind. She told me, "Last month, we all contributed two hundred dollars to send to relatives in Cambodia. They are facing so much hardship, some don't even have enough rice to eat. We always try to set aside twenty to thirty dollars each month to send

home." This strong sense of reciprocity among women was traditional,[49] but
it had survived the war in a remarkable way.

> The only relatives left are my nieces and nephews who lost their parents dur-
> ing Pol Pot time. They are in need of everything. They're miserable. Some went
> into business and were robbed, others got shot at and are now crippled. So I
> worry a lot. I have to send them money because they are orphans. They write
> me, addressing me as mother. What can one do? So I pinch a little here, a lit-
> tle there, and send them money just to keep them from having to engage in
> smuggling and getting shot at.

As Judy Ledgerwood has noted, "in the new world, women earned and kept
cash, which is quite different from owning family land, jewelry, or livestock
[i.e., as they might have in pre-1975 Cambodia]. Cash can be spent according
to an individual's wishes . . . [and] seems to belong to women in a new
way"[50]—including giving them the power for the first time to deliver a steady
cash flow to the extended family in the homeland. Indeed, such transnational
cash flows seemed a predominantly female phenomenon.

At her daughter's wedding, Mrs. Sophat received from the groom a traditional monetary gift known as mother's milk, in recognition of her work
bringing her children to adulthood. Mrs. Sophat said, "I couldn't bring myself to keep the money. I gave it to my daughter." Her refusal of the symbolic
payment for mother's milk seemed to express a sentiment that no price could
be placed on mother's love when it had been expended in the extraordinary circumstances of war and exile. The lessons of mother's milk had engendered resourceful and independent women in war and diaspora.

.   .   .

For the survivors of Pol Pot, encounters in border camps produced a series
of crucial changes, adding up to a radical break from Cambodian cultural autonomy as refugees came to rely on volags for their everyday needs. Integration into volag activities and training programs in preparation for resettlement abroad further destabilized and transformed prior norms of class,
gender, and age. Camp experiences produced a number of lessons pertinent
to the refugees' understanding of citizenship in the United States. First, American institutions were givers of aid and services, and all Americans appeared
to be in positions of social superiority. Refugees learned that they were to
become new subjects who were to submit to the work discipline of American
labor markets, but they also learned dependency on the institutions that
helped them sustain their families and reorganize their daily lives. They
learned the significance of registration and correct labeling as means for gaining access to resources necessary to their survival. Through such daily calculations and strategies, refugees were resocialized into a position of dependence on institutions and officials, a process of clientelism that echoed the

patron–client networks of pre–Pol Pot Cambodia. But the new patronage now flowed from non-Cambodian agencies and patrons who could provide the basic necessities of daily life, help to circumvent bureaucratic obstacles, and provide advice and services for dealing with domestic problems. Women emerged as important figures in managing these patronage relationships.

From navigating the war-scarred landscapes of Pol Pot time to negotiating the bureaucratic rules of international aid agencies, Cambodians learned to become new kinds of subjects, mastering the codes and rules of bona fide refugees, compliant aid recipients, and good patients, for whom well-placed Westerners were aid givers. The dominance of female-headed households, the frequent absence of men, and the focus of aid agencies on women and children made women key agents in these lessons of clientship. Such emerging norms, rules, and strategies seemed an unintended trial run for life in the United States.

PART II

Governing through Freedom

Chapter 3

The Refugee as an Ethical Figure

"Why," I asked Cambodian immigrants I encountered, "did you decide to seek resettlement in the United States? Not France? Or Thailand?" Apparently incredulous at my query, they'd say, "America is the land of freedom—you know, the lady with the light," lifting up an arm holding an imaginary torch. This shining figure was what kept the war-traumatized refugees going in their long nights in Thai camps. By raising their arms, they elected to go to America, the home of freedom and wealth, far away from the demented Pol Pot regime, the chaos, poverty, and political uncertainty of Cambodia. But they were to find that the Lady of Liberty was merely one icon of what it means to be American, and that other images of different kinds of Americas were to play a role in constituting them as new citizens.

For Western liberal democracies, the decades of the 1970s and 1980s saw a resurgence in the immigration of workers and refugees displaced by wars in Asia, Africa, and Latin America. The rising tides of migration across borders coincided with a decline in the welfare state and mounting nationalism. Faced with these conflicting pressures, Western governments began to examine ways to rewrite citizenship, immigration, and asylum laws. Citizenship suddenly became a malleable concept for various regimes intent on tightening the requirements for residence and citizenship. In Europe, governments sought to limit immigration by deporting illegal immigrants (France); making language a criterion of citizenship (the Baltic states); or, in extreme cases, launching campaigns of ethnic cleansing to engineer monoethnic nation-states (Bosnia). In the United States, the response to the outcry against immigrants and refugees was to enact a law cutting welfare benefits to both illegal and legal immigrants. Such laws have led to extreme differentiation among categories of newcomers: aliens (without papers) and undocumented workers on the one hand, and legal immigrants such as certified refugees, work-permit holders, and green-card holders on the other. In states like California, public debates centered on what rights were appropriate for various categories of legal and illegal immigrants, as compared to long-term American citizens.

But citizenship for the disenfranchised American or the disadvantaged newcomer has always been about more than the possession of legal rights—though Native Americans, African Americans, and other racialized minorities have made, and continue to make, great sacrifices in pressing their claims to political membership in the country. As a number of American historians have noted, *belonging* in the United States has from the beginning been defined in part by unofficial social meanings and criteria. These have historically shaped not only the selective reception of newcomers, but also the internal stratifications and unequal access to prestige and power among those already here. For minorities and disadvantaged populations, the lived meanings of citizenship are completely entangled with such systems of exclusion, selection, and judgment.

This is an orienting chapter that examines the spatial and social disjunctions between the border camps where Cambodian refugees congregated in the early 1980s and the United States, their destination country. It also reorients the reader from the world of refugee camps to the context of late twentieth-century America, by focusing on the forms of knowledge and power that have shaped racial and class politics here. These were the technologies that would receive, redefine, and recast Cambodian refugees as modern citizen-subjects. Preexisting categories—earlier waves of refugees, minorities, poor urban folk—were deployed and recast in social programs and techniques to provide the forms through which Cambodian refugees came to be interpreted, managed, and normalized as new ethnics. I trace three technologies of subject-making that intersected in the world of the newcomers: (1) historical racial bipolarism and orientalism, which have conditioned the response to successive waves of newcomers; (2) related processes in the government of poverty, migrants, and moral deviance; and (3) ways that the refugee as a moral figure has determined American foreign policy. Finally, I show how these technologies converged in shaping the reception of Southeast Asian refugees in California. I trace the genealogies of terms such as *black, underclass,* and *refugee,* which have historically been key concepts in the series of intersecting social technologies relating to race, class, poverty, and gender. Neoliberal rationalities for disciplining the poor, controlling welfare recipients, and for producing self-reliant subjects freely avail themselves of the classificatory schemes for positioning racial others, thus constituting citizen-subjects in ethno-racial terms. Later chapters contain a closer examination of the everyday, dynamic processes, practices, and possibilities of subject-making and self-making that were experienced by Cambodian refugees and those who worked with them.

THE LURKING LOGIC OF RACIAL BIPOLARITY

It is possible to chart a continuity in the dynamics of racial polarization throughout the history of the American nation. From its inception, the United States has been imagined as an implicitly racial and classist formation governed by an Anglo-Saxon hegemony that projects white race and class interests as universal for the nation.[1] The concept of America as a specific racial identity has been and continues to be the measure against which all potential citizens are rated as either within or marginal to the nation. As Patricia Williams, among other scholars of race, has noted, "The violently patrolled historical boundary between black and white in America is so powerful that every immigrant group since slavery has found itself assimilated as one or the other, despite the enormous ethnic and global diversity we Americans actually represent."[2]

Within a national ideology that projects worthy citizens as inherently white, the intertwining of race and economic performance has shaped the ways different immigrant groups have attained status, dignity, and thus a perceived racial identity. The racializing effects of class and social mobility were also associated with the emergence of an ideal of white masculinity as the normative qualities of manliness and civilization itself, in contrast to the qualities of "Indian" and "Negro" subjects.[3] David R. Roediger, inspired by W. E. B. Du Bois's ideas about race and class,[4] argues that the concept of "whiteness" developed among the working class within a slave-owning republic during the nineteenth century: "Whiteness was a way in which workers responded to a fear of dependency on wage labor and to the necessities of capitalist work discipline."[5] The founders' ideal of masculine independence found a convenient other in black slavery and "hireling" wage labor. The black population was viewed as embodying "the preindustrial, erotic, careless style of life the white worker hated and longed for."[6] Lewis C. Copeland observes that "[t]he Negro" as a "contrast conception" or "counter-race" is a legacy of white–black relations under slavery and Emancipation that "'naturalizes' the social order."[7] The free working man came to embody republican citizenship, and any immigrant who failed to gain independent livelihood was in danger of sinking into wage slavery, the antithesis of independent citizenship. For not fitting into the dominant ideals of modern industrial labor and entrepreneurship, non–Anglo Saxon immigrants came to be classified as subjugated in both racial and gender terms.

Brackette Williams has noted that both the definition of race and the position of the insider–outsider boundary shift with the influx of populations and changes in racial class formations.[8] By the early twentieth century, nativist assertions of whiteness were intensified by fears of job competition from immigrants, and the racialization of class became pervasive. Reginald Horsman writes in *Race and Manifest Destiny* that the intellectual community "fed

European racial appetites with scientific theories stemming from the supposed knowledge and observation of blacks and Indians."[9] This theory of "racial Anglo-Saxonism"[10] also made acceptance of Irish American (and southern European) immigrants highly contingent, for their whiteness was in dispute.[11] Karen Sacks notes, "By the 1920s, scientific racism sanctified the notion that real Americans were white and real whites came from northwest Europe," as opposed to Eastern Europe or the Mediterranean countries.[12] But whereas immigrant groups such as the Irish and the Jews could over time be assimilated by becoming middle-class and white,[13] groups from outside Europe have historically existed on the outside or in some borderland between the white and black ends of the racial continuum.[14]

The racial logic and framing of American belonging have been complicated by the reality and the ideal of the American imperium. As Horsman has argued, the concept of racial Anglo-Saxonism was tied to the sense of manifest destiny in the nineteenth century, when the nation reached the Pacific coast:

> Without taking on the dangerous burdens of a formal empire, the United States could obtain the markets and the raw materials its ever-expanding economy needed. American and world economic growth, the triumph of Western Christian civilization, and a stable world order could be achieved by the American economic penetration of underdeveloped areas.[15]

American imperialism has been crucial to the formation of an American mythologized identity, one that is based on the romance of the frontier and the land of the free. According to Amy Kaplan, American imperialist domination overseas has been central to ways America imagines its destiny and cultural exceptionalism, not least in providing "the cultural discourses of race, gender, ethnicity, and class at home."[16]

American "orientalism" (which I use in the Saidian sense, of a form of knowledge about the Other that is situated in a geographical and conceptual Orient dominated by the West) has also influenced concepts of belonging. American domination of Asia and the Californian history of racial exclusions have shaped American orientalism, which has been characterized by simultaneous fear and longing. Aversion to immigrants was especially virulent toward the Chinese, and legal exclusions against them culminated in quota laws in the 1920s.[17] Other groups from Asia were subsequently excluded. These measures merely slowed down the steady influx of workers from Asia who worked the fields, railroads, and plantations of the American frontier.

There is a striking continuity in civil society between perceptions, policies, and practices that first emerged in relation to Native Americans and blacks, and those relating to Asian immigrants. Ronald Takaki points out that in the late nineteenth century, early Chinese immigrants were subjected to a process of "Negroization" and compared to black slaves as heathens perceived as a threat to republicanism. Chinese "coolies," like black slaves, were regarded as antagonistic to the free working man.[18] Orientalist images portrayed Chinese immigrants as "a depraved class," "new barbarians" (comparable to the "Red Man"), bloodsucking traders, and a threat to white women—altogether a cancer on American civil society.[19] These attitudes, which cast Asians outside the pale of white civilization, operated within the bipolar racial formation, assigning "primitive" Asians to the black half of the model, on the side of unfree labor and low public status, not belonging to the nation.

The same continuity can be seen in the civilizing mission that was first directed at defeated Native Americans. In the Philippines, the American invasion of 1898 crushed the nationalist movement, and Filipinos were compared to wild men and apes in the American press. Soon, American expatriates there embarked on a compassionate mission of uplifting the "little brown brother" through "benevolent assimilation."[20] The civilizing logic produced a distinct set of technologies that came to be applied to transforming immigrants' attitudes, habits, and goals. Just as Native Americans and African Americans were "reformed" through schooling, Asian immigrants who needed help from service agencies have also been subjected to a process of ethnic reformation, erasure, and cleansing in order to become more worthy citizens.[21] For instance, Chinese prostitutes in San Francisco were among the first Asian immigrants to be assisted and subjected to the subordinating love of church workers.[22] Church workers not only rescued and reformed Chinese prostitutes, they also vetted Chinese immigrant suitors to make sure that they were suitable.

This combination of paternalism and subordinating care, which had a legacy in plantation slavery, was directed toward transforming decadent immigrants into loyal, dependent, and affectionate subjects.[23] Other processes involved in subordinating assimilation were the control and removal of ethnic "tendencies" slaves and immigrants were assumed to have brought with them from their "primitive" cultures. During the process of industrialization of the "new South" in the early twentieth century, welfare capitalism was introduced to reform the "instinctual life" of black workers, aimed at teaching them habits of disciplined industry. Taylorism, or scientific management, became the technology for stripping "primitiveness" from factory workers and transforming them into modern men, or new ethnics.[24] Immigrant masculinity was Taylorized to channel a perceived tendency toward violence into bread-earning productivity. In short, although it is perhaps extreme to imagine a systematic synchronism in the history of the American nation of views on intrepid individualism, the white man, and deserving citizenship, the convergences and overlaps among concepts of race, civilization, and market behavior in shaping claims to citizenship are too routine to be dismissed.

THE GOVERNMENT OF POVERTY

Policies and practices aimed at normalizing the abnormal in order to assimilate the racial other safely into the moral economy of American capitalism ran parallel to the moral politics of poor relief. Racial differentiation in relation to work status is inextricable from racial stigmatization in relation to poverty reform. American welfare reforms, initially directed at poor widows and later extended to include poor immigrants and migrants to industrial cities, created another set of moralizing discourses that increasingly judged the black working poor as recalcitrant or lacking a work ethic; and this formulation came to dog other groups of poor immigrants, who were categorized as being on the black side of the divide.

Judith Shklar has argued that basic, historically derived American values of income earning and the vote define social standing in the nation. Once the franchise is achieved by women and minorities, the social right to work and to be paid becomes the primary source of public respect and prestige. From the perspective of the historically excluded—racial minorities, women, and immigrants—the struggle for American citizenship has "been overwhelmingly a demand for inclusion in the polity, an effort to break down excluding barriers to recognition, rather than an aspiration to civic participation as a deeply involving activity."[25] These intertwined goals—access to income and to voting, which are inseparable from attaining social standing, respect, and prestige—have been central to shaping the meaning and character of American citizenship.[26] This moral construction of citizenship was greatly challenged by the welfare state in twentieth-century America, when traditional discourses about poverty, work, and deserving citizenship came into conflict with ideas about the deserving poor and claims of entitlement to state support. To understand this, we need to pause a bit and consider the broader debates about social citizenship in liberal democracies.

In the aftermath of World War II, Thomas H. Marshall first considered citizenship as a question of modernity, particularly as regards the evolution of civil(ized) society in Great Britain. In his view, the political and civil rights to which each citizen was legally entitled were undercut by inequalities generated by expanding capitalism. Marshall saw the welfare state as the means to compensate for these economic and social inequalities, thus preserving solidarity within the nation-state.[27] In the 1980s, Marxist scholars highlighted the contradiction between democratic citizenship and social inequalities that exist in society, namely, the widening gap between abstract universalistic rights and real-world inequalities generated by market competition, racial difference, and immigration.[28] According to their view, the welfare state becomes the arena in which "interest groups in civil society used the public sphere to demand 'social rights'—the services or protection of the state."[29] Marxists in Great Britain use the term *social wage* to highlight the point that citizenship is shaped by class conflict, because the social wage has enabled the working classes to continue their struggle for improved wages and working conditions.

But the focus on the negotiated social wage misses Marshall's deeper political argument about the ideological assumptions of the welfare state, and about civilization as a process. The welfare state as a technology of disciplining has some unintended social effects. First, concrete steps to relativize social inequalities may diffuse the class resentment of the subordinated by instilling the notion that class differences are a matter of material achievements, not ascribed rank. Second, these steps may attenuate the moral affronts associated with ranked lifestyles by instilling the view that differences are merely a matter of material possessions, which would mask the underlying racialist class logic that informs systematic prejudice and exclusivity. In other words, the institution of welfare may very well reinforce social preconceptions and inequalities by the very process of seeking to reduce material inequalities. Clearly, what is needed is a detailed investigation of how the access of poor people to civil society is structured through market and welfare technologies that deploy, disguise, and redistribute prejudices about poverty, race, and deserving citizenship. My concept of citizenship as the cumulative effects of technologies of government hopes to capture a dynamic process in everyday interactions of negotiation and struggle over key cultural values crucial to the social reproduction of material, racial, and symbolic inequalities in America.

As Michael Katz and his colleagues have argued, historical discourses about poverty, race, and morality are central to the construction of deserving and undeserving citizens in America.[30] Katz argues that before the late eighteenth century, poor-law reformers distinguished between "impotent" and "able-bodied" poor in order to justify the provision of public resources. By the early nineteenth century, discussion of poverty had become thoroughly moralized: the "worthy" poor were seen to have suffered from misfortune, while the "undeserving poor" (paupers) were the result of individual willful habits such as indolence, which came to be associated with crime.[31] By the late nineteenth century, poorhouses had been set up to instill the "labor maxim" and break the cycle of dependence within poor immigrant families. Reformers, legislators, and writers painted a dire picture of poverty, crime, and disease among the poor who had congregated in the industrializing cities. "Among the urban poor, an undeserving subset, dependent on account of their own shiftless, irresponsible, immoral behavior, burdened honest taxpayers with the cost of their support, threatened their safety, and corrupted the working poor. Increasingly concentrated within slum districts, they lived in growing social isolation, cut off from the role models and oversight once provided by the more well-to-do, reproducing their own degradation."[32] The few exemplars of the deserving poor were widows who kept their children clean and disciplined, and able-bodied families cast out of work through no fault of their own. In the 1920s, the eugenics movement linked poverty to race, and while the early objects of scientific racism were certain European immigrants, the color of the undeserving poor increasingly became black after the massive influx of African Americans to the cities of the North in the 1950s. Urban-based African Americans and poverty were fused in a racist image of the undeserving poor.[33] As increasing numbers of recipients of aid to parents of dependent children were unmarried and black, African American women raising children on their own came to epitomize the undeserving poor. Welfare recipients were stigmatized as alcoholic, immoral, and incompetent mothers, and public opinion also turned against unemployed young black men, who were considered unskilled, unwilling to work, and dangerous. Gunnar Myrdal introduced the term *underclass* to describe inner-city African Americans who appeared less successful in integrating into the wider society than immigrant groups.[34]

In the 1960s, cultural difference was more explicitly added to the fusion of poverty and race, especially with the popularization of Oscar Lewis's "culture of poverty," a phrase he used to describe behavioral maladjustments (hopelessness, despair, ineffectiveness) said to prevent some groups from achieving success in terms of the values and goals of the larger society.[35] The debates about the culture of poverty reinforced the liberal perception of passivity among poor people of color and the need for direct intervention to break the cycle of deprivation and degradation that transmitted the culture of poverty from generation to generation. The stigmatization of black women and families accelerated with Daniel Patrick Moynihan's publication of *The Negro Family: The Case for National Action,* which argued that the proliferation of single-parent black families could be attributed to a "tangle of pathology," including "a black matriarchy."[36] Under the Johnson administration, the War on Poverty and Great Society campaigns expanded social programs, but the number of urban poor continued to rise in the decades that followed. In the 1980s, conservative writers such as Charles Murray resurrected the underclass debate, blaming social programs for undermining the will to work and fostering a demoralized way of life among racial minorities in the inner cities.[37] Others saw welfare recipients as feeling entitled to welfare support, or as working the system to their own advantage, or as passive and incompetent individuals unable to function in the labor market. Further debate about the underclass ensued as sociologists sought to define the concept in terms of various social attributes or surrounding social environment. Scholars enumerated categories of the underclass such as long-term welfare recipients, unwed teenage mothers, female-headed households, individuals engaged in petty crimes and other deviant behavior, and unskilled individuals who experience long-term unemployment.

Structuring conditions were identified, including entire inner-city communities cut off from employment opportunities and abandoned by the middle class, resulting in extreme concentrations of poor people isolated from mainstream society.[38]

Overlooked in the contemporary debate was Michael Katz's historical view that "it is only a slight exaggeration to say that the core of most welfare reform in America since the early nineteenth century has been a war on the able-bodied poor: an attempt to define, locate, and purge them from the rolls of relief."[39] Indeed, not only was the underclass debate framed in terms of the expectations of an "overclass"—one that "sets ideological standards under which society in general is expected to live"—but it was also posed in dialectical opposition to the notion of a "model minority" (a racialized minority group that can attain success in those overclass terms).[40] In the 1960s, the term *model minority* was coined to refer to Japanese Americans who, despite their wartime incarceration in camps, managed to gain upward mobility, "leading generally affluent, and for the most part, highly Americanized life. . . . there is no parallel to their success story."[41] The media soon broadened the term to include Chinese Americans, and Asian subjects came to be perceived as minorities who raised themselves up by their bootstraps. Asian Americans were stereotyped as embodying the human capital of diligence, docility, self-sufficiency, and productivity. And the model minority has often been wielded as an ideological weapon to chastise inner-city black communities for persistent problems of poverty, unemployment, and crime.

Critics of the homogenized underclass concept have argued that it has been seen only through the prism of the white middle-class family ideal. In particular, the stereotyped and stigmatized images of black families ignore the variety of family forms existing among inner-city African Americans, and fail to value women's contributions to family life under extremely difficult circumstances. The historical record shows that urban family patterns emerged in the context of racism, the enforced division along gender lines of work roles within and outside the home, and both labor union and employment discrimination.[42] Others point to the continuity of cultural norms and strategies such as extended family networks and fosterage, which suggest more fluid and multifamily models of child care and domestic support.[43] Anthropologists such as Carol Stack have conducted primary research on the importance of networks and strategies that enabled families to form links with wider social structures.[44] Still others have described the more subtle relations and heterogeneity of people and associations that have made inner-city communities more vibrant than the underclass model would allow, and that have made it possible for some families and individuals to surmount the structural conditions of the inner city against all odds.[45] Despite these challenges, belief in the existence of an underclass marked by specific features of disadvantage persisted, and the same set of expectations came to shape the perception and governing of new waves of poor migrants, such as Puerto Ricans.[46]

The model-minority concept was equally homogenized, since it led to the assumption that all peoples of Asian heritage, very broadly defined, could be left in benign neglect and still manage to pull themselves up by their bootstraps. But in the early 1980s, the arrival of refugees from Southeast Asia caused the mass media, especially in California, to refine the idea of the model minority in terms of race and class. Journalists and policymakers came to distinguish between two categories of Asian Americans: on the one hand, the model-minority ethnic Chinese immigrants from Hong Kong, Taiwan, and China along with Vietnamese immigrants; and on the other, the "new underclass" said to be represented by refugees from Cambodia and Laos. This bifurcated model also assumed that racial identity among immigrants to the United States directly corresponded to national origin. And it took for granted that ethnic formation depends on the link between race and class, so that Asian immigrants, like long-resident Americans, could be conceptually positioned in categories of worthy or less-worthy minorities.[47]

STATE DYNAMICS AND THE SPIRITUAL AMBIGUITY OF REFUGEES

Surely, the refugee was one of the most searing figures of the late twentieth century, but despite the news accounts and refugee biographies, little scholarly attention has been paid to refugee experiences of displacement, regulation, and resettlement abroad.[48] Instead, most attention is paid to the threat refugees are perceived to pose to the nation-state. For instance, intergovernmental agencies such as the United Nations Security Council have depicted the massive number of refugees in problematic terms, as a threat to international peace and security. Nevzat Soguk argues that refugees are frequently regarded not as victims of aberrant states, but as "citizens gone aberrant."[49] He maintains that humanitarian interventions on behalf of refugees enforce intergovernmental regimentation that reinscribes the statist hierarchy of citizen–nation-state. Anthropologists have also adopted this model of opposition between refugee and state, viewing refugeeism as a social condition that is fundamentally opposed to the notion of rooted citizens, and thus a challenge to state sovereignty and to the global order of nation-states.[50] Liisa Malkki has argued that imagined nationhood tends to externalize refugees ideologically; thus refugees in general come to be considered morally impure, since they represent "an aberration of categories, a zone of pollution" in the "national order of things."[51] Her assertion is buttressed by other observers who claim that refugees are inevitably objects of suspicion and perceived as threats to state security.[52]

This focus on the nation and its others tends to eclipse the actual complex, ambiguous, and interweaving processes that transform refugees back into citizens. There are millions of refugees languishing in international no-man's-land, but every day, refugees are also being resettled in new countries. The model that polarizes refugees and states as homogenized entities in international relations fails to consider how particular states and their publics may be *for* or *against* refugee influx at different points in time. Nor does it consider the complex ways in which different categories of refugees are variously imagined and received by the host country. For instance, in chapter 2 I showed that nationalist self-perception shaped Thailand's attitude about Cambodian refugees when they first massed along its border in 1979, but that attitude shifted under the pressure of geopolitical considerations. Indeed, individual states do not simply respond to refugee flows in a blanket fashion, but draw on past policies and current interests to respond to pressure for entry from refugees. American policies regarding refugees after World War II demonstrate a dramatic reversal in the moral status of refugees from different countries.

Instead of viewing refugees and citizens as permanently irreconcilable opposites, therefore, this study explores how the refugee and the citizen are the political effects of institutional processes that are deeply imbued with sociocultural values. What are the institutions and social mechanisms that transform people into refugees, and how do they regulate and reterritorialize the displaced? We have yet to produce a detailed understanding of the kinds of mechanisms and practices that assist refugees in returning to citizen status in adopted countries. How do the interpretations and strategies of newcomers trouble the distinction between refugee and citizen, and how do they unsettle the norms and forms of citizenship in the host country?

Most people think of citizenship as the possession of a bundle of rights—a legal condition. This notion of citizenship as nationality is fundamental, and distinguishes citizens from foreigners who are in a country without papers and other illegal residents. The history of American citizenship as nationality has been shaped by a series of inclusions and exclusions on the basis of xenophobia, racism, religious bigotry, and male privilege. At its founding, the country excluded African slaves, Native Americans, and anyone not born in the colonies from citizenship—despite the fact that the United States is a leading example of a "nation of immigrants," in which the naturalization of residents has always been central to the theory and practice of citizenship. Today, the country has millions of legal resident aliens (visa holders and green-card holders), many of whom will eventually seek naturalization.

What are the actual venues and lessons involved in becoming American, especially for the poor and disadvantaged? My approach to this question is to examine the policies and techniques of government that shape the reception, treatment, and transformation of newcomers—such as refugees—

into particular kinds of citizens within the American polity. Various state agencies and private associations converge in facilitating the transition of displaced peoples, with the goal of changing refugee-subjects, perceived as shiftless and suspect, into normalized citizens who can be reasonably integrated into the host society. When Cambodians arrived in the United States in the early 1980s, their status as refugees persisted even as they were being resocialized to become Americans. The relevance of refugee status for Cambodians illuminates how certain institutional processes shape the minoritization process of disadvantaged and at-risk immigrants, who come to depend on the refugee industry, the welfare state, and civic groups. Their position in American civil society as refugee-citizens was also shaped by ongoing debates about American citizenship, the welfare state, and multiculturalism.

Studying state power in the United States, perhaps more than in other societies, requires that we think not in terms of an overarching state apparatus, but in terms of a multiplicity of networks through which various authorities, nonprofit agencies, programs, and experts translate democratic goals in relation to target populations. Here Foucault's notion of governmentality is useful, in that we think of certain state activities as engaged in a project of moral regulation that attempts to give, in the words of Philip Corrigan and Derek Sayer, "unitary and unifying expression to what are in reality multifaceted and differential experiences of groups within society."[53] This role of modern state power in universalizing citizenship is paradoxically attained through a process of individuation, whereby people are constructed in definitive and specific ways as citizens—for example, as taxpayers, workers, consumers, or welfare dependents. A lacuna in Corrigan and Sayer's approach to universalizing the norms of citizenship is their exclusive focus on the state sector, which ignores the various domains, both formal and informal, in which converging forms of rule and ethno-racial discourses produce specific effects that define desirable or undesirable sorts of citizens.

The moral imperative to offer refugees shelter has been a hallmark of U.S. policy since 1945—a break from earlier policies, which privileged race, language, and assimilation over concerns about human suffering.[54] Since 1945, America's rise to the status of a global power has compelled Congress to give up aspects of its isolationist policy and to make up for the country's shameful abandonment of Jewish refugees in prewar years. In 1956 and 1957, the Hungarian uprising led to an influx of thousands of refugees via Austria, and refugees came to be defined as people escaping persecution from a communist state. In his book *A Nation of Immigrants,* John F. Kennedy celebrated highly skilled immigrants from communist countries, such as rocket scientists, inventors, and artists; he urged Americans to accept them alongside the poor huddled masses, and not resent or fear them.[55] Kennedy thus provided moral justification for refugees from communist countries who could be perceived as having little difficulty integrating into the nation.

In 1965, refugees were formally recognized as a special category of immigrants, as it became clear that refugees from communist states were not simply political exiles likely to return home later, but rather new immigrants. *Refugee status*, strictly defined, is bestowed only when claims for entry are made outside the United States to INS officials in third countries. The upshot of this policy is that, from the 1950s until the present, the United States has admitted well over 90 percent of refugees from communist countries.[56] This "calculated kindness" in immigration policy did not favor political exiles from places like Haiti, El Salvador, or Chile, who did not figure into America's global anticommunist agenda but were considered subjects of right-wing dictatorships allied with the United States.[57] Many of these would-be refugees were forced to enter the country illegally as aliens and seek asylum—making them subject to INS executive discretion, which has always been designed to maintain tight borders.[58]

Successive administrations consistently sought to transform each new arrival from communist regimes into a symbolic or literal "freedom fighter." For decades, this label was routinely applied to refugees ranging from members of the Hungarian uprising to Jews fleeing the Soviet Union's "evil empire," middle-class professionals escaping Castro's Cuba, and Afghan guerrillas resisting the Soviet invasion. Fervent anti-communism prompted a significant increase in the country quotas set for immigrants from Asia and Africa in the 1965 family reunification program. Many Chinese were finally able to leave so-called Red China and join U.S.-based families after generations of separation. The number of Asian and African immigrants rose steadily in the decade after the change. Since 1950, more than two million refugees have been admitted from communist countries, of whom three quarters of a million each came from Cuba and Southeast Asia, and more than half a million from Central and Eastern Europe.[59]

But as refugees settled down to become long-term residents, they lost their glow as freedom fighters, and congressional fears of communist subversion began to erode the unconditional welcome offered to escapees from communist regimes. By the 1970s, the image of refugees as politically activist soldiers against global communism began to wear thin, and in the climate of détente more care was taken with controlling refugee influx, which came to represent danger more than opportunity. In 1978, Castro's release of prisoners stirred fears of America admitting "spies, terrorists, and common criminals" among the refugees.[60] Furthermore, the Mariel boatlift of 1980 included for the first time a number of black Cubans (approximately 10 percent), and race began to color American perception of refugees from communist countries, who had until that time been represented by well-educated Europeans, especially Jews.[61]

The U.S. intervention to halt the spread of communism in Indochina ultimately resulted in waves of boat people fleeing Vietnam. In 1979, hundreds of thousands of Cambodians fled to the Thai border after the Vietnamese invasion of Kampuchea. President Carter, in the spirit of his human rights campaign, signed a refugee act that increased immigration quotas for mainland Southeast Asian people displaced by the war. But by then, even refugees fleeing communist regimes had lost their earlier moral aura, and the new migrants compared unfavorably with the mid-century European intellectual elite who fled Nazism, communism, and war. Furthermore, Southeast Asian refugees were reminders of the U.S. defeat in Vietnam. The timing of their arrival in the United States, along with underlying cultural and racial biases against Asians, made their reception a more ambiguous welcome.

Southeast Asians were the most prominent group of refugees to enter the United States in this era of moral limbo. The U.S. withdrawal from Vietnam signaled the beginning of the end of the cold war and the dawn of an era in which the refugee acquired a more ambivalent image. Floods of refugees— both legal and illegal—escaping from natural disasters, civil wars, ethnic wars, and adverse conditions in poor countries, flowed into the country. More and more, refugees came to be viewed as the byproduct of regional conflicts and underdeveloped economies that appeared to have little to do with American interests. Public sentiment gradually began to turn against the "boat peoples" of the world arriving in a recession-slowed United States. Consider, for instance, the heartless response to the Mariel boat people. Many Americans were worried about scarce housing, jobs, limits on welfare, and competition from immigrants. Rioting by Mariel Cuban refugees contributed to their image as "difficult migrants."[62] Compassion fatigue quickly set in, and a climate of antagonism greeted the growing influx of refugees of color from Asia, Latin America, and Africa. The term *economic refugee* came into use to describe people fleeing not political persecution back home, but simply bad economic conditions. Southeast Asian refugees—who ranged from French-speaking professionals to illiterate peasants, from fervent anticommunists to former supporters of the Khmer Rouge, from CIA field guides to hapless tribals—also spoiled the model-minority image of Asian Americans as docile and productive citizens. They arrived just as American domestic policy, under Republican regimes, was shifting away from a welfare-state notion of custodial, collective support of the weak and poor toward emphasis on individuals' civic duty to reduce their burden on the state.

These factors greatly influenced the conditions of the Southeast Asian refugees' reception. Most studies have focused on the gains and failures, at the administrative level, of refugee policies.[63] But refugee politics goes beyond the use of displaced people as a political football between nation-states, or their treatment at the national level. The legacy of racializing expectations with regard to market potential, intelligence, mental health, and moral worthiness came to influence at the practical, everyday level the experiences and understanding of both the newcomers and the long-term residents who assisted them. A number of state agencies were central in the management of Southeast Asian refugees, and these agencies, through their goals, strategies, and practices, came to shape the norms for thinking about and dealing with Southeast Asian refugees.

REFUGEE TRAINING AND RESETTLEMENT: DISCIPLINARY GOALS

Cambodian refugees arrived at a time that a new administration in Washington, which had won election by promising to "roll back the government," was introducing a new climate of limits on generosity toward immigrants and welfare recipients. The Refugee Act of 1980, however—a legacy of the previous adminstration—enabled refugees from Southeast Asia to receive a higher rate of state assistance than any previous group of immigrants arriving on American shores. In fact, a network of processing centers in the Philippines provided training to prepare refugees for entry into the American labor market. As Reaganomics sought to stem the "welfare explosion" that had been building since the 1960s and to stress the possibility of combining welfare and work, Southeast Asian refugees were the guinea pigs in an experimental overhaul of welfare, one front in the war against the underclass.

The Overseas Refugee Training Center (ORTC) in the Philippines prepared Southeast Asian refugees for "successful resettlement" by offering classes in English, cultural orientation, and "other topics like health, transportation, shopping, directions, and personal information."[64] Defenders of the program maintain that refugees were given preparation to meet the employment-related needs of refugee adults with children, adolescents, and homebound mothers, and that the training took into account the various educational backgrounds of refugees to prepare them better for the U.S. job market.

It seems fair to assume that the majority of refugee workers were well-intended toward refugees, seeking to help them adjust to some of the practical issues of survival in the strange new world they thought of, abstractly, only as the Land of the Free. But James Tollefson, who was a teacher at the center, claims that the top priority was to keep the refugees from going on welfare once they reached the United States. Refugee training not only prepared refugees for low-level jobs as janitors, hotel maids, and domestic workers, in an effort to tailor (Taylor?) their training to the needs of economic restructuring at home;[65] it also instructed them in the value of "job mobility," to help them adapt to cycles of employment and unemployment. He makes the further determinist claim that the ORTC was "part of a larger political-economic system that displaces [refugees] from their homes and then provides education suitable only for long-term peripheral employment. . . . Policy and ideology underlying the ORTC ensure that refugees serve the same economic functions as African Americans and Latinos."[66] While it is not necessary to subscribe to a conspiracy theory of warmongering as a way to furnish the postindustrial American economy with cheap labor, it is clear that refugee training in the camps reflected the official perception that regardless of their former backgrounds, the majority of Southeast Asian refugees were going to be members of the working poor in the United States. It also appears that assumptions about the black and Hispanic underclass colored the teachers' expectations about the precariousness of the refugees' self-sufficiency, the limited kinds of jobs they could potentially fill, and their need for social discipline on arrival on the American mainland.

NEW ASIAN IMMIGRANTS: THE LANGUAGE OF RACE AND CLASS

Refugees from Southeast Asia arrived in two major waves. The first came after the fall of Saigon in 1975. Many of the Vietnamese refugees were relatively young, well-educated professional people whose former occupations and skills—as well as their experiences with Americans during the war years—helped them adapt to American society. They soon found jobs and set up family businesses, and have formed business enclaves in San Jose and in Orange County in California. Others depended on welfare support for a time while seeking a variety of employment opportunities in cities like Philadelphia.[67]

The second wave of Indochinese refugees, arriving after 1980, could be divided into two general groups: Cambodian and Laotian peasants who sought refuge in the Thai border camps, and ethnic Chinese boat people who fled Vietnam and were held in temporary camps in other Southeast Asian countries. Like other refugees, Cambodians entered the country with an I-94 document that gave them the legal right to enter, live, and work in the United States. With the document, they could apply for an adjustment of their legal status from refugees to permanent residents and, after a few years, could apply to become citizens. But they soon found that American citizenship involved being framed by policy, practices, and beliefs according to already existing classificatory schemes that identified groupings in terms of race, ethnicity, morality, and market potential.

From the beginning, people working with the refugees viewed Cambodians as less likely than the Vietnamese to attain economic success in the United States. Cambodian refugees arrived during a time of greater anxiety over the ideological, health, and economic threats represented by refugees not only from Southeast Asia, but also from Afghanistan and Ethiopia. A range of social "failures," from welfare dependency to poor performance in schools, were attributed not only to their agrarian background and war experiences, but also to an essentializing construction (that is to say, a definition based on basic, unchanging natural conditions) of cultural difference. In a practice that has been called "surveillance-correction," social scientists writing up refugee reports provided ethno-racial classifications for social workers and teachers that made simplistic causal links between purported cultural features and employment potential.[68] Thus even though Vietnamese and Cambodian refugees came out of the same set of conflicts based on American intervention in Southeast Asia, Cambodians were explicitly differentiated from Vietnamese newcomers, as well as from Chinese immigrants.

In a report to the Office of Refugee Resettlement (ORR), scholars elaborated a "sociocultural" portrait of Cambodians (and Laotians) as more "Indian" than "Chinese" in the "Indo-chinese" identity (which was itself a construction of French imperialists).[69] This artifact drew on an anthropological construct of "loosely structured" society—a term normally used to describe certain features of Thailand, in contrast to the more rigidly organized societies of East Asia—and misapplied it to Cambodian society.[70] Policymakers argued that Cambodians were more individualistic and more prone to place feelings and emotions above obligations and to use Americans as role models than were the Vietnamese (who were more "Chinese").[71] There was no reference to the possible influence of the recent decades of war, social upheaval, and camp life on the behavior and attitudes of Cambodian refugees. But such cultural essentialism became received wisdom, and the view of Cambodians as having an "affectively oriented viewpoint" (in contrast to the Vietnamese) was shared by, among others, a public-health nurse I interviewed, who compared Cambodians to Hawaiians for their "love of children" and "nonaggressive" behavior (the Khmer Rouge notwithstanding). The use of such culturalist typification clearly marked Cambodians as less successful exemplars of the Asian "race," less model-minority material, and more underclass in orientation.

The historical connection between general welfare policies and refugee resettlement also came to shape perceptions of impoverished Asian refugees in the familiar terms already applied to the black urban poor. Economic self-sufficiency was the cornerstone of the Refugee Act of 1980, and by 1982, the ORR sought "to evaluate the progress made in reducing refugee dependence on cash assistance and ameliorating problems of community impact."[72] Many analysts began to assess the differential rates of employment among Southeast Asian refugees, using ORR statistics on prior educational and occupational backgrounds, English-language competence, family structure, sociocultural orientations, and mental health. They concluded that the Vietnamese were the most likely to be employed and to attain self-sufficiency.[73] Such assessments about the economic performance of different Asian immigrant groups thus recast their national origins as discrete ethnicities, and entangled those ethnicities with expectations about self-sufficiency, poverty, mental health, sociocultural deviance, and even "risk for juvenile delinquency."[74]

The metaphor of the underclass was now extended beyond long-resident American inner-city groups to include refugees from Cambodia and Laos.[75]

The term *refugee* came to adhere more tightly to Cambodians, Hmongs, and Miens, and to be synonymous with *welfare recipient;* over time it became detached from Vietnamese Americans. Immigrants from Cambodia and Laos became sharply contrasted to the homo economicus of ethnic Chinese, Koreans, and Vietnamese, who were celebrated for their "Confucian values," family businesses, and can-do attitudes, which were considered closer to the desirable norms of American citizenship.[76] In an eerie echo of the earlier historical beliefs about blacks and ethnic positioning in different regions of the country, social workers came in a sense to feel that because Cambodians were seen as more *disorderly* than other Asian refugees, they should be more firmly regulated as well.

Indeed, the negative associations of the term *refugee* (welfare dependent or welfare cheat) have become so strong that some Hmong and Cambodian Americans have taken to denying their national origins in casual encounters with mainstream Americans, claiming some other ancestry, such as Thai. And some new Thai immigrants, seeking to elude the now-common perception in California that to be Southeast Asian American was to be associated with the underclass, have chosen to identify themselves discursively and in social interactions outside their community with Chinese Americans.[77] This conceptual and spatial distancing of other Asian immigrants from Cambodian and Laotian Americans indicates the extent to which they have been located ideologically at the underclass end of the continuum, a position close to the black pole of the ethno-racial scheme.

By being subjected to a kind of ideological blackening, in contrast to the whitening of Vietnamese and ethnic Chinese immigrants (the stereotyped entrepreneurial self-starters), refugees from Cambodia and Laos came to be perceived as having more in common with other poor newcomers of color, such as Ethiopians, Afghans, and even Central Americans, among whom they were often found in low-wage jobs. They were sometimes compared to African Americans because of being welfare dependent and having high rates of teenage pregnancy, and because of their location and isolation in inner-city neighborhoods. Thus—regardless of the actual, lived experiences and cultural beliefs of Cambodians—social workers, policymakers, and the media clearly demarcated the form and content of their citizenship as low in human-capital potential and in economic productivity, a position detrimental to the normative biopolitical standards of American citizenship.

Brackette Williams has argued that historically, a transformist hegemony constructed racial and ethnic hierarchies based on which groupings have made crucial contributions to the nation. Both classificatory and stratificatory processes have persisted throughout U.S. history, regardless of whether liberal, radical, or conservative regimes were in power. These processes influence the "internal selectivity" of group features, as well as the external configuration of the features thought to constitute any such category and the person who might occupy it. Different ethnic groups are thus continually engaged in "cultural struggles" to claim a higher status within the hierarchy, such contestations merely intensifying the stratificatory processes based on physical and cultural differences.[78] How did the processes of racial formation and underclass stigmatization converge in the experiences of Cambodian refugees? How did this group of newcomers become the Asian American other, seen to embody a mix of alterities: communist contamination, racial primitivity, and welfare dependency?

THE REFUGEE NETWORK IN CALIFORNIA

The Refugee Act of 1980 tried to balance refugee assistance with the expectation of gainful employment, a goal that resettlement agencies and social workers sought to instill in refugees. The strategy to get refugees into employment and off welfare gained urgency by 1987, when the fact that more than half of the eight hundred thousand refugees from Southeast Asia had settled in a few states where welfare benefits were most attractive caused widespread concern. Well over half of those who arrived after 1974 lived in California. Federal officials feared that without a program of voluntary relocation to other states, "a result could be perpetual dependence on the welfare system for many refugees."[79] Refugee leaders in California protested that the government's planned secondary resettlement program was a racially motivated attempt to restrict their freedom of movement, and so remigrations to join relatives, and to benefit from the warm weather and good welfare support, continued.

Compared to other states, California has the most generous package of public assistance for refugees and poor residents. Refugee provisions were time-limited, initially for up to three years from the date of arrival; but by 1987, Refugee Cash Assistance (RCA) was cut back to two years. During this time of refugee support, they had to enroll in one of two refugee employment programs: to study English as a Second Language (ESL) and retool for the American job market, or to receive vocational or on-the-job training (OJT) for entry-level jobs. Most Cambodians from a peasant background who were not yet fluent in English were enrolled in the OJT program, which trained men to be mechanics, electronics workers, and janitors, and women to be caregivers for children. But even when refugee assistance came to an end, the majority of refugees still struggling to cope in this country automatically went on welfare, receiving Aid to Families with Dependent Children (AFDC) benefits, which were relatively generous at both the state and the local levels in California.[80] For instance, a survey found that by the late 1980s, in the Southeast Asian refugee community 61 percent of "nuclear families with two wage earners" received assistance in California, as compared to about 12 percent in other states.[81] Nevertheless, at the petty-official level, suspicion of Southeast Asian refugees was pervasive, and mechanisms of judgment and stigmatization sorted out different kinds of responsible and irresponsible welfare dependents.

In the San Francisco Bay Area, a key agency in refugee settlement was Catholic Charities, which reminded American volunteers that their "commitment to the refugee is a moral one, not a legal one." Volunteers should make refugees "feel welcome in their new home" and offer them "the hope of a new life."[82] One of its pamphlets, *Enriched by Their Presence: America's Southeast Asians* (1980), notes that since 1975, Southeast Asians have accomplished much:

> There aren't yet the accomplishments of exceptional refugees from the past, refugees such as Einstein or Stravinsky; but, as with every group of refugees that this country has welcomed, our newest refugees' accomplishments already range from the sublime—Royal Khmer Ballet dancers offering their gentle graceful steps to this nation's treasury of dance—to the ordinary—hurried steps to work by one who has lost everything.[83]

But besides offering charity, the church agency presents a strong message that accomplishment is the basis of deserving citizenship. Refugee helpers are reminded not to coddle refugees:

> Nevertheless, as sponsor, you should be careful not to consider the refugees as your children, dependent on you for care and protection. They are adults, capable of self-sufficiency; they should be encouraged to make their own decisions and should not be shielded too much.[84]

This lesson in economic self-sufficiency is particularly directed at the second wave of immigrants, the majority of them Cambodians and Laotians. Although all refugees are eligible for cash assistance, "it is recommended that refugees be encouraged to remain independent of public assistance, if possible,"[85] and to become productive as soon as possible:

> Early employment is the key to self-sufficiency for refugees. It is one of the most important parts of the resettlement process. . . . Early employment, even in an entry-level job, is the basic building block of self-sufficiency. Refugees should be encouraged to view their first jobs as steps towards a better employment future and economic independence.[86]

During the first decade after the arrival of the second wave, the ORR conducted research annually on the refugees' progress toward self-sufficiency and on possible barriers to employment. By the mid 1980s, officials were worried because their surveys revealed that despite government training and assistance programs, Southeast Asian refugees showed a high rate of dependence on public assistance, especially AFDC payments. Such findings fueled fears of another underclass in the making, and despite what social workers on the ground knew about the struggles of refugee welfare recipients trying to patch together a living, there was great pressure to weed out welfare cheats and to push refugee populations without adequate employment skills into full self-reliance. (I discuss the travails of welfare recipients in chapter 5.)

Many members of the helping professions who served poor immigrants were themselves second- or third-generation ethnic Americans (Jewish, Japanese, Chinese Americans), or even first-generation Vietnamese Americans. Sentiment in favor of assisting "the poor, huddled masses" often has a nativist undercurrent, which (as others have pointed out) has always been part of the process of becoming and being American. Even first-generation citizens, the children of hardscrabble immigrants, can express anti-immigrant opinions on occasion.[87] Americans tend to share what Sylvia Yanagisako calls a "general folk model" of the old patriarchal family, which they trace to preimmigrant ancestors. Whether they are third-generation Italian or Russian-Jewish or Japanese Americans, long-resident citizens tend to view their current cultural norms—say, about marriage, love, and kinship—as personal modifications of what they see as biologically transmitted traditions.[88] There is a tendency to cast a baleful eye toward newcomers from the old country, who are usually perceived as too tightly knit, too hierarchical, and archaic in their family relations—qualities that are considered part of foreign racial groups, and thus wholly un-American.

Indeed, many workers in refugee resettlement and aid services who were children of immigrants tend to view poor newcomers through the prism of a folkloric image of immigrant ancestors, and to feel that they must be helped to be modern rather quickly. Just as policymakers educate social workers about ethnic differences, so social workers see themselves as having an educative, judgmental, and corrective relation to poor people. As we shall see in the following four chapters, there is remarkable continuity in both policy and practices by the helping professions—clinicians, social workers, policemen, lawyers—to cleanse newcomers of the perceived backward or immoral aspects of their antiquated culture, to govern their everyday behavior, and to make them individually responsible subjects of a neoliberal market society. In the clinic, the welfare office, the household, the police station, and the courtroom, Cambodian newcomers interacted with a variety of professional service providers who brokered relations and provided authorized accounts ("truths") of who the clients were, what was wrong with them, what was to be done, and how to go about doing it in order to succeed in America.

Yet despite the institutional structures of such encounters and the continuities of policy and practice toward urban minorities, I argue, practical citizenship as produced in these everyday domains can be highly unstable and open to modification. There is a dynamic continuum of power in these practices of discipline and deflection, rules and ruses, conformity and chaos; and the political stakes in meaning and conduct are mutually constituted in interactions between refugees and professional experts. By discussing how service workers and their clients are equally participants in these practices, my analysis shows that such fluid power relations produced not only ongoing norms but also their perpetual undoing, creating possibilities for alternative expressions and notions of what it means to be human, not merely citizen.

Chapter 4

Refugee Medicine

Attracting and Deflecting the Gaze

On a sunny afternoon in San Francisco, a young Cambodian man wearing a U.S. army jacket told me the nightmare that recurred in his dreams. Sometime in the early 1970s, he and his brother had been captured by Pol Pot's troops. One day, he managed to escape. Hiding behind bushes, he saw soldiers kill his brother and another prisoner. Their hearts and lungs were torn out and hung on a fence as a warning to others. In the silence following the story, the survivor held out his hands, as if cradling the remains of his brother. Then, shuddering imperceptibly, he pulled his army jacket closer.

Cambodian refugees escaped from a regime that held absolute power over death to a democratic society that defends life. They fled a preindustrial country where the Khmer Rouge attempted to institute a bureaucracy of terror. The central organization, Angkar, depended largely on illiterate, teenage soldiers to enforce rule on an uprooted and traumatized population. They engaged in continual surveillance to seek out enemies and document their crimes before torturing them to death.[1] For Cambodian refugees fleeing the rule of death, the United States was the land of ultimate freedom, yet they came to discover that democratic state power also has a hold on the body, one that is at once benign and disciplinary.

Democratic modernity dominates through the mundane administration and surveillance of individual bodies and the social body, adjusting them to normalizing values and hierarchies. Among the schemes of knowledge/power that regulate individual and social bodies, modern medicine is the prime mover, defining and promoting concepts, categories, and authoritative pronouncements on hygiene, health, sexuality, life, and death. In *The Birth of the Clinic,* Foucault defines the anatomo-clinical method as one based on the pervasive medical gaze, which seeks objective truths embedded in the human body.[2] By healing diseases rather than persons, the biomedical approach is a disciplining practice that produces facts about the body, in the process changing the political status of human life. Scholars influenced by the Foucauldian perspective have taken this argument further, claiming that the health profession has an influence beyond the clinic, producing a new disciplinary space that reworks older divisions between the state and the family. Jacques Donzelot, for instance, argues that the health sciences, along with the ascendance of social workers and the juvenile courts, have served to strengthen, regulate, and improve the welfare of "the social" (the realms of personal and domestic life) in early twentieth-century France.[3] While biomedicine is attending to the health of modern bodies, it is also helping to constitute the normative attitudes and practices of individuals as biopolitical subjects of the modern welfare state.[4]

Also building on Foucault's insights, Arthur Frank notes that "the body is both the privileged site of the modernist will-to-truth and the equally privileged site of the equally modernist display of cultural relativity, if not relativism."[5] For the newcomer from a developing country to the metropolitan West, becoming the modern biopolitical subject entails a two-part process of acquiring a specific set of practices and a specific philosophy of life. With the body, and knowledge of the body, as the focus, state agencies prescribe norms and beliefs regarding health, racialized sexuality, and class comportment. Health practitioners, for instance, impress a biopolitical modality on patients that requires, among other things, subjecting one's body to modern medical attention, yielding up hidden truths about one's embodied existence, participating in medical regimens, and learning self-discipline as a patient-consumer of health.

But these observations on how biomedicine works to define and reproduce biopolitical subjects cannot be left unchallenged. Foucault notes that in social regulation, the body is subtly coerced at the levels of movements, gestures, and attitudes,[6] but he barely explores how the subjects of regulation themselves draw the medical gaze in the first place, or how their resistance to biomedical intervention both invites and deflects control. Using the encounters between medical providers and Cambodian refugee patients, this chapter problematizes biomedical control as a process that is a mix of good intentions and a desire to control "diseased" and "deviant" populations, restricted by the exigencies of limited resources. Many of the caregivers, as children of earlier generations of holocaust survivors and war refugees, often display a deep faith in the efficacy of modern medical care and practices for patients from developing countries. Yet clinicians, constrained by a market-driven health-care system, tend to rely on ethnic stereotypes and simplistic solutions, their gaze on their patients distracted by an eye on the bottom line. Cambodian refugees, for their part, tend to seek specific resources while wishing to elude the control over body and mind that goes with medical care. Thus the biomedical gaze is not so much a diffused hegemonic power as it is a phenomenon generated by the complex contestation of refugee-immigrant subjects attempting to pursue their own goals and needs within the bureaucratic maze of American health and welfare providers. What we have then are body images that "mirror" medical projections,[7] but also game playing and skirmishes that run the gamut of persuasion and assimilation, control and subterfuge, domination and resistance. These negotiated interactions constitute biopolitical lessons in what being American entails for impoverished Asian refugees.

My starting point is an examination of how immigration authorities read the political and diseased bodies of Cambodian refugees allowed into the United States. Their arrival spurred the invention of a field called Southeast Asian mental health that, through the systematic naming and ordering of refugee illnesses, has sought to discipline the behavior, beliefs, and grief of Cambodian patients according to the self-evident truths of biomedicine. Next, I consider a series of clinic encounters in which health workers and refugees are shown to be involved in overt and subtle struggles over medical and therapeutic knowledge, cultural beliefs, and patient objectives. I end by discussing the resistance of patients to being viewed as exemplars of the medical model of the chaotic refugee body, and how this resistance was directed into working the system for specific goals.

SCREENING REFUGEE BODIES

From the beginning, American service agencies, church groups, and immigration officials working with the refugees tended to view them as threats, both ideological and medical, to the American body politic where many were to be settled. The goals of refugee recruitment, processing, and resettlement programs were to socialize refugees to a category of newcomers defined as contagious to and dependent on the civil society.

Germs and Genes

After the INS agents had screened Cambodian refugees for communist sympathizers, those chosen for resettlement in the United States were screened again, this time for diseases, so that they could be transformed into healthy bodies and minds fit for America. As mentioned in chapter 2, a sign at the PRPC in Bataan proclaimed,

> Refugee transformation, the primary goal of the PRPC operations, is achieved through a psycho-social recuperative process involving the "critical phases of adaptation, capability building, and disengagement" which result in changing a "displaced person" into an "Individual Well Equipped for Life in His Country of final destination."[8]

This psychosocial process of transformation not only acclimatized refugees to the intercultural status hierarchy of the camps, but also presupposed the medical image of refugees as the contagious other to the American body politic. A transnational system organized by the Centers for Disease Control (CDC) stationed public-health advisers in asylum countries (Thailand, Malaysia, the Philippines) to monitor the health screening of U.S.-bound refugees. All refugees were given age-specific immunizations, such as DPT, polio, and measles for infants. Everyone above age two was screened for infectious tuberculosis. Those with active or suspected active TB were placed in quarantine and denied departure for the United States until they were certified as healthy. Nevertheless, a health worker in San Francisco working with refugees claimed that the physicals in the camps were very cursory—basically a chest x-ray and possibly tests for leprosy and syphilis.

Upon arrival in American ports, refugees underwent a fairly extensive screening, a process that—much like getting on welfare—was a unifying rite of passage for refugees and a thorough schooling in the bureaucratic and medical definition of the modern subject. CDC officials notified local health agencies of each refugee's arrival, especially those who had had active or suspect tuberculosis, within twenty-four hours of entry. In 1986 alone, the U.S. Department of Health Services allocated $6 million for local refugee resettlement agencies to conduct health assessments.[9]

Indeed, the fear of contagion gave rise to the Refugee Medical Clinic in San Francisco, which was founded to protect the health of Americans, not refugees. As thousands of Southeast Asians arrived in San Francisco and other port cities in 1979, Americans were frightened that they would introduce fatal diseases into local communities. The clinic was generously funded; its mandate was to screen the Asian arrivals, cure them quickly, and then close its doors.[10] But in the late 1980s, the refugee clinic was still busy screening refugees, at the rate of a hundred a month. A nurse told me that the refugees were seen by the health clinic as whole families, and that the screening process took two months. Their histories were taken, and they were given a physical examination and some blood tests. Every adult was given a test for syphilis, for TB, and for anemia. Children received urine tests and audiograms to make sure their hearing was intact. "Everyone gets a stool parasite check, and we find that most of our patients coming from Southeast Asia do have multiple parasites. All that happens on the first day." Return visits included pelvic tests for women and dental screening for everyone; they were given toothpaste and toothbrushes and taught how to use them.

Thus in their first two months in the United States, refugees took their first steps toward being transformed into well-adjusted subjects. They learned the crucial importance of yielding information and submitting to tests in order to generate a health record, and understanding important daily rituals like brushing their teeth. The refugee clinicians saw their work as one of health education, stressing in particular physical examination, prevention, and medication compliance:

> As you know, medication compliance is really important—when you are talking to people who are not used to prevention or to thinking of things over the long run, it is kind of hard to say, "You are going to be taking this medication for your high blood pressure every day for the rest of your life."

Refugees also learned that access to health care was highly dependent on getting Medi-Cal, which was out of reach for the vast majority unless they also obtained AFDC. The refugee clinic referred patients with chronic diseases like diabetes, heart trouble, or thyroid disorders to specialty clinics. Other kinds of illnesses were also taken care of, and patients were sent to doctors only if they had Medi-Cal: "We make that determination about their referrals on their language and insurance capabilities."

For many who had lost loved ones or who had come close to death because of the lack of medical care, access to a clinic became the foundation of family survival. Perhaps more than any earlier generation of refugees and immigrants, medical socialization was important to the Southeast Asian refugees. And from the standpoint of public health, the extraordinary medical attention they received and the money spent on the effort were worthwhile: although more than seven hundred thousand Southeast Asian refugees have settled in the United States since 1975, they never became a threat to public health. This effort to train refugees to use public-health resources fully, however, created a lot of anger among social workers serving other poor people in America, who had limited access to health providers because their health costs were not covered by the federal government.[11]

At the same time, this close medical attention meant that Cambodians, Hmongs, and Miens in particular could not shake the image of their bodies as carriers of exotic and mysterious diseases from the tropics. In the 1980s, many Americans thought that the country was under threat from the inexorable influx of disease-bearing immigrants from all over the world—a view not without precedent in American history. For much of the nineteenth century, Asian immigrants were viewed as inferior racial bodies who should be excluded from the body politic.[12] The reception of Southeast Asian refugees was also consistent with the longstanding American perception that each wave of newcomers, including Europeans, was the source of "germs and genes of an inferior sort."[13] Today, the perception of polluting immigrants is reserved mainly for refugees and peoples from poor regions and sites like Haiti and Africa, whose populations are widely considered to be carriers of HIV.

Southeast Asian refugees came to be viewed as the exotic carriers of mysterious illnesses impenetrable to modern medicine. Not only were they found

to have high rates of tuberculosis and hepatitis, but they were also susceptible to Sudden Unexplained Nocturnal Death (SUND) syndrome. Reports
of sudden deaths, especially among young Hmong men, were attributed to
cardiac arrest during or following a bad dream. The mystery of these deaths
gave rise to speculation about causes, ranging from mineral deficiencies in
their diet to depression and to the effects of the defoliant Agent Orange,
which had been sprayed over much of the Indochinese peninsula during the
war. Many journalistic accounts linked SUND to the supposed cultural primitivity of the Hmongs.[14]

If Hmongs were represented as being vulnerable to death by nightmare,
Cambodians came to be seen as a people suffering from mental illnesses, especially post-traumatic stress disorder (PTSD). This term had been used in
the past to refer to the reverberating symptoms of war trauma among survivors of World War I, the Holocaust, and the Vietnam War. It refers to a cluster of symptoms, including depression, isolation, nightmares, flashbacks, and
vague, chronic illnesses. While there are obvious links between war traumas
and emotional and psychological distress, PTSD and its surrogate, depression, became routine and loose diagnoses applied to any Cambodian person who seemed upset about something—so that being ethnic Cambodian
came to mean as well being medically depressed. *Depressed Cambodian refugees*
became a useful term in a number of situations. It was invoked when the
public became upset about the refugee drain on the health-care system. Con-
versely, treating depressed Cambodians became the justification for state and
local health clinics to obtain much-needed funding from the federal government, especially when they could furnish charts showing Cambodians and
Hmongs scaling the depression stratosphere. For many refugees, being categorized as depressed or sick sometimes became inseparable from getting
health attention and welfare benefits, so that refugee patients came to understand that the stakes involved in the medicalized labeling used by health
and refugee services were but an aspect of the broader regulation of their
daily lives and access to a plethora of resources.

The Empire of the Non-Senses

Soon after arrival, refugee adults were issued a guide called *Facts of Life in
the United States,* which operated as a social-skills passport for navigating
American society. The booklet is available in thirteen languages, from
Amharic to Khmer to Vietnamese. After dealing with the legal status of
refugees, the rest of the pamphlet covers hygiene and safety at home and in
public. The introductory statement on sponsoring families is immediately
followed by instructions to learn American ways of promoting healthy living. Interestingly, the focus on inadvertently offensive bodies dwells on odor:

Americans are very sensitive to personal body odors. Because of this, it is a good idea for people to bathe or shower and put on clean clothing every day, and to wash their hair and clothes often. . . . Our dentists tell us to brush our teeth at least twice a day. . . . Americans use many products to hide their natural body odors. Most of us use deodorants and mouthwashes. People do these things to prevent unpleasant body odors that may offend other people.[15]

So much is made of the masking of smell, this "most animal" of our senses, that it seems as if poor newcomers were being urged to stock up on Listerine and Right Guard.[16] Other instructions include ventilating the home so that strong cooking smells will not offend the neighbors. The irony here is that, compared to most Americans, Cambodians are much more sensitive to the subtle distinctions and meanings of odors—indeed, this sensitivity is important in farming, cooking, and other sensuous activities.[17]

Perhaps smells, like viruses and diseases associated with refugees, were considered by the health agents to be invisible but potentially offensive things that refugees brought with them, inadvertently rescenting Americans' sense of their place. While offensive bodies can be physically contained, smells cannot. The focus on offensive smells, those "invasive" and invisible forces, highlighted anxiety over regulating refugee bodies in social space. Michael Taussig observes that

civilization sniffs out the enemy; uses smell against itself in an orgy of imitation. Racism is the parade ground where the civilized rehearse this love-hate relation with their repressed sensuousity, with the nose of the Jew, their "instinct" for avarice, the blackness of the negro, their alleged sexuality, and so forth. There is furthermore a strange mapping of what is defined as sensuous excess whereby the "minorities" spill out, escape the grid of the normative, and therefore conceptuality itself.[18]

Refugee parents are urged in the guide to use diapers on babies. Other suggestions include not spitting or urinating in public because "Americans prefer clean public places." (This statement does not take into account that most poor refugees were resettled in low-cost, garbage-strewn neighborhoods.) They are also warned about sexually transmitted diseases.

The prominence of desensing and sanitary measures drove home the "cleanliness is next to godliness" message of cultural citizenship—good hygiene as a sign of democratic sensibility. Refugees have to erase the smells of their humanity, submitting to a civilizing process that can be measured out in daily mouthwashes and showers. I remember being greeted at a poor Cambodian home with a woman spraying scent from an aerosol can. When I inquired why she was doing it, she said she had just been cooking Cambodian food, which, she had learned, "smelled bad to Americans." This was about a decade before Cambodian food became nouvelle Angkor cuisine for the Californian cognoscenti. The normalization of refugee germs, genes, senses, and home for the body politic has mainly fallen to the responsibility of the health system, and biomedical concepts and regimes have come to determine what count as biopolitically correct subjects.

THE BIRTH OF SOUTHEAST ASIAN MENTAL HEALTH

In Northern California, the Refugee Medical Clinic was only one site, albeit a major one, in a network of health facilities, which included an Asian mental-health facility funded by federal grants for refugee-related projects. Such government support to local medical facilities gave rise to discourses about something called Southeast Asian mental health, a phrase that referred to a condition allegedly lacking in Cambodian, Hmong, and Mien refugees. Southeast Asian mental health in practice was a set of concepts dedicated to the naming, classifying, and treatment of illnesses in the target population, as well as to the mobilization of resettlement agents, social workers, and academic and medical experts to assist refugees and relieve their suffering. These service providers were also involved in the work of risk management, and through their control of the terms and practices of sickness and healing, adjustment and maladjustment, they sought to put into practice various rationalities for governing the daily behavior of individuals and families. In the process, they also defined their own role as professional workers.

Academics funded by government grant moneys for refugee programs provided the intellectual ballast for the creation of this homogenizing bundle out of individual refugees' woes. Like other poor newcomers, Southeast Asian refugees were said to suffer from something called immigrant psychology. Alejandro Portes and Ruben G. Rumbaut claim that this condition depends to a great extent on the immigrants' "contexts of exit" and "contexts of reception" in the United States.[19] They argue that when war-traumatized newcomers like Cambodian refugees have access to governmental aid and services, their rate of "mental health distress" is less than would be the case in the absence of state assistance.[20] This linear model of immigrant psychology based on class origins and access to state support assumes that the sufferings of diverse populations follow generic patterns, and that mental-health constructs are universally applicable. It does not consider how the power dynamics of acculturation (which needs to be problematized) and the complex micropolitics and consequences of encounters with the health profession may have affected social adjustment. In this line of reasoning, immigrant psychology is taken to be a thing that exists among (non-European) immigrants who enter this country, rather than an attribution by sociologists and health experts, whose discourses play a key role in identifying deviance and proposing rational techniques to reform the other.

Health workers dealing with refugees have used a range of universal diagnostic tools as the lens through which refugees from Southeast Asia are viewed, represented, and treated. I have already mentioned PTSD, the favorite catchall category for the problems of Cambodian refugees.[21] For psychologists, PTSD symptomology includes recurrent nightmares, feelings of sadness, social withdrawal, restricted affect, hyperalertness and an exaggerated startle reflex, sleep disorders, memory loss, guilt, and avoidance of activities that prompt recall of stressful events.[22] An assessment tool freely applied to Cambodian patients was the Depression Rating Scale, which was slightly modified for assessing "cross-cultural psychiatric disorder" among Southeast Asians. Claiming that Asian immigrants have a "private style . . . that suppresses expressions of dysphoric complaints," J. D. Kinzie and colleagues developed the Vietnamese Depression Scale.[23] This scale was sometimes used as the instrument for assessing members of other Southeast Asian groups, such as the Cambodians, even though they have a rather different set of cultural beliefs and practices.[24] Another diagnostic tool, the Children's Global Assessment Scale (CGAS), has also been applied to Southeast Asian immigrants. In one study, Cambodian schoolchildren in Oregon were rated on a scale of behavioral deviance, and the doctors claimed that the CGAS was a better predictor of the children's distress than their own teachers' observations.[25] By these codes, Southeast Asian immigrants were medically defined as socially and culturally handicapped.

While such biopsychosocial assessment tools were intended to help the refugees, it is irrefutable that they played a role in constructing ethnic stereotypes of intellectual incompetence and the need for medical intervention. Cambodian patients have been described as "passive, obedient," but also "non-compliant."[26] The latter characterization was explained as "the unique avoidance of thoughts or activities that reminded these patients of the past. The patients often refused to tell their story in any detail, and many have never told it to anyone else before. There was a conscious effort to deny events of the past."[27] Furthermore, "Many Southeast Asians have an unwillingness or an inability to differentiate between psychological, physiological, and supernatural causes of illness."[28] These statements seem to suggest that Cambodians are "difficult" patients whose noncompliance stems from cultural passivity, the traumas they had experienced in war-torn Cambodia, and perhaps a mysterious Asian malady that made them unable to distinguish between reality and spiritual beliefs.

In general, mental-health experts claimed that Southeast Asians were disproportionately afflicted with depression, overdependency, isolation, psychosomatic illness, somatization, and PTSD, as compared to other groups in American society.[29] In a report to the California Department of Health, an Oakland clinic claimed in 1987 that 16 percent of Cambodian patients suffered from PTSD; the condition was less prevalent among other Southeast Asians in the sample.[30] Cambodians were said to be six to seven times more likely than the general population to be in severe need. More than 40 percent were in moderate or high-need categories, and should be "targeted for dramatically increased services."[31] Although the intention to help new immigrants was genuine, the report interpreting Cambodian refugees' needs was released in time to buttress appeals by the mental-health industry for more federal funds, which had been severely cut back under the Reagan administration. Getting the money was tied to the official designation of Cambodians as a depressed minority.

Attempts to teach refugees medical concepts that would help them understand their experiences have inspired more costly and technologically based innovations by health researchers. A wife-husband psychologist-psychiatrist team produced a videotaped "educational drama about PTSD."[32] It was distributed to selected groups of Cambodian women for viewing, in the hope of sparking a catharsis of their (assumed) suppressed feelings. After viewing the "educational drama," research assistants urged the participants to talk about their feelings and learn the new concepts. The professed aim was to "place PTSD symptoms within their unique sociocultural context and then to teach basic problem-solving skills dealing with major issues of daily living."[33] This videotaped shortcut to counseling was tested among some Cambodian women in San Diego who were diagnosed as suffering from PTSD. Some women claimed to have been cured after watching the videotape, without having to go to a clinic and be labeled "crazy." I watched the videotape and thought it a rather poor version of the Southeast Asian TV soaps avidly watched in Cambodian households, and unlikely to elicit greater emotional release. In any case, this video psychodrama was hailed in the local newspaper for "exorcising the evil that haunts Cambodians," and the psychologists put in a request for more government funding to set up a center for drop-in counseling.[34]

By controlling the medical terms, practices, and funding structure, academic and medical workers were part of an overall scheme of power that defined the form and content of refugee illness and well-being, while producing the truth-effects that seemed to define the public image of Southeast Asian immigrants. Overworked refugee health workers in underfunded clinics, swamped with clients from all over the world, tend to seek an efficient, though unsatisfactory, strategy to reduce the multicultural and personal details of patients' illnesses into diagnostic categories, so that they can dispense drug treatment. Their patients, however, seldom made things easy: a doctor working with refugee patients noted, "Among the Southeast Asians, no one would come in and announce, 'I'm depressed.'"[35] Although health workers solicited refugee stories, they used clinical labels to typecast Cambodians, who were urged to present their experiences in universalizable terms, and to cram the riot of their suffering into little boxes on the psychiatrists' charts. In many cases, the effect of mental-health treatment was to bypass or invalidate the patients' cultural understanding of their lives, as they were taken through a medical acculturation process that moved them from the particular and cultural to the ethnic and the scientific American.

In the course of my research on trauma treatment, I met an Argentine psychiatrist who had treated torture victims in his homeland and was spending some time helping out at a San Francisco hospital. He criticized local mental-health practitioners for labeling Southeast Asian patients as "depressed," but rarely asking them about their war experiences:

> They don't tend to read about the killing fields. But with a little information, you know your patient went through hell, a hell that no human being understands or is able to think about, if they never went through this or something like the mothers of La Plaza de Mayo went through. If you don't know what political repression is all about and you are not interested in asking the question, then you'll never know that the patient has something in his or her past that is horrible.

He noted a similar situation in the way some doctors were ever ready to brand Vietnam veterans as suffering from PTSD, but almost never listened to their traumatic experiences or treated them with the attention they deserved. When I pointed out that Asian American health workers also readily label the suffering of Asian refugees PTSD, he rather harshly observed that they are "victims of their own repression," meaning that despite possible common cultural experiences that might have created more empathy between the clinician and the refugee patient, the Band-Aid approach of biomedicine took precedence.

An important feature of Southeast Asian mental health was the significant number of Asian American health workers whose task included instructing refugees in the American medical nomenclature. It was routinely assumed that their "Asian culture" and experiences as children of refugees from the same continent made them more able to empathize with the cultural predicaments of Asian refugees. But Asian American doctors and nurses were at times even more insistent on the by-the-book definitions of what ailed their patients.

"CULTURAL SENSITIVITY" IN REFUGEE CLINICS

Northern California is the destination of refugees from all over the world, and local clinics are very proud of their "culturally sensitive" approach to health care. There are, for instance, Asian clinics—so called not because they dispense Asian cures but rather because they provide biomedical treatment for Asian patients—and these clinics claim greater cultural sensitivity than mainstream ones. In the late 1980s and early 1990s, news reports lauded such "Ellis Island clinics," funded by federal money, where refugees of the 1980s were met with medical staff highly attuned to their cultural difference, so the clinics served as important halfway houses that made them feel at home. Many of the health workers were American-born Asians "who may have been raised in bilingual households and witnessed firsthand the collision of old Asian customs and new American ones."[36] They understood concepts like yin and yang and the need to balance hot and cold food intake, and supported practices like consulting shamans. As the children of immigrants, refugees, and holocaust survivors, many of the health workers were more accepting of and sensitive to the cultural beliefs, practices, and experiences of war refugees and Asian newcomers. Such cultural discourse, however, seemed used only to bolster the normalizing strategy of introducing scientific and rational thinking about illness and of treating diseases rather than persons. A dissenting Chinese American doctor said, "What we have to do as providers is to be curious. We have to ask again and then again. This is not about these individual [cultural] things. It is about caring, and out of caring searching out what we need to know."[37]

But the biomedical approach to sickness and the pressure of work allowed the health-care workers little time to "know" their patients, only to diagnose where it hurt. Also, many of the clinicians seemed to be true believers in their biomedical methods. As first- or second-generation Americans, Asian (especially Chinese) health workers have earned professional degrees and moved out of Chinatown into suburban communities. Partly as a result of this transition into the American scientific world and into the middle class, they could be among the most ardent believers in rationality, and the most dismissive of premodern "superstitions" and practices. Because they were children of Asian immigrants who had suffered discrimination, some health workers might have considered it necessary to root out non-Western cultural beliefs as a strategy to gain acceptance and achieve assimilation. They might tend to view cultural cleansing or loss as an unavoidable and necessary part of becoming American. At the same time, some acculturated health providers of Asian ancestry expressed an underlying belief in Chinese cultural superiority over Southeast Asians. In short, their claim of cultural sensitivity suggested social skills at dealing with the impenetrable other, but not a modification of their basic faith in Western medicine and rationality.

Thus, although the health providers were well-meaning and sympathetic, the pressure to "do something" with patients often meant in practice the use of the trappings of cultural sensitivity in a limited, strategic fashion to win patients' cooperation, facilitate diagnosis, and buttress the doctors' authority, rather than to give equal time to alternative points of view or to relativize biomedical knowledge.[38] Such health workers were often unable to take a critical view of their own professional role when clinic discourse defined them as ideal care providers for Asian immigrants. Indeed, stereotypical cultural concepts were deployed to construct an intersubjective reality that sought to manipulate, incorporate, and supplant Cambodian notions of healing, body care, and family.

Ronald Frankenberg notes that sickness is a "cultural performance," a sequence of events in which disease narratives interact with patients' beliefs.[39] For Cambodian patients, refugee clinics became the site of a struggle between biomedicine and their own understanding of their experiences, and the skirmishes and standoffs were the key elements in a dynamic process of learning cultural belonging. The following cases of "talking medicine" and "refugee mental health" also reveal, however, that while refugee medicine focused on eliciting cultural talk that could be recast as symptoms recognizable to biomedical diagnosis, clinicians as well as patients were caught up in "webs of power" that structured both the domination of biomedicine over cultural beliefs considered inappropriate and the clinicians' inner conflicts as they tried to control the terms and practices of health care for Asian patients.[40]

"TALKING MEDICINE": REGULATING AND SUBVERTING DRUG THERAPY

At one Bay Area Asian mental-health clinic, the philosophy of culturally sensitive health care was based on an "appropriate use of Western psychiatric methodology in non-Western populations."[41] This approach was inspired by Arthur Kleinman's distinction between disease, which is caused by objective biological processes, and illness, or the cultural experience and understanding of affliction.[42] Other scholars have theorized cultural sensitivity as a "synthesis" between "psychiatry's biopsychosocial model and an often different sociocultural model of human cognition" in the "acculturating group."[43] In practice, however, the two perspectives—biological and cultural—were not in dialectical tension; rather, the effect of culturally sensitive health care has been to subsume and invalidate the cultural beliefs of the minority group. Although doctors and nurses made a show of collecting cultural data and talking about cultural beliefs, their medical knowledge was seldom questioned, revised, or relativized; it was in fact strengthened by the gap between the patients' cultural understanding and the doctors' scientific interpretations (which were not viewed as cultural). By constructing the cultural descriptions of patients as "somatic complaints," the main treatment was "rigorous symptomatic therapy (drugs)."[44]

There were two aspects to what the clinic called talking medicine. One was to get patients to talk about their experiences and beliefs in order to provide information that could facilitate diagnosis and the patients' acceptance of the health-care providers' authority. Doctors and nurses sought to elicit migration histories from reluctant refugee patients, who had unpleasant memories of interrogations by the Khmer Rouge and the INS. Talking medicine was viewed as a way to put nervous patients at ease, and by "validating the patients' feelings about life events," doctors hoped to carry on an ongoing assessment of symptoms and treatment. Cambodian health aides used Khmer terms like "hotness in the body, pressure on the heart, and total body weakness" as substitute "native" terms for what doctors considered symptoms of clinical depression. Furthermore, Chinese concepts like yin and yang were assumed to be universal to Southeast Asian cultures, and doctors invoked yin and yang to explain "that chemicals in the brain can be out of balance and that this can be the cause of their symptoms and sad feelings. . . . anti-depressant drugs will restore this balance."[45]

Talking medicine buttressed a disease narrative whereby stereotypical Asian patients' beliefs were integrated into and transformed within the medical paradigm. In practice, then, cultural sensitivity became a strategy that used cultural difference not so much to understand particular experiences of illness as to read symptoms that confirmed universalized states of biomedicine.[46] A doctor acclaimed for having dealt extensively with Cambodian patients noted that "Depression is depression in all cultures. It has the same vegetative symptoms."[47] Although the intentions of health workers were genuinely to respect patients' pain, their cultural difference was viewed as a distorting screen that would, with difficulty, yield the symptoms that could be identified in biomedical terms so that appropriate drugs could be prescribed. The good intentions of the clinicians notwithstanding, the regulatory force of biomedicine absorbed cultural ideas and transformed them into code words that buttressed medical authority. The caregivers, as much as the patients, were thus caught up in the regulatory effects of biomedicine, and cultural material was appropriated only to be incorporated within the medical framework.

A nurse discussed how health-care workers dealt with PTSD: "We do a couple of things. We make sure that we work the person up medically so that we are not missing some physiological problem that can contribute to depression or somatization and that can actually be treated. . . . When the workups start coming back all negative, which is often what happens, I will say to the people that it is very common for pain in life to cause pain in the body." Here the nurse merely confirmed what Cambodians believed all along—and in a rather more spiritually informed way. Cambodians consider health to be an inseparable aspect of maintaining one's relationships with family members, both alive and dead. For them, illness is seldom a discrete physical phenomenon apart from the social identity of the afflicted. For instance, Cambodian peasants often attribute illness or misfortune to angry ancestral spirits, which can deprive one of the vital life-sustaining essence.[48] But this broader, socially embedded view of sadness as caused by failure or ruptures in one's social networks could not be incorporated into the biomedical view of depression, which tends to be highly individualized in its treatment.

At the same time, for some clinicians eager to provide more than drug therapy, talking medicine was also an opportunity to listen with a sympathetic ear, when patients could be induced to speak about the chaos they were experiencing:

"And now we are going to do something different. Now we are going to have talking medicine." I frame talking about what has happened in terms of medicine because it makes it a lot safer for people. So we talked about your thyroid when you came in, we talked about your pelvic examination, and now we are going to do another kind of talking medicine, about these complaints you are having. Usually I start with the present and what is happening in their current life. "How many people are living in your house? Who did you bring over here with you? What is your community like?" And then, "Are you on welfare? What kinds of financial concerns do you have?" And then go back: "What was it like in the refugee camp? How was the transition?" Then back to the actual flight experience.

She called these "minitherapy" sessions because the nurses were not trained psychotherapists. By stressing their less strictly biomedical role, she revealed the staff's attempts to go beyond the dispensing of drugs, and in a sense even to subvert the limited medical agenda. Talking medicine in this sense sought to provide, along with the aspirins, emotional comfort—as well as perhaps referrals for patients who appeared suicidal. Clearly, the clinic staff saw themselves as trying to give the best possible care to the multicultural patient population, within the bounds set by biomedicine and clinic resources.

Although the strategies of cultural sensitivity and talking medicine to elicit information that would aid diagnosis reinforced biomedical control, they could at the same time be subversive of biomedical treatment, and provide spaces for attending to sick hearts and souls. This conflicting logic of clinic treatment describes a terrain in which some negotiation and empathy were possible, and offered the possibility of attenuating the cold and regulatory nature of modern medicine. Indeed, some refugees felt grateful to receive sympathy for their less-tangible afflictions without having to go to the "crazy house" (mental-health clinic). In practice, then, the biopolitics of refugee medicine—mediated by the strategies of cultural sensitivity and talking medicine—could be accomplished and reproduced only through a daily cross-cultural negotiative and learning process on the part of patients as well as clinicians.

REFUGEE THERAPY: APPROPRIATE(D) TELLING AND MEMORIES

The Asian mental-health clinic, despite its stress on cultural fit with the refugees, seemed to be more strictly regulated by the norms of psychiatry. The approach there was to elicit cultural information in order to invalidate or erase it, so that self-discipline could begin the work of helping refugee minds made chaotic and confused by war and displacement. From my interviews with a Cambodian health aide and some patients, it emerged that a key technique involved distinguishing between appropriate memories that fitted diagnostic categories, and inappropriate memories that must be resisted. Here indeed was the nub of the therapeutic method, guided by the diagnoses in the Diagnostic and Statistical Manual for Mental Disorders III (DSM III): prolonged grief was considered a form of "complicated mourning" that defied the normal stages of appropriate bereavement.[49] The goal of this therapeutic intervention in bereavement was premised on a "self-evident" truth that "there are normal and abnormal responses to death and loss."[50]

In the Asian mental clinic, doctors relied on Mr. Eam, a Cambodian American who was being trained as a bilingual therapist, to gain access to Cambodian patients, most of whom were middle-aged and older women. A former policeman from Phnom Penh, Eam had his own harrowing war experiences, being the only person from his squad to survive the Khmer Rouge. Perhaps his background in intelligence, and his desire to surmount his nightmarish past, made Eam embrace the empirical methods of biomedicine and discourage lingering bereavement. Furthermore, he was being trained for a professional position, and he believed that medicine could help his fellow Cambodian Americans speed their recovery and adjust to American life.

But Eam found it an especially frustrating job to mediate between the Cambodian refugees and the criteria of mental health, which required him to discipline their grief by deciding what were appropriate and inappropriate things to remember and forget. Using the DSM III as the measurement, he sorted the patients according to standardized categories of major depression, schizophrenia, conduct disorder, and bipolar disorder. Asian American psychologists and psychiatrists made the final decision of which category fitted which patient, and prescribed drugs accordingly. Eam noted that his greatest difficulty was finding the truth of his patients' lives: "There is nothing inside their minds thinking that 'Oh, I have this thing called depression, this thing called adjustment disorder,' or whatever. . . . Not only do they not know how to tell their problems, but many do not want to tell the truth!"

In his view, patients lied because of shame over seeking help at a mental-health clinic, which many Cambodians consider synonymous with "a place for crazy people." Often, the shame came from disclosing the collapse of family life and self-respect. He told a story of a Cambodian man whose wife had run away with another man. He got into a street fight with African Americans and was sent to a hospital, which referred him to the clinic. "He didn't tell what his problem was; he had been drinking! He did not want to tell the truth [because it's] so shameful. . . . So my job is to find out exactly. In this country we expect clients to tell us what's going on. It's the client's willingness to tell us what the problem is if they want us to help. But with the Cambodians, we have to dig it up . . . to go deeper." Like his counterparts in other clinics, Eam's battle was simply to get refugees to talk. Cambodians had survived war, labor camps, and flight by becoming masters in the contest between self-willed silence and forced confession. A Cambodian prophecy of doom noted that only by playing dumb would people survive: "Only the deaf-mutes would be saved during this period of misfortune."[51] Silence and opacity become a shield of defense in the face of authority. Many refugees viewed Western medicine in the light of a magic bullet that would ease their pains, but they detested the talking part of the clinic culture. Some said to Eam, "I want to cooperate with you, but the method you use is so difficult, it involves discussion. . . . I feel dizzy, feel so exhausted."

The clinic's quest for hidden "truths" was made more difficult when Eam tried to get female clients to yield information that could fit psychiatric categories. Female patients, accustomed to values of female modesty, probably found it too humiliating and painful to share stories of war violence and suffering, as well as current health problems, especially with a younger man. Thus in practice, treatment often entailed a struggle between silences and truths, a "truth-game" that if played correctly could gain refugees access to medicine.[52]

Eam saw his job as getting patients to say things that suggested symptoms identified in the DSM III chart. The next step was to prescribe medication, which, though desired, was carefully administered by the patients. Outside the clinic, women complained that the drugs might be too powerful, and had the effect of blurring memories they might wish to retain, no matter how painful. This effect seemed to coincide with Eam's understanding of the goal of mental-health treatment: "Our medicine is to knock you down in order not to think, not to think about what's going on, about the family . . . just to knock you down, to go to bed. We believe that the more the patients sleep, the better the chance they will feel better. So they forget whatever stuff that upset them." Genuinely concerned with the suffering of his patients, Eam subscribed to the therapeutic belief that grief was a time-limited linear process, and that becoming healthy required letting go of painful memories.

His patients, however, resisted such losses. They took their prescribed drugs according to their own judgment of whether they helped with their daily aches, but the treatment failed to discipline their grief. As in many cultures, grieving for the dead was considered part of life, and indeed could be a lifelong process as one searched for meaning in the death of a loved one. Freud himself opposed the pathologizing of mourning:

> The distinguishing mental features . . . are a profoundly painful dejection, cessation of interest in the outside world, loss of the capacity to love, [and] inhibition of all activity. . . . It is easy to see that this inhibition and circumspection

of the ego is the expression of an exclusive devotion to mourning which leaves nothing over for other purposes or for other interests. It is really only because we know so well how to explain it that this attitude does seem to us to be pathological.[53]

I had the sense that other than getting medicine for everyday aches and pains, the Cambodian women kept their own counsel about their sorrows. One of Eam's patients was Mrs. Tech (introduced in chapter 1), a widow in her fifties who had had high blood pressure and stomach problems for a long time. She suffered from dizziness, and felt weak most of the time. When we met, she was sitting on the mat in her living room, showing me a shoebox of medicine bottles: "The medicine I got from there is good and it sometimes relieves the headache. . . . He tries to make all the women who have mental problems happy. But I think a lot. [He] told me to forget about the past and not to think a lot. But how can I forget?" She told me the story of losing her husband and two sons in the war. "I have felt sorrowful and sick since." In the United States, she reconnected with one of the sons; the other had died at the Battambang hospital where she had left them. Such memories were the connecting tissue to her past, and her ongoing grief. Her Buddhist faith might be defined as a "deathlife" philosophy in which consciousness of suffering and death was a moral condition of existence.[54] Biomedical treatment sought to blot out her memories, so that she could be freed from the shadow of death and participate more fully in her adopted country. But although she needed medication, Mrs. Tech resisted the medical dislodging of her past life and what remained of her cultural self.

Both the refugee clinic, with its conflicting goals of talking medicine, and the mental-health clinic, with its judgment of what constituted normal mourning and appropriate memory, provided the kind of treatment that allowed very limited opportunities for the telling of stories in a full and uncensored manner. Overall, since American medical settings "constrain Khmer in expressing their own culture,"[55] Cambodian women sought catharsis through talking of past traumas only in the presence of sympathetic relatives and friends, whose community provided the cultural context for the experience of pain and healing. Traditional Cambodian therapies were community activities, reducing social isolation and strengthening social bonds. This collective approach to suffering and healing was in contrast to the Western biomedical and psychiatric focus on the afflicted individual, but it was nominally encouraged by physicians, who readily acknowledged the limits of their time, resources, and ability to heal the spiritually ill. Nevertheless, within clinic walls biomedical practitioners sought only the evidence of what they defined as the truth of particular conditions, and distrusted any aspect of the patient's experience that might permit an alteration of the relationship doctors have with psychiatric logic. All games of power are games of truth, but not vice versa, so that there is always the possibility in a truth game for the discovery of alternative stories and truths.[56]

MODERN BODILY REGIMES

Daily encounters between refugees and health workers were lessons in new "bodily regimes" relevant to the cultivation of behavioral traits, such as learning the routines of checkups, vaccination, family planning, and drug treatment—the temporal structuring of life that refugees were first subjected to in the transit camps.[57] Medical regimes thus not only socialize people to expected norms of patient behavior but also instruct patients about the rules and rights that constitute the proper biomedical and juridical subject.[58] Here again, Cambodian refugees were considered among the most problematic patients when it came to learning medical routines. Their responses to medical orders were found to be unsatisfactory, and were labeled irrational, passive, and face-saving. Some Asian American health workers interpreted Cambodian smiles as expressions of their "fear of authority"; yet there was also the suspicion that the smiles disguised intransigence about medical discipline. Cambodian refugees deployed a range of tactics—silence, polite smiles, the resistant body, and faking illness—to subvert and thwart clinic rules but still retain the medical attention and resources they desired. These cultural performances as patients were important lessons in citizenship, as Cambodians learned that the politics of subordination entailed figuring out how to obtain resources controlled by experts.

Taking Medicine

A primary concern of the poor immigrants was gaining access to prescription drugs. As mentioned in previous chapters, many refugees and the poor stayed on welfare in order to safeguard their children's access to Medi-Cal. They reproduced in the United States the patron–clientelist orientation learned in refugee camps, where American service providers and experts often became the focus of deferential behavior because they could provide access to important things like medicine.[59]

Of all Western medicines, Cambodians were most interested in injectable drugs, intravenous drips, and pills, in which they have a high degree of faith. This faith was based on the Khmer culture's idea of putting good things into the body. A former pharmacist in pre-1975 Phnom Penh told me about Cambodians going to the hospital regularly for injections if they felt sick. Pregnant women wanted injections in order to become "strong and healthy." But during the Khmer Rouge years, not only were people deprived of modern medical care, but untrained so-called medics injected toxic substances called *ach tunsiy*, or rabbit's secretions, into the sick, causing their death.[60] Nevertheless, that experience did not dissuade Cambodians of the efficacy of injectable Western drugs. Lindsay French reports that in refugee camps, Cambodians injected themselves with vitamins and treated themselves with stolen antibiotic drips. This limited aspect of Western medicine was viewed as uniquely effective, while other aspects of Western healing were considered unnecessary and obstructionist.[61]

In clinic encounters, Cambodians' respect for Western medicine was not matched by their respect for American doctors, whose techniques and interpretations they often found baffling and controlling. Older Cambodians expected healers (like the Cambodian *krou*) to have special insights into illnesses without performing tests or cross-examining the afflicted.[62] Yet in America, the doctors submitted patients to an interrogation about many unrelated topics concerning themselves, their relatives, and their migration history. A nurse in the refugee clinic saw it this way:

> People sometimes doubt our abilities because we ask so many questions. "Well, what's the matter? Don't you know? If you have to ask these questions, then maybe you're not very good." In this culture, we think the more questions you know how to ask, the more skilled you are. Oftentimes when I see patients I say, "You may not be used to this, but I am going to be asking you a lot of questions. This is how we do medicine in this country. I know that in the country you come from, people didn't ask you so many questions." So we start from there.

Not surprisingly, clinicians complained that Cambodian patients seemed to display skepticism when faced with questioning. They wondered whether the doctors were fakes, concealing their lack of knowledge by asking many questions and relying on many instruments. In contrast, the Cambodian *krou* are men and women of few words. They set about their healing by prescribing herbs and setting bones, but their primary work is in divining the cause of a person's illness and mediating with spirits to heal illnesses and remove misfortune. In the United States, the *krou* continue to do a flourishing trade attending to sick people who are simultaneously using Western drug therapy.

A nurse pointed out that aside from having physical checkups, medical compliance and the importance of prevention were the two major lessons that the refugee clinic hoped its patients would internalize in the process of becoming the good patient. The goal was not only to foster health, but to shape and direct patients' behavior so that they would become responsible, self-monitoring subjects. But too frequently, Cambodian patients resisted the doctors' authority by ignoring medication instructions. They complained that doctors prescribed too many drugs and gave them dosages that were "too hot" for Asian bodies. Even after clinicians reassured them that their dosage was

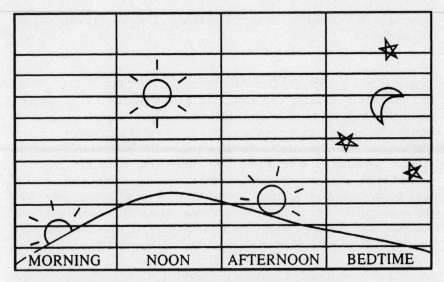

Figure 3. Card to indicate the daily schedule for taking medicine.

proportionate to their "smaller size" relative to Americans, Cambodian patients routinely reduced their drug intake, or took their medicine irregularly. This self-administering was not surprising, considering that in their homeland women's repertoire of domestic skills included health management; but it was clearly a blithe disregard of medical rules.[63] The nurse continued:

> Some people only wanted to take drugs on days they felt bad. Or some people have unusual sets of reasons why they decide to take medicine. I have one guy who only took yellow pills on Monday and he took the green ones on another day of the week, so he split his medicines up into a color-coded system of his own that I have yet to understand. The people do different things with their medications, so we do a lot of teaching around how to take the pills.

To instill a respect for medical regime, the clinic gave patients with little knowledge of English a card divided into columns represented by moon and sun symbols, to indicate appropriate times of day for taking medicine (figure 3). Pills were glued to the appropriate columns so that the patient knew which pill should be taken at which time of day. But some patients misread the linear representation of time and substituted their own schedule. Taking the diagram to represent the lunar cycle, they took their medicine according to the waxing or waning moon phases. Another strategy was to stop taking drugs a few days before their next visit so the doctor could see that "I am still ill." Instead of directly challenging doctors' advice, Cambodian patients took the drugs while protesting that the illness lingered on, and that they remained unhealed. They drew a fine distinction between taking the medicine and taking medicine.

Passivity of Women, Bodies of Resistance

In Cambodia, women played a major role in the daily care of their families, but in the United States they found themselves dependent on a medical system in which they operated as ignorant recipients. Working with a Chinese-influenced humoral theory, Cambodians believe that hot and cold winds affect the health of the body. Bodily aches (including headaches) are often treated by pinching, cupping, and coining in order to relieve pain and bring toxic winds to the body's surface, thus restoring balance among elements in the body, and between the body and the environment.[64] Hot and cold foods were variously prescribed to prevent imbalances in the body, and to restore the sick body to health. Women's care of the body through dietary and healing practices, together with their rituals commemorating dead ancestors, were social obligations that ensured the health and safety of the family. The link between physical well-being and nurturing one's social relations in this world and the next is clearly central to Cambodian healing practices.

Perhaps not surprisingly, in American clinic encounters, Cambodian women were viewed as a special category of "difficult" patients, perceived as being more "traditional and superstitious" than men. Furthermore, clinic workers characterized them as passive, silent, and fearful of authorities. Even Asian American nurses could seldom talk to them in a such a way as to break through their silences. But while the health workers saw Cambodian women's passivity as simply a sign that they were downtrodden and mired in outmoded cultural mores, it can be read in a variety of ways—as a tactic to deflect control while maintaining a relationship, or as an attempt to shield a vulnerable self.

In Cambodian culture, authority figures should not be questioned or otherwise embarrassed, so both men and women tend to display passive obedience before authority.[65] This pose of passivity was further honed during the Pol Pot years, when Cambodians' silence avoided disclosures and exposures that could result in terrible consequences to oneself and one's loved ones. In refugee camps and in American institutions, Cambodians found that by being passive with powerful authority figures, they could dissemble about what they wanted to do and their reasons for doing so, while still maintaining the patron–client relationship. Often, the customary obedience was "compounded by fear and ignorance of our legal system," as Cambodian patients worried that by yielding up information about themselves to an American official, or by deliberately disregarding rules, they might be threatened with deportation.[66]

But as survivors of war traumas, these women might have been using passivity to mask suicidal tendencies or the loss of self-respect. For instance, in the course of my interviews with dozens of refugee women, many told me painful stories of flight and the suffering of family members, and a few implied in the most oblique way that they themselves had been abused. But I could never be certain how many had actually been tortured in their flight from Cambodia or raped by Thai soldiers "guarding" the refugee camps, or what kinds of compromises they had made in order to survive and care for their children, or how deep was their sense of dishonor. A survey of two hundred Southeast Asian refugee women, including Cambodians, found that 50 percent had been raped. The lethargy noted by clinicians might be attributed to the women having been raped, with the irreducible sense of dishonor it brought to themselves and to their families. An aid worker of Cambodian heritage said, "Cambodian women face many problems, but rape is the worst of all for them. In Cambodia, girls are compared to flowers that can wither at a hurtful touch, like the rose and the jasmine. It's different from the United States. Your women talk about it. They take measures to protect themselves." But fearing ostracization by their families, many Cambodian victims were silent sufferers.[67]

Indeed, encounters with modern health measures were not always reassuring, and in fact could be rather unnerving. Regardless of whether they had been victimized, young girls arriving in the United States faced the ordeal of physical examination required of all refugees. Most Cambodian girls had rarely been naked before anyone, except perhaps their mothers. I was told that refugee girls arriving in Los Angeles were horrified to be told to strip and lie under bright lights, with open legs raised up in stirrups. Pelvic examination by a male physician, even with a female nurse standing by, was a painful introduction to the American medical system. The San Francisco clinic understood Cambodians' sensitivity about exposing their bodies to the medical gaze. "We have a policy here that we don't do pelvic exams on single women or women who are not sexually active, because there is so much cultural stuff that is attached to virginity and an intact hymen." Only female clinicians did pelvic exams on married women or those whom they suspected had had sex or been raped. The patients were told the medical reasons for gynecological examinations. Whenever possible, young women who had been examined were reassured that they were "still virgins."

Nevertheless, Cambodian women remained opaque to the medical gaze— a kind of docile body, made passive through what Foucault called "a microphysics of power" and yet repelling the supervisory instructions and meticulous care the medical sciences required.[68] The refugee clinic tried to instill in women the notions of calculated risk and preventive action that go with being a prudent citizen in an insurance-buttressed society. Refugee women must be taught responsibility about their bodies and the fate of their children through a kind of calculation that links present action with future consequences. Yet Cambodian women seemed resistant to the minute self-observation necessitated by that method, as well as to the idea that such micro-practices regulating bodily forces could be part of a larger scheme to control one's fate.

This skepticism was reflected in Cambodian women's strong rejection of certain medical interventions into hidden bodily processes to control the spread of diseases or to regulate pregnancy. A nurse complained, "I teach women how to do their own breast exams, which is kind of radical for them because they are not used to touching themselves in a specific way."

More radically, Cambodians drew the line at cutting their bodies or inserting foreign objects into them, since in their Buddhist beliefs, the body should remain intact. In Cambodian Buddhism, the body is considered to be in unity with the social self and the soul; all three are closely interrelated. A sacred essence resides in the head of each individual, and the head must be treated with special respect. After death, the soul separates from the body and continues its existence, hopefully in a higher reincarnated form. In her study of Cambodian amputees in refugee camps, Lindsay French observes that to be born able-bodied and then lose a limb represents a sudden downturn in one's fortune. It is a sign of bad karma, which not only betokens a fall in status but also bodes ill for the future.[69] Besides, for Cambodians, surgery unavoidably stirred up memories of torture during the war years. During the Pol Pot time, soldiers on both sides routinely cut open the bodies of fallen soldiers to eat their livers or mutilate them further.[70] Many Cambodians witnessed family members injected with fatal substances, or dying under torture and dismemberment. Now patients in America, Cambodians had to rethink the relationship between bodily integrity, social status, and war memories on the one hand, and biomedical interventions on the other.

A nurse told me about a Cambodian woman who, when told that she had a breast mass, refused any medical procedure. Even after seeing five specialists and being shown the x-ray image, she resisted a biopsy. The nurse said that her patient saw no connection between her current feeling of health and the idea of the diseased body she could neither see nor feel. Besides, the idea of being anesthetized frightened her. It seemed an unnecessary and costly risk to submit to surgery that might lead to the mutilation of her body. For her, having to sign permission for the operation was the last straw. Signing a form recalled situations under the Khmer Rouge in which being interviewed and signing forms often resulted in one's torture, dismemberment, and death. Her fears were so great that the clinic could do nothing, but they worried about whether the patient's resistance to preventive surgery would also dissuade her from pursuing a lawsuit further down the line. Fortunately, the director of the clinic had developed some equanimity about resistance to surgery. He recalled the case of a retarded boy whose parents rejected surgery for his defective heart: "I couldn't go against them. They're the ones who were caring for him, feeding him, changing his sheets—not me. In America, we pull out all the stops to save someone. But they see death as part of living. It's a more realistic approach. They don't prolong a painful, dismal existence."[71] For many Cambodian patients, following some medical instructions might actually consign one to a karmic misfortune after death.

Beyond teaching general preventive measures, clinicians focused attention on disciplining women's bodies in order to regulate childbirth. Lessons in family planning reflected the widespread political concern that Cambodians, like other poor working-class and refugee populations, were a new underclass in the making. A refugee-resettlement social worker reported that many social workers were upset because the local health departments began to treat refugees based on their expectations of American minorities, assuming that they were "coming here in hordes to have babies and take advantage of the health system or welfare system. They were people in crisis who were brought to this country by the political events that we participated in and who have, because they are here, some rights to have service providers be somewhat sensitive to them. There have been a lot of problems that we have tried to work on but were not successful."

Since sex is such a culturally sensitive subject, Asian American nurses played a major role in reproductive health education. For instance, a Japanese American nurse who made home visits told me that her instructions about reading body signs for pregnancy were often met by silence: "They don't say anything. They . . . feel we're some kind of authority." Using a maternal and teasing manner, she urged Cambodians to engage in family planning. In one family, after the birth of a sixth baby, she said to the father, "'Papa, no more babies' . . . no one ever challenges or refuses you." But the next time she visited, there was a new baby. In this case, the nurse accepted that her good intentions would be subverted by a people whom she saw as grateful to America for accepting them as refugees, and yet determined to follow their own desires about family size. The nurse continued to visit them. Through their passive pose as clients of the state, this family subtly negotiated a space for making their own decisions and yet still eliciting the bureaucratic attention that helped secure medical access. Even more powerless than the men, Cambodian women learned not to express personal opinions but played off authority figures in their own community and in American institutions.

In the refugee clinic, Southeast Asian women were seen as epitomizing the fecund premodern woman who must learn self-discipline and new knowledge in order to make rational decisions. A Chinese American nurse saw her role as promoting "patient participation in the decision . . . to empower them as parents." Collecting groups of refugee and immigrant women together for health classes, she discussed the idea that one could plan pregnancies, the

THE PILL

Figure 4. Learning the facts of life the multicultural
way (California Family Health Council, Los Angeles).

different methods of contraception, and prenatal care (figure 4). When her
instructions were received in silence by Cambodian women, she took it to
mean their "not wanting to lose face by asking an authority figure questions":

> And I say, "Wait a minute, you have a right to ask questions, you have a right
> to refuse, you have a right to another opinion." They say "yes," but do not com-
> ply with my orders. . . . Even though they are passive, they are even more de-
> manding [than other patients] because we don't know what they are ques-
> tioning, or what issues are there for them.

In her estimation, Cambodian women were more passive than Chinese
or Russian refugees. After her presentations, Chinese women would ask questions, soliciting medical information. In one meeting, "the Russians ask, 'Can
I have a sonogram?'"[72] Instead of seeking the latest medical technology, Cambodian women "turn their bodies over to authority figures. They will say yes
to everything, leave, and then come back pregnant . . . they're just saying it
at times to placate us." Cambodian women displayed polite smiles and a seem-
ingly detached attitude toward their own bodies. They appeared uninterested

in lectures on contraceptive use, birth spacing, the stages of pregnancy, and phases in the birth process—basic lessons for modern would-be mothers. The nurse hoped to "empower" them via birth control but was unable to persuade Cambodian women to go so far as to learn to use a diaphragm. Despite her patient coaching, she concluded that Cambodian women became used to "having things done for them." They seemed impervious to medical interpretations of their problems, needs, and goals.

Family-planning advice stressed individual decision-making. Female patients were given comic books called "The Pill," "Natural Family Planning," and "A Planned Family Is a Happy Family," to be used in concert with instructions from a health worker.[73] Female readers were instructed to treat their bodies as manipulable machines, divorced from their emotional, social, and political contexts. Because of their own limited access to patients' families, clinic nurses tried to "empower" individual women in decision making about having children, but failed to reduce the husband's control of his wife's body.

Outside the hospital, I heard about a couple of cases in which the woman rejected her husband's desire to have more children; but in general, it appeared that Cambodian women went along with the decision to have children. Indeed, these women managed to thwart obstetric interventions even more than the "empowered" female patients did. They were engaged in a complex contestation that both invited medical attention and repelled it.[74] One might say that the medical gaze was reproduced by such silent resistance, which compelled further medical attention and use of resources to make them better patients. Because the unregulated fecund Cambodian body seemed both premodern and unruly, it confirmed the image of a new Asian American underclass already stigmatized for its unwed, pregnant teenagers. Social workers complained about the increasing number of pregnant Cambodian girls dropping out of school, and workers in the WIC program also noted the increasing number of pregnant Southeast Asian teenagers among their clients (see the next chapter).

Here, once again, the experiences of war and of enforced dependency in the United States must be part of the context for understanding patient behavior. The loss of children to starvation and disease during the Khmer Rouge years increased the Cambodian immigrants' desire to have more children. Cambodian health workers told me that family planning was an unknown concept among the majority of Cambodians, though women knew secret methods for aborting unwanted fetuses. Women never talked to their husbands about sex, an area that was viewed as a male prerogative. Older women believed that the number of children they had was predestined, as a reward or punishment for past lives. They thought a woman becomes pregnant after dreaming about a man who presents her with a gift that signifies the sex of the child.[75] Although these ideas indicate a moral or religious system of self-regulation, they differ radically from the medical model that subjects bodily forces to minute supervision and control. Aside from the cultural issues, there was also the stark reality of inadequate household income, and many immigrants were aware that having more children in the United States would ensure access to medical services, which was yoked to receiving public assistance. So although pregnant women attempted to deflect medical discipline and rejected self-observation by internalizing the medical gaze, they wished to retain their claims on health care and, through their babies, on the larger welfare system.

WORKING AROUND THE MEDICAL SYSTEM

Refugees then were engaged in the management of ongoing crises that drew from but also undermined the normalizing procedures of biomedicine and market-driven care. Patient resistance was seldom articulated, both because of language problems and because of an aversion to disagreeing with Americans, who were viewed as having greatly helped Cambodians and who continued to be providers of everything from over-the-counter pills to a living income. Instead, the locus of resistance was in their bodies, in the refusal and subversion of medical discipline. Despite their thwarting of medical regimes, refugees hung on to the clinic because it was a key institution that helped secure their other needs. Because they felt the need to repel the perception that they were living off the system, Cambodians used nonverbal strategies to negotiate their specific goals with the medical authorities.

Clinics were the gateway to other forms of supplementary benefits. Pregnant women were asked to get a clinic clearance in order to qualify for a supplementary food program that provided food and diaper vouchers for a child up to five years of age. Older refugees, or those unable to work who hoped to receive social supplemental income, had to get a clinic to endorse real and imaginary disabilities. Many older Cambodians I met had tried to get doctors to examine their eyes, ears, limbs, and even mental condition in order to qualify for this supplemental income. Young and old Cambodians made repeated visits to doctors to get drugs and health certificates qualifying them for additional support. In some cases, Cambodians fearful of life in the streets faked madness in their clinic examinations, creating dysfunctioning bodies and minds that mimed their lack of sufficient social support. Some doctors made money selling their signatures for disability benefits. I was told about people who went into clinics to obtain such papers, then came out and did perfectly normal things like driving away in a car.

For a while, the desperate scramble to be defined as depressed and thus eligible for health benefits made it hard to disentangle the many practices that produced sickness. Being sick became a state induced by the health system itself, rather than by causes recognizable by the biomedical model. One of the most celebrated cases of exotic illness appeared in the early 1990s when a group of old Cambodian women, by definition a category suffering from PTSD, claimed they were blind even though doctors found nothing physically wrong with their eyes. The mysterious blindness afflicted about one hundred women in the Cambodian enclave in Long Beach, California, but nowhere else. Doctors pointed to a combination of factors for the mysterious vision loss, including dissociation, survivor's guilt, PTSD, and (reluctantly) the desire to be tested for disability benefits, which were among the highest benefits paid in California.[76] I asked a health worker based in Northern California who worked with Cambodians about the symptom, and she dismissed it as a strategy among helpless and lonely old women to get cash support. In my fieldwork among hundreds of Cambodians, I never met a single person who claimed this condition or heard reports about it. Indeed, after receiving some life-skills coaching, some of the formerly blind women in Long Beach gradually regained their sight.[77] By submitting to the trope of "depressed Cambodians," refugees elaborated illnesses that enhanced their access to health care and social support.

Encounters in clinics then involved social contestations that went beyond skirmishes over medical discipline. Although doctors and health workers were in a sense socializing agents, the refugees were not "normalized" in quite the ways intended—as self-monitoring patients and life-planning citizens. Instead, acutely aware of their own limited rights and security in America, Cambodian patients constantly negotiated with health providers for a variety of resources. Engaging in such institutional practices was an unavoidable set of rituals and routines for impoverished newcomers along their road to learning and resetting the terms of belonging.

SACRED BODY, SOVEREIGN BODY

I have argued that community clinics constituted an early training ground for Southeast Asian refugees, where they learned that the biopolitical aims of medicine entailed the disciplining of everyday behavior in order to orient and transform patients into self-surveilling modern subjects. Foucault's concern was with the generalized effects of biomedicine, and his analysis stopped at the complex intentions and manipulations of medicalized subjects who, as Foucault himself noted many times, could use their bodies to disrupt normal expectations and explore other possibilities. My inquiry into the encounters between refugees and American clinics shows that the subtle subterfuges of the cultural other both frustrated and compelled the medical gaze. Biomedical management and control were achieved and reproduced only through a process of negotiative, cross-cultural learning on the part of refugee patients and clinic staff alike. Cambodians, war-traumatized and canny survivors, showed themselves to be masters at dissembling, a skill that had helped them survive wars and that continued to be relevant for their

everyday survival as the most disadvantaged newcomers in American society. Their negotiatory and manipulative tactics were also a product of the
market-driven focus of health care, and the spread of the model of Southeast Asian mental health, which depended on real and virtual traumatized
refugee subjects. Although clinics were a necessary part of their lives, biomedicine failed to produce the healing that was sought.

One final example reveals the complex intentions at work in dealings with
clinics. An elderly Cambodian widow, Mrs. Yem, went to a mental-health clinic
for her headaches, as well as to a private Vietnamese doctor, hoping that he
would sign a form that would qualify her for disability benefits. The clinic
gave her shots and drugs. "The more I take them, the more trouble they give
me. Like here [tapping on her temple], it feels like someone is drilling away,
and it hurts so much that I black out." Eventually, she decided to stop taking her medication. She sought out the *krou khmer* who had foretold her husband's death on the voyage over. He advised her that she might have offended
ancestral spirits—a diagnosis in line with the common Cambodian belief that
protracted illnesses could be attributed to the "hungry" spirits of those who
had perished but had not been appeased by the living.[78] Mrs. Yem said, "Yes,
I might have said something wrong. It is possible that I didn't think of the
spirits, that we arrived in America and we didn't make any offerings." The
krou instructed her to make offerings to a monk as a way to appease the angry spirits. Because the bodies of the dead were missing, Mrs. Yem could not
offer the proper funeral rites that would have converted the sacred and uncertain beings into friendly ancestors. Everyday objects had to stand in for
the missing or dead persons who occupied the threshold between the realms
of the living and the dead.

An enlarged photograph of a young girl hung over Mrs. Yem's head—her
youngest daughter, missing in Cambodia. She lived with two grown-up daughters but pined for her youngest. Gazing longingly at the photograph, Mrs. Yem
sought comfort in the belief that she herself had been born with a caul draped
over her head, an auspicious sign that marked the infant as blessed with a
spirit guardian. Hearing this, the *krou* advised her to set up an altar in her bedroom, offering incense, flowers, and fruits to her protector spirit, who could
watch over both Mrs. Yem and her daughter in Cambodia.

With the performance of Khmer-Buddhist rites, Mrs. Yem as surviving
devotee could continue to hover on the margin between the worlds of the
living and the dead. More able-bodied Cambodians, when it became possible to visit their homeland again, made trips to give their loved ones proper
burials; if not entirely healed by this experience, they could at least begin to
lead more normal lives.

Thus Cambodian Americans' need for ritual modes of healing—treatment
by the *krou,* altars to the dead, physical therapy, herbal medicines, and
prayers—coexisted with an equally desperate need for modern medicine.[79]

Ultimately, the first-generation refugees eluded being governed as patients, and seldom learned to act on themselves in the way the medical regime directed. Nevertheless, biomedicine continued to be a very powerful aspect of the process of normalizing and directing refugees in the rules and aims of biomedicine and the medical bureaucracy, and in effect armed them with lessons for interpreting and navigating other areas of life in America. In Giorgio Agamben's terms, the sacred body is both included in and excluded from the sovereign body, and medical practice can be said to have a role in keeping the *homo sacre* "separated from the normal context of the living."[80]

The preceding discussion also indicates that the disciplining mechanisms of biomedicine are less powerful and all-pervasive than we give them credit for being. The clinicians themselves appeared to be both agents and objects of biomedical regulation. They sought to reduce patients' cultural beliefs to biomedical terms, but at other times subverted medical procedures in order to provide emotional support. They instructed patients in the norms of medical regimes, and yet sometimes had to adjust to patients' insistence on "deviant" behavior. Perhaps the overwhelming suffering of refugees daily reminded doctors and nurses about the limits of biomedical care, even when they believed in it as the best medicine for life in modern society. Health workers found themselves as much caught up in the regulatory processes of biomedicine and refugee care as were the refugees themselves. The community clinic thus became a primary site of dynamic citizenship-making for both newcomers and long-term residents, for "clueless" refugees as well as for professional experts.

Through such medical encounters, poor immigrants learned the links between their medicalized bodies and the making of political claims, everyday practices that promoted their constitution as subordinated subjects; while doctors and nurses found their sense of themselves as good caregivers defined in part by their unwitting role as socializing agents of the state. Thus, besides restoring the well-being of refugee bodies, refugee medicine became a mediated process for transforming postcrisis subjects into self-scrutinizing sovereign actors.

Chapter 5

Keeping the House from Burning Down

Phauly Sang, who was from a petit bourgeois family in Phnom Penh, told me about her arrival in San Francisco in 1980:

> I was with five other people: my younger sister, her husband, my nephew, and two boys, who were my brother-in-law's brothers. Our sponsor was the International Institute. At the airport, the man who met us was not Cambodian. He said, "I am Laotian." His name was Tamni, and he took us to the house of a Cambodian landlady in Oakland.
>
> The next day, I and my sister were sick. We had flu. It was cold, and my sister, she was pregnant too. They took us to Highland Hospital, and we waited from ten in the morning to ten at night. No translator! They said they were waiting for a translator. After we spoke a little bit, the nurse [who had volunteered in Khao-I-Dang camp], she said I spoke some English. And then she asked me to start a job, but at that time I was so scared, and I spoke only a little English. . . .
>
> We stayed in the landlady's house for ten days. The money we received from International Institute, eighty dollars, I gave to the landlady to buy some food for us. I was worried, thinking, *After II stops giving us money, how will we live?* Then Tamni came and took us to the welfare department.
>
> I met a Cambodian there and I told him, "I don't speak English!" We were so happy to meet another Cambodian. He asked me what kind of job, and school, I had in Cambodia. He did not say if you fill out the forms, you will get money. The Cambodian landlady, she didn't tell us either. And then, after maybe three months, we started to talk to people and they said, "Did you go to apply for welfare?" That's how we knew, from that time! When the check came, I didn't know how to cash it! [laughs]

Despite their training in border camps, it took a while for even well-educated Cambodian refugees arriving in the States to figure out how to cope in their transition from a preindustrial society to the most challenging postindustrial economy in the world. They gradually learned, as they had in the community clinics, that filling out forms, yielding up information, and fitting authoritative categories in many ways determined the flow of material and social resources toward them. Over time, the refugees became familiar with a constellation of public assistance offices and programs and their complex and sometimes contradictory rules, by which what is given with one hand is taken away by another, and assistance with getting a job is undermined by deductions in public assistance. Settled in some of the worst neighborhoods in Oakland and San Francisco, the Cambodian immigrants were isolated from the wider society and far from the low-paid entry-level jobs in hotels, middle-class households, and the factories of the Silicon Valley.

Cambodian refugees' living arrangements were dictated by the structural conditions of public housing in rundown neighborhoods that were poorly served by public transportation and far from supermarkets, schools, launderettes, and other normal urban facilities. The everyday chores of earning, buying, spending, and distributing resources among family members required a great deal of work on the part of people who mostly couldn't drive, or didn't own cars, or didn't even understand the morphology of the cityscape. Older women told me they were afraid of venturing out because they might get disoriented, lost, or mugged. Fathers walked to the bus stops to meet their children coming home from school, to protect them from being jumped on and pummeled by other kids. Initially, there were tensions with long-resident blacks in the neighborhoods, and some resentment over what was seen as competition for welfare support.

Above all, the recombined refugee families were obsessed with survival—in particular, the absolute need for health care for their children. The network of public-assistance programs became the main and often the only structure of information and communication for these poor newcomers, who were otherwise cut off from the cultural information of the marketplace and of civil society. Cambodian refugees were sucked up into the vortex of uncertain, low-paid work that had trapped poor blacks and other minorities in the shift from a manufacturing to an information-based economy. As the new immigrants struggled to gain a foothold in the service industry, they learned that their very survival, especially that of their children, depended on remaining part of the welfare structure of information and access.

This chapter follows Cambodian refugees through the maze of social services and traces how the interactions between social workers and their refugee clients shaped the social workers' perceptions of good and bad refugees, those who were worthy and responsible versus those who were unworthy and irresponsible. Refugee experiences became absorbed into the framework of a historical practice of racial classification in welfare policies that separated minorities into good and bad ethnics. As Robert Lieberman asserts, "The politics of race and the politics of welfare are linked" not simply because inner-city African Americans came into more frequent contact with social workers, but also because "the institutions of social policy were sculpted out of stone already hewn by racial division." Furthermore, racialist policies do not always or necessarily stem from self-conscious intentions, but have been shaped by "the racial structure of society."[1]

But I maintain that in welfare policy it is not just structural positioning but also specific rationalities and techniques that overlap with or deploy pre-existing raced differentiations. Here, I will show how in daily encounters, poor newcomers like Cambodian refugees were constituted as particular kinds of unworthy subjects who must be taught to become self-reliant, to be accountable for their situation. The processes intended to produce self-disciplining, provident subjects often rely on ethno-racial notions as the basis for discriminating among, assessing, and penalizing welfare clients. The interplay between policy and practices is part of a reflexive process whereby the participants—both social workers and welfare recipients—reflected on the categories, both explicit and implicit, that informed everyday procedure and conduct.[2] Cambodians interpreted the rules and aims of welfare programs through the lens of their own cultural predisposition and orientation, but their options and decisions were directed and constrained by the diverse technologies within which they found themselves ensnared as members of the urban working poor.

THE MICROPRACTICES OF THE WELFARE OFFICE

Because of their image as helping institutions, we are accustomed to thinking about social services as providing assistance to the down-and-out, but tend to overlook their role in governing less-powerful members of society. As Foucault has noted, "What is important is that social work is inscribed within a larger social function that has been taking on new dimensions for centuries, the function of surveillance-and-correction: to observe individuals and to redress them, in the two meanings of the word, alternately as punishment and as pedagogy."[3] I discussed earlier that in the United States, almshouses, church workers, and welfare reformers have played a major role in shaping the discourses, policies, and practices for racializing and normalizing new urban migrants. These moralizing templates also came with preventive measures intended to thwart the development of unconventional families and dangerous classes.[4] Thus the helping professions have always been one of the spaces in which established discourses are applied to everyday practices to construct "the social." I would stress, however, that the resulting set of relations is mutually though unequally produced. We can see this clearly in the power dynamics of a welfare office, where social workers along with the welfare recipients struggle over different kinds of truth, the terms of exchange, and the condition of possibilities for staying in the system.

Refugees' access to public assistance was initially organized by the Refugee Employment Social Services (RESS) program, which—as its name suggests—took care of the social benefits tied to the obligatory employment training program. At the local level, a targeted assistance program in counties heavily settled by refugees assisted them with vocational training, ESL, and adjustment issues such as taking the bus, using banks, getting housing, referrals to clinics, and so on. Initially, RESS supported refugees for up to three years, but as time went on, this aid was reduced to one year. As the federal funds for refugees were gradually cut off, many of them went on welfare (getting AFDC checks), already carrying with them the image of reluctant workers. A Vietnamese American refugee worker I call Nguyen explained the rules to me:

> If you are on refugee aid, they automatically encourage you to go to work. These programs are designed for people on aid so that they can become self-sufficient. They want to get them off welfare. You can make money, but you have to report it to your office. If you work part-time and your income is small, you are still eligible for welfare. But they deduct whatever it is that you make. They will still give you the difference in welfare. Say you get eight hundred dollars per month in welfare. You work and get four hundred. They have a formula to calculate how much they will deduct. You continue to receive food stamps and Medi-Cal. The penalty for not reporting your earnings will be fraud.

But combining public assistance with less than one hundred hours of work per month would barely raise a family of four above the poverty level. At Catholic Charities, a Vietnamese American nun discussed how poor people who worked more than a hundred hours a month stood to lose welfare benefits and medical coverage in one of the most expensive places to live in the nation:

> The problem with the AFDC is that the system is not helping them to become self-sufficient. The system is penalizing. One of the reasons welfare recipients tend not to work is if, say, I have five kids—a wife and five kids, that means seven people—I get one thousand to twelve hundred per month plus food stamps and Medi-Cal. So how am I, without skills, going to make a thousand dollars a month? If I work one hundred hours a month, I forfeit everything! I have to report everything! . . . That is why many people are hesitant to work, because they cannot make enough money, and their earnings will be subtracted from the AFDC payments—they have to copay for Medi-Cal and everything. Their food stamps are cut off. But if men decide to get off welfare and work full-time, then the wife has to go to work too in order to support the family. I have families who quit welfare and the husband and wife went to work, and it was difficult to survive.

The refugees are caught in the mismatch of low-wage entry-level jobs, variations in payment levels from public-assistance programs, and the federal government's minimal standard of living. Robert Bach says, "There is a growing realization that wage rates must increase significantly if independence from public programs is to mean anything except self-reliant poverty."[5] In California, however, semiskilled jobs continued to be compensated at a level that did not raise families to the minimum standards, despite the explosive growth of the economy in the last decades of the twentieth century.

We see in the refugee welfare debate the legacy of established discourses about the underclass and the racial other, and of anxieties about irresponsible citizens. Even though they obtained a firsthand picture of the travails of the working poor and sympathized with the catch-22 situation of refugee families, social workers were caught up in the logics of the state's preoccupation with qualifying, classifying, and punishing individuals who entered the territory of the welfare state. The primary role of the social workers was, in Ken Moffatt's terms, to aid "in the management of the poor and helping to control the dangerous classes," separating the normal from the abnormal, the good from the bad refugees, the responsible from the "welfare cheat."[6] The exercise of power in the welfare office entailed surveillance of the would-be recipients and an active process of decision making on the basis of information gathered.

While Nguyen seemed a kind person who, having gained an official position from helping earlier Vietnamese arrivals, now wanted to serve Cambodian refugees, he could not refrain from assessing these late arrivals in relation to "better" and better-adjusted refugees:

> Most of them [Cambodians] are not highly educated. They were farmers, and their tendency is to be lazy. We're talking about old people without education. They have never before even worn a pair of shoes in their country. So with the income they receive from welfare right now, it is easy for them to be lazy. They are not motivated to go to work. And I think mostly from word of mouth and people talking to each other, they find some way to get out [of employment and language training]. . . . You know that may happen, but how to motivate those people can be very difficult. . . . They do not want to improve their skills here. For those people it is very difficult to change them. Maybe the young people will grow up here and become educated and want to change, but for them they don't want to change.

Nguyen was in part expressing his frustration over getting the later refugee arrivals to sign up for and remain in English-language and vocational classes, not merely over welfare benefits; but he was also ventilating a bias toward Cambodians and Laotians. For instance, he claimed that in Southeast Asia, Cambodians were less-effective agriculturists than Vietnamese. In his view, this ineffectiveness accounted for their being passive welfare dependents, as opposed to Vietnamese boat people who quickly slipped out of the refugee category and came to be identified with the Asian model-minority image. I noted that his picture of Vietnamese refugees seemed more favorable than that of Cambodians, and he qualified his statement:

> I believe that most of the refugees, if they are able to do something, they don't want to be on aid. There are a lot of factors that affect the lives of refugees here. I suspect a lot of discrimination at the workplace. You don't see or hear it, but it is still happening. Sometimes there is conflict and discrimination among the refugees themselves. And then there is difficulty in adjusting to the new life in this country. Loss of parents, friends, relatives, brothers and sisters, you have nothing. You only have yourself. And your mind is still in a state of shock. You are not able to cope with life, the language, to be able to go and care for yourself. . . . [Compared to the Vietnamese] for the [Cambodian] refugees, it is harder for them to catch up. But I hope the next generation will be sent to school and hopefully they will learn and assimilate to the new society faster and better than their parents. For the parents' generation, it is too late. I meant that it is hard for a person who is fifty or fifty-five years old to change. They are farmers and have no education. . . . You have to have a foundation, and then you spring up from that foundation and go on. It is a long process of learning. [This applies] not only to Cambodians but even Vietnamese who did not have education in Vietnam. It is hard for them to adjust to this country too.

This welfare officer himself was an educated Vietnamese immigrant who had arrived in the first wave of refugees out of Indochina. When Vietnamese refugees arrived in 1975 (five years before the big influx of Cambodian refugees), they did not receive massive refugee aid, and despite their great losses and the stings of discrimination, they doggedly built a life through self-employment. This claim must be set alongside a study of Vietnamese refugees in the same period that revealed a significant degree of dependence on welfare checks (see below).[7] Yet despite such overlaps in family strategies and dependence on public assistance, Vietnamese Americans, as far as I know, while the target of other slurs, have never been accused of being passive or lazy. The widespread assumption seemed to be that all refugees deserved support (given their sufferings linked to the Vietnam War), but they could be differentiated in terms of responsible and irresponsible clients. We thus see an elaboration of racial polarization interwoven into underclass discourses to produce new categories of deviance and unworthiness.

The assessment of refugees' eligibility for welfare was also determined by purported group characteristics, including forecasting their potential market performance. Nguyen noted that with their limited skills, most refugees (especially Cambodians, Laotians, Afghans, and Ethiopians) were qualified only for jobs in electronics assembly, child care, and janitorial services, so refugees tended to be classified as menial workers. In fact, this practice of targeting ethnically marked groups for certain low-wage positions, and not for others that they might have the skills for, was consistent with a broader pattern of practice in twentieth-century America that has had profound effects on the shaping of the urban black working classes.[8] The poor refugees were being assimilated into the lower reaches of the American labor market and society:

> Basically, the job market needs those skills. Certain jobs the men can do, and other jobs the women can do. Like clerical work. Traditionally women can go into that, but men do not want to be working as clerks. Not even one out of a hundred men chooses to go into clerical training. Women do not go into mechanics. Women and men go to electronic assembly training. It depends on what kinds of things men and women can do. Like assembly work. You just sit there and assemble components or solder some wires, so men can do it and maybe women can do it faster than men. When they get out of training, they get at least four or five dollars an hour.

In Nguyen's view, then, refugees were ideal labor for electronics assembly, but women were more suited to the job—not only because of his personal gender bias, but also because the wages were minimal.

Historically, poor immigrant and black women have been penalized for working, and not conforming to the nuclear-family ideal of the stay-at-home mother. Driven by an ideology of deserving versus undeserving women, AFDC initially was a substitute for the male bread earner, so that families headed by unmarried mothers could approximate "normal" ones. This patriarchal principle was gradually overturned in the era of deindustrialization; by the 1980s, the shift to a service economy and increased demand for low-wage workers made female employment outside the home tolerable, and even respectable.[9] At the time that Southeast Asian women encountered the welfare state, welfare subsidies were being reduced as a way to push women into the labor market. Their experience paralleled the earlier situation encountered by inner-city African Americans, as changing conditions in the labor market—discrimination against colored men and a decline in blue-collar jobs, paralleled by a rising demand for cheap female labor—had consequences for family strategies, divergence in gender roles, and ethnic formation as a whole.[10]

Cambodian men were generalized as being shiftless (echoes of the depiction of poor black men) and were distrusted by many officials in the employment program, so most of the trainees ended up being female. The best-attended program was the one training refugee women to be child-care providers. The employment program operated on the assumption that a single income earner in a poorly paid job such as janitor or child-care worker provided sufficient support for a family of six—and that didn't take into account providing child-care support for the worker. As mentioned earlier, even

for Cambodian American families with two income earners, making do without AFDC was a tremendous struggle. Additionally, welfare policy was based
on the assumption that the normal family unit was nuclear, and failed to take
into account the need to support other relatives who might be scattered, because of overcrowding and high rents, in other households.

Hidden take-home work spawned by the booming electronics industry
concealed part of the income of many low-paid members of Southeast Asian
households. Some well-intentioned individual social workers, genuinely
concerned about helping their clients, turned a blind eye to such additional
earnings and did not dock the family's AFDC check. Nevertheless, social services in general were premised on a technology for making judgments based
on information gathered, and regulating clients according to some calculus
of limits to entitlements and the autonomy of individuals and of families. As
Moffatt has noted in his study of another American welfare office, "Every interaction between the welfare worker and the client is one in which the
worker sits in judgment on the client's eligibility. . . . Through the examination the individual is given a status and then linked to any number of markers and measurements meant to characterize each individual client. Finally,
the individual is reconstituted as the case. The individual case is the result
as well as the object of power."[11] And another power structure is at work:
many social workers are children of recent poor immigrants, and they operate within the institutional dynamic of successful immigrants who, having
themselves surmounted victimization, become oppressors of more recent
waves of newcomers. The time it takes to progress from victimized to vic-
timizer status has become compressed in our age of neoliberalism, and rather
recent arrivals are already caught up in the power vector of oppression, pushing impoverished people as underpaid or unemployable workers into the
turbulent capitalist economy as soon as possible.

GENDER FRACTURE AND FAMILY STRATEGIES

Gender bias is institutionalized in the welfare state, and it has roots in American republican ideals and women's politics in the early twentieth century.
In the early welfare state, gender ideology mediated the perceived problem
of racial difference, and social policies were directed toward the female citizen, who was seen as the source for racial uplift and the reproduction of the
republican order. Gwendolyn Mink puts it succinctly: "Women's citizenship
justified women's separate—and disparate—treatment under the law until
the 1970s. And animated by the twin anxieties of race and republic, men's
citizenship denied legitimacy to governmental mitigation of men's economic
dependence."[12] For the Southeast Asian newcomers, the stress in welfare practices on women's role in uplifting family and race, and the stigmatization
of men on welfare, resulted in women becoming more thoroughly inte-

grated than men into service structures. These factors also shaped women's strategies in forging political and economic links that would safeguard their children.

This section addresses the concerns of gender fracture in household contribution and in public assistance, and family support beyond the nuclear unit through the interpretations and experiences of Cambodian refugees. Welfare norms and market forces, combined with the lingering effects of war traumas, compelled refugees to cope in distinctive ways, which had both strengths and weaknesses. These multiple effects shaped refugee and family strategies and gender relations, but not all in the same way.[13] Cambodian refugees had few skills, or the wrong kind of skills, to find employment easily in the new economy. While all adult family members struggled to make a living, women could make use of their connections to the welfare state as a source of economic and moral power often denied to men. This split in gender integration contributed to gender conflicts and the strengthening of female-headed households.

Even educated Cambodian men and women had a difficult time, and their routes to economic stability often depended heavily on working in social services helping their own people. For instance, when Peter Thuy arrived, he was immediately recruited into work as a menial laborer. The son of a Cambodian scholar in South Vietnam, Peter had spent five years at a Buddhist college in Cambodia. In the early 1960s, he worked for the U.S. special forces in South Vietnam. For a while, he worked under Alexander Haig, who was a colonel in the Green Berets. His role was to recruit thirty thousand Cambodians in Vietnam to fight the communists in Cambodia. When Phnom Penh fell to the Khmer Rouge in 1975, Peter was in military training in Bangkok. He and sixty-eight Cambodian soldiers were flown to Camp Pendleton. From there, they were sponsored by a hotel operator in the Poconos who wanted cheap labor.

> At that time I learned that the minimum wage was $2.30 per hour, but we got only $1.51 an hour. So we had to work nine hours, six days a week. So we thought that's not fair, so we didn't work anymore. Even though I spoke some English, I didn't know the system. I didn't know how to use the bus system, I didn't know how to use the telephone well . . . [the only person I knew was] in California, and it cost $3 to talk three minutes and you made only $1.51 an hour.
>
> They said no welfare. We didn't know nothing about food stamps, about welfare. I didn't know until I wrote to a friend in San Francisco, and they sent me a newspaper. So I got it and I saw a job opening that pay like $2.50, $2.88, and I was so happy. I really saved money. After two months I saved $200, and I got a plane ticket for $175 from Pennsylvania to Chicago, and then I came to San Francisco. So I found a job [as a busboy in a hotel] for about $2.80. I was so happy about that.
>
> I kept on going to adult school to study more. And then I moved to Oak-

land, because it is less crowded and the rent is cheaper. And I kept on work-ing and going to the Berkeley adult school. And when I finished, I went to Laney College. At that time I studied only two nights a week, and I worked on weekends.

His many jobs included cabinetmaking, electrical wiring, carpentry, and cut-ting down trees. He was eventually hired by a resettlement agency, helping newly arrived refugees with things that he himself was never told when he arrived:

> Mostly you help refugees to fill out affidavit forms that their relatives are here in the U.S. But first when they get to the airport, you have to be there to pick them up and find them a temporary place to stay, with food, blankets, and shel-ter, until they find their own place. If not, we find them a place. And then we help them apply for welfare, food stamps, Social Security numbers, Medi-Cal, whatever.

Later, he held a job as a community health worker for two years. When I in-terviewed Peter, he had been working for the state of California for seven years as an unemployment claims assistant.

For educated Cambodians like Peter Thuy and Phauly Sang, their first moves were to learn English and begin seeking a job before their refugee cash assistance ran out. After graduating from her English class, Phauly started to look for a job and learned to drive a car in case she needed to commute. Her Cambodian lab-technician license was not recognized at the local hos-pital, and she found part-time work as, successively, a clerk in Chinatown, a teacher's aide, and an Asian family-planning officer. When I met her, she was working as a Cambodian translator for a Bay Area hospital. Her work also in-volved setting up an on-call system through which hospital personnel could use the services of Laotian, Mien, Hmong, Vietnamese, and Chinese trans-lators to communicate with the large number of Asian immigrant patients.

But for the majority of Cambodian refugees who were not qualified to be social workers, health aides, or teacher's aides, it was almost impossible to live entirely off earned income—even if they were in a state to obtain employ-ment. Cambodian men as a rule survived the war in smaller numbers than women, and in the first generation, few coped well with the transition to America. As recounted in chapter 2, male authority in the traditional Cam-bodian family was never questioned, but now their war traumas were com-pounded by their lack of economic or social skills that could help them sup-port the family adequately. From their perspective, much of the work of health and social workers was focused on the weak—that is, refugee women and children—and the men themselves did not know how to ask for help from American institutions. Indeed, the traditional American republican gender ideology that saw receiving social services as incompatible with manly independence lingered on in the attitudes of many social workers, who tended to consider underemployed or jobless men among immigrants and minorities as a threat to motherhood, and hence to the reproduction of the social order.[14]

A female health worker who had a big caseload of Cambodian Americans described her view of Cambodian gender dynamics. On her visits, the husband

> is usually taking care of the little kids, watching TV with them, getting a little food or something for them. There are lots of times they are not in the apartment; they are down in the foyer or courtyard visiting with other men. Sometimes they take the kids down there, and they are all socializing together. They all spend a lot of time fixing up cars. If they have a car, they take the wife and all the kids to Women, Infants, and Children (WIC) to get vouchers and to all the wife's appointments, and they sit outside the clinics . . . and smoke and just seem to be okay. Why I am saying that they suffer from what appears to be depression of some sort is that many of them have complaints of headache, dizziness, backache, feeling weak, and so forth. . . . I am sure that back in their own country, they were hardworking, on farm or autoshop, and now their role is relegated to taking care of children and so forth.

Many Cambodian men who lived through the war found coping with American society a major burden. As a rule, no Cambodian men sought therapy for depression unless forced to do so after getting into an altercation. Language problems and the cultural fear of the shame of seeking help intensified their isolation. Some simply wanted to stay at home and hang out with close relatives and friends. It was not surprising that such war survivors sometimes rebelled against intensive job training programs, and the pressure to get off cash support as quickly as possible. They found it very difficult to comply with the requirement to take classes; adult men in particular found English lessons torturous. After the refugee provision period ended, many older refugees signed up for welfare benefits, which did not require training and were less regulated than was the refugee cash program.[15] One such person was Mr. Heng, who had volunteered in the refugee camp but never sought a job after arriving in the United States. In his late fifties, Mr. Heng was sponsored by a son who had settled in Florida earlier, with the help of his in-laws. After six months in Florida, Mr. Heng decided to move to Oakland, to join his second son. He considered himself too old to start over: "I figured that I was too old and would not be able to learn the language. And I no longer had the stamina to work for others, and as we all know, here [in California] if one can't work, one simply has to rely on public assistance. . . . We have no education, so what kind of work can we do?" In Oakland, he and his wife shared an apartment with an unrelated family of six. His son, who had eight children, lived in the apartment just above them. With their combined AFDC checks ($1,300) and supplemental security income ($1,280) spread over two households, his extended family was barely making ends meet.

In truth, these Southeast Asian immigrants lived in a state that, though well known for its generous welfare support (relative to other states), had a high cost of living and a postindustrial economy that paid below-living wages to the semiskilled. The public-assistance system assumed that having a single income earner (whether male or female) in the family was sufficient for any family's survival, and that they could go off welfare and purchase Medi-Cal on their own. But for all of the families I interviewed, basic survival required that they get welfare support and health coverage. A single woman could not get Medi-Cal, but mothers with children could. Cambodians very quickly learned that social provisions were focused on dependent motherhood (AFDC, Medi-Cal, WIC, food stamps) and thus women (even if not single) rather than men were the ones to obtain AFDC and health benefits for the children.

In the late 1980s, a family of five could receive about $600 a month, besides food stamps and Medi-Cal. People who were sixty-five years of age and older and would never be able to work again, or those with long-term disabilities could receive supplemental security income (SSI), amounting to about $640 a month. When children reached age eighteen, their AFDC support ended, so their family's overall income decreased. If people were temporarily disabled, they could apply for General Assistance (GA), which paid about $341 a month in 1989. Regardless of their health, some young people considered GA a form of support they could apply for (it needed a signature from their health-care provider every three or four months) before they obtained jobs, so many who received GA were also enrolled in workfare or some other training program. All those who received AFDC, GA, or SSI were automatically eligible for Medi-Cal. Further support was extended to pregnant women and nursing mothers, who could sign up for vouchers to buy baby formula, other food items, and diapers at the WIC offices. Most families also relied on food stamps. Cambodians who could hardly speak English sprinkled their everyday conversations with terms like AFDC, SSI, GA, ESL, and Medi-Cal, codes for their daily struggles to survive in America.

A Cambodian woman employed by the WIC program described the situation for arrivals:

> Fresh off the plane, Cambodians are sent by their friends and relatives to government offices to apply for AFDC, Medi-Cal, SSI, and WIC vouchers, often on the second day. They are eligible for AFDC and WIC if their monthly income is less than fifteen hundred dollars a month before taxes for a family of four to five persons. The problem is that persons on welfare automatically get Medi-Cal, but not a low-income worker. Thus, it is better to be on welfare than to work for a low-paying job with no security and health coverage; there is also no child-care support.

Because of Cambodians' concern with access to health coverage and the health of their babies, many families felt that, regardless of outside earnings, it was imperative to sign up for AFDC because Medi-Cal came with it. They understood that mere cash income could not buy them the medical protection they needed, especially for their children. The lack of affordable health care was for many families the biggest barrier to getting off welfare.

It is important to note that many Cambodian refugee families who went on welfare also had family members earning income from a variety of jobs. On my visits to families on welfare, I frequently missed seeing teenage boys and girls, as well as young men, who were away working as baby-sitters, office cleaners, day laborers, or car mechanics. Parents also said that young people traveled long distances to work in doughnut shops, microchip assembly factories, or garment sweatshops. Older men formed groups and hired themselves out for odd jobs like gardening, hauling away refuse, and construction. I was told about forays into the Central Valley, where refugees could earn some money picking vegetables for friends who were lucky enough to be operating farms. Only the old, the infirm, and mothers of young children were at home. Sometimes, welfare mothers sold snacks such as roasted corn and cakes to children in the courtyard.

In her study of Vietnamese refugees in Philadelphia, Nazli Kibrai uses the term *patchwork* to refer to such household strategies of combining incomes, welfare payments, and resources from different sources, including extended kin.[16] Similarly, Cambodian women and female networks pooled as well as distributed various resources in ways that ignored the welfare-defined nuclear family unit of parent(s) and children. But this strategy of getting income from multiple sources and distributing it beyond the nuclear family was frustrated by the welfare policy forbidding welfare recipients to work more than one hundred hours a month. To the refugees, this requirement seemed to be a penalty for earning an income, since welfare benefits were insufficient for making ends meet, and since only a few family members could find (usually part-time, low-wage) work. Because Cambodians often shared income and expenses within an extended kinship network (usually including grandparents or grandchildren), they needed to patch together welfare checks and multiple earnings to support a larger network of kinsmen more efficiently. The result was that many refugees declined to report extra earnings by some family members, many of whom in any case did not fall within the nuclear model the AFDC used as the basis for determining cash and medical coverage. The public perception of refugee unemployment as a pervasive problem was, therefore, more an illusion than a reality.

Nevertheless, social workers continued to be vigilant about finding "welfare cheats." Educated Cambodians who had obtained well-paid jobs as social workers sometimes disapproved of the strategies used by the low-skilled refugees to obtain public assistance. For instance, the WIC worker commented, "Technically, only a person over sixty-five years can get social supplemental support, but Cambodians who can demonstrate disability get it too. So some Cambodian teenagers and many adults between thirty-five and forty-five years have gotten SSI, i.e., supplemental support, for the rest of their lives." Another social worker noted that "when refugees go through the public support system, they are smarter than we are and they know every program that is out there and they avail themselves of it." While some Cambodians did take advantage of public assistance, many others were caught in a situation in which they needed both welfare, with its medical coverage, and paid work just to make ends meet. But because of the ideology that work is the basis of responsible citizenship, the helping profession was focused on enforcing the self-supporting nuclear-family ideal on the one hand, and weeding out welfare cheats on the other. Social workers sought to instill the kind of responsible self-monitoring they saw as missing in improvident refugees. They did not pause to pose the question of whether getting off welfare could give dignity and self-respect to impoverished, unskilled newcomers who could barely support their children or secure health coverage, on incidental, minimal pay. For all their claims on public assistance, these families were excluded from the kinds of knowledge and communication skills that could make them effective players in the postmodern economy.

WOMEN KEEP THE HOUSE FROM BURNING DOWN

Two Cambodian proverbs spotlight woman as the source of her family's happiness, prosperity, and security:

> Wealth is there because the woman knows
> how to save and be frugal; a house is comfortable
> and happy because the wife has a good character.

> Better to lose one's father, than one's mother;
> it's better to lose one's goods when the boat sinks in the
>   middle of the river,
> than to lose one's goods when the house burns down.[17]

Khmer Buddhism makes women the center of family morality, but also its guarantee of the family's material security. In the poor areas of Oakland, Cambodian female-headed households thus had a dual meaning—many families literally had no surviving or effective male head, but also women were ones holding the cards when it came to managing the economic, social, and moral life of the family. There was a lingering sense that the entire society had come through a collective karmic experience in which the very survival of their people was in question. Some Cambodians, looking to fables to make sense of what had happened, invoked the folktale of a *kaun lok* bird who abandoned her children in the forest to forage for food as an indication of what might have led to the catastrophe.[18] As Khmer Buddhists sought collective responsibility for such a historic cataclysm, female survivors struggled to make sure by any means possible that their children were fed and that their house did not burn down again. Thus while welfare rules sought to discipline refugees for not conforming to the nuclear-family ideal and scapegoated them for their range of family strategies, women reconfigured relations and resources in ways that conformed to their own interpretations of needs and values.[19] As was often the case with inner-city black families, women on public assistance were at the center of a wider family network, so more people depended on welfare benefits intended for the use of a single nuclear family than met the professional eye.

Women and men experienced welfare provisions differently. Cambodian mothers, plugged as they were into the system of financial aid and health coverage, demonstrated creative ingenuity in trying to overcome the odds against them and their children. By contrast, some men, depressed at their loss of status and unemployed, became alcoholics, living off the aid secured by female family members. Mrs. Sophat, the mother who saved a portion of her welfare checks to send to relatives still in Cambodia, explained how the patchwork of AFDC, Medi-Cal, and wages provided resources to care for her family. Her family had relocated from Florida because they could not afford to raise a young family while earning minimal wages without health coverage, as social workers had expected them to do. Mrs. Sophat had stayed with the man the Khmer Rouge forced her to marry. Together, they had six children, including the two oldest, who were from her previous marriage.

> We were on refugee assistance for only two months. From the time we arrived in the U.S. [in 1983], we worked right away, because there were only working people. There was nobody just living off welfare in Florida. I worked in the cannery. It was a huge warehouse, and all we did was pack the crates. But my husband worked by installing car windows because he was a mechanic. When he left, they really felt a loss. His supervisor still calls him to go back and work.
>
> We had to pay in cash for the younger boy's birth—close to four thousand dollars. We were broke, so we fled here so that we could get Medi-Cal for a while. My husband's waiting for the children to be a little older, because if we leave California now, we would not have Medi-Cal. There was no Medi-Cal in Florida.

I asked how her second marriage had been faring since her husband took to drinking.

> There are some problems, but I didn't want to have one marriage after another, and so I just put up with it. But currently, I am not very happy. He drinks and then looks for trouble with his stepchildren. It's natural with stepchildren and such. As you know in our culture, it's not the same with other people's children. As the mother, I always try to protect my children, I try to give them good guidance. And with the second set of children, it would be difficult if we separated. The children would be without parents. So these days, I just try to put

up with it. He never beats me or anything. He just looks for arguments over the children from my first marriage. I am currently very unhappy, but I try to put up with it. After working for three years in Florida, he does nothing now.

Most households came to be headed by women, widows or divorcees preoccupied by a major worry: how to arrange for the older children to help bring in enough money that the family could eventually rent a home outside the ghetto or, better yet, buy their own house. If they succeeded, they would spend their old age in a secure home and neighborhood, hopefully being cared for by one of their children. This long-term strategy required the pooling of income generated by as many family members as possible from a variety of sources—a form of interhousehold cooperation common among peasants in Cambodia.

But this strategy was constrained by the welfare policies that discouraged long working hours, and by public-housing policies that permitted only nuclear families to occupy their housing units, discouraging apartment sharing. Despite official disapproval, however, different families, sometimes unrelated, often lived together in cramped two-bedroom apartments, with their personal belongings stacked in corners. People might have meals on the verandah or in the corridor, because food was shared with kinsmen living in other units. Mrs. Sophat said, "It is difficult to live like this, because the places are small. We don't have enough money to live in a bigger place. So people just live apart and only take their meals together. Family members do live apart; but it is not as if the family is broken up or anything. People go back and forth and visit each other." As Carol Stack has reported, among inner-city African Americans similar strategies for coping with the welfare system increased the networking among female kin and neighbors, but also contributed to the shifting membership of households.[20]

For instance, Mrs. Young, a widow, received monthly cash contributions from a son and a son-in-law who shared her two-bedroom apartment. An elderly cousin and her granddaughter, who also lived with them, contributed a portion of their AFDC check for food and rent. The goal of most families, especially if headed by a widow, was to receive as much welfare aid as possible for as long as possible so that they could save for the future. Sometimes, aged relatives or friends were boarders so that they could split their SSI checks with the extended, pseudo-kin networks.

Some families sought to prolong the time they received welfare by disguising the age of children and by concealing their marital status and income-generating activities. Another reason for misrepresenting the age of children was to keep them in school longer, to give them a chance to catch up with their American counterparts. At age eighteen, when children were taken off the AFDC roll, they could apply for a GA stipend for about eighteen months.

The stipend, which operated like an unemployment benefit, would be reduced if they got a job or got married. Recipients experienced this termination of benefits as an arbitrary cutback, plunging them into the void of no protection merely because of a theoretical change of status, with no consideration for their actual employment condition. In desperation, some young recipients misreported their age, address, marital status, and employment in order to ensure the continuation of some public support. In practice such attempts to work around the rules of public aid arose from the exigencies of a situation in which refugee families were struggling to support as many people as possible in a very insecure environment.

Beyond seeking to shape family form and conduct, welfare policies also sought to discipline female bodies, the site of physical and social reproduction, outside the clinic context. A program already in place to teach African American girls "correct" terms for "body parts and functions," as well as "life-planning," also legitimized the surveillance of Southeast Asian teenage females.[21] Operating on the assumption that "pregnancy is undesirable for adolescents," social workers kept a lookout for pregnant girls. A public-health worker told me that the rate of teen pregnancy was higher among the Mien than among the Cambodians, and that Mien grandmothers were happy to take care of the babies: "They feel that so many of their people were killed in the war that they are duty-bound to replenish their race, so they rarely practice family planning." From my own observations, there were few pregnant Cambodian teenagers, but they nevertheless drew a lot of attention from social workers.

In Cambodia, premarital sex, especially among girls, was almost unheard of. Cambodian parents carefully sheltered unmarried daughters, and girls' marriages were arranged affairs; the virtuous daughter and the well-made marriage both reflected on the honor and status of the entire family. But in California, the frequent absence of fathers and the influence of American high-school culture have led to an increase in premarital sex, especially among boys, Cambodians told me. As will be seen in chapter 7, parents attempted to control their daughters' sexuality, teaching them to mute their "natural" seductiveness, but worried that conditions did not allow for raising virtuous daughters.[22] Although Cambodian parents were preoccupied with the moral surveillance of their daughters, they were unable to supervise their children in the same collective fashion as they had back in their homeland. Nevertheless, the wider community continued to exercise a kind of moral censure, and parents felt a great deal of shame if neighbors gossiped about a wayward daughter, bringing dishonor to the entire family.[23] Parents who still had influence over their children demanded a Cambodian marriage if a daughter had a Cambodian boyfriend whom she was seeing frequently. And if a girl got pregnant, usually—after a thrashing—she would be compelled to marry her boyfriend, if he was Cambodian, in a Cambodian ceremony, thus legitimizing their sexual relations and saving the girl's parents' face. In some instances, pregnant teenagers continued to live with their mothers for support, and seldom obtained a marriage certificate. The young women registered for AFDC and Medi-Cal; meanwhile, their Cambodian grooms, who might hold down factory jobs, moved into their brides' families' homes in order to save on rent. This practice echoed the norm among peasants in Cambodia, where young married couples spent some time living with or close to the bride's family, and contributed to the extended family's income while saving for the future. Possibly for some girls, becoming pregnant was a first step toward gaining independence from their parents' household, and young couples spent their first few years saving to win that independence. In some cases, a number of young couples rented a single apartment together, sharing the rent but buying their food separately, though they might eat together on occasion, like an extended family. When they could afford it, couples found a place of their own.

Madam Neou lived with two sons, seven daughters, and a son-in-law in her one-bedroom apartment. Her eldest daughter was eighteen and pregnant. She had undergone the Cambodian marriage ceremony but decided not to obtain a marriage certificate so that she could continue to receive her GA check. Her husband concealed the fact that he lived with her. He worked in a fast-food restaurant. The hope was that by the time both their GA stipends ended, they would have saved enough money to move out and become legitimate, by registering their marriage and reporting their own address.

I learned of one case in which the mere suspicion of welfare cheating made a social worker feel entitled to intervene in a couple's private reproductive decisions. It involved a young couple living with the bride's mother and making a monthly payment to the household. The social worker advised the Cambodian mother to let her recently married daughter use contraceptives so that she could continue to go to school, and have a career later on. The girl's husband, however, who was employed as a mechanic, refused to practice family planning. The social worker also warned the mother that her goal of saving to buy a house might not be realized, since even families with members working for income were not able to buy their own house.

Although teenage pregnancy was not common, social workers tended to suspect it as part of a household strategy to prolong welfare dependency. Furthermore, they were upset that pregnant teens would go back to school but not get married. A Cambodian health worker, embarrassed by the situation, explained,

> You can't get AFDC if you are married. So we track them down. Sometimes they are living with the father of the baby, but they are not married. This is what I meant when I was talking about knowing the system. . . . We've seen this slippage in America. Premarital sex is open now, and it is just a way of life. . . .

So now we have these refugees coming here, and I've asked many of them, "Is this the kind of thing that goes on at home?" They'd say "No," because in the village situation or in a family-kinship situation, these things were monitored. But now that they are here, they are starting to go this other way, and it is because of economics, because you don't get any aid or Medi-Cal or anything if you get married. So that is what I was talking about before—learning the system.

She continued, "They need to find money, right? They don't know how to find money by working, [but] they know how to find money by working the system." She was especially unhappy with young girls dropping out of school. "They become pregnant again and again, and have no time to go to school."

A few girls in the Cambodian apartment complex I visited did get married at sixteen, a couple of years younger than was the norm in Cambodia. But not all pregnant girls were married, or had a boyfriend to support them. I met a fourteen-year-old girl who was pregnant, shy and proud at the same time. Despite parental disapproval, American high-school culture and the mass media encouraged teen sexual explorations. Social workers claimed that parents were of two minds about pregnant daughters: a few refused to support their daughters anymore because they had boyfriends, while others welcomed the additional source of welfare aid. But it seems presumptuous to assume that the refugees could have learned to be so cavalier about new babies, and to consider them primarily in terms of their economic value—after all, these are people who had lost many family members in a recent war.

But once girls dropped out to have babies and live on welfare, many began to lose the incentive to get a job or plan for college later on. In the housing complex where I did research, the majority of Cambodian teenage girls were not pregnant mothers, but enrolled in high school. So this strategy of getting extended AFDC benefits through early pregnancy and unreported marriage was *not* a general practice, but it was perhaps common enough to draw the attention of social workers always on the lookout for what they regarded as a common mode of adaptation by young women across all ethnic lines. It also occurred to me that the vigilance of social workers in stigmatizing teenage pregnancy as deviant might have lent it greater prominence than it would otherwise have had. Such prejudices racialize teenage female bodies, depicting them as unruly and dangerous, and may very well end up promoting the very welfare dependency through precocious sexuality and pregnancy that is decried. Perhaps it was more permissible for social workers to tolerate the lack of health insurance for children, whether born in or out of wedlock, than to permit one more pregnant teenager to live her own life.

It is useful to remember that up until the 1960s, the United States had the highest rate of teenage mothers in the world, and it was considered a normal thing in the middle class. But for decades now, Americans have had an unreasonable fear of single teenage mothers, who are made out in the media to be "monster mothers";[24] these fears link to a host of baseless claims that "illegitimate" children do less well in school or are at risk of becoming criminals. This demonization of teenage mothers continues side by side with acceptance of, or even a fashion for, well-off single mothers expending huge amounts of medical and social resources to have children. In welfare terms, teenage mothers are treated as members of defective families without male providers, thus contributing to the image of female recipients as "the undeserving poor," or "clients of the state."[25] One can only surmise that the supervision of female bodies and other aspects of welfare-dependent families are an outgrowth of the welfare agents' own self-surveillance and struggle to internalize contemporary norms and forms of the middle-class ideal.

·   ·   ·

In summary, then, for the immigrant who didn't speak English or had few skills, the welfare office with its myriad contradictory policies was a disciplining maze through which refugees had to pass in order to gain entry into the wider society. The welfare system gave much-needed cash as well as a prod to become self-reliant citizen-subjects; it encouraged employment and yet penalized those who sought to increase family income; and it became a basic source of female power at home, and further marginalized men. Welfare agents both supported and suspected welfare mothers.

These contradictory pressures are consistent with the way American welfare policies and officials have historically helped shape a category of economically precarious urban people, regardless of their national or cultural point of origin. For the majority of welfare recipients, it is impossible to make a quick transition into the kind of higher-wage employment that will sustain an entire family. Like many poor urban migrants, the Cambodian refugees seemed destined to be California's new servant class, responding to the demands of an expanding underground service economy—a topic to which I will return in the final chapters.

For the Cambodian refugees, welfare procedures and practices strengthened the role of women in caring for and planning the family, and in making basic household decisions. Women much more than men were integrated into this structure of aid and services, and this connection created a feminizing patronage system that had ramifications across all areas of life. And the effects of dependence on the helping professions included learning to be a reflexive subject, to come up with the right story in order to fit controlling narratives about being a refugee and a welfare recipient. Nevertheless, this newfound position and subjectivity did not preclude efforts to deflect and question American values.

Chapter 6

Refugee Love
as Feminist Compassion

In a rundown part of San Francisco, the police were briefing a group of Cambodian refugees at the Self Help Center about crimes in the Tenderloin neighborhood.[1] Suddenly, Mrs. Mam, a tiny old woman standing beside her husband, blurted out, "My husband abuses me all the time. What should I do—should I remain calm about it, or what?" The audience gasped in surprise. Then Sarah, a community activist who was acting as the mediator between the police and the Cambodians, replied, "I would not in my life allow anyone to harm me. If the police are not a good support I'd find a support group, and then someone to work with my husband." She then read out the phone number for the women in crisis hot line.

The audience was made up of about twenty to thirty Cambodians, some with their children, who met each week at the untidy community center, which also served as a drop-in place for the homeless, prostitutes, drug addicts, refugees, and other denizens of the neighborhood. The center was opened in the late 1980s to provide a streetwise alternative to conventional hospitals and clinics, emphasizing peer counseling, crisis management, and ongoing support for the down-and-out and those traumatized by war. Some Cambodian refugees who came by regularly had been organized into a self-help group by Timothy Hale, a white-haired church worker who used to work with Central American refugees, and Sam Ngor, a young Cambodian American student turned social worker.

After the pause that followed Mrs. Mam's outburst, the discussion returned to thefts and muggings in the mean streets.

Shy man: My son had a bad time with police when he got into trouble at school. The police officer said to him, "If you're not happy, you should get a ticket and return to Cambodia."

142

Thirty-something guy with a cap: Many here don't respect the police, but we Khmers do.

     Sarah: We will meet with the police chief to discuss their handling of domestic-violence issues. How they can help the specific needs of this group.

   Shy man: I want the chief to talk to officers so that what happened to my son won't happen again.

 Young woman: In my building, my son was taken by an American man from our fifth-floor apartment to the basement. I reported to the police and also to the manager.

Sarah, perhaps automatically assuming that Mr. Mam was an abuser, reminded everyone to report crimes against the family to the police. As the meeting was breaking up, the Mam couple broke into a quarrel, drawing comments from a tipsy old man. Mrs. Mam turned to the social worker and said that her husband was verbally abusive, and sometimes he hit her as if he were striking wood. "Thump, thump!" she said, hands chopping at her leg. Mr. Mam, red with anger, made a slashing gesture across his throat, and screamed that she had committed a blasphemy against his dead parents. She was out of control, and the children too. He blamed her for his loss of control over them. Hale broke in and told him to discuss his problems in the group, and not take them out on his wife.

FEMINISM AND WELFARE REGULATION

The conversation described above typifies the kinds of issues faced daily by Cambodian refugees, and highlights the complex pattern of their relationships with social workers and the police. Community and social workers saw themselves as mediating between Cambodian families and the police, but also, frequently, between women and children on the one hand, and men on the other. A meeting intended to make Cambodians more streetwise about crime had turned into an occasion for venting families' dirty secrets. The very presence of a feminist community worker encouraged women who might not ordinarily speak up about battering to do so. Of the myriad issues that made survival such a daily struggle for the refugees, domestic violence became the main cause and excuse for the interventions by service providers, police, and the courts. The spotlight on domestic violence, and the shifting lines of power between the sexes and the generations, became the prism through which social and legal discourses developed a theory that Asian male power oppressed women and children. Through such interventions, American constructions of race and gender were applied to social and legal practices that became the disciplinary technology through which Cambodian women gained autonomy, and children rebelled against their parents.

Feminist analysts have focused on the gendered dimensions of the welfare system, especially on the "feminization of poverty," whereby women have tended to predominate among welfare recipients and state dependents.[2] More recently, scholars have explored the disciplining aspects of the welfare system that confer second-class citizenship on women, defining them as wives and mothers so that their relation to the state must be mediated by their husband or father.[3] Historians show that early female political reformers played a major role in bringing this about, as they struggled alongside but not in alliance with racial minorities to fight for equal citizenship with white men in the republic. In the early years of the welfare state, women's politics turned on motherhood, as middle-class female reformers argued that government's responsibility for addressing social needs must focus on women's different needs. Gwendolyn Mink notes, "But by welding motherhood to women's citizenship, women's politics problematized claims for gender equality. It further compromised the possibility of racial equality when it offered motherhood as the solvent for diversity in America. Arguing for policies tied to gender difference, women's politics interposed women reformers as managers of racial difference."[4] Not only have women become the paradigmatic welfare subjects, but as time goes on, female social workers have become the chief mediators of motherhood, gender, and race relations within social-services programs.

In the 1980s, with the growth of the service economy and Reaganomics— as well as the expansion of the social-work profession's influence and the second-wave feminist movement—the role of the AFDC program in regulating the nuclear family was undercut. Mimi Abramovitz points out that "[i]nstead of upholding the [patriarchal] family ethic, [the AFDC program] increasingly legitimized the female-headed family by providing it with the economic resources to establish independent households."[5] For the first time, feminists began to argue that AFDC benefits could be viewed as a set of social rights for female recipients, increasing their bargaining power vis-à-vis the men in their lives.[6] But Nancy Fraser has argued that the gains in social rights for women from "welfare-state capitalism" are ambivalent, because the social rights that channel the entitlements, benefits, and social services also "disempower clients, rendering them dependent on bureaucracies and 'therapeutocracies,' and preempting their capacities to interpret their own needs, experiences, and life problems."[7]

There has, however, been little ethnographic investigation of how welfare benefits have transformed domestic patriarchy and yet situated women in a kind of clientship to social programs. Neither has the role of the social-work profession in producing this conflicting dynamic of female domestic empowerment and public dependency been examined. We know very little about the contemporary micropolitics of social work, or the quotidian effects of welfare practices involved in constructing the racial, gender, ethnic, and class character of new immigrants in late twentieth-century America.[8] There is a widespread impression that feminism stands outside welfare regulation, when in fact, since the 1970s modern feminist logic has become embedded in technologies that foster poor women's empowerment and clientship.

In the previous chapter I discussed how social workers dealing with refugees strove to instill in them the norms of self-discipline and productivity, and yet welfare policies that limited the number of hours a recipient could work frustrated refugees' strategies to attain self-sufficiency. In this and the following chapters, my attention shifts to a more focused consideration of the workings of feminist "pastoral power"—the kind of caring political relationship that promotes the well-being of its subjects by means of detailed and intimate regulation of their conduct; in this case, immigrant women on welfare.[9] Frequently, feminist agents identify "culture" as the basis of problems in Asian families, and thus tend to ignore the ways that Asian women exercise power, and the effects of wider institutional forces on families trying to cope in a violence-ridden environment.[10] By exploring the micropolitics of welfare dependency and interventions by social workers, we can identify the categories and mechanisms that daily produce the norms of differential belonging for refugee clients. How do the caring and disciplinary practices of social agents delimit the gendered Cambodian subject as a client, even as they embolden women to resist domestic patriarchal power? Feminizing technologies are central in constituting minority subjectivity, shaping gender ethnicity (which I discuss further below) by teaching women about the ethic of self-empowerment.

REFUGEE LOVE AS COMPASSIONATE DOMINATION

Compassionate love has had a long and varied history in the United States, but the different narratives have all been based, sometimes more explicitly than others, on the concept of paternalism toward subordinated populations; and historically debates have centered on concepts such as their "readiness" for political sovereignty. Issues of slavery, colonialism, and immigration have all been argued in this context. Historians describe how in the nineteenth century, as antislavery criticism mounted, slave owners waxed lyrical about their "enlightened" paternal slave management "founded on pity and protection on the one side, and dependence and gratitude on the other."[11] The transformation of "savage" Africans into "docile, happy" Sambos was the leitmotif of slave owners' civilizing ideology. Eugene Genovese has written eloquently about how paternalism in the subordination of slaves was differently perceived by slaveholder and slave, and how the notion of an implicit exchange forced the recognition of the latter's humanity, denied in slavery and racism.[12]

After the United States reached the Pacific, American frontier ideology came to be couched in terms of paternalistic domination and guidance of Asia's "inferior" and "incompetent" races.[13] Vicente Rafael has employed the term *white love* to denote the intertwining of American colonization and civilizing love in the Philippines. An expression of the inseparability of violent conquest and the moral uplifting of the natives, white love in practice enforced discipline and surveillance on the natives, while seeking to instill in them desires—"democratic aspirations, sentiments, and ideals"—defined by the colonizers.[14] Rafael takes care to show that Filipinos resisted the colonizing effects of white love by promoting their own cultural identities and nationalist aspirations.

A contrasting and more deterministic notion is found in Frank Chin's term *racist love*. He identifies the Christian cultural colonization of nonwhite Americans as a process whereby "the stereotypes assigned to the various races are accepted by the races themselves as reality." He asserts that "the people of Chinese and Japanese ancestry stand out as white racism's only success."[15] In Chin's view, converted Asian Americans, unlike African Americans, do not resist racist love, but eagerly embrace its promise of white approval and acceptance by becoming deracinated and Christianized subjects. Chin of course misdirects his admiration for the civil rights movement by grossly exaggerating and simplifying African American resistance to racist love.[16] Besides, by proposing a rigid division between "fake" and "real" Asians, Chin's argument leaves no space for the complex strategies of dealing with racist love, or for the destabilizing of the perceived division between imposed rules and techniques of self-making. Ben Tong, for instance, argues that the "groveling" of Chinese Americans was faked submission, part of a creative strategy of subterfuge that sought to deceive and outwit the domineering compassion of white institutions.[17]

Refugee love may be considered a liberal variation of humanitarian domination, as enacted by refugee workers, social workers, the police, and some health providers, who in their various capacities provide pastoral care in the broadest sense of the term to refugees.[18] Although refugee workers do not oppose different kinds of public and welfare support for refugees, they see their work as driven by American values of instilling a sense of autonomy and self-reliance in clients, and stimulating them to seek eventually productive lives. It is in the very nature of social work to intervene in domestic affairs, and inevitably to trouble the boundary between public and private, thus transforming institutional arrangements within the family as well as its relation to the wider society. When driven by an explicitly feminist agenda— as tends to be the case in Northern California—social work has both disciplinary and nurturing elements that promote the installation of cultural rules that reorganize gender power in the refugee or poor immigrant family.

Feminist social workers (who may include men) have sought to break down the separation of the private and the public domains, which in their view nurtures refugee or minority patriarchy. They intervened not only to regulate poor families, but also to empower women, including encouraging battered women to leave their families. Implicit in these social-work strategies was the construction of undeserving patriarchal subjects and deserving female and child victims of patriarchy, who should be taught such American values as autonomy in decision making, gender equality, and nuclear family relations. Indeed, this form of civilizing strategy seemed justified by the perceived Asian patriarchal otherness of refugee subjects and victims, but it subjected refugees and other poor immigrants of color to a kind of ethnic cleansing in the process of becoming Americans. Sau-ling Cynthia Wong has used the concept of ethnicizing gender to describe a process whereby "white ideology assigns selected gender characteristics to various ethnic others"; she cites as an example the contrasting images of effeminized Asian men and ultra-feminized Asian women, a variation of the black stud and Mammy figures in American popular culture.[19] Here, I am suggesting a process of "genderizing ethnicity," whereby the Cambodians as a group were feminized by a strategy of ethnic transformation that aimed to empower weak refugee women and marginalize patriarchal-deviant refugee men.

The structure of refugee love based on racial difference and female clientelism was mutually if unequally produced by clients, since refugee women compelled and even invited the intervention of social workers into their lives. They sought not only to gain access to material benefits, but also to effect changes in their status and power at home and in society, perhaps in ways not always clear to the social workers cheering them on. Nevertheless, Cambodian Americans were ambivalent about feminist thinking, and as often as they made use of feminist prodding, they also criticized what they saw as excessive materialism and individualism.

This discussion first presents the changing gender dynamics of Cambodian refugees as they struggled to support their families through partial dependence on AFDC benefits. Then I examine how feminist social workers sought to empower Cambodian women vis-à-vis their men, and how refugee women, emboldened by connections to public services, sought to gain gender power by setting the authority of state agents in opposition to the authority of the husband. Feminist-infused refugee love—which goes back to the work of good church women among poor people at home and abroad—is merely the latest transformation of the civilizing mission to educate and "uplift" populations considered not yet quite American. Refugee love produced a structure of strategic support—defining individual material and social needs—within which Cambodian women made practical as well as moral choices that transformed the power dynamics within their families and community.

FAMILY REUNIONS, BREAKUPS, AND SURVIVAL

Cambodian women enjoy the freedom they find here. They can explode in anger when their husbands put too much pressure on them. Men like me try to change, not to expect absolute compliance with their wishes. They may try to accommodate their wives' wishes, but they don't like it. I think "yes" here [pointing to his head], but I don't feel right in here [pointing to his heart].

    Cambodian social worker PETER THUY

Even as Cambodian refugees struggled to hold their families together, they found themselves grappling with changing norms of gender roles and relations, both within the family and in the wider society. Domestic patriarchal power over women and children in Cambodia had been shattered by the war, flight, and camp life; and in diaspora, men struggled to reclaim their domestic authority even though the majority could not support their families, often suffered from the aftereffects of torture and illness, and had no public role in the United States. Although most Cambodians still considered patriarchal power to be the ideal, women had become more assertive in criticizing Cambodian masculinity and challenging conjugal relations. As mentioned earlier, women had been forced into painful self-reliance in the war, flight, and refugee camps. Frequently without the help of husbands or male relatives, they gained a greater sense of control over their own lives, and in the world of the camps, they figured out what they needed and how to get it from the aid and service agencies. Once they reached America, welfare agencies provided a new structure of resources and services, and defined new needs and norms that compounded power struggles between husbands and wives, and between parents and children. Because AFDC benefits went directly to women, they gained an immediate source of power that further undercut male authority, already reduced by the inability of many men to find gainful employment. And the unstable composition of family groups— caused by loss of family members, fictive relations formed in the camps, frequent migration within the United States, and newly reintegrated households—further weakened family networks and support. In Cambodia, the direct rule of male power over the family and the complementary codes of female compliance, as well as sexual, social, and economic norms, were features common to most agrarian societies dominated by family farming. For Cambodian men, however, life in America was a major threat because of both public and private challenges to male authority.

    Many Cambodian families were afflicted with marital conflicts, some with roots in the war and the flight to safety, and most struggled with the difficult circumstances of adjusting to the new country. Many Cambodian men—with a background in farming, limited education, and suffering the aftereffects of shell shock—could not negotiate the transition to job training and employment in the United States. For many of them, the American dream was

not going to happen: they were poor and unemployable, and they were going to live in crowded apartments in crime-ridden neighborhoods; the dis-
appointment and frustration could be overwhelming. This set of experiences
is not unique to Cambodian refugees; for many immigrants from developing countries, coming to the postindustrial economy of America may mean
being funneled into an underclass. The frustration these men felt contributed to cases of wife battering and women seeking refuge in shelters; but
there was no way to tell whether domestic abuse and family breakdown occurred at a significantly higher rate among Cambodians than among other
populations living in inner-city neighborhoods and facing a similar set of
daunting circumstances. One refugee worker, who reported some cases of
elder abuse and of incest, stressed that overall, incidents of abusive behavior among Southeast Asian refugees were not too frequent, "but it always
seems to happen in a situation that is ready to boil over anyway."

Among Cambodian refugees, many wives often lost respect for men because of their inability to make a living, and men's refusal to share household chores and child care only compounded the anger. The Cambodians'
customary family roles and gender norms became, if not irrelevant, at least
severely undermined, as men failed to support their families and wives became more assertive in seeking help. Relations between husband and wife,
parents and children came to be dictated, to a significant degree, not by
Cambodian customs of unchallenged male power, as they remembered
them, but by the pressing daily concerns: access to state resources and other
forms of income, and achieving a measure of respect from the society around
them.

Welfare dependency dealt a major blow to male power in the family. Again
and again, male informants remarked that "In America, men feel they have
lost value because they are no longer masters in their own families." A *krou
khmer* who was often consulted by unhappy couples noted that "Money is the
root cause of marital problems in the U.S." He explained:

> For instance, most of us who came to the U.S. are recipients of welfare assis-
> tance; the majority of us are nurtured by the state. Oftentimes, it is the wife
> who gets the welfare check but not the husband. She is the one who takes care
> of the kids. But when she receives the check, her husband wants to spend it.
> When she refuses, and wants to keep the money for the children, that's what
> leads to wife abuse.

Scholars have established links between economic insecurity and family
violence among different disadvantaged groups, and have shown that when
combined with substance abuse, poverty can lead to domestic violence.[20] Indeed, like their counterparts among European immigrants to the United
States in the early twentieth century, Cambodian women were caught in what
Linda Gordon calls a "double position" as victims of wife abuse and as guar-

dians of their children; they stood up to their husbands in order to ensure the economic survival of their children.[21]

Some Cambodian men lashed out at their wives in order to restore their sense of male privilege. Besides struggling over control of welfare checks, they sought to compel wives to return to their former deferential behavior by physical force. And many women still tried to support male power, for the sake of family unity, despite the occasional beating. Mrs. Mok confided,

> There are many cases of wife abuse. Yes, everyone gets beaten, myself included. But sometimes we have to just keep quiet even after a disagreement. Like in my case, I don't want to call the police or anything. As the old saying goes, "It takes two hands to clap. One hand cannot sound itself." I just shed a few tears and let it go. If it gets out of hand, then you can call the police. But the men still think more of themselves than of women. They never lower themselves to be our equals.

This acknowledgment of a degree of responsibility in marital conflicts indicates that Cambodian women did not think of themselves as passive victims, but were aware of their own role in struggles over domestic power. Mrs. Mok seemed to imply that she tolerated the occasional beating because men could not adjust to their change in status, and she knew she always had the option of calling the police—as some other women did.

Another view of marital conflicts is that they arose not so much from husbands' attempts to revive their former authority as from their abandonment of the traditional husband's role. A Cambodian health aide disputed the stereotype of pervasive PTSD among the refugees, claiming that Cambodian men's emotional problems stemmed primarily from their living conditions in the United States, worries about family conflicts and cultural dislocation, and feeling trapped in their apartments. What appeared to be purely self-centered behavior might have been rooted in feelings of failure.

Many women were dismayed at their husbands' diminishing sense of responsibility toward the family. There was a definite shift on the part of many male refugees to the American culture of individualism, and away from the Cambodian emphasis on family unity. Men tended to spend their time away from the apartments, spending money, playing games, and gambling with friends. Few had jobs, though many were required to take ESL classes in order to receive welfare benefits. Following resettlement in the Bay Area, divorce and separation rose as married men carried on affairs. A woman I met at a wedding seemed to confirm this observation: "Some men leave their wives and kids to take up with other women. Perhaps the AFDC, which provides for the family, makes them feel freer to do so. They look for younger women and change wives like they change clothes." In such comments, Cambodian women criticized men's emphasis on individualism and materialism as a factor contributing to their family woes.

There were many female-headed households among the refu-
tion, not only because of widowhood, but also because men w...
tated or deserted them. Mrs. Lai told a story that was in some ways typi...
forty-year-old woman who had never been to school, she was a quick study,
and had picked up English by watching soap operas on TV. The Khmer Rouge
had killed her first husband, and five of her six children had died of starvation. During her flight to Thailand, she met her second husband; they had
two young boys. After arriving in this country, her husband got a job as a waiter,
then a carpenter. When he was laid off, he got so upset that he abandoned
her. She decided to get some training in the refugee program for child caregivers. She started working full-time, making seven dollars an hour. The AFDC
barely covered her rent and gas for her car. Her husband visited on and off,
and wanted to get back together, but she refused: "Just go, I don't want it."
She said he had spent a lot of her money, leaving her and the kids hungry at
home. She was thinking of starting her own child-care business at home.

In another case, a woman was abandoned by her second husband in the
United States because she no longer fitted into his new life. Mrs. Preng, an
attractive woman in her thirties, had been the wife of a soldier who was killed
shortly after the Khmer Rouge took over. In 1980, she married a man who
participated in the anti-Khmer Rouge resistance movement, and they adopted
a baby in the refugee camp because "my husband wanted a son." After they
arrived in Massachusetts, her sister-in-law, their sponsor, urged her husband
to divorce her:

> She told me that in America, whoever eats must also find money, and ignorant
> persons like myself cannot make any money or find jobs. This is a country of
> educated people. . . . They said that I was dumb and illiterate. Don't even know
> Khmer writing or English, so how can I find a job? Americans—you may be
> husband and wife, but each contributes equally to the rent and other expenses.
> I thought about it, but I let them say whatever they wanted because it is true
> that I am ignorant and because it is my parents' fault that they didn't send me
> to school.

Mrs. Preng trembled and wept profusely while recounting her story, seeming still in shock that her husband could have abandoned her and their son
in America. After the divorce, Mrs. Preng moved to Oakland to join her married daughter, but could not live with her because the authorities would not
allow extended-family members to live in her tiny government-subsidized
apartment. She and her seven-year-old boy were living with friends when I
met her.

> I can't afford my own housing. Even if I were to rent a one-bedroom place, it
> would cost me $475, and my [AFDC] income comes to only $500. And what
> about electricity and food . . . ?
> So these people were nice enough to take me in. I am very grateful to them,

but we don't dare let the manager know about this. In Cambodia you can live anywhere you want as long as you don't burn the house down. Here it's too difficult.

Her current travails became interwoven with the violence she was subjected to during the war years. She lifted the hem of her sarong and said,

See, this is where the Khmer Rouge hit me [showing her left leg]—this scar— but before I could get stitched up, the flesh was already rotting. They also brutalized my entire body. I am full [of suffering]. Sometimes, my whole body would tremble uncontrollably. When I came to America, I could not study [English] because my heart was burning [with anger]. I still cannot learn anything.

It was obvious that in her situation, welfare support was barely sufficient to keep her and her boy from drowning in their problems. She was suffering from sickness of the heart and body, but had not figured out how to apply for supplemental security income. With her permission, I called a social worker to see whether she could be helped.

But it was not always the men who abandoned their spouses. Some women also learned to play the game of divorce, serial monogamy, and other practices unheard of in Cambodia. Peter Thuy knew of cases involving couples over sixty-five years old in which the wives kicked out the husbands and then applied for supplemental income. Mrs. Sophat reported some rather unusual cases of women abandoning both husband and children:

Some men have realized, though, that things are not the same as when we were back home. Some women have left their husbands for American men, leaving their children behind. And so the men are worried; they are afraid that the women will leave them for American men. There are quite a few cases, involving Cambodian women in Florida, Long Beach, and so on. The Cambodian women and American men met while working together. Then they got together and left their families. Some were never abused by their husbands; they just didn't love their husbands anymore, and so they left them. Some were beaten and mistreated and left for that reason.

This fear of Cambodian American women betraying their families caused some men to become paranoid and controlling. Mrs. Sophat confided that since their arrival in America, her husband had become extremely possessive of her and would not allow her to go out without him. Phauly Sang also noted that many Cambodian women had left their husbands because family morality had collapsed. Wives left their husbands because they "look[ed] down on them . . . for not working, for not being as clever as other men." They felt free to do so because the AFDC supported them and their children, in any case. In an optimistic tone, Mrs. Sophat said, "Cambodian women are very happy living in America, because they now have equal rights. . . .

We can start up businesses more easily here. If we want to work, we can pay for day care." Being a single woman—unthinkable in Cambodia—was becoming a small trend in California. As the number of divorced and separated people increased, violence became more common in everyday life.

One example involves two young women who had recently separated from their husbands. Catharya, a stylish woman in her thirties, told me that another woman had recently threatened to kill her. She suspected that the woman was having an affair with her estranged husband. The woman's son was a gang member, and both mother and son were well known for being violent. Catharya reported that a few days earlier she and her boyfriend had been coming down the stairs in her apartment building when the other woman, standing in the lobby, reached into her purse for something. Catharya's boyfriend thought that the woman was about to lunge forward with a knife, and he hit her. Subsequently, he was arrested when the woman charged him with trying to rob her. In general, younger women on their own seemed to need men, whether boyfriends or sons, to provide protection.

Some older Cambodian women were quite independent and had adjusted happily without a partner. They did not seem to be stigmatized for their independence. At a party, I met one such woman, Mrs. Kim, a friendly and attractive woman in her early fifties. Her family had been rice farmers outside Phnom Penh. She got married at seventeen and was married for twenty-eight years, but her husband had died a few years after they arrived in America. Three of her grown children were working in electronics factories, and living elsewhere. She lived with her school-age daughter in West Oakland. Her neighbors were African Americans, and she got along well with them. There were also a dozen Vietnamese American families in her low-cost apartment complex. After her husband died, she enrolled in a local community college. She liked being in America because "one can keep growing, learning things."

One of the things Cambodian women learned was to fight for child support if their husbands divorced them. I heard the following story from Mr. Sok, who was one of the Cambodians born in South Vietnam who had worked with U.S. forces during the war. After the fall of Saigon, he was sent to a reeducation camp for more than three years. He felt so strongly that he could not live under communism that the second day after his release, he left his wife and children and escaped from Pol Pot's Kampuchea, finally making his way to Bangkok, where he connected with some American army friends. He was later sponsored by a cousin who ran a grocery shop in West Oakland. Using money he sent, his wife and children left Saigon and finally joined him in Oakland. "She did not like me anymore," he said. They separated, and she told the children not to see him because "'For five years he had been depressed,' . . . so I have this friend," he explained, pointing to his female companion. His wife had more than $750 a month in AFDC but took him to court to force him to pay child support. Mr. Sok was kept busy holding down three jobs—as a waiter, a school translator, and, with his companion, a housecleaner in the Oakland hills.

These stories illustrate some of the complex reasons why Cambodian families who managed to reunite in America broke up again, as well as the crucial role American values played in shaping the motivations and actions of women and men as their Cambodian family ethics faded and they gradually became American persons. Although some of the family conflicts were linked to sufferings inflicted by war, most marital problems grew out of gender-specific difficulties in adjusting to a new society and out of the breakdown of Cambodian marital norms, especially the father's role in supporting the family and maintaining moral authority at home. Many dispossessed Cambodian men refused to help out at home, and stayed away gambling and drinking with friends. In that regard they were perhaps not very different from some American exemplars of patriarchal masculinity, but their families were not economically secure enough to support their behavior. Some Cambodian women, enjoying the autonomy represented by a welfare check or a new job, left their husbands. Cambodian men—economically marginalized, lacking proficiency in English, and sometimes charged with domestic abuse—compared unfavorably to the native-born American men for whom some women abandoned them.

Gender tensions among Cambodian Americans arose from a range of forces and motivations—abandoning the family, divorce, new desires—and welfare support made available the opportunity to act on those tensions, though not necessarily the motivation. Some Cambodian refugees opted for individual makeover, but others muddled through their unhappy marriages. Some leaped at freedom and self-advancement, while others chose to stay with their families, tough going though it was. Clearly, Cambodian families were struggling for more than material survival: they were struggling with the conflicting values of being simultaneously Khmer-Buddhist and American. This conflict came into sharp focus when the structuring of opportunities to make personal choices was skewed by the availability of feminist thinking as an alternative to traditional Cambodian views of husband–wife, parent–child relations. Poor women found that they had more options than men for getting social workers and the police to help them in their family power struggles.

SOCIAL WORKERS AND THE EMPOWERING OF WOMEN

In her important study of family violence among new immigrant groups and African Americans in early nineteenth-century Boston, Linda Gordon argues that women's rights movements were most influential in the fight against domestic abuse. Indeed, the welfare state, as enacted by professional social workers, has in modern times subjected poor, migratory, and alien families to social regulation, and played a role in constructing family-violence problems.[22] But social control was jointly produced, by the social workers and by the women (and, to a lesser extent, by the children) who elicited their support. Gordon argues,

> In historical fact, most of the invitations for intervention [by professionals, bureaucrats, and charity workers] came from women and secondarily children. In other words, the inviters were weaker members of family power structures. . . . In their struggle to escape the control of the [immigrant] patriarchal family, women not only used the professions and the state but helped build them.[23]

Earlier generations of professional social workers held specific ideas about the ethnic cultural patterns that contributed to family violence. Gordon considers these supposed patterns, based on ethnic stereotyping, to be negligible influences compared to the common experiences of poverty, migrancy, and helplessness among immigrants from agrarian societies caught up in a world of loss and flux.[24] Nevertheless, social workers continue to lean on claims of ethnic cultural differences in dealing with contemporary immigrants. When it came to Cambodians, social workers were influenced by a policy guide that claimed that Cambodians possessed "a looser sense of discipline, obligation, and loyalty, in contrast to the Vietnamese and Chinese. Cambodians were at the same time viewed as more "affectively-oriented" and thus open "to create an emotional mutuality with Americans."[25] Their "warmth" and "friendliness," when combined with the belief that Cambodians suffered from a disproportionately high incidence of mental problems, made them a special refugee group for service providers.[26] At the same time, many church and social workers also viewed Cambodians, compared again to ethnic Chinese and Vietnamese, as "more prone to divorce and separation," their families rife with patriarchal power and violence. Social workers, who have repeatedly dealt with domestic violence, saw their role as instructing Cambodians about the illegality of wife battering, the proper parenting of children, and—especially for women and children—their particular needs and rights as individuals. In the context of this professional perception of cultural difference, social workers sometimes lost sight of Cambodians as a refugee population traumatized by war and facing the practical problems of adjusting to American culture. Instead, by focusing narrowly on the Cambodians' "patriarchal Asian culture," they sought to impose new norms of gender and parenting behavior.

Feminist activism since the 1970s has converged with a whole range of public-service agencies involved in assisting women and families, especially in California. Coming out of the civil rights, anti-war, and New Left movements, feminists dissatisfied with the male chauvinism they encountered in those groups took on their own struggles and causes, focusing first on abortion and soon on rape and domestic violence. The first rape crisis hot line was set up in Berkeley in 1972, and soon women's shelters proliferated in major cities across the country.[27] The influx of immigrants into California in the 1980s intensified feminist interest in assisting foreign and minority women, who were viewed as especially vulnerable to domestic abuse, not least because of their cultural differences, social isolation, and ignorance of their rights as Americans. The rediscovery of child abuse and wife battering since the sixties led to the allocation of federal funding to family-violence–prevention centers and associated programs.[28] Middle-class feminists played a major role as advocates, fund-raisers, and workers in the fight against wife battering, based on the belief that domestic violence cuts across all ethnic, racial, and class lines. An Asian women's shelter was set up in the mid 1980s in order to assist Asian women, "particularly immigrants, refugees, and military brides," who could be helped "in rebuilding violence-free lives for themselves and their children."[29] Asian American advocates, like their Hispanic counterparts, set up feminist agencies that sought to counteract images stigmatizing poor female immigrants as welfare mothers or passive wives and empower them by providing an alternative structure of access that would help overcome male oppression at home.

Critics of family-violence reformers have charged them with class domination, because the majority of professional workers were middle class, and their clients mainly women and children from poor or working-class families. There seems to have been a greater willingness to remove children from poor homes than from middle-class ones; indeed, children in any juvenile court tend to be predominantly poor, and in most cities mainly nonwhite.[30] Assistance to abused women and children "has also been accompanied by efforts at social control and class domination."[31] But few of the critics have focused on the race and gender dimensions of strategies to rescue abused women and children, or on the underlying logic of cultural cleansing and reformation.

The late eighties in California was an era in which the emphasis in welfare programs on normalizing motherhood became linked to a strategy of empowering women as individual decision makers, with the implicit assumption that this empowerment would bring the family and ethnic communities more into line with the egalitarian ethos of American society. Feminist social workers became more explicit in their discourse of empowering immigrant women and teaching them "their rights in this country." An Asian American deeply involved in social-service issues affecting poor minorities defined her goal as being to "eliminate violence through the empowerment of women" because domestic abuse is a problem of the "power and control dynamic" within the family. Guided by books like Lenore Walker's *The Battered Woman,* feminist immigrant advocates stressed teaching clients, especially

Figure 5. "You or someone you know may live in a home where domestic violence is a problem" (Family Violence Prevention Funds, San Francisco).

women, to break out of "learned dependency" through resisting male oppression, and even to break up the family, if necessary.[32] Their ultimate goal was to "save" women from abusive family situations and teach them to seek the right of individual freedom. At women's organizations in San Francisco, there are large collections of booklets and suggested readings for women seeking to struggle free of family abuse (see, for example, figure 5).

Health workers at the San Francisco refugee clinic were especially sensitive to the issue of "patient rights," though it was often a struggle to impart this concept to refugees, including some Southeast Asian women. A nurse told me that when cases of domestic abuse came to her, she took the opportunity to coach female victims about seeking help:

It takes a lot of education and counseling for women, because complaining about such things didn't get you anywhere in the homeland. In many places, such as Cambodia, you were the property of your husband. And here we do a lot of talking: "You don't have to stand for this! You can leave. You can get a restraining order, we can get you into a shelter." So we try to help women get some of that autonomy that they've never experienced before. Another amazing cultural contradiction!

This statement reveals that social workers exaggerated the weakness of married Cambodian women, and often lost sight of refugees' recent experiences of war and dislocation, both physical and cultural. Indeed, wife abuse in many cases stemmed from the husband's defensiveness, not from his overweening power at home. But driven by their feminist assumptions of unchallenged patriarchal power in Cambodian families, social and health workers became champions of women and children, while men were either ignored or punished for behavior perceived to be resulting from cultural patriarchalism. But it must be noted that the helping profession's stress on female independence from male domestic power was paradoxically predicated on female dependency on the structure of social services. In the following sections, I present two cases among many I gathered over an eight-month period in 1989 and 1990 that typify the conflicts and pressures faced by the Cambodian refugee couples in America.

Mrs. Sin Seeks Shelter

That Mr. and Mrs. Sin, a couple in their fifties, fought for years was no secret to their friends and neighbors. For some time, Mrs. Sin had been seeing a female health worker in Chinatown who advised her to seek social intervention as a means to deal with her husband. An opportunity seemed to present itself at a Friday dinner when, in Mr. Sin's words, his wife "lost control and pushed him."

He pushed her back. She fell and knocked her forehead on the table. Her son said it was an accident, but Mrs. Sin retorted, "If he had not intended to hit me, how did I get this bruise?" The next day, she visited the health worker, who urged her to call the police.

On Monday, the health worker arrived with the police to take Mrs. Sin to a women's shelter. Her five children begged her not to go. Mr. Sin was taken aback and confused. He pleaded, "I want the police to arrest me, to let my wife go." As he tried to keep Mrs. Sin from leaving, their little girl burst into tears. The health worker chided Mr. Sin for "frightening" his children as well as his wife.

Soon afterward, a tired and disheveled Mr. Sin, accompanied by his twenty-year-old son, attended the Self Help Center discussion group and confided their problems. The son said, "It has happened before. Ma gets angry easily; she has mental problems. The children, especially the little ones, want her home." A young woman who shared their apartment agreed that Mrs.

Sin was sick. She reported that on the evening of the quarrel, Mrs. Sin was "doing big mouth talk," ranting at her husband as she was serving him rice. Mr. Sin pushed her, and she fell on the table, sustaining a small bruise on her forehead. Mr. Sin interjected, "If I have to go to the police station, let me go now. She wants to come home."

That desire was not so apparent in Mrs. Sin's behavior. Ensconced in the shelter, she had agreed to talk to her husband on the phone. She told her husband to come and take her home, but would (or could) not give the address of the shelter.

At this point in the discussion, the Cambodian social worker Sam Ngor tried to explain the conflicting versions of the fight in terms of cultural difference. He noted that there is a difference between "oral and literate cultures. In oral cultures, people always change their minds about what happened." Here Ngor was apparently speaking of Cambodians with rural origins who were sometimes not literate in Khmer, but his account slighted the glorious achievements of Cambodian civilization, as well as presuming that in a literate society, people did not or could not change their minds. He went on to claim that furthermore, in a literate society like the United States, men could be jailed for abusing their wives and children (covert smiles lit up the faces of the women, while the men looked down). Mr. Sin crossed his arms and said, "I respect her, but it is she who controls me." His female co-tenant nodded.

Then the group broke into a debate about marital relations in Cambodian families. The women said husbands and wives should respect each other and share power equally. One woman claimed that she and her husband shared power. The men disagreed. The live wire of the group, Mr. Pang, said—only half in jest—"A man must control his wife; if not, he'll have to find another." Ngor cautioned, "The man is the decision maker, but maybe that is changed." The protests came fast and furious: "Man is the decision maker." "He is responsible for everything in the family." "According to Khmer law, he is king." Ngor appeared to agree: "Man is responsible for everything in Cambodia, but. . . ." In the brief silence that followed, there was mute recognition that much had changed in gender behavior, if not ideals, since the Cambodia of before 1975.

A few days later, I talked with Mr. Sin's younger boy, a sophomore at a community college. He was very upset and scared. He called his mother at the shelter every night: "She wants my father to do certain things before she comes home. She wants to come home, but she does not want to [as long as things remain the same]. . . . If she comes back, I think my dad will treat my mum better, will have learned his lesson. I will also treat her nice." In the past, he had pestered her for a car, and she had refused to get him one. "Now," he said, "forget it—I just want her back." His father had not eaten or slept in days. The son blamed the health worker for bringing this calamity upon his family.

It's not a big deal, this give and take [between my parents]. It has been blown up into a big thing. My parents, they're always [fighting]. I don't think she really hates my dad, I think she's trying to play games, to force him to throw away his bad attitude. She should know that none of her kids can live without her. My dad is old, is getting older. When he hears that something is endangering the family, his blood runs cold. Back in Cambodia, Dad did something bad. Now he has time to think of the past, of the bad thing he did, and she wants this time to teach him a lesson.

Then he added, as a way to explain his sense of being caught in the middle between two cultures:

They adhere to customs and stick to the Cambodian family system in some circumstances. I can't follow them. I can't follow her rules at all. We the children are independent, but are still not independent. I like my parents, more my mom, because she gave birth to me. I want to repay them, when I become a man. I guess I still stick to Khmer ways.

Mrs. Sin decided to return home ten days later. The family immediately closed ranks and did not want to talk to outsiders anymore. Despite her health worker's urgings, she did not press charges of battery against her husband. She seemed to have some psychological problems, and was somehow caught up in the machinations, perhaps well intended, of the social worker on the one hand, and the men in her family who understandably strongly resisted such outside interventions. They viewed the welfare state and refugee love, especially in this case, as interfering with the family and creating havoc, while stripping away the tattered remains of male authority. Ngor found himself caught between his liberal views as a newly minted social worker and his empathy with refugee men in trouble:

Many men can't take it that their wives work and become more assertive at home. I have intervened in many cases of wife battering and told the men about wife-battering laws, only to have them shout at me, "I don't care! This is my wife!" A social worker I know had to use tear gas to protect himself from a furious husband wielding a gun. In fact, during [the chaos following] the 1989 earthquake, a Khmer man shot the boyfriend of his estranged wife.

Refugee men were having to grapple with the implications of their predicament now as subjects of a legal system, not of family honor codes. The intrusions of service agents and the police into domestic affairs made Cambodian men feel even greater uncertainty in their already precarious position. In the public mind, Cambodian men, like their counterparts among Hmong and Mien refugees, had apparently come to symbolize Asian peasant or tribal patriarchy from which refugee women and children must be saved. Not only were these marginalized men dealing with the dissolution of their former power in the home, but they were also confronting a legal system that appeared to favor women.

Mae Gets Her Husband Locked up, then Released

In the next case, we see two male social workers, Tim Hale and Sam Ngor, sympathizing with the disempowerment of a husband who was constantly out-maneuvered by his wife, who routinely used the law to discipline her wayward husband. Since 1985, Mae, a good-looking woman with wavy, shoulder-length hair, had threatened to divorce her husband, Pang, because his alcoholism created havoc at home. Somehow, family counseling and the self-help group kept them married, despite frequent fights and separations. When I first met them, Pang was still on probation for an incident of wife abuse earlier that year. In late spring 1990, the Pangs appeared at a group meeting together, though he had been ordered out of the house days before. They gave different versions of the conflict that had led to their latest separation. Pang—a slim, middle-aged man with a rakish grin and sinuous gestures—reported that his wife had ordered him out of his apartment after he danced with a Laotian woman at a wedding party. The people who had been at the same party agreed that it was "a very dirty dance," but they saw that Pang, who had forgotten to zip up his trousers, was obviously drunk. Pang tossed a remark in his wife's direction: "You gave me such tight pants; I felt uncomfortable." The next day, he reported, his wife called the police to have him removed from the apartment.

> *Mae:* I called Sam [the social worker] to report that my husband had sold his gold chain to buy alcohol.
>
> *Pang:* Why call him—is he your husband? [Some friends chimed in, expressing concern for what would happen to him.]
>
> *Pang:* I want to be happy at the wedding. When I drink, I am happy.
>
> *Young woman 1:* Why don't you dance with your wife?
>
> *Pang:* Freedom *(Serai)*! To dance with whomever I please. Doesn't she want to feel free too?
>
> *Man:* Suppose if she dances too close to a man.
>
> *Pang:* No problem. This is a free country, an open place.
>
> *Hale:* But you can get into an enclosed place, like a prison. We are concerned you may get into trouble.
>
> *Pang:* She has called the police four or five times to harass me. I want to be happy at a wedding. I want to "open the room." Today I am happy. I just want one more day to be happy, free. I want to go back home. I miss the children.

Ngor: His wife lost face at his sexual gestures while dancing in public. Then he went home and sold his gold chain. So they got into a fight.

Young woman 1: One should not have too much freedom at a party. Dancing is okay, but not the way Pang did it. Traditional dancing is friendly, not sexy.

Old man [gesturing with his walking stick]: I believe that most Khmers have problems with Western clothes, the zippers and so on.

Sino-Cambodian woman: Pang did not know that his zipper was not closed. He's okay—dancing, drinking—okay. The zipper's a mistake.

Pang [turning to me]: I gave forty dollars [to the wedding party]. I have pain in my head and arm [showing me his scars]. My head's no good. I'm getting old, thinking a lot about the children. If I don't care, my children won't be good.

Young woman 2: It seems that nothing but handcuffs are good for my children.

Hale: Pang's mind is okay, but the combination of injury, drink, and party is not good. Our goal is to share and help each other. Pang is smart, and he makes people laugh.

Pang went into a reverie about how, when he was in Cambodia, American soldiers parachuted from the sky and hugged him, saying, or indicating, "I am good." He said he wished he knew specifically what his wife Mae did not like about him. He was afraid to go home again because she might call the police again. Hale told me that until the recent flare-up, the Pangs had been okay together for the previous six months. But now, Pang seemed to be in a situation in which the police were ready to come after him, and his wife was often threatening to call them.

A few weeks later, the Pangs had another fight. The police came and threw him in jail. At the next meeting, Mae told the group that someone had mistranslated for her, erroneously reporting that she was hit by her husband. She insisted that she never said such a thing, but that by waving her hands before her face she had been trying to say that Pang had not hit her. A Cambodian male witness to the quarrel was sick, and the social workers were trying to get his statement that Pang did not beat his wife. Hale prepared a statement from another Cambodian witness confirming this. When Hale presented the story to the judge, however, he would not believe it, but relied on the police report. A Chinese American policeman insisted that at the scene, Mrs. Pang had told him the many ways Pang hit her. The police suspected that Mae later changed her story in order to get her husband out of jail. We never learned whether she had merely intended the police to break up the spat, but not throw her husband in jail.

Mae called her husband in prison to say that after he got out, he must join

Alcoholics Anonymous and attend the self-help group meeting regularly. Pang got incensed, and they had another squabble. Mae then called the social worker to report that she wanted a divorce. Pang, confused about why he was in jail, accused his wife of having delusions of power: "I think the judge is the one who will decide to release me, but she thinks that she is the one who is controlling the situation. She thinks that by telling the police I did not beat her she is securing my release." Contradictorily, he thought that Mae, using the mediation of her social worker and lawyer, had somehow kept him in jail for three more months. Back at the meeting, Mae—all decked out in red silk and gold jewelry—said, "I have a lot of problems: headache, bad appetite. I'm afraid that when my husband comes back, I'll have problems again. I don't know how to solve the problem. If he doesn't drink, I'll feel very happy, but he'll do it again." Recently, she had also become worried about their eldest son, who had been detained once by the police. She was trying to keep him under curfew in the evenings, when gang fights broke out regularly.

After a few weeks, Pang was released from prison because his wife refused to press charges. They got back together. He stopped drinking for a few months, and Hale urged him to join Alcoholics Anonymous. Pang was asked in group how he would change.

> *Pang:* I can't promise to stop drinking, but I will try. Most Cambodian parties offer drinks, so—? [Laughs] First, not to drink. B, not to talk too much, or walk outside. Then come to the group to talk about our problems. Jail has been good for me, cleared my mind! [Laughs] Yes, and being single too! I received good service in detention, good clothes, and a mattress. I got no blame from anyone, not like at home. Staying in jail is better than at home. The things are clean, and there is a cigarette machine. I can watch TV. The best thing is, you can save money! No need to pay rent. Next time I'll have to hit Mae harder to get back in. [Laughs at his own joke] I missed my children.

> *Matronly woman:* I heard from Mae that you phoned her about not going out or going visiting. Jealous that you could not go out yourself? Because even though you were in jail, your mouth spoke out, causing trouble.

> *Pang:* I also worried that the kids may be alone, if there's a fire. . . . Sometimes I called, and Mae was not there.

> *Matronly woman:* One of your daughters said she wanted her mom in jail and you, Pang, at home. [Chortles]

> *Pang:* The prisoners were nice to me, and wanted to meet me. They felt sorry because I didn't speak English. I shared a cell with a white guy. He loaned me some money and pushed me to eat when Mae could not bring me supplies. Before I was re-

leased, the prisoners showed *The Killing Fields* on a large screen. In my honor! I got medical treatment every day for my hand injury, from playing basketball in jail. The doctor told the warden to let me sleep on the lower bunk.

Man in the back row: There are always fights in the family, but after a short while, things get sweet.

In both of the cases of purported wife abuse described here, the women's strategy involved using a public institution—the woman's shelter, the prison—to widen the arena of conflict that originated within the family. Mr. Sin was apparently oblivious to his wife's (or rather his wife's health worker's) stratagem, and he was so shaken by the police taking his wife to the shelter that the promise of a change in the marital relationship was enough to persuade Mrs. Sin to return home. In contrast, Mae and Pang had a long-term on-again, off-again relationship with each other, and with the police. Mae's threats to call the police were a familiar disciplining measure that was bitterly resented by Pang. Her decision whether to charge or not charge Pang with battery became a weapon that was ultimately successful, in that it compelled Pang to make a serious effort to give up drinking and go for counseling, in order to return home and be with his children. Despite Pang's public bravado, the power Mae wielded was recognized even by her young daughter, who speculated that if Mom was that tough, perhaps she should be the one in jail. It was clear that Mae was a shrewd woman who expertly used social workers, the police, the court system, and the self-help group to turn things in her favor, while her husband, desperately unhappy, could use only mockery to undercut her new authority. Their worries about their children haunted the family drama.

THE SELF HELP CENTER GROUP THERAPY

It was unusual for Cambodians who came of age in the home country to speak publicly about their problems. These were families seriously in trouble, and in reaching out to the self-help group, they participated in another form of imposed compassion that came with a price—self-exposure and subjectivization. Working with Cambodians in trouble, both Hale and Ngor had many opportunities to observe the changes in the Khmers' distribution of domestic power, and how those changes linked to differential experiences of dislocation and methods of coping. They noted that Cambodian men complained that women benefited more in the United States, while men relived their suffering in their minds and often lost control over their own families. Hale saw the gender-specific problems as typical of refugee status, especially among those fleeing war-torn countries: "I always try to link their past with the present—their experiences of torture, of losing families with current problems with kids, assimilation. Often, among refugees of all nationalities, men have lost their place in society. They don't like to ask for help, and it seems like they've lost control over their families. Women tend to ask for help more."

Ngor, the trainee social worker, faulted American society for privileging minority women over men, so that the former had easier access to resources and jobs. "Cambodian women adapt more easily to the new society and are more flexible, quicker in learning English than are the men. I blame affirmative action for making it easier for women to get jobs than for men. The service economy favors women perhaps unfairly over men." Ngor was caught between trying to emphasize nonviolence between spouses on the one hand, and feeling deep empathy for the men's displacement and loss of authority on the other. Perhaps too he felt ambivalent about this intervention into the intimate heart of Cambodian culture, this reordering of their ethical space by American do-good social tinkering. Regardless of their sympathy for the men's loss of status in society and power at home, both Hale and Ngor agreed that Cambodian women tended to reach out for help more than men, thus gaining access to more external sources of power. Despite some niggling doubts, the social workers were central to this process.

·   ·   ·

In this chapter, the state is brought into the study of citizenship not as a monolithic structure standing outside people's everyday concerns, but in the form of social workers, policemen, and judges through whose interpretations of social norms and the law new subjects learn about the dominant culture of belonging. Refugee love, as a regulatory form of compassionate intervention and surveillance of the refugee family, was often backed by the law. Humanistic values, middle-class norms, and feminist concerns were channeled through it, producing a paradoxical situation that promoted an ideology of individual autonomy realized via public paternalism.

Some feminists have argued that social-work interventions, whether to provide welfare or to mediate domestic conflicts, have the effect of simultaneously undermining "private patriarchy" and bolstering "public patriarchy."[33] Cambodian refugees, like other poor immigrant and minority groups, became feminized not only because the majority of welfare recipients were female, but also because women quickly learned to turn to the authorities for help with trouble at home. The gender-specific provision of welfare and the feminist ethos of social services have reworked the private–public split, further dissolving whatever remained of a family code of masculine power.

The cases described here show that welfare clients, as much as service agents, played a role in building the regime of social regulation. Refugee women sought more than material benefits from the state agents; they used their interventions to alter the distribution of domestic power. They came to use links with social workers as bargaining chips with their husbands, and learned that domestic disputes could take on larger political overtones that would invite the state in. The law became part of their strategy to redefine their own position as wife, mother, or daughter. As outsiders, we can of course never know the complex personal intentions at play in any domestic situation, but what are of analytical interest are the divergent truth claims of parties to a particular conflict, as well as their different access to state agents. It was not clear from the cases described here whether the women got what they really wanted from legal interventions: did they want their families broken up, or their husbands in jail, or something less drastic? In her study of domestic violence among earlier generations of immigrants, Gordon concluded that social-worker interventions often helped victims, but professional blaming of victims and interpretation of their needs led to social discrimination and domination: "Often, the main beneficiaries of professional interventions hated them most, because in wrestling with them one rarely gets what one really wants but rather, is asked to submit to another's interpretation of one's needs."[34] While contemporary feminist social workers might assume that in cases of wife battering, the women were victims of "learned helplessness" and that theoretically, a family breakup would be advisable, many female clients disagree. Cambodian women in different ways demonstrated a resourcefulness that grew from a whole set of transformations associated with war, flight, and resettlement in a new country. They were active planners seeking to use the law to punish and discipline their husbands, so that they would reform; in most cases, their goal was to keep the family together under new conditions of gender power. (In Mae's case, however, there was a suggestion that she was operating mainly in her own self-interest, rather than that of her family, and that she had other cards up her sleeve.) In other words, refugee women learned the option of using state agencies to combat some aspects of Cambodian masculinity, without necessarily breaking up the family. Whatever the outcome, however contestable male authority, these refugees came to view citizenship as a highly gendered set of practices and possibilities.

At the same time, whatever their motivations, Cambodian refugees were coming to recognize and even to an extent adopt what they understood to be American values—materialism, greed, self-centeredness—learning what it might mean to be American or to take advantage of life in the "land of opportunity." They realized that availing themselves of different kinds of material resources and services in their strategies for daily life entailed a moral cost to their community, but they were caught up in bureaucratic power structures that in major and minor ways shaped and constrained what otherwise would have been selective decision making. In struggling to keep their families and lives together, Cambodian refugees—especially the abandoned wives, frightened children, and unhappy husbands—were critical of aspects of American society, despite their gratitude for having been accepted as new citizens, and for the material goods and practical help they received. Pang, in spite of his irascibility, made some telling comments about freedom and its dangers.

In turn-of-the-century California, progressive social workers are administering such regulatory attention primarily to native-born minorities and immigrants of color. The middle-class and liberal aspirations of service agents play a role in defining and resolving domestic disputes that have implications beyond gender abuse in the family. Although the service providers studied here were aware of the structural and material reasons for the problems that tormented Cambodian refugee families, their interventions nevertheless inflicted symbolic violence on the specific intentions of their clients and on Cambodian culture. They were quick to project wife and child abuse onto Cambodian culture, which was variously described as "oral," "authoritarian," and "patriarchal." Social workers sought to push Cambodians along the path to a "different cultural value system" by teaching them middle-class cultural norms like negotiating with spouses and children rather than commanding or beating. Through their daily encounters with the welfare system, refugees unintentionally reinforced lessons in unequal ethnic gender citizenship for their American supervisors. The identity of the social workers depended on their daily work of "empowering" and "liberating" refugee women, even when they were also sympathetic to the men. By having the right to intervene in domestic disputes and to set new norms of gender behavior, service workers were able to redefine refugee ethnicity morally, a process that also legitimized their professional domination over impoverished, disadvantaged, and racialized Americans. Thus the helping professions have an overall effect of reforming the character of the immigrant group (with the participation of the subjects themselves), and of subordinating the men and also the community as a whole. Whatever the good intentions of individual social workers, the internal logic of compassionate domination produces this double submission—majority women dominating minority women, who dominate minority men. Various rationalities involved in shaping modern subjects have historically been entangled with and dependent on processes of subordinating "less-civilized" races, with the effect of feminizing ethnic men and masculinizing ethnic women.[35] A key aspect of feminist civilizing efforts is the desire to construct the "woman of color" as an ethical figure, a poster child of recent liberation from foreign male oppression who carries the promise of a contemporary version of the American dream. One might say that female immigrants of all classes are vulnerable to such feminist projections, as the popularity of novels about long-suffering Asian women and their postarrival liberation attest.[36]

Chapter 7

Rescuing the Children

While most poor Cambodian American families adjusted to the demands of life in urban America, conflict between parents and children became a recurring theme for some families. The previous chapter provided a glimpse of estranged and battling spouses in the community, but even more heartbreaking were struggles with children. Although fights between couples often resulted from disagreements over welfare checks or outside liaisons, conflicts with children usually stemmed from the parents' loss of moral authority over them, and the children's efforts to develop their own identities when faced with the daunting contradictions between parental expectations and the influence of the wider American society. Especially children born after 1975 lacked a shared interpretive discourse between parents' Khmer-Buddhist traditions and their own American experience that could have nurtured greater understanding and trust between the generations.[1] Many Cambodian American children (like children in general) felt that they could not learn ways of being modern by following their parents' guidance. Children of refugee parents struggled to free themselves from what they regarded as outmoded and irrelevant Cambodian family codes, while daily exposure to consumer culture, television, schools, and street gangs came to have a disproportionate influence on shaping individual identities.

Just as welfare dependency increased women's power relative to men's, so children's capacity to adjust rather quickly to American language, media, markets, streets, neighborhoods, and institutions increased their social power relative to their parents'. These external forces both undermined parents' authority and stretched their economic resources in their desperate attempt to hold the family together. Frequently the household was headed by a poor, single female. Many parents were housebound and unemployable, or living on welfare checks, or overworked in low-income jobs. Their moral authority as parents could be easily challenged by children growing up fast and eager to join the wider world. To an uncomfortable degree, parent–child relations focused on how children should save and spend their time and money. For parents, these were issues central to the collective needs and future security of the family; for children, these concerns centered on their attempts to shape their own individual American identities. They evaluated the way their parents spent time and money on them in American terms, as a measure of love. As happened with conjugal battles, cases of child abuse or threats of abuse often drew the attention of teachers, social workers, and the police. As we saw in cases involving wife battering, the helping professions blamed what was perceived to be Cambodian culture, and emphasized disciplining and reforming the parents, while taking a therapeutic approach to the children, which focused on helping them develop their self-identity.

SAVING AND SPENDING TO HOLD THE FAMILY TOGETHER

The generational divide was often unconsciously displayed in Cambodian home interiors. Lined with grass or plastic mats for communal gathering and eating, the living room was usually dominated by a huge television, a VCR, and a stereo system. This command center provided the refugees' connections to the outside world: Southeast Asian soap operas for the parents, and American TV shows and rock music for the kids. The walls were often covered with symbols of this culture clash. Sentimental pictures of Angkor Wat and of lush landscapes, a cluster of faded family photos, and drifting incense were all redolent of the lost world of an irretrievable homeland. Juxtaposed to these traditional icons were posters of fast cars, scantily clad white women, and calendar pinups of Asian starlets. The latter images seemed to provide silent assent whenever parents complained about their children's interest in spending and sex. To the teenagers, the parents' home culture did not seem to have much relevance to their desires and problems, and they complained that their parents could not help them understand or sort through their experiences of growing up in America.

Parents were now unusually dependent on their children, and struggling desperately to hold on to them. They had lost their economic independence and were acutely aware of their current devalued status in American society. Most could not speak English at all, or not well; they depended on their children to translate for them, and this relationship mildly humiliated the adults while giving school-age children unexpected power. In addition, older Cambodians could not get around easily and were afraid of the society outside the apartment complexes in which they lived. Indeed, both older and younger Cambodians were viewed as easy targets by muggers. Parents depended on their children to read street signs and to take them places. Handed such chores as dealing with the building supervisor, paying utility

mediating with people outside the family in countless ways, it is
ising that some teenagers felt that they were raising their parents,
ersa. Social workers noted that children felt that "their parents don't
know anything about the United States," and often found themselves making decisions on their parents' behalf. Even youngsters lucky enough to have
working parents found themselves often left at home unsupervised, because
their parents tended to spend long hours in low-paying jobs.

Aside from the change in the power relationship between parents and children, many children felt frustrated because their parents were unable to help
with their everyday problems of homework or growing up in America, and
could not act as models for future behavior. At the time of my study, Cambodian adolescents had either been born in the United States or arrived as
very young children, having been born in refugee camps. I met preteens who
said that although they knew in theory that their parents cared for them,
they sometimes felt unloved because their parents did not verbally express
their love to them "the way American parents say 'I love you.'" Besides, their
own parents did not interact with them the same way or engage in the kinds
of play they observed between friends and *their* parents, who took them on
picnics or to play ball in the park. At home, parent–child relations were
shaped by adult expectations of unquestioning obedience and limited verbal communication. Whatever the children learned in school about middle-
class American behavior, they were not finding it at home, and this increased
their sense of alienation, adding to the burdens of having to take on the lion's
share of household responsibilities and having fewer resources than most of
their American peers for enjoying being teenagers. Not all Cambodian families had such difficulties, of course; indeed, some young people felt happy
with their family situation and did very well in school. But as children grew
older, they sometimes felt ashamed of their parents (which seems a rather
common American phenomenon) and their inability to offer guidance on
life in America.

American high-school culture had upended the respect and gratitude
Cambodian parents expected from their children.[2] Among my informants,
many of whom were middle-aged women and single parents, the most frequently cited problem with their children was their lack of respectful behavior
toward their parents. Parents were often kept in the dark about what went
on in school—or perhaps they rarely asked, since they had had few similar
experiences themselves, and often could not read school announcements or
teachers' reports. Some children felt that their parents' input was so irrelevant that they forged their parents' signatures on their report cards. Parents
also complained that school culture taught kids to talk back, something totally unheard of in Cambodia. Some children greeted their elders like equals,
for instance by waving casually and saying "hi" instead of using the *sompeah*
(greeting by keeping the eyes down and bowing over hands held in a Bud-

dhist gesture). Although parents were exquisitely aware of their irrelevance in many aspects of their children's lives, they felt that they had made major sacrifices and endangered their own lives to bring their children to safety, or to give birth to them in a free country; so they at least deserved basic respect. Thus children's insubordination was a major source of pain and conflict that sometimes tore families apart. Although more boys than girls rebelled against their parents, the symbolic importance of a girl's virtue for the family honor caused some parents to treat girls' adventures more harshly, and also to suffer more deeply if they lost their daughters to American culture.

Consumption and sex were intertwined areas of disagreement between parents and teenagers. To teenage boys especially, money, flashy goods, and sex were part of becoming American and gaining acceptance in the wider society. Such desires threatened to drain the limited resources in many Cambodian homes. A *krou khmer* who had tried to help many families saw it this way: "When the children come to the U.S., they go to school. The schools are taught by Americans. [Consequently] they don't respect their parents very much. They follow the American ways. And then the parents get angry and beat the children." Most parents did not resort to physical punishment, especially if the father was ineffective, sick, or absent. The *krou* mentioned his sister, who was married to a crippled American soldier. They had two teenage boys who frequently brought girls home for sex. The father could not discipline the boys, and the mother was unable to refuse their demands for money to spend on their girlfriends. Once she gave them money so that one of the girls could get an abortion. Sometimes even the *krou* gave them money. He explained that in Cambodian culture, mothers sometimes so doted on their children, especially boys, that they could not discipline them:

> The mother cannot just not give. She just has to get the money somehow. The boys don't understand Buddhist tenets; that's their mores. They are like animals. I said to them, "If your mother were an American woman, you would have no right to stay here with her." You see, if their mother were an American, she would have thrown them out. But the mother is Cambodian—she loves the kids too much. She feels sorry for them far too much. Whatever they want, she gets for them. . . . If they want a car, she'd buy them a car; if they want a bike, she'd buy them a bike; if they want clothes, she'd buy them clothes. And the mother works night and day [as a bank accountant and a store owner].

This was perhaps an extreme example of the tensions between mother love and rebellious teenagers and the continual renegotiation of the Cambodian parent–child relationship. Increasingly, parents tried to compel their children's compliance by promising gifts of consumer items. For instance, a widow, Mrs. Chat, lived with a teenage daughter and a son who had just turned eighteen, and gone off welfare support. Nevertheless, he made constant demands for money to spend on movies, clothes, hairstyles, and consumer items. Mrs. Chat felt trapped between her desire to give him money and the need to save her limited income. According to her, he did not seem to have trouble in school, but he went out frequently spending money and having a good time. An older son worked as an electronics technician, and she worried whether the second son would find a job too when he graduated from high school. Her welfare support was going to cease in a few years, and she depended on her sons to take care of her when that happened.

The contrary needs of teenagers and their parents created tensions that reflected two radically different sets of survival concerns. A youth counselor touched on problems between Cambodian parents and teenage boys: "You can't say to them, 'Don't do this, don't do that'"; he explained that they desperately desired cultural conformity and acceptance, and sought it by dressing and acting like American teenagers—who were represented, in their milieu, by Vietnamese gangs and African American verbal styles.

Elderly parents, obsessed with their material needs and security, considered their children's embrace of American youth culture both distasteful and dangerous. Mrs. Suong, a sixty-two-year-old widow, had been the mother of eight children, but only a daughter and two sons had survived the war. She suffered from severe headaches and a back injury sustained in a fall.

> I worry about myself, that I am getting old and sick most of the time. And another thing . . . I am an old-fashioned woman. I don't like the way my son acts in the new style [New Wave clothing, moussed hair]. I told him not to wear an outfit I don't like, but he doesn't listen to me. He does not have a proper hairstyle, according to my way of thinking. His schoolwork is okay, but the things that bother me are his way of dressing and his going out a lot. He spends money on those clothes I don't like.
>
> I worry that when he goes out a lot, he may get into trouble with someone, or that he may get involved with bad friends. I have had three sons killed by the communists.
>
> I have two other sons, three brothers, and one sister, all missing somewhere in Cambodia. I worry about how they are living, if they are alive.

Parents wished to see their children grow up guided by basic Cambodian values, especially those of respect and gratitude toward parents, as expressed in daily behavior and in Buddhist rituals. In the past, sons could become temporary monks to gain merit for their parents, and girls could offer food and services to monks. These rituals expressed obedience and gratitude to the parents who had raised them, and enhanced the standing of the parents in the eyes of society. But in the United States, young Cambodians had little or nothing to do with Buddhist temples, and were generally ignorant about Khmer-Buddhist teaching (though with the building of more temples, a revival of some form of Khmer-Buddhism was under way). Boys' disrespectful behavior and sexual adventures were thus especially painful to parents. Despite their loss of practical power over their children, parents sought to demonstrate their moral authority by forbidding dating and by offering to arrange a "proper" marriage for them.

Phauly Sang told me that her twenty-five-year-old brother, Sichantha, fell in love and got married in the proper Cambodian way. He had obtained a certificate in electronics, but found a better job as a translator for a lawyer. For a while, he corresponded with a girl in Cambodia, but a female cousin told him to break it off with her: "She told him that he would have to start over again with the girl, and spend a lot of money . . . why not get a girlfriend here?" He finally met an eighteen-year-old girl at school. One day, when Phauly and her nephew stopped at a gas station, they saw Sichantha with his girlfriend, accompanied by her niece, in another car. When he saw them, he drove off without filling his car. He knew that Phauly, who in the United States acted as his mother, did not approve of dating. A few months later, after Phauly determined that the bride came "from a good family, not of farming origin," Sichantha and the girl were married. Phauly ticked off the reasons why this was a good match: the girl's family was polite, had no problems with friends, and got along with people. They were also "half Chinese, and had lighter skin" than other Cambodians.

The proper handling of children's courtship and marriage was a key expression of parental power and moral reputation, and it upheld the parents' status in the community.[3] For older refugees, courtship and marriage became the cultural practices that preserved their identity, and the primary way to combat some elders' fear that in America, Cambodians had lost their culture. This story seems to highlight a difference between parents from urban backgrounds and those from rural ones. There was some indication that many of the families with severe problems had peasant origins, and the adults in such families were perhaps less effective in controlling children growing up in an urban American society.[4]

Acutely aware of their eroding power, Cambodian American women resorted to old strategies—gossip and fearmongering—as a way to curb their children's more outlandish desires and adventures. Anthropologists have noted that women in agrarian societies exert social power by producing and shaping public opinion, often as a way to direct and control unacceptable behavior such as wife beating and premarital sex.[5] In Oakland, Cambodian American women revived their sisterly networks, meeting frequently at weddings and parties to exchange information and gossip, and generally to comment on what was going on in the community. Spreading urban legends about child abduction or girl gangs was a way to shape the behavior of their children, warning them of horrible things that would happen to them if they did not listen to their parents.

In fact, at the time that I was conducting research, there was a rising wave of crime against Asian children in the Bay Area, and rumors implied that

Figure 6. Children in San Francisco's Tenderloin district.

there were many unreported cases of incest as well as sexual abuse and kidnapping of Asian children in poor neighborhoods. Community-based agencies set up a program to fight the sexual abuse of Asian children; they distributed flyers, a comic book, and even a videotape in a variety of Asian
languages, including Khmer, to provide practical information needed to protect children. Social-service workers, well aware that Southeast Asian refugees
tended to avoid the police or the government, were particularly vigilant for
cases of child abuse in that community. It was not clear how reliable were
the available statistics—the press reported a 50 percent increase in child sexual abuse and kidnapping in Chinatown and San Francisco's Tenderloin district over a three-year period—or whether such statistics were compiled to
produce risk-assessment models that would help agencies gain government
funding, or as a strategy to justify interventions into the family and preempt
blame if things went wrong.

Teachers were trained to recognize signs of child abuse, and if they failed
to report their suspicions, they might be penalized by the authorities. Children of Southeast Asian immigrants were often reported as possible abuse
victims because teachers could not distinguish among bruises left by beating, the blue-black marks made by coining and other traditional forms of

dermal treatment, and even birthmarks. But the widespread suspicions and talk about harsh Southeast Asian parents intensified the perceived need for social work. A variety of community organizations also spread warnings about the dangers of allowing children to hang out, but it was never exactly clear how common such dangers were, or to what extent the nonprofit agencies were also monitoring the behavior of the parents.

RISK MANAGEMENT IN CHILD WELFARE

Nigel Parton has claimed that in neoliberal societies, child welfare has become a more "ambiguous, uncertain, and contested arena."[6] In recent years, the focus on disciplining single-parent households has expanded to include the fragmented world of other at-risk groups, such as substance abusers, the homeless, and delinquent children. Social-welfare strategies now incorporate risk education into their interventions, in order to make individuals responsible for their own prudent or imprudent actions and their consequences.[7] There is less reliance on direct disciplining (though the persistence of police beatings should warn us that strong-arm techniques are still important) than on teaching citizen-subjects techniques for dealing with risk and to take responsibility for their failure to manage risk. Because children are viewed as not yet able to manage themselves, child-welfare workers now see themselves as engaged in the management of risk to children. As part of this strategy, parents of at-risk children must be taught skills for managing the family. In my research on Cambodian families in San Francisco, social-work techniques for regulating appropriate family and individual behavior operated primarily through talking, confession, and the interiorization of norms and modes of self-expression.

The Cambodian self-help group discussed in chapter 6 provided a social-work format for troubled parents to learn to talk about their troubles, express their emotions, and take responsibility for managing risks to their children. The caseworkers, Timothy Hale and Sam Ngor, operated as partners negotiating with families in order to teach parents how to negotiate with their children. These social workers were ready to evaluate and adjust family norms, and to suggest ideas for managing children, so that some of the families determined to be at risk would not become clients of the state. Their first step was to try to teach refugee parents new techniques for talking to their children in a way that promoted a sense of autonomy within a regulated freedom. As the users and customers of such techniques, Cambodian Americans had to struggle with their own different sense of parental responsibility.

At one meeting, Mrs. Sym, a middle-aged, heavy-set woman who had been looking dejected for weeks, finally spoke up. Her forehead bore an inky mark the size of a quarter. Scraping the skin with a coin was a common Cambodian practice to release "bad wind" from the body. Mrs. Sym's vigorous scraping had engraved a scar that attested to her anguish as a refugee widow raising her children in the crime-ridden neighborhood. She began by telling about her nineteen-year-old son, who frequently cut class and hung out with a Vietnamese gang. He had smoked crack since ninth grade and had been in jail three or four times. Recently, he had broken into a car and stolen the cassette player. He was now on probation and working in a sweatshop stitching labels on Levi Strauss garments. In the past, he had worked for a short time, but had returned to gang life. He carried a gun. She complained, "He won't listen to the old people. I feel like his working does not amount to anything. He gives his money to his friends, but not to me even though he sleeps and eats at home. I can't sleep at night, and I take a lot of pills." Her sixteen-year-old son had started to hang out with another Southeast Asian gang, and had learned to steal. Mrs. Sym had a retarded teenage daughter at home, and despite receiving some outside help with the girl, she was barely coping with her many children. She also saw a counselor, who did not want to take on her entire family. Now she was requesting that the self-help group allow her eldest son to join.

Man in a green jacket: One of my sons also cuts classes. He hates the math teacher, and gets bad influence from other kids. He was a good student until he went to high school. I try to save as much money as I can, for instance, to buy him shoes, but the kid wants to buy other [kinds] that are too unattractive or too expensive.

Pang: My sixteen-year-old son wants his parents to support only himself, not others in the family.

The social workers' initial response to the breakdown of parental control and the children's alienation was to teach parents a new set of communication skills. Ngor explained that the children feared social rejection; they wanted the running shoes and clothes the other kids had. He reminded them that there were social-adjustment problems for refugee children as well as for their parents in America:

Ngor: Be more like friends; be open to the kids. Explain your reasons to them. Do not behave in an authoritarian way; be more egalitarian. We should treat our kids the middle-class way, not the commanding way. We should reason with the kids, not in a low-class way that is rigid, not open. Don't be authoritarian; listen to them, talk to them. For example, the middle-class way is to talk with reasoning; the lower-class way is "I tell you what to do."

Sino-Cambodian man: Everyone should talk to the children when they are young in order to develop an understanding with one another. When the kids are over sixteen, one should talk to them confidentially, not in front of others.

Old man: I agree, but it's a little tougher than that. Parents should
know what kinds of friends they have. One should "break"
them when they are young. Break the pattern.

Ngor: Not physical punishment, I hope.

Hale [aside to me]: The parents need to express their frustrations, and so on,
but I think they are very sensitive to children. I have actually been impressed by the men being respectful to what
women say. I guess there is equality at that level.

Ngor, who was being trained as a social worker by a refugee agency,
reflected its welfare philosophy of teaching refugees a certain set of Spockian supposedly middle-class attitudes and values. He counseled that instead
of corporal punishment, there were different parenting options that could
be used to control and guide the conduct of children—such as setting cur-
fews or taking away social privileges—that would give children the moral responsibility of working toward an agreed-upon goal. Such planning engaged
children in their own regulation; it also helped parents to identify and assess risk, and to reduce the possibility of misfortune or conflict. Ngor and
Hale struggled to teach parents such skills—the very negotiative and calcu-
lative relations that the new social work encourages between caseworkers and
client-customers.

Maybe they recognized that the parents concerned would not be effective
in adopting strict strategies because teenagers were making their own money,
and thus were in greater control of their own movements and resources—
phones, TV, music—than even their parents were. Ngor, especially sensitive
to the inversion of the conventional Cambodian parent–teenager power dynamics, emphasized the appropriateness of conciliatory parenting behavior,
while typecasting their cultural norms as lower-class and authoritarian. But
Cambodian parents felt that such methods further reduced their already
shaky authority vis-à-vis their children, and questioned the wisdom of allowing
children to play an equal role in decision making about their lives and fu-
tures. They were also concerned that children seemed to have become empowered by social workers taking their side in any conflict.

There are many long-resident Americans who would agree with the Cambodian clients that parents need to maintain their authority to set rules, and
not merely negotiate with their children. Hale, who had a different experience with refugees because of his long involvement with a sanctuary movement, was less caught up in the liberal parental ideology. He used his interpretive understanding of refugee subjects and situations as a central technique
of his practice. Instead of criticizing the parents, he valued the Cambodians'
cultural sensitivity to personal relations as something that could be a source
of strength in dealing with their children. But the message was clear: both
men advised parents to recognize the pressures their children were experi-

encing, and to negotiate with them in order to anticipate and forestall risk. This risk-management technique reconstituted the nature of the parent-clients, seeking reform by cleansing their cultural attitudes about what it meant to be parents and by substituting reasoning as a way to deal with children—who, as Americans, were considered rational subjects. Reasoning, rather than imparting the distilled wisdom of parents, was the way to get to children to change their risky behavior.

When the meeting broke up, there was a melancholy moment as people silently pondered the fact that they were losing their children to the hurly-burly world of inner-city America. Parents complained that children did not obey their wishes automatically. "The kids think, *Why should we listen to you when you did not go to school and can't speak English? What can you do for us?*" Parents now had to learn to treat their children as equals, even to promote their individual desires apart from the family's collective interests.

GIRLS AT RISK

Perhaps more than losing their sons to crack and armed robbery, losing control over their daughters' sexuality produced deep anguish and anger in parents. There seemed to be a sense that a boy who ran afoul of the law still had the possibility of being straightened out, but a daughter who lost her virginity before marriage struck a blow to (what remained of) the family honor that could seldom be overcome. As Nancy Smith-Hefner has observed among Cambodian Americans in Boston, double standards for sexual behavior in boys and girls continued to guide parents' treatment of their children. While sexual promiscuity in boys could be interpreted as a sign of virility, girls had to maintain sexual purity because it was the basis of family honor. Young boys' sexual adventures were tolerated even if not encouraged, but young girls who dated or engaged in premarital sex caused parents humiliation for losing control of their daughters, and by thus failing to guard family virtue, earning public disgrace.[8] But like many of their high-school peers, some Cambodian teenage girls started dating and having sexual relations, often without the knowledge of their parents.

The control and abuse of daughters was the major catalyst for social workers to vent criticisms of Cambodian parents and culture, and was a major source of disagreements and power struggles between parents and social workers. When it came to teenage daughters, Cambodian parents discovered that they were subjected to strong pressures to conform to middle-class norms of the freedom to date. Scholars point out that American dating—which evolved out of the notion of companionate family, a concept of family relations based more on friendship than on unequal power—began in the 1920s as a form of middle-class courtship. The practice was rooted in a rating game for displaying male money and female sexual appeal in public:

Figure 7. Little girls must stay close to their mothers.

Linda Stone and Nancy McKee say that "American prewar dating was often a frenzied, competitive, materialistic, impersonal, individualistic struggle to continually demonstrate popularity among peers."[9] After World War II, the average age at which people got married dropped, and dating began even in the early teens, as a kind of training for (serial) monogamy (American teenage mothers received a warm welcome then!). The goal of dating was not sexual gratification, though sexual activity did happen, but rather to provide training for individual girls to set sexual boundaries.[10] Teenage dating became standard middle-class conduct, but parental strategies about dating ranged from the most permissive to regulation of age limits, types of friends and outings, and curfew hours.

In contrast, Khmer notions about courtship in the 1980s required the potential suitor to come calling (as in nineteenth-century America), and to demonstrate respect and general usefulness to the girl's parents in their home. Little or no interaction between couples was allowed before engagement. Phauly Sang, who was college educated, told me that in Phnom Penh in the early 1970s, it was only after she got engaged that she was allowed to stroll along the river bank with her fiancé for the first time. In other words, the parents, not the girl herself, set social and sexual barriers until their daughter's marriage; and these norms had changed little in parents' minds as the families moved to America. Furthermore, in an environment of relentless gossip about women's compromised virtue in America, parents of young girls were especially vigilant. Compared to their Americanized daughters, they were more concerned about the honor of the family, and did not see the need for daughters to explore and test their responsibility as growing sexual subjects. Indeed, they viewed with horror the idea of girls exploring sex with boys. Too many Cambodian American girls, in their parents' view, wanted to become like other American teenagers.

American officials working with Cambodian families, however, regarded such Khmer views about teenage sexuality as a problem to be managed. In conflicts over controlling teenage behavior, culture came to be objectified as an element to be used—by social workers or lawyers—in ways that demonstrate that immigrant groups such as Cambodians were judged rather differently from long-resident American groups.

Runaway Girl, 1

One hot and muggy day, I arrived at the downtown community center for the meeting of the self-help group. Negotiating my pregnant body through the untidy tangle of chairs rescued from the street, I anticipated another afternoon of listening to the usual litany of problems that came with being poor and living in the ghetto. Flamboyantly dressed sex workers, transgendered people, and street activists were milling around the door, getting ready for their meeting, as an austere, middle-aged couple discreetly took seats at the back of our room. Mr. and Mrs. Chou were a Sino-Cambodian couple who operated a family business in the neighborhood, but I had never seen them at the meeting before. While the self-help group had a set of regular participants, it had gradually become as well an informal drop-in meeting for other Cambodians who needed emergency help and a stepping stone to the authorities. When the meeting ended, the Chou couple came up to the social workers and in stammering tones reported that a few days earlier, their fourteen-year-old girl, Lynn, had not returned from school, and they had not heard from her since. Children in the neighborhood did get lost occasionally, and they feared that Lynn, who was sociable and fun-loving, might have been abducted.

Over the next few days, Ngor and Hale talked to officials at Lynn's school and to her friends. They soon discovered that Lynn had moved in with her boyfriend's family, who were Salvadoran refugees. Hale was relieved and elated. He had known Lynn since she was a little girl, and he showed me a picture of a curvy young woman in a fuchsia gown, her vivacious face framed by highly moussed hair. He said, "It's wonderful; the kids are madly in love!" Ngor noted dryly that many such cases of interracial romance did not last. He pointed out that Lynn was Buddhist and could not speak Spanish, while her boyfriend was Catholic and could understand neither Khmer nor Chinese. Their English was still not very good, and neither was yet old enough to drive a car. But Hale was tickled pink; there was something quintessentially American, he felt, in this Cambodian-girl-meets-Salvadoran-boy tale. The boy's parents had treated Lynn very nicely, and told him that if the pair were getting married, they should tell her parents. School officials sent Lynn for counseling, and she was finally persuaded to call her parents. Mr. and Mrs. Chou had been so traumatized by Lynn's running away from home that they tried to do what she wanted and accepted the affair—which eventually became a shotgun marriage, causing them much anger and shame. They began to attend the group meeting regularly, not to talk about Lynn but to draw on the communal support in silence.

If this case had involved nonimmigrant Americans, a marriage involving a fourteen-year-old girl would have been annulled, and her older boyfriend (who was not yet twenty-one) would have been charged with contributing to the delinquency of a minor or with statutory rape. I do not know the details of the arrangement between the court and Lynn's parents, but it seems clear that some kind of "cultural defense" appeal (a claim that the young people's cultural assumptions justified, at least in part, their actions) might have been used to make an exception in this case of juvenile truancy. Indeed, with the influx of multicultural immigrant cases flooding into courts, more and more defense attorneys in situations involving Hmong kidnap-marriage practices *(zij poj niam)*, Japanese rituals of parent–child suicide, and even wives killed by husbands who suspected them of adultery—have resorted to the cultural-defense argument in order to reduce the defendant's sentence.[11] In a Brooklyn case, a "Kampuchean man and his Kampuchean girlfriend" kidnapped and killed her mother, who had allegedly opposed their relationship. According to a journalist covering the case, the girl's defense attorney planned to use a cultural defense by demonstrating that "she was just following orders, submitting to the dictates of her man—in accordance with the roles indigenous to her native Kampuchea."[12] The stress on the exotic Kampuchean worldview, and the assumed passivity of the "girlfriend" seemed intended to reduce her culpability as a partner in murder.

In these cases, the expertise of social scientists such as anthropologists has been used to reinforce or refute cultural difference as a mitigating circumstance in the adjudication of criminal cases involving new immigrant and minority groups. Clearly, the *culture* used in this fashion is often invoked as a wholly static, homogenized, or stereotypical entity, just one more weapon in the arsenal of legal combat. The cultural defense has become a highly contested issue among immigrant advocates and legal-aid societies, including those that are supportive of immigrants' rights. Indeed, when cultural difference is raised in court cases, the tendency of experts such as attorneys and psychiatrists has been to dismiss, or to demonize, it as an obstacle to teaching newcomers about the supposed impartiality of the American legal system. In Lynn's case, whatever cultural motivations inspired her actions or those of her Salvadoran partner, their Californian update of *West Side Story* stirred the sentiments of social workers, who sought to make sure that no one got hurt when star-crossed lovers transgressed the lines between different communities.

A few months later, a big Cambodian-Salvadoran wedding celebration was held at what the Cambodians considered the best Chinese restaurant in the neighborhood. The entire self-help group was invited. The Cambodian and Salvadoran parents of the happy couple could not speak to each other, and I was told that the Chinese restaurant, rather than a temple or church, was considered a neutral enough place for Catholicism and Buddhism to meet. Despite the obvious differences, the two communities—as war refugees arriving in the same era, living in the same part of town, and being to an extent socialized in the same local schools and even by the same set of social workers—probably had more in common (welfare dependency, eroding parental authority, assertive youngsters, the pressures of American youth culture) than one would have suspected at first glance.

In this case, the strategies of the young lovers respected neither the customs nor the cherished wishes of their parents. Perhaps even more urgently in diaspora than in their homeland, Cambodian parents wanted to have proper marriages for their children, especially daughters, as a way to raise their social status in the eyes of the community. Lynn's escapade resulted not only in a humiliating loss of face (premarital sex, shotgun wedding) but also in the loss of their daughter to a different cultural community. Because of the institutional similarities in refugee ethnic formation in the Bay Area, Lynn and her husband had much in common, but her parents grieved over their sense of the irretrievable loss of her cultural identity. In their view, American culture, institutions, and officials had abetted in this loss.

Runaway Girl, 2

America in the 1980s saw a crisis in child welfare, with widespread allegations of child abuse in day-care centers as well as in homes. State agents, whose encounters with refugee families happened mainly in the context of domestic violence, saw their role as protecting children on the one hand, and preserving the family (after it underwent some sort of treatment) on the other. In dealing with other American families, social workers might have been more worried about balancing the need to provide supportive, preventive service with trying not to undermine parental responsibility. But in the case of poor minority families, they were more ready to impose specific norms and constraints on the parents' treatment of their children. Social workers, for instance, were on the lookout for at-risk children and for signs and symptoms of child abuse among minority populations. Indeed, they were made morally culpable for failing to report any suspicions, and their zeal sometimes resulted in embarrassing and humiliating experiences for innocent par-

ents. In the case described here, the child beating was real, and various social, judicial, and medical experts and agencies got involved in trying to balance power and responsibility. But in the process of teaching the parents
lessons about children's rights, they also profoundly demoralized the parents, who came to feel that they had lost all their own rights.

Anita Mouly left home after her father beat her for secretly going on dates
and staying out late. Anita only wanted her parents to stop beating her, but
the involvement of Child Protective Services (CPS) in her case magnified
her power vis-à-vis her parents, creating a rift that could not be mended. This
case illustrates the wide gulf between Cambodian and American attitudes
about teenage girls and their responsibilities regarding public behavior and
sexual conduct.

The following account is told entirely from Mrs. Mouly's point of view.
She told me the story a couple of months after Anita was returned to the
family, and though her daughter was back, her mind and heart remained
troubled. The family had arrived in the United States sponsored by Mormons,
and they converted in 1985. According to her mother, soon after Anita
turned sixteen, she began coming home from school late in the evenings,
sometimes after ten-thirty at night. Mrs. Mouly complained that Anita's excuse always was that she went to the Mormon Church to get help with her
homework after school:

> Her father was mad because she was out gallivanting with a boy, and she never
> called to tell us where she was going. But people had seen her and said she
> wasn't at the church but with a boy. At this lie, he grew madder and beat her.
> She was always out quite late, and we were ashamed . . . this went on for six
> months before we first beat her. That's when my husband really beat her; he
> beat her until the electrical cord snapped.

A few days after the beating, Anita was visited by a Mormon church worker.
The next day, she left for school and did not return, presumably taking initial refuge in the church worker's house. Later on the night that Anita did
not return home, the police came to arrest Anita's father, but he was not in.
Mrs. Mouly quickly phoned him to stay away for a few days. Mr. Mouly was
finally charged with resisting arrest, and his wife borrowed money from
friends to bail him out of jail. Still shaken by the shock of what had happened,
she tried to explain to me why Anita was beaten:

> According to our customs, if you go gallivanting with a boy, people will say
> that your parents have not brought you up properly. When she goes around
> with a boy, the neighbors, they watch her and laugh at us. Our customs . . . we
> don't allow kids to fall in love with each other like that. The parents would
> first observe each other, and if they approved, they would approach the par-
> ents to ask for the daughter. . . . But you just don't let them go off by them-
> selves, just the two of them. For us Cambodians, that is very shameful. From

what I have observed, my daughter has slept with her boyfriend, perhaps. This kid follows the American way through and through, and not one bit of Cambodian ways.

The day Anita did not return home, her teacher called to inform the parents that their daughter was safe, but she did not want to talk to them. Acting on a report, perhaps filed by Anita's teacher with the advice of the social worker, CPS obtained a court order to detain Anita. She was subsequently declared to be a dependent child of the juvenile court who was to be temporarily removed from the custody of her parents. For several months, the Moulys could not talk to their daughter, nor did they know her whereabouts (they suspected that she was staying in the home of the Mormon worker). Mrs. Mouly showed me the court papers. The CPS caseworker reported,

> The minor has shared her pain at being intimidated by family members in some phone calls and is very uncomfortable when she is harassed about coming home or dropping charges of felony abuse, or called a person who is shaming her family. She feels shamed, but more because she cannot feel like returning to her parents as long as they are without counseling help and they do not understand her struggles.

Since the 1960s, child-protection practices have been primarily concerned with the physical safety of the child victim, but CPS still adheres to the belief that the family, with therapeutic intervention, can be saved as well. "Modern policies favor 'temporary' removal from the home, either of the victim or the abuser, combined with therapy for both. . . . The battered child remains in protective custody while the parent enters a treatment program."[13] In Anita's case, the court determined that she was to be reunited with her parents after six months if they demonstrated compliance with orders to seek mental-health counseling and promised to refrain from beating their children again. Mrs. Mouly described her weekly lessons at the Asian mental-health clinic:

> They told us not to beat the kid. They would say, "Can you stop doing it? Stop beating the kid, or the wife. When you're mad, can you refrain from beating them?" My husband says it is difficult to have trouble here in America. Even when they lecture to us the same things over and over again, it is difficult. "They shake us mentally and would not let us live in peace, and it throws our hearts into turmoil."

In seeking to resolve Anita's case, social workers, therapists, and court psychiatrists all insisted on teaching the parents three things: not to beat their children, that American teenagers have a god-given right to go out dating, and a narrow set of parenting options for supervising teenage dating. The strictness of the conditions for releasing the girl back to her parents was heavily influenced by the view that Cambodian mores of parenting and supervision of daughters had to be entirely erased, in order that the children might become autonomous American subjects.

It was not clear from Mrs. Mouly's account whether CPS had intervened to sweeten the mental-health regime by having the authorities offer the family government-subsidized housing. But the use of material resources as leverage to encourage poor families to overcome their moral failures and become deserving citizens has had a long history.[14] The Moulys simply learned that they were going to get state help that would make them "better parents." They received a subsidized three-bedroom house in the suburbs, which was a vast improvement over their previous crowded apartment. When their daughter returned, she was to get her own bedroom. Social services helped Mr. Mouly, who had been unemployed, get a job as a yard worker. The trade-off, they understood, was their submission to social disciplining and moral makeover.

In the clinic and the court, the experts went beyond punishment for child abuse to what seemed to the Moulys to be destruction of their authority as parents. Over time, as they requested visitation with Anita, the focus of the officials' concerns shifted from child abuse to letting children go out dating; they had to become like mainstream American parents. The outcome of such requirements could only be interpreted by them as a state attack on their culture itself. Beyond defending Anita's rights not to be abused, the court encroached on the rights of her parents to be her moral guardians:

> They told us that the American way here is different from the Cambodian way over there. You cannot apply the rules from over there to here, because the kids grow up here. They have to be allowed to have boyfriends. The doctors told us how things are in America, how our kids can go out and that we cannot stop them from going out. They just teach us these things, once a week.

At the clinic, the parents had the therapists' mantra, "They have to be allowed to have boyfriends," drummed into their heads—something therapists would think twice over before ordering native-born parents to allow. To Mrs. Mouly, this loss of control over her daughter's social life seemed a total abdication of her power as a parent:

> The doctors asked what Anita wants for her to come home. She just wanted to be able to go out to eat after school and for us not to be mad at her, and that she'd call to see if it's okay. And that Fridays and Saturdays when they want to go out together, if it's okay to go out till 11:00 P.M. or midnight. So I asked the doctor to help me think through the situation, because for me, if I won't let them go, I'm afraid it would be against the law. The doctor says [our daughter's request] is appropriate, it sounds right. So I signed the paper because there had been so much trouble.

It seems that the therapists and the court came up with a very impoverished model of parenting for the Moulys, who were subjected to the kind of reg-

ulation that no American-born middle-class parents would take lying down.
There is a wide range of parenting options between beating and giving in
entirely to the wishes of children. The only parental authority the social workers allowed the Moulys was the dating curfew, and even that limit was set by
the court and not by the parents themselves. The rules for Anita's dating
seemed very Spockian and ones that even "liberal" middle-class American
parents across the racial-ethnic divide might find excessively permissive. They
were advised to be their children's friends, and were put in the position of
having to justify their values and norms of responsible parenting, which constitutes a very serious breach of family privacy. It seems clear that while social workers and therapists might shrink from imposing such norms on the
"average" middle-class family, they had no such qualms in their zeal to reform or remove what they saw as Cambodian cultural practices, addressing
issues that went far beyond the beating. Ironically, Mrs. Mouly's complaints
about the intervention of social workers sound by contrast very "modern"
and no less up-to-date American than do the wishes of Anita and her complaints about her parents' antiquated family values.

Meanwhile, for much of the year, gossip in the Cambodian community
swirled around the family, mostly casting blame on the girl for bringing her
parents such shame. The case ignited fearmongering on a grand scale, as
parents took the opportunity to warn their would-be adventurous daughters to think about the shame they would suffer for such foolishness. A friend
of the family reported that Anita finally agreed to see her parents after a
few months:

> She just visited, and her parents sat down and talked to her. They said if you
> come back, we'll buy you a car or something like that. But she said, "If I come
> back, you don't look down on me or my boyfriend when he comes to visit me."
> See, her parents don't like her ways, but she always asks them to follow her
> rules. The parents of her boyfriend, when they see the girl like that, they won't
> want her either. They'd say she's the type who finds it easy to have boyfriends,
> they'd say that "she's no good." That's my culture.

In other words, although Cambodian women I spoke with did not like the
fact that the girl was severely beaten, they felt in retrospect that it was somewhat justified because she had brought great shame to her family, especially
after the court got involved, giving her an inordinate amount of power relative to her parents. She was also viewed as someone who totally rejected the
key values of Cambodian culture, and some women thought they should pressure her boyfriend's parents to reject her as well. A friend of Mrs. Mouly's
felt that this would be the right thing to do, because Cambodian Americans
had to retain their basic values of parental moral authority and children's
obedience: "I can say that this is a problem. Some of the families right now,
they copy from the American lifestyle. They say that if they're just going out

on a date, it's fine, just tell the parents. Some are still really Cambodian, and they feel that you don't have to do like the Americans." Clearly, the refugee community was beginning to think through the whole issue of parenting, and considering whether parents should forgo any form of physical punishment and permit their female children to date. There were, after all, many other cases of parent–child disputes over dating in which the families succeeded in working out some accommodation without resorting to the kind of beating administered to Anita. Some also suggested that maybe the community should not be so critical of young people who acted like other American teenagers; better to give them some freedom than to lose them entirely to "American culture." At the same time, they felt embarrassed that Cambodian culture was made to look bad as a result of this case.

The court order to allow Anita to date was reinforced by supporting documents that used the language of cultural difference to justify disciplining her parents. The caseworker's deposition presented the parents as uncaring people living by barbaric rules. It detailed Mr. Mouly's abuse of his daughter as lasting for four hours, saying that he hit her in the face and on the head, breast, and legs, leaving welts and open wounds. "The mother failed to protect the child or to get medical treatment for her." The caseworker noted that Mr. Mouly had suffered "tremendous stress" under the Khmer Rouge in Cambodia and because of the child-abuse charges. Nevertheless, the assessment went on to describe Anita as a victim not only of parental abuse, but also of Cambodian culture:

> The therapist sees the father as very possessive of the minor and primitive emotionally toward her and still operates under the cultural rights in Cambodia to rule over, demand of and perhaps even be justified in killing the minor, himself and other family members when he is shamed and angered. The father has acknowledged that this is unacceptable and punishable behavior in this country, but he is in the middle of two different systems and emotionally traumatized. He will require further counseling to understand why he used corporal punishment over time and how to cope with raising children and the stresses of life in a different cultural value system, and how his past stresses feed into his current adaptive behavior.

Thus, using the Moulys' ethnicity to punish them, the court recommended continuing counseling. Only by cooperating with the child-welfare workers could they hope to be reunited with Anita. Cambodian observers also chafed at the idea that the parents were reduced, in materialist American fashion, to the position of trying to buy Anita back with a car, just as the new subsidized house had bought their compliance with the permissive parenting rules imposed by doctors and lawyers. While this system of unequal exchange may seem to bear some similarity to traditional Cambodian notions of patron–clientelism, those relationships existed in an atmosphere of respect. From the perspective of the Cambodians, CPS's removal of the child, the court injunctions, and the mental-health stipulations represented a profound departure from the ethos that they believed should shape the flows of resources and services.[15]

Meanwhile, Anita stayed with the Mormon worker who had contacted CPS for her; there she led what under ideal circumstances Americans would consider a normal teenage life. An A student, she received a scholarship to attend a private high school and was enrolled in an advanced college-preparatory curriculum. She also attended a summer camp for refugee children and spent a day at Disneyland. She even had a supportive boyfriend. The caseworker's deposition continued,

> The minor's boyfriend is sensitive to the minor's anxiety and has provided support for her. He is able to comply with the foster home rules of being home on time from social activities with the minor. The minor shows much strength in attempting to form an identity as a Cambodian young person in an American culture, and one who is motivated to achieve high grades in school to prepare for college.

At the six-month reunification hearing, Mrs. Mouly's fears that Anita had been culturally transformed while in foster care seemed confirmed when they were finally allowed to see her in court. "When we saw our daughter for the first time in months, she didn't cry. The parents saw the kid and started to cry, but the kid saw the parents and just ignored them like an American. She didn't cry." The court ruled that Anita's parents had changed and were willing to comply with the therapists' guidelines on how to deal with her. Henceforward, they were not to beat their children, and were to negotiate with their teenage daughter rather than demand that she follow their rules.

Mrs. Mouly showed me a letter that Anita wrote to the judge, a letter that perhaps reflected a process of having thought through the voices and views of her sponsor and doctors rather than having truly come to terms with the complexity of the situation. Indeed, I tend to read the letter as evidence of the influence of social workers who were invested in the child's individuality, focusing on her potential and their knowledge of her emerging subjectivity:

> I wish the criminal charges on my father be dropped. . . . My father has gone through terrible times here in America. Also, he doesn't understand me nor himself. . . . I finally accept the fact that he is my father and no matter what he does to me he would always be still my father, my flesh and blood. . . .
>
> My father need not be punished more for what he did. All he needs is time and guidance which he is getting now. He just needs to learn about the Westernized way of raising children. He has grown up in an environment where parents always abused their kids as a way to discipline them. . . . I'm willing to give my father the opportunity to improve. . . . I believe that counseling is the

answer to my parents' needs at this point. I know I'm not perfect. I'm a pretty
rebellious young woman.

Unlike her parents—who were judged, disciplined, and punished by the
courts and medical services—Anita was encouraged to be an autonomous
subject, within the limits of regulated dependency on child experts. She came
to internalize the views of her helpers about what being a normal American
girl was like. She learned to express herself as an independent subject, who
had a future for which she was planning.

I could not speak with Anita, and in fact her mother did not want me to
talk with her. But the note reveals considerable ambivalence about the punishment and humiliation dealt to her father: "My father need not be punished more for what he did." Like so many children of immigrants, Anita
was caught between her parents' class background and her own class aspirations. In fact, as a study by Maggie Scarf reveals, this generational disjunction has affected family dynamics in many troubled American middle-
class families as well.[16] For poor immigrants' bright children like Anita, and
perhaps Lynn, having access to middle-class expectations and material conditions contributed to their view of their own parents as overly strict, stingy,
and more—attitudes that appeared to their parents as simple disrespect
and selfishness. Cambodian American teenagers, especially girls, confessed
to me their sense of material and cultural deprivation after learning—in
school, in church, on TV—about what was possible for them in America, while
their parents could not even guess at, much less guide, their aspirations. But
many immigrant children quickly learned their legal rights, and they realized that they could compel changes in the treatment they received from
their parents.

At a parent–teen forum held in the Tenderloin, Southeast Asian teenagers
performed two skits about parent–child disputes arising out of dating and
sex. Both ended with parental tirades or the threat of worse punishment. One
of the teenage performers said, "We don't know what we're supposed to do.
We do what's cool. If you yell at us, we'll get mad back. We just want to act
our age. This is how we are," which garnered applause from the audience. A
man defended the parents, remarking, "There is a saying in Vietnamese that
goes, 'If you love your children, don't let them know.' So even if they can only
express their love by showing anger, you must keep in mind that there is always love there." The mediating psychiatrist advised the parents to listen to
their children's problems and to refer the children to an older sibling or a
counselor if they felt too embarrassed or uninformed to help.[17]

After Anita returned home, Mrs. Mouly confessed to feeling estranged
from her and having to be careful about her wishes and desires. She felt especially uncomfortable when Anita's date came over, and she tried to shield
her younger girls from the young couple's necking and more on the sofa

in the living room. Indeed, such behavior would not be tolerated in many middle-class and working-class families, no matter what parenting model was being imposed by social workers. In some parts of the country, parents unable to correct such behavior in their children, boys and girls alike, have resorted to sending their troublesome children to state institutions. The Moulys had no choice but to tolerate it, since they themselves were under the eye of the authorities.

> Now, with all these problems, I don't pay much attention to the Khmer customs. They are as different from American ones as the earth from the sky. So I have stopped adhering to Cambodian ways. Your heart tells you that you can't apply the Khmer ways to the children, but when the children do this, the heart is still Khmer, it is still angry, still resentful. In his heart, my husband is troubled, truly troubled, but he doesn't know what to do. He just has to put up with it—having to see with his own eyes her staying out late, that she has the legal rights, because we have already signed all those things.

The Moulys felt they had signed away their rights over Anita, and potentially over the younger children. They tiptoed around Anita, imagining that they were still on probation. From their perspective, the loss of their child seemed like an excessive punishment for the child's abuse: they had been thrice humiliated, first by Anita's concealment of her dating, then by the gossip mill in the Cambodian American community, and finally by the entire institutional assemblage of church, court, and clinic. Not only had they lost face, they had been associated with a mental-health facility, which Cambodians viewed as a place for crazy people. Worst of all, even though Anita had physically returned home, they no longer felt they had custody over her. She belonged to the state. The bigger lesson for the Moulys was that they lost privacy just when they were becoming American enough to appreciate it. They also discovered that while their parental authority could be defended in terms of cultural difference, the same term could be invoked to discipline them. Indeed, while social agents and experts sought to guide and advise them about being better parents, at the end of the process they found themselves to be, for lack of a better expression, culturally unfit parents in America.

· · ·

In this and the previous four chapters, I have discussed how various and even contradictory rationalities intersecting in the refugee industry, the medical services, the welfare office, the drop-in neighborhood center, and the courthouse converged to shape Cambodian refugees into some kind of American citizen-subjects. These encounters comprised a complex mix of labeling, disciplining, and regulatory technologies for, on the one hand, remaking the subjectivities of the newcomers and, on the other, a self-construction on the part of the clients and customers as they variously internalized, rejected, or criticized the norms and standards for becoming autonomous, knowing subjects. In various domains, the programs and practices included defining refugee subjects in racialized, classed, and gendered terms; medicalizing disease and disobedience; reconstituting family and gender relations; promoting a feminist concept of self-empowerment; and risk-management strategies for dealing with children. These regulatory regimes not only restructured family life, they also issued dominating judgments about Cambodian patriarchy, and directly and indirectly promoted the interests of women and children over those of men. Overlapping fields of knowledge—refugee studies, medicine, welfare, law, and feminism—were technologies of power that defined and directed their clients in everyday life, with the goal of constituting citizen-subjects who were self-reliant, productive, provident, and free. Cambodian Americans in turn learned to assess, use, deflect, and combat the forms and norms of regulation, depending on their specific interests and reading of the values encoded in these citizenship lessons.

Such encounters with state bureaucracies—many of which were occasioned by domestic conflicts—produced complex lessons about individual autonomy within structures of patronage, about the limits of supposedly universal citizenship rights within ethno-racial hierarchies, and about self-empowerment within a regulated freedom. Clearly, one crucial lesson of ethnic clientship was that the assertion of individual independence seemed most effective when the law could be invoked, with the help of teachers, social workers, and the police. Social workers and therapists disseminated middle-class norms of parenting along with messages that could only be read as cultural cleansing, even when a cultural defense was invoked. Their preferred clients were women and children, who learned the social necessity of dealing with social workers in their efforts to obtain outside resources and power, as well as how to navigate and manipulate the rules and sources of authority (patriarchal, psychiatric, legal) in pursuit of their own interests. There was a particular investment in young people, aimed at fostering self-actualization through the internalization of dominant codes and the pursuit of personal projects.

These technologies thus shaped an ethical subjectivity for the autonomous, self-knowing citizen. While other studies have stressed the economic motivations and effects of the helping professions, these chapters have focused on the mundane ways they variously constitute the relations, ideas, and actions of new citizens. The next section looks at how, for some young Cambodian Americans, the project of remaking one's interior self, and of redefining one's relation to self and to others, was pursued in religious and market spheres.

PART III

Church and Marketplace

Chapter 8

The Ambivalence of Salvation

Pilots flying over the night skies of the northern San Francisco Bay Area seldom miss noticing a multispired temple looming out of the Oakland hills, a beacon of light that helps guide some safely to their destination. At night or in broad daylight, this white temple, evocative of a fairyland palace, can be seen by Cambodian Americans living in the flatlands of East Oakland (figure 8). For many young refugees, the temple of the Church of Jesus Christ of Latter-Day Saints (commonly called the Mormon Church)[1] represented a guide to the mysteries of salvation and redemption to be found in middle-class America.

Although most Cambodians were introduced to a range of Western churches in the refugee camps, the Mormon Church became a major institution providing a refuge for young Cambodian people from inner-city blight, and an initiation into what suburban American dreams can be about. Indeed, Protestantism appeals to many non-Western immigrants for providing, among other things, the idea of belonging not only in this life, but also in the afterlife.[2] In a late twentieth century dominated by population flows and migration to metropolitan areas, the Mormon Church, which Harold Bloom has called "this most original and imaginative product of American religion,"[3] has become a powerful force in the process of converting poor immigrants to white respectability, just as it has been extraordinarily successful in recruiting converts located throughout the Asia Pacific to an American middle-class ethos of clean living, hard work, and success. Although the Mormon Church has had a problematic relationship with American society, to many disadvantaged newcomers, the Mormons seem to represent the white bourgeois image and values that epitomize success in the majority society.

As Bloom has noted, Mormonism is not orthodox Christianity, and

Figure 8. The Mormon Church is a kind of promised land: the Church of Jesus Christ of Latter-Day Saints in Oakland, California.

throughout their history Mormons have been maligned as spiritual counterfeits by mainstream denominations of Protestantism, as well as being regulated by the state for the practice of polygamy in the nineteenth century and beyond. Most Americans have always viewed Mormonism as a religion on the American spiritual periphery, a deviant, clannish, and acquisitive countercultural challenge to modern American society. But in Bloom's view, America is a post-Christian nation, and Mormonism is the main example of what he calls the "American religion," which fundamentally celebrates the pre-Christian tradition of individual divinity. While Mormons would be offended at being described as post-Christian, Bloom makes a compelling argument that the church is actually deeply American. Far from being deviant, this homegrown religion of a pariah group—precisely because of its history of striving for assimilation in the American mainstream; its adoption of the tenets of the nuclear family, matrimonial sanctity, and individual material success; and its spread among affluent Westerners—is very attractive to contemporary outsiders and newcomers to the country.

We have considered how Cambodian refugees are normalized as refugee citizens, and their own active role in inviting and deflecting the schemes of control in health and welfare agencies. Outside the state sector, Cambodian Americans, especially young people, seek other forms of guidance to cultivate a modern self in some American fashion. It should not be surprising that religion is the other domain in which compassionate care can be found for disadvantaged and impoverished newcomers seeking to make it in the land of the free. The Christian paternalism invoked by slave owners found new life in the post–New Deal constellation of faith-based institutions that, willy-nilly, provide material and moral help to the disadvantaged. Recently, Christian paternalism was given a boost by members of the Republican Party who invoke "compassionate conservatism," an ideology that rejects the welfare state and directs the poor to seek help outside the federal safety net in faith-based programs. The hope is that such private charitable institutions will treat people not as clients or dependents, but as moral individuals with responsibilities and duties, and capable of self-governance.[4] For some Cambodian refugees, the Church of Jesus Christ of Latter-Day Saints provided lessons in the forging of an American moral discipline, patriarchalism, and individual responsibility, along with access to white middle-class mainstream society. Thus the Mormon Church offered an alternative modernity to that of secular state institutions, seeking to inculcate modern methods of discipline and situate newcomers within a sacralized global hierarchy of ethno-racial positioning and possibilities.[5]

For poor immigrants like the Cambodians, turning to dominant institutions is often a way of gaining majority white acceptance and, not unexpectedly, of finding the language to articulate an individualized identity. Earlier chapters considered the ways Cambodians learned to negotiate institutional rules that provide access to resources; this chapter focuses on ways they learned to negotiate cultural rules to gain the signs of white respectability that were crucial to realizing an American success story. For the first generation of young Cambodians, becoming American entailed an obligatory submission to American institutions, but also the obligation to invent themselves in contradistinction to both their own cultural backgrounds (as represented by their parents) and the dominant norms of white society. As should be clear by now, the processes of being-made and self-making do not entail a simple opposition of hegemonic American culture and minority culture, but rather a reworking of the tensions between paternalistic compassion and self-reliance, spiritual discipline and racial subordination, and church regulation and the crafting of a moral personhood. This interlacing of assimilation and self-invention always bears the traces of cultural loss, and we will see how, in their turn toward the Mormon Church, Cambodian Americans attempted to reinterpret Khmer-Buddhist values and integrate them into Mormonism. This process can be seen in the context of an American tradition identified by Max Weber, that church membership endows moral qualification for business activities.[6] Young men and women in rebellion against their parents sometimes found in Mormonism an alternative moral order that taught obedience to the church as a way to build up creditworthiness, a kind of entrepreneurial individualism for the market society. What did Cambodian Americans find appealing about the Latter-Day Saints (LDS) Church, and how did they balance its compassionate domination with their search for a modern self? How did young Cambodians respond to church discourses about an entrepreneurial ethos and a conservative sexuality? Why are there distinctively gendered strategies as Cambodian Americans explored the possibilities of class mobility through gaining churchgoing respectability? By considering conversion testimonials, religious practices, and gender differences, I found that Cambodians not only turned to the church for resources and lessons in class mobility, but also sought a language for expressing their individual truths, within an implicit racial ranking.

THE MORMON CHURCH AND ITS ASIAN RECRUITS

The Mormon Church was founded in 1830 by Joseph Smith, a Protestant revivalist driven out of New York first to the Midwest, and then the West.[7] With its headquarters in Utah, the church today is organized in geographical units subdivided into areas, regions, stakes, and wards. In the northern Bay Area, the church is organized by stakes, which are city-based units; they are further subdivided into local branches (wards) for each ethnic or racial group. For instance, the Oakland stake has separate wards for Tongans, Japanese, Chinese, Vietnamese, Filipinos, Hispanics, African Americans, and white members. In other parts of California, there are also Mormon wards for Laotians, Hmongs, Koreans, Samoans, and mixed Asian groups. While Mormons stress that the composition of wards is determined by language spoken and geographical location, nevertheless, in practice these wards tend to be structured along ethno-racial lines, and thus reinforce these differences in the constitution of American middle-class belonging.[8] In any case, this is the understanding of Cambodian refugees, who accept that different cultural or ethnic groups belong to different wards. The northern Bay Area stake represents, in microcosm, the church mapping of ethnic and racial hierarchy under the moral leadership of white American men, who at the pinnacle are represented by the Quorum of the Twelve Apostles and headed by the president, who is believed to be a living prophet.

The decade of the 1980s saw major growth for Mormonism in California, partly because of the large influx of peoples from all over the world; during that time, the church became truly multicultural, bringing even the smallest groups, such as Tongans and Hmongs, into its fold. A Mormon officer for the western states noted, "We are not just proselytizing the suburbs. This is an era when we're getting into the inner city, creating small church units and re-establishing a sense of neighborhood among African Americans in Los Angeles."[9] In the northern Bay Area, there were two wards for the Cambodians, each led by a white bishop, with overall membership fluctuating between five hundred and eight hundred. Although each ward organized its own services and activities, it appeared that young members from the different wards were encouraged to mingle on the basketball court, in the gym, and at dance parties held each month in an affluent suburban Mormon center. In everyday church activities, interactions across wards tend to be limited to those with white Mormons. Besides the wards, all Mormons are organized by age and gender groupings: teenage girls (twelve to eighteen years old) into the Young Women Society, their male counterparts into the Aaronic Priesthood.

Patriarchy is central to the religion, given the male priesthood, which entitles males to special powers on earth and in heaven. At twelve, boys considered worthy are ordained to "hold the priesthood," which endows them with supernatural powers such as the ability to exorcise evil and perform miraculous healing. All worthy ordained Mormon men believe they possess the power to act on behalf of God, and to be the "head of the house." Deborah Laake quotes from a lesson manual for fourteen-year-old boys:

> The patriarchal order is of divine origin and will continue throughout time and eternity. There is, then, a reason why men, women, and children should understand this order and this authority in the households of the people of God. . . . It is not merely a question of who is perhaps most qualified. Neither is it a question of who is living the most worthy life. It is a question largely of law and order.[10]

While boys are schooled to believe that they can become gods, girls are taught that they can also become immortal, but only by bearing their husbands' "spirit children throughout eternity."[11] Adult women, referred to as Sisters, are excluded from ultimate decision-making authority, but they carry out church work through the Relief Society. Among the Cambodian converts, most were Young Women and Sisters; there were very few Cambodian men who had been ordained to the priesthood.

In recent years, this racially ordered and gender-stratified religion has spread throughout the Asia Pacific, becoming "a vast, global ethnoscape mandating and facilitating movement between various . . . communities and the Mormon core."[12] There are currently about eleven million Mormons, increasing numbers of whom are overseas converts. It may be helpful to mention briefly the racial history of the church and its contemporary attitude about people of color. The early adherents of Mormonism were radical antiabolitionists, a position for which they were violently attacked and chased from place to place. Later, the church leaders backed off from the antiabolitionist stance and invented a "racial cowardice" idea that African Americans (believed to be cursed with the mark of Cain) had been equivocal in the battle between good and evil, and as a result did not deserve to reach the higher rungs of the secular and the celestial orders. This antiblack attitude clashed with the Mormon mission to proselytize and reform "benighted savages," which made the conversion of Native Americans and other peoples of color considered to have primitive cultures a highly prized achievement. It was not until 1978, when the Mormon president had a revelation, that black men were allowed to be ordained to the priesthood. This obstacle to racial discrimination removed, the next decade saw an explosive growth in Mormon missionizing work in the multiracial Caribbean, South America, and Africa. Part of the appeal of Mormonism was its claim that Native Americans and South Pacific Islanders could trace their ancestral origins to migratory lost tribes mentioned in the Book of Mormon.

In recent decades, Mormonism has also spread like wildfire throughout the Asia Pacific. At a church service, a visiting minister talked about his thirty years of missionary work in Asia. When he and his friends first started, he said, they were learning Asian histories and getting their doctorates. At first, they could not speak Asian languages, and had to mime their testimonials. "At that time, there weren't many missionaries in Asia. But since that time, the church has grown very strong in Asia. Temples have been built in Korea, Japan, and Taiwan." He mentioned that his friends have been named temple presidents in these countries.

> So if we look over the last thirty years, much has happened. If we look into the distant future, anything can happen. Some of us sitting in this room can become presidents or bishops . . . or perhaps someone sitting in this room might be put in charge of the mission in Cambodia. Anything can change, and God only knows how it will change. Thirty years ago there weren't many memberships in Taiwan and Korea, but today there are many. God has chosen us to be in service on this earth, so I hope that we are all preparing to serve Him. If you do, you will be greatly blessed. I say all this in the name of Jesus Christ. Amen.

It is this kind of dedicated and dogged missionary work, mainly on the part of young men between nineteen and twenty-two years old, that has made Mormonism one of the fastest-growing religions in the world, with new recruits mainly in Latin American countries.[13] In Asia, the largest populations of converts have been among the Filipinos and the Japanese. Another measure of the church's vast growth is its $8 billion annual revenue, much of it provided by the obligatory monthly contribution from members called tithing (10 percent of gross income).[14] The transnational appeal of Mormonism has been its reaffirmation of patriarchal values and discipline, which nevertheless is situated within a vertical structure that assimilates less-successful peoples to American values of strict morality, hard work, and middle-class success. Thus various Asian-Pacific groups caught up in unsettling social change have found reassurance and structure within the framework of Mormonism. Even so, it is worth asking whether the attraction to Mormonism, with its structure of racial domination, was merely a form of titular conversion for impoverished Asian immigrants, and not something that reached deeper into the management of the soul.

"CAMBODIANS GO TO THE MORMON CHURCH IN ORDER TO GET THINGS"

Susan, a Cambodian working in public health, complained about the Mormons being "so aggressive!" in going from door to door in the apartment complexes where most of the Cambodians live, combining offers of help with proselytizing. Many of the seven thousand Cambodians in Oakland "hated them," she said, because they came by so frequently. In her own case, when she told her unwelcome visitors that she was a Catholic, they "demanded" that she convert to Mormonism, declaring all other religions to be "evil." This coercive view of Mormon missionizing was shared by a Cambodian Baptist priest, Petros Tha, who has a small congregation of Cambodians. He observed that "the Mormons pressured Cambodians to be baptized." Susan worked for the WIC program, which provides free food vouchers to poor mothers. In her work, she met many newly arrived Cambodian women who, urged by their friends, signed up immediately for coupons to buy formula, food, and diapers for their children. In Oakland, the Mormon Church was a major competitor with government agencies in providing resources to refugees. The accusation of Mormons' "coercive" proselytizing and "psychological and economic pressure" to win converts has also been made by Christian churches.

There is intense competition especially between the Catholic Church and the Mormons for members among new immigrant populations from Hispanic and other countries in the developing world.[15] A major area of concern for the Catholic Church is the "loss" of Hispanic immigrants, who have been flocking to join Protestant churches, attracted by messages that emphasize victory and success in this world, instead of the Catholic focus on Jesus's suffering and death.[16] This interchurch competition for Hispanic converts has concealed a smaller trend of Asian immigrants also streaming toward Protestantism.

Within the refugee community, the widespread view was that some Cambodians gave in to Mormon pressure in order to obtain things like used clothing and furniture, sometimes food, and even on occasion money to help pay rent and utility bills. Once Mormons had helped refugees settle in and furnished their household, they worked very hard to convert the family. Susan insisted that despite receiving help and converting to Mormonism, most older Cambodians continued to believe in the Buddha and to practice Buddhist rituals at weddings and funerals. They continued to eat Cambodian food and make food choices according to the traditional concepts of the hot and cold winds affecting the body. Nevertheless, Susan's father-in-law and some other elders were very worried about the low attendance at the Oakland Cambodian Buddhist temple. Working within a very limited budget, the temple organizers wanted to hold more gatherings and cultural performances that could attract the interest of young Cambodian Americans. Cambodian mutual-aid associations had tried to attract the young by holding weekend parties, but the older folk hated the disco music and dancing. On some occasions, youth gangs had attended the parties armed with drugs and guns. On one occasion shots were fired, apparently to impress the pretty girls. The police were called, and the dance events canceled. In any case, the youth center soon had its hands full mediating between young Cambodians and American authorities like the police and the school system.

Petros Tha noted that Mormons attracted the young because the church on the hill held Friday night disco dances where white and Asian teenagers mingled. Often Mormon missionaries were clean-cut young men in ties and business suits who regularly visited Cambodian homes where there were teenage girls. Most of the Cambodians who had converted were girls and young women, who sometimes joined the church over the objections of their parents. Thus although leaders of other churches tried to reduce the attraction of Mormonism for some Cambodians to a matter of strong-arm methods and self-interest, among the young, especially women, there was a pattern of gravitating toward the Mormon Church.

TESTIMONIES OF TWO SISTERS

Mormonism as a set of ritual practices instills an evangelical drama and also a capitalist rationality into the everyday experiences of new and would-be Americans.[17] The "wildfire conversion of Latin America" by Protestant sects continues in California, where tens of thousands of Hispanic immigrants convert to Mormonism and other denominations each year.[18] Did Cambodian refugees, who were predominantly Theravada Buddhists, turn to the Mormon Church primarily to gain resources, as some claim, or were some flocking to the church in order to resolve unanswerable questions or to heal their spiritual wounds?

On a Sunday morning, I attended a service for Cambodian Mormons in the temple complex. There were about thirty adult Cambodians, mainly women, and about an equal number of children. Midwestern-looking whites, most of whom were middle-aged or older, sat among the Cambodians. Mormon Elders and Sisters also sat at the ends of pews, perhaps to keep an eye on the Cambodians and their sometimes restless toddlers. More white Elders sat up front, and they were joined by a young Cambodian couple, an Elder and a Sister, who expertly translated sermons and testimonies from English to Cambodian and back for the congregation.

The service opened with an Elder urging the Cambodians to be more like Jesus, and he reminded them that "God granted that you be free to be in this country." After prayers and two hymns, the Cambodian Elder broke bread into tiny pieces. Four Cambodian boys from the congregation came forward and passed trays of bread pieces from pew to pew. After the taking of bread and holy water came the monthly ritual of providing testimonies of faith. A basic tenet of Mormon theology is that direct, personal revelation is received through prayer. Two Sino-Cambodian sisters took the stage to offer their testimonies.

The Heng sisters, both single mothers in their late thirties, were from a middle-class family in Phnom Penh. Although their father died when they were teenagers, their mother managed to support the family comfortably by operating grocery stores. Their brothers and sisters were professionals in the capital until the Khmer Rouge took over. In the aftermath, the family scattered, but both sisters finally made it to the Thai camps in 1979. On this Sunday morning, Mely Heng, looking neat in a white dress and heels, nervously stepped forward to give her testimonial. She recounted how she turned to Christian churches in Khao-I-Dang camp. Before the war, she had been forced to marry a man intended for her older sister, who had run away. (At this point, she burst into tears.) Although they survived the Pol Pot regime and flight together, her husband started beating her and the children once they arrived at the refugee camp. On one occasion, her children ran away and hid in the bushes until she found them. Seeing that the missionaries provided some protection to his wife and children, her husband protested, "What is this church? They won't let me drink or smoke. I'm not going to join them." Nevertheless, the church sponsored the family to settle in Texas; the family later joined relatives in Northern California. One day, when Mely and her children were at church, her husband took everything from their apartment and moved in with his mother in another city. Without letting up on her crying, Mely went on about how the church helped her:

> In 1987, Sister Foster and Sister Smith helped me go to court. I got help from the Elders to go through the court hearings. Later, Elder Sister Smith settled the matter. I want to thank you all for being my friends and helping me when I was in need. Now that all the marital problems are settled, I have found a little apartment for myself and my kids. But I was always scared that my ex-husband would come by and harass me.
>
> I was always feeling sick. Then Sister Smith brought the other Elders and Sisters by to pray for me. We sat around holding hands and praying. Then Brother Joseph came up and blessed me. Brother Joseph put his hand on my forehead. I closed my eyes, I saw a very bright light, and since then, I am no longer sick, afraid, or weary. I have heard the testimonial of the church and the Gospel!

Mely's testimony revolved around the church's help in ending a miserable arranged marriage, and in providing the emotional support and magical power to heal a single mother with young children. Although she had some relatives in the Bay Area, they could not help her with her divorce, or to deal with the American court system, or even perhaps with her feelings of damage and despair. Only the church provided both charity and emotional support in dealing with her crisis. In particular, Mely found the help of Mormon women, who emphasized values such as kindness and friendliness, very gratifying in managing her emotional turmoil. By providing both spiritual and legal guidance, church members constructed a kind of hierarchical reciprocity in which Mely played the subordinate role of a convert seeking shelter in the church.

Mely was followed by her sister Lily, who had to be urged on by the congregation to step forward:

> I am so nervous. Today I want to tell you about the first time I encountered the faith. When we arrived in Khao-I-Dang, we did not know anything about the church. I was crossing the jungle [into Thai camps], and I looked up and saw the cross. I thought it was a dead body. I was scared to death. My friends [in the camp] kept on telling me to go to church; I would have a chance to get to the U.S. faster. So I went along. . . . But as I read the Mormon Book, it started to make more sense; I began to believe that there is a God and that those who have done good deeds will go with Him, and those who have been bad shall not.

Lily's account of her conversion experience seems to resonate with the experience of another refugee woman, whose story was reported by Carol A. Mortland. After arriving at a Thai refugee camp, this woman had a dream about a church. "I didn't know about the church. I saw the lady with long white clothes. I asked her, 'Can I go across the river?' She talked to me, but I don't remember what she said. After that I woke up. I wanted to go to church." She converted because she decided to "believe in Jesus," but also noted that "people said you go faster to America if you become a Christian."[19]

In the refugee camps, when many Cambodians, including the Heng sisters, first encountered Christianity, they could not distinguish clearly among the different churches. It was not until they arrived in the United States that they began to identify the different denominations. Christianity seemed effortlessly to bridge the distance between the lady with the lamp and the lady with the torch, and perhaps conversion visions had as much to do with the traumas induced by war and flight as with reaching salvation. Many Cambodians interested in Christianity still considered themselves Buddhists. Although refugees at the camp and in the United States encountered many churches, the Mormon Church seemed to have elements that allowed for interpretations that blended with the Buddhist faith.

In Lily's account, she selectively syncretized features of the two religions, interpreting one in relation to the other:

> It is like our Kapi [religious text], which says that after the bloodbath "those who had survived will seek shelter under the Bo tree" [under which the Buddha attained Enlightenment]. The book also says that "those are the truly blessed ones" who have been sheltered by the Lord. That story reminds me of the one in the Mormon Book about a boy under a tree. It reminds me of my

story, of how we escaped and all, and the story of the shade of the Bo tree. It's just like when I listen to our Elders, it's like what is said in the Buddhist book. Because we were good, we had survived and escaped to live in this free country, whereas others were killed.

In fusing elements of Buddhism with Mormonism, Lily insisted on the salience of her original faith, which suggests a form of religious adjustment that was not simply conversion. Yes, the Mormon Church provided help, but she seemed to be justifying her conversion by showing how Mormonism offered the elements and the language to help her make sense of her horrendous experiences and her subsequent self-transformation.[20] The testimonials of the Heng sisters narrated their journeys through loss, suffering, and finding shelter—plots that echoed Buddhist stories of suffering and resolution, except that in their experiences, the sisters found redemption in a new society, and a new religion.[21] Through the language of religious conversion, the Heng sisters made sense of their sufferings and transformed themselves into new kinds of women in America.

At the same time, as converts, the sisters expressed their ambivalence at being inducted into an alien ethno-racial hierarchy. Thus, at the end of her testimony, Lily provided an ironic defense of Cambodians joining the Mormon Church:

> People often say that the church is bad, that it cheats you of your money and such [referring to the tithes]. I've been in this church three years now. I know this church is truly good, and that all the Brothers and Sisters and Elders really care for me and my children. I know this church is truly good. I also want to thank them for persisting in coming to visit our homes although we are poor. Although our houses smell bad, and we are of a different color, they still persist. When we need help, there is no God who can come down to help right on the spot. There are only the Brothers and Sisters, who are like God. It doesn't matter which Brother or Sister. Whenever there's a problem, we just call on them to service our needs. I know this church is true, and that is why we are all here today.

A burst of laughter greeted her ending, and the congregation rose in a hymn, covering up any lingering suggestion of sarcasm or doubt. Indeed, whereas Mely's testimony was of the expected kind, a story of salvation at the hands of the church that ended with the blinding light of revelation, Lily's testimony was an ambivalent and ironic commentary on the lot of refugees, especially mothers, seeking the help of the church to make ends meet and help the family survive in the new country. Her new faith, she suggested, consisted of an interweaving of ideas echoed by both Buddhist beliefs and Mormon teachings. The towering Mormon temple now stood for the sheltering Bo tree, but Lily insinuated a critique of racism in church workers who, even when they dutifully made home visits to Cambodians, could not hide

her conclusion, she did not say the customary words, "I want
imony that I know this church is true, and I say this in the
Christ." Instead, she said, rather ambiguously, that "I know
true, and that is why we are all here today." By "we," did she
mbodians, and were they all present simply because the church
had been ᵤᵤ efficient in its charitable functions? A Cambodian monk said
to me that to the young in America, "Buddha appears to be hiding"; so where
else can one find shelter in the land of the free?

The evangelical drama of bearing witness—including the rhetorical ending, "I have heard the testimony of the church," or "I know this church is true,
amen"—created a community out of new converts and long-term church
members, uniting both white and Cambodian Mormons into a single,
stratified moral order. The ceremony closed when four old white Sisters ca-
joled the Cambodian women into going to the front of the chapel, where
they sang, with piano accompaniment, "America the Beautiful." Before the
congregation dispersed, an Elder reminded them to attend the baptism of
a Cambodian couple that afternoon, and that *The Killing Fields* would be aired
on TV that evening.

Anthropological studies have suggested that church rituals among new converts in the Asia Pacific must negotiate the uneasy issue of imbalances between gift givers and gift receivers, between the powerless and the powerful.
In Papua New Guinea, Edward Schieffelin maintains, the social and economic
support provided by missionaries was not a sufficient reason for the Kaluli
people's rapid embrace of evangelical Protestantism. He points to the centrality of "the drama and rhetoric of the evangelical process itself" as a moral
force in winning converts. The "key Bible stories seemed to parallel and
confirm important elements in the Kalulis' own mythological and religious
tradition." At the same time, the incorporation of Kaluli traditions into Protestantism radically shifted the direction of their moral reciprocity "from the
horizontal plane between people to the vertical between man and God, mediated by the pastor and the church organization."[22] Hirokazu Miyazaki notes
that in Fijian churches, gift giving is balanced by speeches that celebrate the
generosity of the gift givers but also stress mutual respect and "mutual love"
as the ultimate gift, thus offsetting feelings of being dominated on the part
of poor parishioners. Fijian Christians focus on the limits that church rituals placed on their agency, this abeyance leaving them with the hope for an
ultimate response to their wishes.[23] Church rituals thus function to even out
unequal exchanges, and at the same time offer the promise of a privileged
access to power currently denied to new converts.

There was a similar moral reframing in the Heng sisters' testimonies, as
they described their transition from Cambodian modes of kinship support,
now lost to them, to a support system based on a vertical reciprocity structured by the Mormon Church. In the Bay Area, Cambodian temples were

just being built to serve the fragmented immigrant community, and these institutions were hobbled by limited funds that prevented their providing enough help to the many sufferers in their congregation. Instead, a powerful institution such as the Church of Jesus Christ, with its aura of white respectability and know-how, was better able to provide the promise of institutional integration for disadvantaged newcomers of color into the dominant culture. The Mormon Church's stratificatory division into ethno-racial segments reinforced the Asian converts' sense of being inducted into a vertical reciprocity within which they are subordinated minorities.

FAMILY REUNIFICATION ON EARTH AND IN HEAVEN

Another Buddhist theme that Cambodians wove into Mormon theology was the intense desire for family unification with relatives separated by war or lost in death. In testimonials expressing their desire for reconnection, Cambodians saw in the structure of the church, and in the objectified vertical relations with God, a transcendental force linking Mormons with non-Mormons, the living and the dead, those who belonged with those who did not. This profound desire for suturing fragmented relations was expressed in the testimonial of a seventeen-year-old girl:

> Good morning, everyone. I am grateful to be here. I am thankful for the opportunity to bear my testimony. I would like to talk to you about the experience that my family and I had. When times were hard, my family and I wanted to find freedom. That's when I got to come and live in the U.S. . . . Since we've settled in the States, the Lord has been our inspiration. He helped us in many ways, and one of these was to write a letter to my grandfather in Cambodia. Later we tried to find ways to send him some money so that he could have some support. While we tried to send him some money, we could never make it. . . . There was no other way that we could do except ask the Lord for help. We decided to kneel and pray to the Lord so that we could send our Grandpa some money in order to buy some food. . . . I felt the Spirit so strong as we all together asked the Lord for help. . . .
>
> About a month or two later, we got a letter—but it was not from our grandpa. It was from a neighbor. It said that Grandpa did receive the letter and the money, but at the very moment he saw the money and the letter he was so happy, and he died. [She broke down, weeping.] This broke my heart, and also my family's. But however I feel happy because I know for myself the power of prayer.
>
> If I will do my part, I know the Lord will do His part too. I know that the Church of Jesus Christ of the Latter-Day Saints is true. I say this in the name of Jesus Christ. Amen.

In the absence of a revived Theravada Buddhist temple that could reach people in their thirties or younger, the Mormon Church provided the hope that helped salve family wounds of separation and loss. It also enabled Cambodians to transcend the barriers between this world and the next through the structure of church power. Many of the converts found special comfort in the Mormon belief in the continuity of the family unit in the afterlife. A major tenet of Mormonism is that good behavior, such as prayers, sexual purity, and a temple marriage, will qualify converts and their families to an afterlife in heaven, where they can be reunited. Cambodian converts pointed out how these ideas resonated with the Buddhist belief in the power of good deeds (karma), and its link to reincarnation. Indeed, for most young Cambodians, besides filial piety and respect for their parents, this is the residue of Cambodian Buddhism that they have retained. Simon, a twenty-one-year-old student, explained,

> I don't know anything about Buddhism. I was just born into it. Ma just prays on her own and does not tell me anything about Buddhism. However, in my view, the two religions [Buddhism and Mormonism] are similar, teaching guides to live a good life, to get closer to God. In Mormonism, there is belief in the afterlife when one rejoins God in the Paradise World. In Buddhism, we believe in reincarnation.

Furthermore, the drama of Mormon ritual practices struck a chord with the Cambodians' deep yearning to reconnect with family members so recently lost in the war. There is a Mormon ritual of proxy baptism that allows young converts to become living substitutes for dead souls who, thus baptized, can enter heaven. A major goal of some Cambodian converts was eventually to baptize all their dead relatives so that the entire family could be reunited as Mormons in heaven. This was the principal reason Simon's mother had supported his decision to join the church. According to him, she said, "We have to assimilate. A lot of people are going to church. We mustn't stay home on Sunday." Within four months of their arrival in Oakland in 1984, his mother, his sister, and Simon himself, despite his early reluctance, were baptized. His mother then urged him to extend the baptism to his dead father. "I went to the temple and submitted his records. An Elder blessed me in his name. It was Ma's idea to do this, in order for family unification after death." This baptism of dead souls was even more meaningful because many Cambodian refugees were unable to return and find the bones of loved ones, in order to give them a proper burial. In this way, proxy baptism became an alternative practice to Theravada-Buddhist customs commemorating the reciprocal relations between the living and the dead.

Sophie, another young convert and first-year student at Brigham Young University, loved the idea of "family forever" for a slightly different reason. As a single woman, Sophie was less concerned with dead relatives than preoccupied with the question of permanent marriage and everlasting families. She explained that there were three levels in the Mormon heaven (purgatory, middle level, and the celestial kingdom). "The celestial kingdom is the highest. One can become perfect. One can also have children." All good Mormons aim to reach the highest heaven eventually, but their chances depend on action taken in earthly life. She compared this Mormon emphasis on performing good deeds in order to reach a higher level in a reincarnated life to Buddhist tenets: "I think Buddhism is just another branch of interpretation of the Bible. Buddhism is similar to Mormonism, but also different. Mormonism emphasizes temple marriage; it's another step to heaven. Do good in this life and we will be together in heaven." She especially endorsed the Mormon emphasis on sexual purity and permanent marriage. Only by going through a temple marriage can a Mormon hope to reach the highest heaven. The married couple, pledged to lifelong fidelity, "have the chances to go together, but there is no guarantee that both will end up in the same place." Unlike Simon, whose conversion was driven in part by the family desire to reunite with the dead, Sophie's belief in the Mormon afterlife was motivated by her desire for a permanent marriage and everlasting family in the afterlife. Sophie persuaded two sisters to become Mormons, but failed to convince her parents to get baptized. She felt sad about the tension this created in her family: "Every time I talk to Dad he thinks that it's good, but he's not ready to convert. We end in argument." The church ideology of permanent love had unexpectedly created a self-centeredness in Sophie, something she could make up for by hoping that "after this life, we can be together in heaven, and be sealed in the temple."

Mormonism appealed to some Cambodian Americans because of their unresolved grief over the dead, their unanswerable questions about what happened during the war, the practical difficulties of adjusting to life in the United States, and—especially among young people who arrived as children—a kind of psychodrama with echoes of Theravada Buddhism, which they frequently knew only in the abstract. The church resonated with the traditional Buddhist need to worship ancestors, but also created new desires for an afterlife that one can control (through good personal conduct and the mediation of the church) and for making permanent the family relations that are so easily threatened in this uncertain world. But concern for others in this and the next life perhaps cloaked the fostering of a new self-centeredness—something that Sophie's father may have detected, since the girls' baptism drew them away from the family in this life, even though they were thereby assured family unity in the next. Perhaps more than any other Western church, Mormonism emphasized the kind of family values that resonated with refugees, immigrants, and other peoples in upheaval. The liturgical dramas provided catharsis for deep pain, and the compassionate structure of help and advice provided a guide that promoted learning practical behavior for personal and economic success in the modern world.

RACIAL BIPOLARISM AND GENDER HIERARCHY

Becoming Mormons entailed forms of domination for the Cambodian refugees, thanks to their status as new Mormons at the bottom of the LDS hierarchy, but it also offered the promise of mixed marriages as a civilizing mission directed at foreign converts. For the Cambodians as members of a minority group, becoming Mormon was one path to integration into the Christian world; for the young women, there was the expectation that the Mormon Church would provide chances for acquiring the forms of cultural capital that would allow them to attain upward mobility. For them, marrying a white Mormon would have a further whitening effect, in the sense of raising their status and dignity as Americans. Church workers played along by pushing Cambodian recruits along the Mormon paths to economic and social mobility that would situate them closer to the white pole, in contrast to unconverted Cambodians. Young Cambodian American women were more likely than men to become converts, to acquire the forms and rituals of white womanhood, and to differentiate themselves from Cambodian men, thus having greater opportunities to marry white.

The bishop of one of the Cambodian wards in Oakland had extensive experience as a missionary in Asia. Bishop Lawton sought out and welcomed multicultural populations that were at first glance very different from white Americans. His experiences in Asia had taught him that non-Westerners who worshiped ancestors found Mormonism appealing, and he was very tolerant of their erroneous conflation of ancestor worship and reincarnation with Mormon notions of the afterlife and the celestial kingdom. He noted that the Mormon temple (figure 8) reminded some Cambodians of Angkor Wat, and indicated that he did nothing to discourage this association. Other Cambodian recruits still struggled over the difference between the Buddhist belief in reincarnation and the Mormon concept of eternal life. They had been brought up to believe that there were multiple stages of reincarnation, not just the three-tiered heaven of the Mormons. This uncertainty about and dissatisfaction with the efficacy of Mormon worship convinced many of the female converts to continue to take part in Khmer-Buddhist rituals as well, in the hope of ensuring their accumulation of merit for at least the Buddhist afterlife. The church tolerated such practices as cultural difference, but regarded them as a mark of the inferiority of Cambodians as Mormons.

The Mormon Church's tolerance for and recruitment of multiracial converts operate as an assimilative force that absorbs non-Western others into one stream of the American success story, helping them to be positioned near the whiter end of the continuum. Through its elaborate organizational structure and strategies of overseas conversion, the church situates peoples of color as primitive others who must be civilized as a way of entering the modern world. In practice, therefore, it is a system of modern disciplinary power, analogous to global corporations, that orders the poor and up-and-coming masses of the world within an American structure of white domination. The church organization, stratified by gender and race, is geared toward recruiting future generations of a truly international congregation. Unlike that other religious empire, the Catholic hierarchy, the Mormon structural system seems so effective because of its modern methods of operation, and because of its focus on self-cultivation, which is so thoroughly this-world oriented.

Compassionate domination and conservatism are the Mormon Church's twin appeals to the new urban migrants of the world, arriving on the doorsteps of affluent society. The church has been absorbing a variety of ethnic and racial groups at an increasing rate, and converts reach different levels of leadership depending on experience, not race. The only exceptions are the Quorum of the Twelve Apostles and the first presidency, positions that for now are all filled by white men. John Hawkins claims that much of what comes to be perceived as Mormon racial hierarchy is the "residual of American and [minority] cultures interacting," and not church policy.[24] Racial bipolarism is no longer the result of policy, but rather an effect of norms about ethno-racial ranking in society at large—a kind of classificatory rationality that intersects in this case with the very structure of the LDS Church, in which disadvantaged groups starting out at the bottom are guided toward integration, by means that include what may be called raced hypergamy.

Bishop Lawton noted that there were about 450 Cambodian members in his flock, but their church attendance fluctuated, and that some converts had actually faded away after a few years. His hopes, he said, lay with the young ones, especially those who started out in the church's primary school. On Sunday mornings, little Cambodian boys and girls attended Sunday school at the temple complex. Besides teaching English, these classes socialized the youngsters to transfer moral authority from their parents to the church. At one class, the teacher wrote "I can obey" on the blackboard, right next to a poster depicting a kneeling Jesus Christ's Agony in the Garden. Many children and even their parents found the church a more effective place to learn English than the state-sponsored ESL classes. Such instruction, especially for the very young, provided the context wherein the church could pry children away from the authority of their parents and integrate them into the hierarchical structure of white authority. Just as racial logic informed various regimes of truth about clients in the welfare office, the community clinic, and the courthouse, so the idea of "primitive" difference was a way to appropriate the moral authority of parents and to realign young, vulnerable Cambodians with the white church hierarchy.

It may be important to situate the stigmatizing of people of color within the Mormons' history of persecution as a pariah group and their own slow climb toward white respectability. To nineteenth-century America, the most damning thing about Mormons was the practice of polygyny at a time when the urban middle classes had begun to valorize the bourgeois nuclear family and its code of white manliness.[25] The pioneer farming community was often on the run from arson attacks by Americans who viewed polygynous Mormon families as an abnormality, and a moral challenge to the ideal of the nuclear family as the best means of reproduction, stability, and material advancement. The Supreme Court ruled against polygamy in 1879, and Utah, where many Mormons had found refuge, was excluded from statehood. A timely revelation in 1890 brought the practice officially to an end. Nevertheless, stigmatization persisted, and early in the twentieth century, the habit of denigrating plural families stereotyped Mormon men as having abnormal sexual appetites—an attribute that had previously been applied mostly to African American men.[26] So the Mormon adoption of the nuclear-family ideal, as reflected in the model of the "celestial marriage," became linked to the attainment of respectable white masculinity.

Their image was further improved when a strict code of sober living (forbidding alcohol, tobacco, drugs, or gambling) reinforced the emphasis on traditional roles and the nuclear family. In a sense, one could say that through the adoption of these changes in gender and family forms, the Mormons—already famous for their business acumen—became whitened. This wedding of middle-class ideals with "old-fashioned" sobriety attracted many disadvantaged but driven new immigrants, who had no time to waste on the more liberal and self-indulgent aspects of American culture that critics linked with the 1960s youth rebellion. Mormons thus have a lot to show the Johnny-come-latelies of the world about how to reach white respectability quickly, by providing a specific path toward success in the American environment.

Bishop Lawton told me that he had two main goals regarding his young Cambodian converts. Both dealt with marriage, the key relationship between men and women for procreation and family formation, and a central institution in Cambodian culture. One goal was to help Cambodian women who had had their marriages arranged for them by their parents when they were teenagers in Cambodia. Mely's testimonial is an example of the kind of help the church provided for Cambodian women wishing to end their marriages. Apparently oblivious to the irony, Bishop Lawton claimed that the church was a crucial agent for fighting the patriarchy of Cambodian culture and for teaching Asians about marriage as a partnership. Such interventions, legitimized by the concept of Cambodian culture as primitive, were essential to the reproduction of social distinctions between whites and nonwhites and to the status hierarchy of Christendom in America.

The other goal, directed at the young, was a much more complex task. The bishop explained that the church provided all kinds of activities through which young Cambodians learned to be single American women and men in a safe environment. The temple is a vast complex with many rooms specially equipped for games, dances, and religious meetings. There, young

women and men could become friends, have a date, arrange their own marriage, and learn how to interact with white society. Indeed, for many young
Cambodians living in high-crime areas, there was nowhere else to go on weekends except the streets, which had been commandeered by drug pushers,
young gangs, and prostitutes. The Mormon temple provided a safe haven,
especially for young women out on the weekends.

Vanna, a sophomore at Hayward College, explained, "Half the Asian kids
in the U.S. don't have any form of recreation or place to socialize. The church
provides all forms of recreational activities. Also, Mormon couples take kids
to the movies, et cetera. My sister enjoyed going along with Mormon couples and helping to translate for them when they visited Cambodian homes."
After she was baptized, Vanna followed in her footsteps. "I got interested because I wanted to get involved in activities—baseball, basketball, swimming.
Initially, the religious lessons were boring and I hated them, but as I kept on
going to church I started to get serious." The Mormons "persuaded" her to
get baptized after she had a "conversion experience" in class.

In addition, there seemed to be a trend toward raced hypergamy that was
encouraged by the bishop.[27] He was not surprised by the incidence of interracial marriage among the converts: "the girls are beautiful, you know." He
mentioned with satisfaction a recent marriage between a Cambodian woman
and a Mormon soldier, against her parents' wishes. The temple performed
the ceremony, and the young couple had since left for Germany, where the
soldier was stationed. Marriages between Cambodian girls and white Mormon
men were especially painful for Cambodian parents because of the agnatic
filiation of the Cambodian community. But for some Cambodian women,
white men—and especially the Mormons—represented the middle-class
norms that they were aspiring to attain. (I return to this theme later.)

Part of the appeal of Mormon marriage lay in the religion's clear conjugal roles and tradition of the spiritual leadership of the husband. By his status as priest or Elder, a Mormon man has moral authority in the domestic
sphere. A recent proclamation by the president of the church reminded that
"By divine design, fathers are to preside over their families in love and righ-
teousness and are responsible to provide the necessities of life and protection for their families. Mothers are primarily responsible for the nurture of
their children. In these sacred responsibilities, fathers and mothers are ob-
ligated to help one another as equal partners."[28] This conjugal division of
labor places the family under the spiritual power of the male household head.
A Cambodian man showed me a flyer that read,

> Families who have a father, or other family member, who holds the priesthood
> are most fortunate. There are many times when this priesthood may be used
> to bless the family as a unit, or to bless individual members. . . . A father's bless-
> ing might also be desired when a child, or other family member, is having a se-
> rious problem, or needs to make an important decision. When a family mem-

ber is leaving home—to go to school, or to go on a mission, or whatever, the father should bless this individual. Just having the priesthood in the home is a great blessing. [There was an accompanying translation in Khmer script.]

For girls and young women growing up in the chaos and uncertainty of resettlement, there was something comforting in the gendered division of labor, and in the idea of the father as a moral guardian of the family. In such messages, converts learned about the domestic gender configuration wherein the Mormon man is both the leader and the beneficiary of the family; and they took his leadership of a gendered modality of power to be the essence of Christian civilization. By comparison, Buddhism did not appear to offer any guidelines for practical living in America.

BUDDHA IS HIDING, BUDDHISM IS DEPRIVATION

For some young Cambodians, their ignorance of Buddhism and its seeming immateriality propelled them toward Protestantism. This point was brought home vividly when I met with some Cambodian American college students who were involved in an oral history project to gather the stories of Cambodian refugees in the Central Valley. They expressed frustration over interviewing the refugees about Cambodian traditions, and I was not sure whether they were talking about the difficulty of translation, the limited responses of the informants, their own confusion about Cambodian culture, or all three. I then asked them what Buddhism meant to them. A sophomore, who was dressed in a black top, neon-green skirt, and matching plastic sandals, said that Buddhism did not explain anything in America, nor was it a religion written down in books that you could read. I suppose she could imagine that Buddhist texts do exist somewhere in the world, but her point was that there were no books on Buddhism written in English and readily available, the way the Bible is. To her and her friends, who had very faint memories of Cambodia, Buddhism was something intangible, and perhaps irrelevant to the lives they wanted to lead in America. She complained that Buddhism did not explain the world the way Protestantism did, and was not taught from books, but merely practiced at home. She wanted to be a Protestant because there were books to guide her, whereas when she asked her parents about Cambodian Buddhism, they were unable to tell her anything except to say, "Do this; don't do that." Besides her rejection of Buddhism as an expression of parental control, there was a faint disdain for what appeared to be merely oral traditions and the prejudices of peasants.

This attitude was also noted by Peter Thuy, the social worker: "In Cambodia, parents told their children Buddhist stories on an irregular basis. Even though boys entered the monasteries for short periods during their puberty, they didn't learn the scriptures but spent most of their time learning to bow, cleaning, and cooking. Thus, it is not surprising that in America, the children have no sense of what Buddhism is all about. Maybe that is why they are eager converts to Protestantism here, which stresses regular, book-based instruction."

There is a Cambodian temple outside Stockton in California's Central Valley, a converted farmhouse filled with Buddhist pictures, icons, candles, ritual objects, and air scented with incense. When I visited, the yard was being used as a dusty makeshift workshop for making Buddhist figurines. A row of plaster Buddhas, yet to be colored, placidly observed visitors entering the temple (figure 9). Inside, we met the Venerable Dharmawara Mahathera, a monk of the highest order in Cambodian Buddhism and spiritual father to the refugee community (figure 10). Bhante Bharmawark, as he was also known, claimed to be one hundred years old, but he appeared to be a youthful octogenarian. In his youth, he spent many years studying and working in India, including living for years in the jungle in silence, but "speaking to animals," until he learned the art of psychic healing. I was accompanied by oral historian Jackie Rainer,[29] who asked Bhante about young immigrant Cambodians drifting away from Buddhism. Bhante answered,

> The spiritual world has power. The material world also has power. And we all seem to be captured by the power of the material world. We think that Buddhism is conducive to peace, to understanding, to well-being. The young think it is different, they think differently. They think that Buddhism means deprivation, preventing them from being joyful, from a happy life. They think differently. . . .
>
> They come to the temple sometimes when the elders come, but not with a view to understanding things and following what is good. They don't understand how to judge what is good and what is bad. We have great difficulty with this subject. We do not know what to do. . . . I tell them that at their age, they must not think about anything except education.
>
> It is difficult. It takes time for them to understand what paths they should follow. Now I feel that even the parents do not know where to go. They are confused; they were already confused when they came to America—about their destination, their faith—they don't know what to do. This is due to the fact that they suffered so much in the killing and destruction, in war after war after war. That is why I've said many times that the Cambodians need almost everything. They need material health, but they need spiritual health more.

While many young Cambodians avoided him, the monk was venerated by his American sponsors, who promoted his healing powers to a segment of the white public that had lost faith in both Protestantism and modern medicine. He was sent all over North America and Europe to heal patients and teach his secrets of a healthy life (meditation and a strict vegetarian diet). He talked about curing, without medicine, all kinds of rich and famous people, but bemoaned the fact that he could not reach young Cambodians in America. His earnings on the lecture-healing circuit produced the money

Figure 9. Plaster Buddhas manufactured in the California farm country.

to build the temple, which he hoped would remind the young of Buddha as the guide to life and of their need for Buddhism even in America. Were young Cambodian refugees too impatient to seek a balance among physical, mental, and spiritual health? Bhante gently told us that it requires so much of the spirit to know that the true healing does not need drugs. "I am actually healing but without using any medicine. I understand that so many people lost their faith. I feel that reform is very badly needed now, but there are people who are trying to find an alternative in this country and all over the world. Even in England, France, and India." But in the immediate, hurly-

Figure 10. The Venerable Dharmawara Mahathera (with sunglasses) and a fellow monk, California.

burly world of Cambodian immigrants, Buddhism appeared to be one more tradition that demanded sacrifice and suffering, whereas the image of Jesus Christ, as presented by the Mormons, was that of a winner.

JESUS AS A SUCCESS STORY

For the young who have no time to waste, the theatrical glamour of evangelical Protestantism—akin to barbells and eyeshadow—is the promise of quick change. Three teenagers from Central America tell me they became evangelicos because the gringo preacher always wore a suit and a tie. In this case, the visible sign of faith and grace is at once a sign of success.

RICHARD RODRIGUEZ, *"Catholic Latin America, 'Born Again'"*

Writing about the appeal of evangelical Protestantism to Hispanic youths, Richard Rodriguez notes that the central experience of faith—"an individual standing alone before God"—appeals to the peasant migrant, the refugee, the young person "making the journey into modern cities."[30] Similarly, one observes among some young Cambodians how conversion became a rite of passage to self-reinvention, a breakaway from the parents' Southeast Asian agrarian culture, a plunge into the new world of middle-class America. The promise of achieving personal success in the diaspora was carried in a Sunday sermon by a middle-aged white Mormon that was based on a story in the Book of Mormon about Jacob, who was born in a little town near Jerusalem:

> Today I want to talk about things that happen in our lives, things that seem out of our control. Does anyone ever wonder why some people are smarter than us? Or can run faster? Or are richer? It seems that sometimes things are unfair, but it is something that our Heavenly Father has planned for, and it always works out right. . . .
>
> Jacob had many brothers, and some of them were nice, but the others were mean to him. When they all grew up, Jacob came to America where he realized that all the pain he had suffered was for his own good. He knew what it was like to be put down, and he resolved to help others.
>
> Jacob became smarter and smarter just because of all the things that had happened to him. As a result, Jacob went through all of the West and preached the Gospel of Jesus Christ. . . . If we weren't sad, we would not know what it means to be happy. If we weren't sick, we would not know what it means to be healthy.
>
> In my life, I have also felt that. I had a great job, but after a little while I was laid off. I didn't feel very good about that, but I got another job. I had learned the importance of work, and I had learned the importance of saving money. . . . I ask God in prayer so that I might receive, but I was given Hope that I might learn to obey. . . . I asked for inspiration so that I might be happy; I was given poverty so that I might be wise. I had asked for strength so that I might win over men, but I was given weaknesses so that I might feel the need of God.

This speech intertwines two messages: the lesson of victory over adversity through helping others in diaspora is linked to a lesson about the importance of overcoming adversity through hard work and saving money by oneself. Life struggles are to be overcome, with the help of God. Helping others is indistinguishable from becoming competitive—in work, intelligence, and making money—just as Jacob in helping others became a successful man. Jacob's compassion is an idiom for the message that church membership bestows the moral qualification to ascend to the entrepreneurial class. And perhaps most important of all, sermons such as these fostered in newcomers the capacity and desire to express themselves as autonomous selves, separate from their families. Converts learned to develop the kind of self-discipline and regular habits that are part of being a modern subject, only here the individual morality was regulated by church leaders, rather than by the street-level bureaucrats who sought to govern other areas of their lives.

YOUNG MEN SEEK AND DEFLECT CHURCH DISCIPLINE

There is a white masculinist aura about Protestantism that adheres to all of its practices, rituals, and artifacts. To nonwhite immigrants, Protestant men are the unmistakable symbols and agents of success: the business suit and tie, the polished shoes, the clean-cut appearance, and the remote politeness. Today, Mormon Church regulation, perhaps more than that of other Protestant sects in America, works with "penetrating efficiency," accumulating awesome riches not lost on hungry immigrants.[31] Although many Cambodians received help from churches, the few who had converted and become practicing Christians were from urban backgrounds in Cambodia. For the potential young male converts, Christianity provided daily lessons in American middle-class conduct and values.

David, the son of a French-educated Sino-Cambodian professor in Phnom Penh, looked like any Asian American high-school senior in Berkeley. When he was a little boy, his family was driven out of Phnom Penh to work in labor camps, where he witnessed many brutalities, including killings. Soon after they arrived in Berkeley, his parents converted to the Presbyterian Church, which had helped them settle in. David was often mistaken for a Chinese or Korean American. "What does it mean to be Cambodian?" I asked. "I'm not sure," he replied. "To be Cambodian is to obey my parents. To obey your parents is the biggest thing in Cambodia. That's what my grandma told me, anyway. It's very hard to draw out what's specifically Cambodian about my family, because my father is very educated in terms of the Western world. I guess my father's pretty Americanized. He has a picture of the Angkor Wat, which he is going to frame nicely and put up."

David's father had retrained as a technician, but now operated grocery stores in good neighborhoods. In contrast to most Cambodian boys, David had been directed by his father to go into engineering, like his cousins in France. The family was very clear-sighted about gaining (or recovering) middle-class status, and the church was crucial to helping them acquire the cultural competence for acceptance by white society. David confided,

> I don't allow myself not to be American. Whatever society I live in, I have to adapt to it. You have to live according to that society or you won't survive. It's very hard to live in a society where you have your own values and beliefs and try to be separate from society. But to be American is not an easy thing. I don't want to keep being Cambodian. Imagine you go to a party where you don't know anybody, what would you do? . . . It might not sound so hard because now I speak fluent English, and I know the culture. I know how to shake hands, I know when to say "hello," when to say this or that. But it was very hard. I remember my first year in high school. I used to sit and cry because I felt so lonely and such an outcast. But the church people came to talk to me, because one of their values is to be courteous and polite. I was shy. I used to hate girls; I was scared of girls, but at church, a lot of girls came to talk to me. . . . I acted really funny or jerky because I did not know how to be myself then.

David was not ashamed of his past: "I treasure what happened to me in Cambodia very highly. I think that made me a more mature person, but being young I was able to adapt to what was happening here." His family had vivid memories of Cambodia, but now they felt the need to adjust to this society. Learning how "to be myself" was part of the self-invention for which Protestantism provided the script, a cultural reform that was crucial to David's becoming relatively popular in high school, where he had once been ostracized. "I learned, besides what Jesus or God is, how to help other people, how to talk to other people. That is, if someone has a problem, you listen to their problem . . . I learned that you don't necessarily have to say anything, but just be there to listen to their problem, and that would help them a lot. I learned those kinds of things from the church."

He also learned strict Protestant values about not having sex before marriage, and about not swearing or fighting. "Those are my values . . . I feel very strongly about them. . . ." I interjected, "Are these values part of being Cambodian too?" He replied,

> I could say that the value or belief I have being a Cambodian is the same value as being a Protestant. Because for a Cambodian, you're not allowed to have sex before marriage or even date, but I've learned or believe that dating is not bad because you get to learn about other people and to prepare yourself for marriage, learn how to deal with the opposite sex. That's why I date all the time, even though it goes against my parents' rule; they just think that dating is bad for me in terms of [distracting one from] school.

The other values from the church that David agreed with were "refraining from drinking, and learning to dress and talk properly." Protestantism offered a kind of social discipline compatible with his parents' desires, but for David, it also provided the language for developing a voluntary inner asceticism, along with daily "habits of the heart"[32] that allowed him to prove himself before God.

Simon, who had earlier talked about baptizing his deceased father in the Mormon Church, was another young man who found Protestantism an important modernizing culture in America. His father had been a high-school teacher in Phnom Penh, and his mother a property owner. Their first contact with Protestantism was with Baptists who taught them English in the refugee camps. Later, in Oklahoma City, the church provided clothes, food, and money, and taught him about "what to do, how to behave; not to hit people, but how to greet them." For Simon, conversion to Mormonism was the crucial move that helped him situate and orient himself in the new society. Looking neat in the business suit and tie worn by Mormon men, Simon explained,

> Mormonism taught me "Wheresoever God exists, he lives." By learning that I can communicate with him and develop a companionship with him, I can ask for help. A lot of times he helps only when I do what I'm supposed to do. I wasn't doing very well in school, academically, as well as in getting along with

others. I did not know how to study for tests. Now I pray before and after exams. Before, I didn't feel any confidence at all.

The self-direction and self-discipline inculcated by the church helped Simon in his entrepreneurial ambition. He was a student at Hayward State University, but that summer he was working at Jack-in-the-Box and a doughnut shop, and was looking for a third part-time job. He was on financial aid, and his major was business administration. His immediate plan was to open a grocery store that his mother, who was currently living on SSI, could operate as a livelihood. "My goal is to get a good job, buy a house, and have a family. Also, I want to sponsor my sister from Cambodia." Something he might have to do before all these plans could be implemented was to go on a mission, a rite of passage that is optional for young Mormon men after they complete their schooling.

The very reason that Protestantism appeals to upwardly mobile men makes it distasteful to men from peasant backgrounds. For many of them, the price of church discipline and white respectability was too high to pay. Many of the Cambodian refugees came from provincial or peasant backgrounds, and the young men in such families had been trained for jobs as car mechanics or factory hands. Very few wanted to go to college.

Some Mormon young women blamed their brothers' lack of educational success on their parents. It was part of Cambodian culture to be strict with young girls, keeping them "pure," but to allow young boys to do whatever they wanted, like roaming freely outside the house. Sophie told me why her younger brother had not followed his sisters and joined the church. He was sixteen, and spent most of his time hanging around with Cambodian gangs, drinking, and smoking:

> Cambodian parents don't know how to love their children. They don't explain their rules, and sometimes they are not strict enough. They don't punish boys. There is a lack of love by action and by words. A lot of parents don't care about kids going out, and don't ask about their homework. A lot of the kids feel bad. They see how Americans treat their kids, taking them on picnics, caring about their homework. Our parents are on SSI, and living in government housing in East Oakland. [My brother] helps them with American culture, with English. In the beginning, he came to church. He was a good boy, for two to three years. He went to school, and his teacher said that he was the smartest kid, but he didn't care. I asked him why, and he cried. He needs to get away from his peers. More girls join the Mormons than boys. Girls are more teachable, to become good women and housewives. They stay with the church. Guys are more stubborn; they find it hard to keep the rules.

This is a pretty devastating commentary, its baldness perhaps only possible from a young person growing up in a cultural world so different from that of her refugee parents. Young people were hungry for concrete guidance to help them cope with the demands of school and social life, as well as for affirmation of their individual identity within a less-hierarchical family model. Teenage boys were also pressured by their families to earn an income. This pressure often resulted in young men taking one of two paths: dropping out of high school to make money in low-paying jobs, or joining street gangs. Sophie said that her brother thought that the gang would take care of him, not his parents. Young Cambodian boys found church morality—forbidding premarital sex, drinking, gambling, and smoking—oppressive. To Sophie, such prohibitions were values central to becoming American. "It's harder for boys to become American and easier for girls, because they're taught to be subservient, like responding to things such as 'Honey, do this.' Boys rebel." She could not think of any Cambodian men who went to college; in fact, most of the Cambodian men her age were already married, raising families, jealously possessive of their wives, and in her view, heavy drinkers, like some working-class American men. They fitted neither her image nor the Mormons' of what being American was all about.

YOUNG WOMEN MANAGING THE UPWARDLY MOBILE SELF

Why does Mormonism have a special appeal to some Cambodian women? Older women, stripped of family support, turned to the church for material and social resources. But women in their late teens and early twenties who joined the Mormon Church sought something less tangible. They wanted to be Mormon Young Women. By surrendering themselves to church discipline, they learned to manage their own subjectivity as clean-living young women, to develop a new status that commanded respect and facilitated hypergamous unions with white Mormons. This section draws on interviews with four Cambodian Young Women: Vanna, Jackie, Sophie, and Rita. Sophie and Rita came from a family of five girls, three of whom converted to Mormonism. Sophie was a sophomore at Brigham Young University (BYU), and Rita was married to a Mormon in the U.S. army. As mentioned earlier, Vanna was a college sophomore, and Jackie had just graduated from high school and was bound for the same college. While most young Cambodian men seemed to chafe at Mormon rules, these women were eagerly embracing the church discipline and white power as a guide to finding their way in the world. They were the church's Cambodian success stories.

When I met Sophie, she was home from BYU for the summer. It was Sunday, and she was dressed in a frilly black chiffon blouse, red miniskirt, black mesh stockings, and party shoes. She was holding a check for $190, the tithe she gave to the church (10 percent of her summer earnings as a bank clerk). In Cambodia, Sophie's family was Thai Cambodian, and her father had been a village leader near Battambang. After escaping to the Thai camps, the family had been sponsored by the eldest daughter to Oakland.

As a teenager, Sophie saw that her friends were already "learning English and American culture" every Sunday at the church. She invited Mormon missionaries to her home, and soon she and her sisters were baptized, against her parents' wishes. "The older Mormons pushed me to go to college. I just wanted to be on the same level as Americans—to learn to speak, to be knowledgeable, to be educated. At first, Cambodian people were put down for not speaking English; that made me want to do so." The Mormon Church, more than the public schools, seemed to provide the range of lessons that would enable young Cambodians like these women to acquire the skills that would win respect from Americans:

> Mormons have good values, and they teach you how to be a good woman, i.e., Young Women's values. I started out as a Young Woman. Learned to dress modestly, not a short, short skirt [gesturing self-consciously at her mini]. Learned to keep yourself clean, to keep your chastity. A lot of kids don't know that. This is where I belong; it is like my parents' teachings.

This statement about learning self-discipline from Mormonism was echoed by Vanna in a separate interview:

> Being Mormon helps me to operate better in the U.S. When I was in high school, many Cambodian girls married in the twelfth grade, about half of them to older Cambodian guys whose jobs were not so good. They got pregnant or simply married to get away from strict parents who wouldn't let them out of the house, but they then found that it was worse in marriage. The husbands won't let them out; they are jealous about other guys, and worried about having no control.
>
> If I had not become a Mormon at sixteen, my life would have been different. I'd have two kids by now. I'd be cutting school, mixing with the wrong crowds, falling in love with the first guy, and feeling peer pressure.

For both women, the strict morality helped them to negotiate the teenage years with a focus on their studies instead of being distracted. The goal of maintaining sexual purity, which resonated with Cambodian values for young women, discouraged them from teenage pregnancy and early marriage to Cambodian men, most of whom were in the working class. Both women set their sights higher.

Jackie too found the church very important in helping her to manage her feelings. Her father had been a doctor and was killed by the Khmer Rouge. After the family (mother, Jackie, younger sister, and brother) arrived in Oakland, they visited the Mormon Church, liked what they saw, and got baptized. When I first met Jackie, she was dressed for Sunday school in a pink blouse and tight satin skirt, both setting off her tumbling black hair. Her long nails were painted the same shade of pink, and tipped with glitter. (Cambodian girls dressed up for church as though they were going to a wild party; the goal seemed to be to look like suburban teenagers but with an element of bad-girl subversiveness in it. The Mormon officials apparently tolerated this mode of dressing on the part of new "ethnic girl" converts. (Long-established black Mormon women, like white ones, always seemed to dress conservatively in pastel or dark colors.) Jackie explained,

> The church has helped a lot. They only teach you the good stuff. In the past, I used to lose my temper easily, but after I came to Sunday school, and the teachers taught about how to be nice to your neighbor and stuff, then my whole attitude changed. I became a calm person and really nice. It's really interesting, like, every time I have problems in school I always kneel down and pray. It seems my prayers are always answered.

Clearly, the management of emotions and their appropriate expression were very important lessons for girls struggling with their family war traumas and adjusting to a new environment. Sophie talked about how the church helped her gain a sense of self-control and direction:

> My life has changed ever since I was baptized. Before, I didn't know who I was. I now believe that I am a spirit that came to earth to have a body, and will go back to heaven to be tested. I became happier and got closer to my family, learned to appreciate my family more. I was taught that we should just help each other. My dad risked his life for us, but I didn't know why he did it. After the church became part of my life, I learned step by step that he loved us. The church taught me to be more sensitive, to express my feelings verbally. They always talk about love, to show it, to tell it.
>
> In our family, we never did that. The culture is such that families do not say "I love you," "thank you." Now we Thais express more about love. At first we felt uncomfortable, but they're getting used to it. They still don't hug or kiss us [children].

In contrast to their parents' commands and silences, the church provided the vocabulary and gestures of love that the young women welcomed, giving them a language of sociability and belonging in white society, and a way to talk about who they really wanted to become. "Premarital sex is really discouraged. One leader says that she notices that Cambodian girls get married early, and she encourages us to go on to college and finish our education." These lessons in balancing self-control with an affectionate personality socialized the young women to old-fashioned American values of emotional work within the family and academic discipline to ensure a promising future. The cultivation of a virginal sexuality helped them not only to resist peer pressures in school, but also to prepare themselves for their future roles as loving wives and mothers.

For instance, Vanna said she was busy attending college, and not dating. She wanted to wait and marry a returned missionary; young Mormon men are all encouraged to serve two years as missionaries, after which they are considered ready for marriage. She described her plans:

I really like the Mormon idea of being married for eternity. There is less divorce among Mormons. As far as sex is concerned, being Mormon and being Asian are the same—not to have sex before marriage. You have to be morally clean; it applies to the men too. . . . We should marry between twenty-three and twenty-five years old. It is more than likely that I'd marry a Caucasian. I want someone who is well educated, doesn't smoke and drink, and who respects me for who I am.

Vanna's parents wanted her to marry her "own kind," but she did not believe that there were Cambodian men who possessed these qualities. "Most Cambodian guys say, 'I'm a man. Whatever I say is right.' I find Caucasian and Chinese men more attractive than Cambodian. The tall Chinese guys who look Caucasian, who are light-skinned and more into American traditions like dating, whereas Cambodian men hardly do that, like my brothers-in-law." The latter also had working-class jobs, such as glass manufacturing and packaging goods. Vanna sought middle-class status, a strategy that apparently was inseparable from marrying a white man. Through the lens of the church, she saw masculinity inscribed in class and ethno-racial terms:

As Mormons, we're more matured, there's trust between us. Non-Mormon Cambodian men don't trust their wives, and vice versa. They have a different kind of marriage. I'd feel more safe with Mormons because it's guaranteed that the marriage will last forever. Not with those Cambodian guys!

The Mormon Church's stepped-up missionary work among people of color resulted in increased numbers of young American missionaries marrying exotic women they met during their missions overseas or in minority communities in the United States. Two of Sophie's sisters married returned missionaries, whereas her getting a scholarship to BYU made her defer marriage:

After my older sister was baptized, she went on a mission to teach Cambodians, Laotians, and Americans in Utah for one and a half years. She was the translator for a missionary from here. Upon their return, she dated a returned missionary and got married in the temple. The bishop interviewed them first. Now my sister is a housewife, with one kid, and pregnant again. Her husband is an engineer. The Mormons believe in big families as a joy and a blessing. The more people are born, the more spirits come down to have bodies.

Sophie's younger sister Rita expressed the same values:

One thing they really stressed in the Young Women's classes is purity; to keep yourself clean before marriage. Our body is a temple, given by God. To keep it clean; this is similar to Cambodian values. They teach us about marriage in the temple. Find the right guy and lead him to it. It's forever!

When Sophie went to BYU, Rita, wanting "a change of scene from Oakland," visited her. In the first semester, Rita met Mike in the apartment complex

where they were staying, which he was helping to paint. He had been back
as a missionary from Korea for a year:

> He had a Korean fiancée but broke off with her before we got together. He
> was really understanding. Two months after we fell in love, he was sent to the
> U.S. army base in Germany. So we decided to get married immediately. His
> parents were on a mission to the Dominican Republic and said to us, "Go
> ahead." Then we went to Germany, where Mike was with the Mormon unit in
> the U.S. army there.

Her parents were not pleased that they got married in a hurry, with very few
Cambodian relatives present. But when I interviewed Rita, the young couple had returned to Oakland and were carrying an infant, on whom the
grandmother doted. Rita said she wanted to teach her baby about Cambodian values. "It all boils down to respect for the parents, but not a lot, because we live in America and our parents are not lenient. We are very different from non-Mormon friends. Most of us look for people who don't
smoke, or drink. My husband doesn't, and he is very patient. It is easier to
find someone who has some religion." Rita spent her free time teaching the
Gospel to Cambodian women and telling them how to understand their children, to be "reliant and open-minded."

Sophie was more ambivalent about finding the right match:

> I'm very picky. I date guys once or twice. I'm looking for a very strong person
> who is worthy to take me to the temple, who will love children, will love my
> parents, my culture [meaning food, dress]. I want both a temple wedding and
> a Cambodian wedding. Sometimes I think I'd want my husband to speak Cam-
> bodian, but a Mormon guy is my choice.

When I asked whether she had ever considered marrying a Cambodian man,
she simply said, "No. Because the Cambodian men, none goes to college. I
want someone at the same educational level as I am. Besides, most of the
Cambodian guys my age are already married."

These Cambodian women were learning not only to be good Mormon
wives and mothers, but also to embrace the idea of the nuclear family, and
to turn to their white Mormon sisters for some of the emotional support Cambodian women traditionally receive from their female kin. This search for
social and emotional networks among church women accelerated the process
of hierarchical incorporation. Mormon feminist Jill Mulvay Deer writes that
after the Mormon Church abandoned plural marriage, "the Mormon female
kinship network became less extensive and less essential," while the male leaders strengthened "the hierarchical chain of command" and "de-emphasized
the partnership of men and women outside the home."[33] The nuclear family represented a higher class status for the women, and within that configuration, they were socialized into the church-sanctified gender asymmetry.

If these examples indicate a broader trend in the career and marriage strategies of Cambodian teenagers, then there appears to be a bifurcation in the ways girls and boys negotiated their adult status. Most young men were either married men supporting their families by taking working-class jobs, or else had been pulled into the orbit of street gangs. In contrast, young women like those I interviewed placed a stronger emphasis on education and moving up into the middle class. As Sophie said, "Cambodian parents don't encourage men to go to college. My mum wanted me to work and make money too. But I've learned what's good for me—education. Without a degree, I can't have a career." This upwardly mobile path was forged with the help of churches that provided the middle-class mores, conduct, and self-scrutiny that eased the entry into higher education. Regulated within the racial hierarchy of the Mormon Church, Cambodian American women also came to acquire a racialized gender subjectivity that was shaped by a sense of white masculine superiority.

.   .   .

The Mormon Church, as an alternative modernizing force, was only the most successful of Christian institutions to wed religious asceticism with habits designed to accumulate economic status. While mainstream urban Americans may have lost this message, communities in the American heartland and poor immigrant groups see a connection between moral sobriety and business worthiness. In Asia, the Buddhist ethos has also become allied to capitalist conduct—get-rich Buddhist movements have emerged among the middle classes in Thailand and Taiwan—but in the United States, many poor immigrant communities turn to Christian churches and movements for revitalization and for learning to acquire the values and practices of economic individualism and citizenship.

The paradox is that Mormonism encourages a secular and individualized sense of self within a hierarchical structure. While racial discrimination has not been a church policy for some time, new immigrants are integrated through differentiation, producing a subordinating racial subjectivity among nonwhite converts that marks them as the Third World component of a global religious order. The recruitment and conversion of displaced populations like Cambodian refugees operate within a system of compassionate domination in which social support is accompanied by racial disdain, kindness is blended with cultural superiority, and acceptance is ordered by racial and gender configurations. Even as the church teaches recruits the initiative and self-discipline for negotiating the market economy and attaining the good life, this is done within a structure of white power that is more sharply inscribed than in the wider society, though continuous with it.

For some Cambodian women and men, "freedom" in America—in the sense of being released from Cambodian family rules—has made the church an indispensable structure of power that provides the social means to attain upward mobility, and a kind of dignity as a citizen. Buddha may be obscured, but young Cambodian Americans did not cease to wrestle with him as they engaged in an inwardly oriented search for the true self. Many insisted that they remained Cambodian and were drawing on their roots in Buddhist traditions when they interpreted Mormon doctrines and sought to reconcile or to bridge the two religions. Young women expressed contradictory impulses of desiring Mormon models of middle-class female subjectivity while feeling ambivalence about losing their own culture embedded in family relations. For young women following Mormon prescriptions for reinventing themselves, raced hypergamy sometimes became a further stage in the converging trajectories of social, class, and symbolic mobility that moved them closer to the white end of the prestige and dignity continuum.

Chapter 9

Guns, Gangs, and Doughnut Kings

FOR THE PRICE OF A CUP OF LATTE

My family and I emigrated from Cambodia to the United States in 1981. In 1982, at the age of 12, I began sewing in factories. I was paid by the piece. Initially, I made about $10 to $15 for 10 hours of work. I worked in these sewing factories until the age of 18, when I was making about $25 to $30 a day (for 10 hours of work). Then I went away to college. . . . I am not surprised that these sewing sweatshops still exist. I have refugee friends and neighbors who still work in these factories to supplement their income.

These factories usually pay wages in cash, untaxed and unreported. This "underground" money is desperately needed to supplement the monthly $900 welfare check for a family of four. Everyone involved is trapped. The sewing factory owners I worked for were not driving Mercedes Benzes or BMWs. They were working as hard to scrape a living as we workers were.

The preceding is a letter sent by a Berkeley resident to *The New York Times,* in response to a report about criticisms of immigrants going on welfare.[1] As it points out, the labor contractors for garment sweatshops were often Asian immigrants themselves, forced by the terms set by manufacturers and retailers into cutthroat competition with one another, and often unable to pay workers the minimum wage.[2]

Cambodian refugees, including children, tried to work; but for the majority—having less than a high-school education and limited proficiency in English—remaining on welfare was their only option,[3] because their skills relegated them to the class the resettlement authorities had mapped out for them: cheap labor for America's postindustrial economy. A recent study reported that about 30 percent of the one million Southeast Asians in the United States were on welfare even after a decade in the country.[4] Among Cambodians and Laotians in California, the number reached 77 percent.

But it is erroneous to assume that current newcomers to the United States are less self-reliant than were earlier generations of immigrants, the grandparents of many of the Americans who complain about immigrants today. A review of government censuses reveals that

> Contrary to popular myth, for example, more than half of public welfare recipients nationwide in 1909 were immigrant families, making new arrivals three times more likely than natives to be on the public dole, according to research accumulated by a 1911 commission on immigration. In Chicago, two-thirds of those receiving public assistance were foreign born. . . .
> Today, the weight of newcomers is proportionately far smaller. According to calculations from the 1990 census, 9% of immigrant households received welfare payments, compared to 7.4% of households headed by natives, although today's elaborate welfare system is costly.[5]

The widespread perception of Southeast Asian immigrants as shellshocked refugees or welfare dependents reflected the public dialogue of the 1990s, which increasingly called for a kind of biopolitical security against the influx of poor newcomers. One major argument holds that the unceasing influx of non-European immigrants will have the effect of producing a nation alien from its existing self.[6] In a special issue of *The New Republic* devoted to immigrants, sociologist Nathan Glazer supports slowing down immigration; reflecting common fears that the new immigrants are out of step with the nation's European roots, he wonders whether they will produce excellent students and scientists.[7] He questions whether non-European immigrants are going to acquire appropriately American cultural capital, and produce the kind of economic contribution that will make them worthy citizens.

The rosy picture of earlier immigrant generations has them scrambling up the rungs of the educational and economic ladders, reaching parity with natives in three generations. A statistical study of early twentieth-century immigrants embellished the myth by stating that it has taken them a century to become rich, as reflected in the later achievements of their descendants.[8] But contrary to the simplicity of the myth of ethnic succession on the one hand, and its partner the work-ethic succession on the other, social histories of labor and ethnicity provide evidence that both before and after the implementation of formal welfare programs, strategies for getting by within and across generations form a more complex picture. These strategies contain many common elements—uncertain low-wage jobs, the dole, illicit operations—though these elements have been ethnicized as "the Irish, Pole, or Italian pattern."[9] Generations of poor immigrants have also depended on wages earned as field laborers, factory workers, restaurant employees, gardeners, and housecleaners. Women's earnings were especially crucial when a male breadwinner was not making enough, was a migrant worker, or was otherwise missing.[10] Male immigrants had access to a succession of blue-collar jobs, and many did manage to establish basic security for their families, especially in the automobile and steel industries.[11] But, despite a seeming surfeit of blue-collar jobs, prejudice, exploitation, and exclusions pushed many poor immigrants into illegal activities instead. Criminal gangs were not uncommon among the first few generations of Irish, Italian, and Jewish newcomers, among others, who employed racketeering, gangland robbery, and white-collar crimes as a path to upward mobility. Stories about such outlaws have been celebrated in print and on film for expressing a kind of American heroic exuberance, a colorful part of the nation's past (when European immigrants were less white). As the underclass debate has shown, when African American migrants from the South joined European immigrants in the industrializing cities, such criminal activities became stigmatized and racialized as black. Race became part of the technology for defining and disciplining illegal activities in conditions of rampant unemployment.[12] Contrasted to the two figures of the immigrant hustler—the low-wage worker and the outcast hoodlum—is a glorified image of the tradesman, an independent entrepreneurial figure pulling himself up by the bootstraps who launched generations into the middle class (or so the Horatio Alger fable goes). Of course, some gangsters and robber barons, or their descendants, have historically been able to move on to become legitimate and respectable Americans.

Today, blue-collar jobs are no longer an abundant entry point for even high-school graduates, many of whom can look forward only to low-paid service jobs such as working in fast-food restaurants, cleaning hotels and offices, making deliveries, baby-sitting, and other junk work with no benefits or security.[13] Indeed, transnational labor markets, with a startling tolerance for un-American working conditions, rely on flexible and temporary labor regimes. Workers are compelled to be flexible in the sense that they are supposed not to be tied to a single line of work, but to be open to taking a variety of low-wage jobs as they become available. The stress is also on their agility in responding catch-as-catch-can to low-wage opportunities in conditions of unfettered competitiveness. Such short-term, part-time piecework cannot provide the basis of a lower-middle-class standard of living unless—as many Asian immigrants do—the family pools earnings from all working members to live and share things in common. But the existential insecurity is acute, and it is reflected in the way American cities no longer invest in an industrial center that brings together blue-collar workers and where "broad shoulders" are prized.

The new globalized city is a highly fragmented space dominated by a cosmopolitan elite, with few connections to highly localized ethnic neighborhoods and ghettos filled with people from around the world. Saskia Sassen has noted that

Corporate culture collapses differences, some minute, some sharp, among the different socio-cultural contexts into one amorphous otherness; an otherness that has no place in the economy; the other who holds the low-wage jobs that are supposedly only marginally attached to the economy. It therefore reproduces the devaluing of those jobs and of those who hold the jobs. The dominant economic narrative, by leaving out these articulations, can present the economy as containing a higher-order unity by restricting it only to the centrally placed sectors of the economy.[14]

Southeast Asian Americans are disproportionately represented among the new immigrants who are intermittently employed in the decentered, devalued, and subterranean industrial sectors of the Silicon Valley—surely the hub of the most globalized knowledge-based economy, in which opportunities for ordinary, routine, steady jobs for the working poor are shrinking rapidly. Although microchip assemblers, janitors, gardeners, and maids are crucial to the day-to-day running of the high-tech citadels, these workers have become invisible, laboring in back rooms, backyards, and private homes. They are marginalized as the kind of people that industry has no need to invest in because they can be replenished by newer, more desperate immigrants. The perception that new immigrants are good enough only for poorly paid, labor-intensive, and often unpleasant jobs (such as food packing) also helps to shape them as laboring subjects who, despite their best efforts, are highly vulnerable to the shifting tides of dead-end jobs.

The gaps are greater than ever between the minimum wage and middle-class living standards, between the social isolation of the hidden, inner-city ethnic ghettos and the information economy, between the regulating, scaled-down welfare state and the thoroughly unregulated, turbulent economy. Thus the welfare-receiving family and the ethnic community in general are compelled to subsidize these low-paid and irregular forms of wage work, and to absorb as well additional costs of child care and supporting laid-off or injured family members—in other words, the social reproduction of the laboring class.[15] Many of the working poor in the Silicon Valley cannot afford housing, and even in the best of times, thousands of ordinary workers have to make long commutes. Increasing numbers of working people are homeless, and some sleep in buses and shelters at night.[16]

Like other poor immigrants from Mexico and South America, Southeast Asian immigrants have found that America's service economy makes it impossible, for the non-English speaker or low-skilled immigrant, to make a quick transition into the kind of employment that will sustain the entire family. As poor refugees whose ethnic identity has been pigeonholed by the welfare system's perceptions, policies, and practices as belonging in the low-wage service economy, Cambodians seem bound to be California's new servant class. As the Californian economy surged in the 1990s, Southeast Asian Americans—like their Hispanic counterparts working in jobs whose hourly rate is about the price of a cup of designer coffee—have become a major element of the hidden labor force. Labor advocates have uncovered garment factories that pay workers sewing at home for ten-hour days, seven days a week, less than half of California's minimum wage ($5.75). The Department of Labor estimates that at least 60 percent of the 150,000 garment workers—mainly Asians and Hispanics—in the Los Angeles area are underpaid.[17]

Ethnic garment sweatshops have become a template for high-tech factories that employ people to do piecework at home. Poor Southeast Asian immigrants, mainly women, are contracted to assemble components in their homes at piece rates of $1–$5. They work in isolation, often in unsafe or unhealthy conditions, and lack contract security or grievance procedures. An electronics assembly manager for a Silicon Valley firm explained why he favored Southeast Asian immigrant female workers: "Just three things I look for in hiring . . . small, foreign, and female. You find those three things and you're pretty much automatically guaranteed the right kind of work force. These little foreign gals are grateful to be hired—very, very grateful—no matter what."[18] Such workers do not have overtime pay or other benefits of regular employees, but they seldom complain for fear of losing earnings.[19] Altogether, approximately half of the Southeast Asian population in and around the Silicon Valley has little choice but to assemble electronics components.

Other emerging ethnic enclaves include specialty food industries, which have greatly expanded to serve an affluent upper-middle class increasingly oriented toward gourmet cuisine,[20] and the child-care industry. Hispanic and Asian immigrants are hired as back-room workers at restaurants and supermarkets. Supermarket megachains operated by immigrant ethnic Chinese have used kinship, language, and cultural ties to control and exploit other Asian immigrants. Cambodian American women have also been trained to be baby-sitters; many care for children in their own homes, and have become popular as nannies for well-off families in California. The underground manufacturing and service labor market is turning out to be dominated mainly by Asian female and Hispanic male workers.

It is thus no longer clear that wage employment or nepotism in family businesses operates today under the same conditions that applied to previous decades of America's industrialization. With less support for human welfare as a political problem and more stress on individual competence and competitiveness, poor people are forced back on the moral economy of family, street, and community in a fluid economic environment. Market volatility itself becomes a form of labor regulation, requiring parents to work long or irregular hours as long as a job lasts. Such precarious employment and income conditions among adults add to the problems of undersupervised teenagers as the family daily searches for cash. Family-type gangs tend to flourish in ghetto neighborhoods; there young boys learn to deal with and to inflict violence, as well as picking up tough forms of masculinity along the way.

THE DANCE OF MANHOOD IN THE STREETS

While their mothers and sisters ran the homes and took in poorly paid work, many teenage Cambodian boys took to the streets. This was the public arena in which they had to establish themselves as young American males—tough, self-reliant figures who commanded some respect from other ethnic groups, and perhaps from themselves, in an unforgiving world of poverty, violence, and racism. The streets were a contrast to the home, where they were for the most part dependent on women and their welfare checks. Some children felt disassociated from their school, a terrain dominated by tougher kids from other ethnic groups, where they had to deal with dangerous and humiliating encounters with bullies. Faced with the lack of discipline in inner-city schools and uncertainty about the future, a variety of gangs sprang up, forming improvised societies for the gaining of street smarts, access to easy money, and protection from rival gangs. We might think of minority gangs as ethnicized networks of entrepreneurial subjects—creative, stylish, risk-taking, violent—who produce a street-based alternative to the conventional wage economy, and thus play a major role in shaping the impoverished multicultural slice of the American cityscape.

The police definition of a gang is a group of three or more persons that has as one of its primary activities the commission of criminal activities (assault, robbery, homicide, trade in controlled substances, shooting, arson, witness intimidation, theft of vehicles), and that has an identifying name and other trademarks.[21] This definition is too narrowly focused on types of crimes, and does not allow for the variety of associations that go by the name *gang*. It also fails to recognize the wide variation in degree and type of criminal activity within particular gangs and across gangs. Here, I use *gang* as a common term for a variety of same-sex groups and loose networks that, while connected to criminal activities, also includes social groups engaged in entrepreneurial and cultural activities. Some gangsters have become street entrepreneurs because the easy availability of guns and drugs provides illegal ways of gaining wealth. It is important to note that not all gang members participate in crime, that criminals are not always gang members, and that people migrate among different ethnic gangs. Furthermore, street gangs participate in a variety of licit and illicit activities, and they evolve over time in a variety of circumstances.

Early twentieth-century California was dominated by Hispanic, white (mainly from "Okie" communities), and African American gangs. By the late 1960s, easy access to guns had made city gangs more violent, as competitive gangs engaged in crimes and fights over turf. In Southern California after the Watts riots in the mid 1960s, the Bloods formed as a racial brotherhood at least partly motivated by the need to join together to fight when attacked by Hispanic cholos and white racists. They also engaged in criminal activities such as auto theft, burglary, and other crimes against property as a means to support themselves and to acquire weapons. Hispanic and white gangs were just as violent against people and property, and the continual influx of poor Hispanic immigrants contributed to intense turf warfare with African Americans in Los Angeles. Nevertheless, the Crips and the Bloods, originally from the South Central district of Los Angeles, were singled out by the police as the embodiment of gang violence. This image gained national prominence despite the fact that African American gangs also participated with the "radical civic police" such as the U.S. Brotherhood for community protection.[22] In 1966, the Black Panthers for Self-Defense called for full employment, decent housing, free health care, breakfast for schoolchildren, and an end to police brutality in Oakland. The media, however, dwelled on their (registered) guns and gangster rap, a combination that was frightening to the white majority. By the 1980s, African American gangs had become more violent, especially after the Crips and the Bloods seized control of the crack cocaine trade and spread their economic and cultural force to ghettos in other major cities.[23] Vietnamese gangs, sometimes with links to Chinese gangs in Chinatowns, also grabbed national headlines for violent crimes, mainly against their own community. But for Cambodian kids, African American gangs, more than any other ethnic grouping (including the Vietnamese), represented the iconic figures of street glamour and working-class masculinity.

In recent years, authorities in California have sounded the alarm that "Southeast Asian gangs" were among the fastest-growing criminal groups, but the groups most responsible for the image are violent Vietnamese gangs that prey on their own community. The most notorious gangsters are those street entrepreneurs who traffic in the economics of violence and death. Vietnamese criminal gangs began to emerge in the late 1970s, and they generally target members of their own community, who tend to keep wealth at home and don't report crimes to the police for fear of retaliation. In time, Vietnamese gangs such as Born to Kill traveled to cities across the country, engaging in auto theft, extortion, firearms violations, home-invasion robbery, witness intimidation, assault, and murder. Vietnamese gangs tend to be well armed and to use extreme violence to deter victims from reporting crimes. They operate as highly mobile, cross-country criminal enterprises, sometimes with links to ethnic Chinese gangs. Other Southeast Asian criminals also join Vietnamese gangs.

In Southern California, some Cambodian gangsters from Long Beach have teamed up with Vietnamese gangs against the Chicano Bloods, their feuds sometimes resulting in gunfights. In the late 1990s, a home invasion ended in the death of two Asian gangsters in Stockton. The two young Cambodian American men killed in the shootout were suspected of belonging to the Asian Street Walkers, a group that had in the past committed a variety of petty crimes but not violent home invasion. In the same year, also in Southern California, a Laotian man belonging to the Tiny Rascal Gangsters was sentenced to life in prison for participating in a bloody home invasion that took five lives.[24] The public learned from these two high-profile crimes that violent Southeast Asian gangsters are not all Vietnamese; some Cambodian and Laotian gangsters have copied their methods. Another copycat group was The Cambodian Killers, who were famous for armed robbery, murder, and drive-by shootings; they also ran a protection racket to squeeze money from local shopkeepers.

According to the police, the majority of Cambodian (and Laotian) gangs are not hard-core criminal syndicates but rather small groups of neighborhood predators, seldom well armed, confining themselves to a variety of petty crimes against property and managing turf issues by battling with neighboring gangs.[25] Cambodian gangs arose in the 1980s; they generally consisted of five to twenty members informally organized by leaders in their middle to late twenties. Some Cambodian kids, alienated from school or needing protection in school and on streets dominated by other ethnic groups, dropped out to join gangs. Many families told me that they were worried about their young teenage sons being induced to join street gangs. Some were attracted by the opportunity to make pocket money by breaking into cars. Because of their low earnings, the majority of these kids continued to receive some form of welfare payment, since as one teenager told me, "It is the only real [sure] way to survive." Most Cambodian gang youngsters were not violent, but rather kids who hung out together outside the home sharing camaraderie on the school playground and in the street. Sometimes Cambodian American gangsters stole cars for the radio, or for a lark, got drunk, or took drugs together. These gangs drew the attention of the police, probation officers, and Cambodian leaders, who cooperated in efforts to relieve some of the problems of young people. Asian police officers in Oakland occasionally offered to resolve conflicts among small-time thugs, or their disputes with other ethnic gangs.[26] But it seems clear that the rate of crime-related gang activities rose and fell in inverse proportion to the gyrations of the economy. For many teenage Cambodian Americans, becoming a gang member was primarily the most immediate way to get cash, to have some pocket money that would buy a measure of self-respect, as well as things such as sneakers that could win immediate admiration on the streets.

Cambodian gangs then are networks for trading mutual obligations among youths, as well as with older hoodlums who can guide them in the wider world, which their own parents (if they have any) cannot navigate with cultural assurance or political savvy. They also serve to provide social structures that construct and reinforce social norms. Boys told me about fights over girlfriends, sexual competitions that were part of the ritual for establishing the street-level masculine pecking order. Such gang activities regulate gender relations, in which boys internalize big-guy-gets-the-girl lessons and their implications about competition based on age, brawn, and economic power. Young women participated in gangs mainly as trophy girlfriends of gang leaders, but apparently, Cambodian girl gangs like the Asian GirlZ (AGZ) have arisen in other cities, such as Long Beach, California. Cambodian gangs seem to be developing out of a fusion of kinship and patron–client systems to organize activities for making wealth and managing risk in poor neighborhoods.

Gangs engage in economic work that is not recognized as such by society, because this work often operates outside the law, and generally outside the norms of routine, monotonous labor. Gangsters are people who spurn the regulation of local authorities, the moral reform of churches, and the work discipline of industry. Nevertheless, the Cambodian gangs described to me were not entirely dependent on petty crime as a mode for making income, and many gang members went to school, earned wages, and were legitimately employed in other ways, as well as being dependent on families and their welfare checks. But for Cambodian American youths, perhaps not unlike other minority street kids, becoming a gang member was the most obvious way to explore what it takes to become an American man.

Inner-city streets are the site and the situation for an alternative masculine sociality in opposition to the female-centered home, and for building an image of masculine toughness in place of the weakling image of the welfare kid. Generational conflicts and misunderstandings at home also intensified desires for a peer-oriented experience that would allow the immigrant boys to develop a tough, urban attitude in the intersecting crosscurrents of urban American culture. The streets offered a relatively regulation-free environment where young males could assert some economic independence from their parents, cope with uncertain economic and cultural options for their future, confront their marginality in society, and explore their budding American personalities, all away from imposed adult supervision by parents, social agencies, or the Buddhist temple.[27] In the swirling culture of violence, young men had to learn to protect themselves from everyday forms of racism and urban intimidation by tough posturing. As hoodlums and thugs, they marked and protected their own turf.

Street gangs provided informal social groupings for this isolated and impoverished community, as they have done for earlier generations of immigrants.[28] From what I could learn, Cambodian gangs were loosely knit groups of young males (fourteen to twenty-seven years old) that were modeled on family relationships and led by older men, whom younger members addressed as *bang* (a term of respect for an older relative). This structure can also be seen as a recasting of the Cambodian patron–client model, with youngsters looking up to an older male as guide, patron, and provider of resources. I was told by a former gangster that about 90 percent of Cambodian American boys in Oakland, where he grew up, joined street gangs at one time or another. Each boy formed a kind of dyadic relationship with the *bang,* who was both initiator into a streetwise adulthood and protector in the streets. It was clear, though, that much of this mentoring focused on identity formation rather than on violence, though one might have to resort to the latter to shape the former.

All gangs take their brand names seriously. For new minority gangs, the challenge was simultaneously to borrow and to differentiate from the semiotic language of other ethnic urban toughs, in order to select and sustain a fierce but distinctive ethnicized gang identity. The names of the Crips and the Bloods, their brand colors (blue and red, respectively), their rituals such as displaying colors and monikers, and their initiation rites soon gained national notoriety and were adopted by emerging ethnic gangs, such as the Hispanic Bloods. Cambodian and Laotian street gangs took inspiration not only from African American and Hispanic gang nomenclature but also from Vietnamese gang names, especially Born to Kill. Thus, Cambodian gangs had names such as Cambodian Killers (CK), Cold Blood Crips (CBC, a fusion of the two top African American gang names), and the more benign Asian BoyZ (ABZ). The naming form seems to suggest a wordplay that stresses a tough attitude, but also a kind of esprit de corps. Cambodian kids used the acronyms rather than the full names of their gangs, in a kind of intraethnic secret code.

Young boys confided that they were regularly jumped from behind by other ethnic gangsters throwing dirt and wielding broken bottles, knives, and even guns. Hispanic Bloods or Vietnamese gangs asserted their superiority by, as one former Cambodian gang member said, "showing signs, wearing colors, and giving bad looks." At the same time, such symbolic forms and rituals projected urban toughness and defined boundaries in the tense dance of turf protection and urban masculine one-upmanship. The gang names, colors, and trademarks at once negotiated relations with their counterparts from similarly subordinated minority groups such as the Laotian Oriental Crips and the Mien Asian Pride Crips, with whom they were in some competition, and also mutually signaled ethnic pride.

Gang activities in all of their manifestations are centrally involved in shaping and regulating the public personae of boys from a weak and resource-poor ethnic community. Gang leaders and would-be leaders sought to build up their public power not only through socializing younger boys in criminal activities and through their urban strut or styles, but also by using gangster rap and ghetto talk to shape a reputation through the exaggeration of personal achievements. Cambodian kids referred to ghetto talk as a "second language" that they used outside school. Encounters with the law or a stint in prison were badges of honor that drew impressionable boys and girls.

Much attention has been given to gangland attire, how it signals membership and can become a target of rival gangs' bullets if worn in the wrong neighborhood. Gang clothing—especially jackets, caps, colors, and insignia—is a primary form of identification. Among Hispanic gangsters especially, attire is supplemented by unique trademarks such as tattoos, hand signs, hairstyles, brand names, and even graffiti as codes of membership. In recent years, hip-hop music and the association of sports and gang insignia have crossed over into middle-class youth fashion, lending gangster style and gangster rap an uncertain but tolerable respectability. After all, as one California police report cautioned,

> The gang attire in and of itself does not mean that more crimes are also being committed. . . . Growing out of the "grunge" look and with the adulation of the hip hop culture with its "attitude," baggies and shaved heads, or gang attire, has become popular nation-wide among teens including upper and middle-class white adolescents as well. Gang attire is displayed everywhere as the chic fashion statement for young people. It is shown all over MTV and other teen videos. Of course, teens have for many years adopted the dress of one another, particularly in ways found offensive to teachers, parents, and other authority figures—nothing is new about that. Today, however, gang attire is displayed with fanfare; it is widespread even among the wares of some of the very posh, expensive designers. But in the wrong neighborhood, gang attire can get a youth in a lot of trouble, and maybe even get shot! On the other hand, white teens in upper and middle class white suburban neighborhoods who sport the look will probably not be rounded up in "sweeps." In addition, focusing too much on attire as a tool for gang identification clearly leads to outright discrimination giving authorities license to apprehend and investigate young people when there is no rational basis for either inquiry or arrest.[29]

Of course, recognizing gangster attire as an emblem of youthful rebellion does not guarantee that minority kids "in the wrong neighborhood" experimenting with a tough gangster persona will not be automatically suspected by the police.

In his study of youth culture, Paul Willis notes that there is a "symbolic work" that daily draws on the raw resources of the body, language, cultural framework, and consumer items to define and recode symbols, giving them specific meanings. To his mind, this is "necessary" cultural production because many young people feel more themselves in leisure than they do at work, and they are constantly engaged in the work of forging "visible identities and styles outside or against work and working respectability."[30] Minority gang members do not draw their repertoire of symbols and signs from white gangs (the Aryan Nation, Skinheads, Hell's Angels) not only because most white gangs are fundamentally driven by racism and commit hate crimes, but also because they represent white forms of countercultural production. For many minority youths, at stake are the material and the symbolic forms that sustain individual and community in opposition to dominant white cultural prescriptions and meanings. The expressions and styles—sartorial and verbal—borrowed from the Crips and the Bloods encode an urban, gritty, stylized "don't mess with me" masculine identity. It is important to remember that African American men historically suspected of being sexually ambiguous or aberrant were pressured to be "more manly"—a trend that saw its fullest expression in the hypermasculine arena of gangs and sports that has been marketed by corporations as black culture. The term *BoyZ* became a positive tongue-in-cheek symbolic reversal of this supersaturated image of toughness and an embracing of the dominant culture's term of denigration.

Cambodian youths incorporate such elements into their self-fashioning as Cambodian American *BoyZ in the 'Hood*. I met Joe—a seventeen-year-old former gang member, attired in a large torn T-shirt, earrings, low-slung baggy khakis, and heavy shoes—sweeping debris in his uncle's doughnut shop. Joe had a silver Cambodian earring in one ear and a Buddha amulet on a gold chain, and with his spiky, colored hair and insouciant look, he could have posed for a Benetton "cross-cultural" commercial. By thus locating himself in the universe of gangland insignia, Joe was shaping himself as a youthful consumer, projecting an individualized urban masculinity that was at once distinctive, stylish, subversive, and definitely not white.

Joining a gang was mainly a rite of passage for many second-generation Cambodian kids, a means for engaging characteristically minority forms of masculinity, and a creative way to use consumer elements to make themselves visible in urban America. Petty crimes furnished pocket money to supplement low wages earned at Levi Strauss or the take-out joint. At the same time, interactions with other ethnic gangs (rather than with their parents) provided the opportunity to develop ideas about manhood and gender relations. There was a recognized ethno-racial ranking of powerful outlaw symbols, with African American gangs supplying most of the original naming forms, sartorial styles, language, and gestures that constituted a constellation of aggressive and subversive meanings in ghetto neighborhoods. Drawing on elements in these complex sign systems, other minority youngsters crafted their own public identities, and learned to negotiate turf issues and build ethnic pride of place, often in a manner that was creative, humorous, and not always violent. These boys were also attracted to gangs for the social and cultural materials that provided for shaping their own personalized identity within an inner-city youth ideal of a masculine counternation. The gangs' vital expressions of street dynamics and cultural vibrancy, however, cannot be disassociated from the disruption, delinquency, and violence in public life that increase their "nuisance power" in the eyes of authorities.[31] In this way, street gangs participate in the vicious cycle of social exclusions. Even the trappings of their masculine otherness depend on the committing of petty crimes. The commercial appropriation of their violence-saturated forms— rap music, brutish song lyrics—both exploits the gang figure as designer fodder and condemns him as criminal outcast, intensifying the mutual estrangement between street toughs and the public.

THE DOUGHNUT EMPORIUM

America is a miraculous country.
TED NGOY, *the "Father of Doughnut Entrepreneurialism"*

In recent years, Californians have noticed that more and more doughnut shops are being operated by Cambodian Americans. By the late 1990s, the Winchell's Donut House chain was being replaced in many places by independent doughnut shops owned by Cambodian Americans.[32] The story has it that a Ted Ngoy—identified as a former Cambodian ambassador to Thailand or a former Cambodian army officer (or both)—found refuge with his family in Orange County, where he first encountered an American doughnut. Ngoy applied for a job as a trainee in a Winchell's shop. After a year, he borrowed money to buy his own shop, Christy's (named after his wife), in La Habra. By the mid 1980s Ngoy owned a chain of fifty doughnut shops, stretching from San Diego to San Francisco, and a luxury home on a private lake in Mission Viejo. "America is a miraculous country," Ngoy told the *Los Angeles Times* in 1989. He has since returned to Cambodia to "enter politics."[33] Ngoy is credited with training hundreds of his countrymen. He made loans available to workers to help them start their own shops. By spawning an ethnic industry, he came to embody the Cambodian American success story.

What this legend underplays is that Ngoy was a Sino-Cambodian, one of the old Phnom Penh social and economic elite who survived the Pol Pot slaughter. Among the Cambodian refugees, they are perhaps the best able to take advantage of the American economic scene. Before 1970, Sino-Cambodians composed one-third of the population in Phnom Penh, and were also found in Battambang and Kampot. They controlled the rice trade, retail trade, and import–export businesses.[34] With their background in running family businesses and experience at pooling resources, Sino-Cambodians felt that they did not need to rely on American institutions in order to find their legs in this country.

In the San Francisco Bay Area, including Stockton, there were in the 1990s

Figure 11. Randy Yu's doughnut shop, also serving designer coffee.

120 doughnut shops operated by Cambodian Americans, 80 percent of whom were of Chinese ancestry. Sino-Cambodians also opened shops in Modesto (eleven) and Sacramento (eight). Cambodian Americans operated doughnut shops in Los Angeles and New York as well. Many have pointed out that it was in some ways an ideal business for newcomers: one did not need to know good English to learn to make pastries; the job required only hard work, and a willingness to work odd hours and accept being apprenticed at little or no pay to the shop owner. A Cambodian American manager of Donut Star in San Francisco was quoted as saying, "Getting hired at a place where your boss and colleagues speak Chinese was a real incentive for my wife and I to take on this work five years ago. The prospect of working without language barriers and amongst the comfort and familiarity of our own folk is attractive."[35] These family businesses did not need to bother with union rules, and apprentices were trained for up to a year without pay, often working at night. Shops depended on unpaid or underpaid family labor. The combination of opportunity to learn from one's ethnic compatriots, apprentice system, hard work, and fortuitous circumstances enabled displaced Sino-Cambodians to take on an established restaurant chain and reenact the classic American story of immigrant family labor. But is this a classic American story of the mom-and-pop enterprise, or is it a tale of nepotism in a "family business" that grew into a franchise chain?

I interviewed Randy Yu, because his doughnut shop (see figure 11) was on my way as I went to pick up my daughter at school. It took me a couple of phone calls to fix a date with Yu, because he was always busy traveling among his many different shops. As I waited in one of his shops, nursing a cup of standard American coffee, Yu drove up in a red Cadillac. Practically the first thing he said to me was that he usually drove a green pickup truck, but that day he was using his wife's Cadillac. The car had been his gift to her for working so hard to help him get started in the business. Now that he had succeeded, she could stay at home or go shopping. These are new Cambodian American figures—the entrepreneur and his consumer wife, a Cambodian woman who drives her own flashy car.

Yu said that 30 percent of Cambodian refugees in the United States were ethnic Chinese, and that they were the ones who were in business. Sino-Cambodians, he said, quickly took over the doughnut business because it was "too hard work for the 'natural Cambodians.'" In Phnom Penh, the Chinese commercial elite had a leisurely life, attended by servants. But the Pol Pot time changed everything. Having spent two years in Khao-I-Dang, Yu noted that many people from privileged families like his learned to make money there. "During the war, people got very smart, smuggling goods across Khmer Rouge lines and selling them in Khao-I-Dang. They worked very hard, not like before." Yu went on to describe how he became a minor doughnut king.

Yu and his wife used to work sixteen-hour days, and for years spent nights in doughnut shops, taking turns every other night. He apprenticed himself to a friend for six months with no salary to learn everything—mixing batter, baking, setting out the wares, sales, and the financial end of the business. Then, in 1983, Yu bought his first store for twenty-five thousand dollars, using loans from family members. Next, he bought a shop in Albany, near Berkeley, and trained his half-brother, Joe's father, to be the baker—a job that required him to come in at two in the morning to prepare that day's batch of doughnuts. Yu said that for a family man, owning and operating two shops is the optimal strategy, because if you have more than that, labor costs and the amount of time each spouse has to spend at each shop (ten hours a day) will be too much to make the enterprise truly profitable.

At this point, the by-the-bootstraps family operator transformed into the mobilizer of an ethnic labor pool for building up a chain of businesses. Yu started loaning money and training relatives to operate shops in other towns. When he ran out of relatives, Yu recruited individuals from other minority groups whom he partially absorbed into his kin-based business network. The sales clerk in his Albany shop was a Laotian teenager. He employed a Hispanic man in the same capacity for another shop he recently bought in Daly City. By the time I met him, he was the owner of at least ten doughnut shops.

Yu's story echoes the stereotype of the mobilization of family labor, the recruitment of relatives or pseudo-kin, and the circulation of money in the making of a traditional American ethnic family enterprise. As newcomers with no credit history, Cambodian Americans—like other impoverished people—could not rely on American banks. Sino-Cambodians mobilized cash and savings from their relatives and friends through a rotating credit system called *hui* in Mandarin and *thong thing* in Khmer. A typical lending circle is made up of relatives and friends. Meeting once a month, the club awards a loan sometimes to the bidder with the highest interest rate, and at other times to the bidder with the greatest need. In this way, small-timers can get startup capital of twenty thousand dollars or so to make a down payment on a shop, and then they pay back the lenders from earnings each month. By the late 1990s, it cost fifty thousand to sixty thousand dollars to establish a doughnut shop, but twice as much in cities such as San Francisco.

Here we have a classic American family business, making and selling doughnuts in the neighborhood, but with a twist. There are Cambodian American family-operated doughnut shops, but the rotating credit system allows a mom-and-pop operation to expand into a franchise system. As Marilyn Strathern has argued, commodification allows the money that sticks to a family to circulate beyond the immediate family, within the wider kinship group.[36] Entrepreneurs like Yu become the capitalists who seed new business units that are partially based on exploiting the unpaid labor of relatives and minority friends. Yu would establish a shop, then sell it after a year or two to a relative or friend who had worked for a while without pay, while Yu would move on to a bigger shop. This way, thousands of Cambodian American families in California managed to set up family doughnut businesses, and many more are running units in franchise chains owned by energetic fellows like Yu. These chains, based on nepotism and kinship networks, eventually allowed Cambodians to control the doughnut industry in the state.

The very circumstances that led Cambodian Americans to carve out an economic niche for themselves in the doughnut business also produced a similar success story among Vietnamese, who have come to dominate the nail-salon industry. Like doughnut making, doing nails offers an easy entry point for hardworking immigrants without a good education. Vietnamese immigrants in Southern California first opened nail salons as a sideline employment for young women (between the ages of twenty-one and thirty-five). By the late 1990s, the nail manicure industry had grown into a more than $6.5 billion industry, with half of the nation's manicurists being of Vietnamese descent. In many cases, nail salons are family-operated affairs, with mothers teaching daughters and cosmetology certification tests administered in Vietnamese. Fathers or husbands may own the family salons and have shares in other nail shops. Kim, a licensed manicurist in San Francisco's Pacific Heights, said, "The younger people, they go to school and learn English. They don't want to do nails. They work in offices."[37]

After having learned to operate doughnut shops, many Cambodian families wanted to try other American mom-and-pop businesses, such as running gas stations or hamburger joints or Cambodian-cuisine restaurants with names like Angkor Wat and Battambang. For Yu, however, doughnut shops are a better business than restaurants, because restaurants are even more labor-intensive. And besides, there is "loss from sales tax, about eighty dollars per thousand, that works out to three thousand dollars per year for the government!" In doughnut shops, most of the business is take-out. Nevertheless, he pointed out, "Doughnut shops are finished now as a way to make good money." There were too many in the Bay Area, and the cash price to buy an existing business had risen to a hundred thousand dollars. He had already turned his entrepreneurial energy in another direction: "Better to buy a house—a couple hundred thousand, and wait for the value to rise before selling it. In five years it will make a lot of difference." Pause. "I am always thinking about making more money," he said with a big grin. He confessed that he was in debt again, having borrowed money from relatives to buy eight houses for rental.

Yu's story is a wonderful example of how different these contemporary mom-and-pop operations are, because they go beyond being stand-alone family enterprises. Instead, they are units in a chain that develops from the entrepreneur's use of nepotism to mobilize unpaid and overworked labor to build an empire within the ethnic labor niche. Yu is a small-time homo economicus who has been able to leverage value garnered in a low-status take-out business into the higher-yielding, more prestigious sector of real estate. Already, Cambodian franchise chains of doughnut shops are moving to cities such as Detroit—"The auto workers, they want lots of doughnuts." Cambodian doughnut king Ning Yen has a multimillion-dollar business that includes the principal distributorship of doughnut-making ingredients and equipment to his compatriots' shops.[38] He plans to introduce the pastries to China and South Korea.[39]

The next generation may not want to invest in the labor and ability of relatives, or to circulate money among a circle of pseudo-kin as a way to make a family business. They may want to stress the individual acquisition of knowledge and become highly paid professionals, more like the now-standard image of Asian Americans, or they may prefer to become a different kind of businessman. Joe confessed that his childhood was spent living in different Cambodian enclaves around the West, as his father moved from doughnut shop to doughnut shop to learn his trade. Yu gave him the best pay, so he decided to work full-time in the Albany shop. The family moved a lot because Joe's parents did not think that children should be limited by the local conditions of ghettos. Observing how hard his dad worked, however, Joe did not see a future for himself as a doughnut king. He wanted to go to business school and later operate a launderette instead, "because this would be easier than the doughnut shop; the laundry machines do the work. Besides, you get cash immediately from the machines." His goal was to be a different kind of American entrepreneur, operating a chain of cleaner businesses, perhaps.

THE HELPING PROFESSIONS

The majority of Cambodian Americans could afford to take few risks, and, like other poor immigrant and minority communities, they still relied on a range of helping professions to get their needs translated and wants met. This demand for social services provided an opening for a small group of Southeast Asians—working as translators and aides in schools, hospitals, and government offices—to ascend to the middle class. Phauly Sang's career trajectory is fairly representative of how educated Cambodian Americans climbed into the middle class. As I mentioned before, after she arrived she tried to get a hospital job as a lab technician, but local hospitals would not accept her Phnom Penh license. She learned to drive and to type, and soon became a public-school bilingual teacher's aide. Still on welfare, she moved on to a part-time job in family planning, teaching Southeast Asian women how to use birth-control devices she herself had never used. A few months later, Phauly found a full-time job as a translator in a prestigious hospital, and bought herself a nice car. For the next few years, she and her relatives pooled money to buy a house, and she devoted much of her energy to sponsoring relatives still in refugee camps to come to America. Because she signed an agreement with the INS that those relatives would not depend on government support after they arrived, Phauly started a home business, in addition to keeping her hospital job. She converted her living room into a workroom, putting her newly arrived relatives to work sewing pieces for Chinatown's garment factories. While her pressing financial needs were understandable, she became in effect an agent in supplying cheap exploitable labor for the sweatshop economy.

Like many Cambodians in the helping professions, Phauly came to reflect deeply on how her actions mediated between her community and the dominant institutions, and how they shaped norms within her own community. This mediating role engendered profound personal ambivalence, as the experiences of mental-health worker Mr. Eam (chap. 4), and of social workers Peter Thuy (chap. 1) and Sam Ngor (chaps. 6 and 7) have also shown. They were supposed to instill the very normative regimes among their compatriots that they themselves were still uncertain about, and they recognized that they were disciplining instruments for remaking their own people into appropriate kinds of American subjects. The ethical uncertainties associated with being a helping professional were compounded when they felt that their community was the brunt of antiwelfare criticisms, and that they had to explain and justify the needs of terribly helpless people to receive welfare. Phauly was also upset when newspapers claimed that 65 percent of Cambodian refugees were "depressed"; she protested that in her experience, this was not true, and that such branding of Cambodians was part of a range of tactics on the part of intractable individuals and mental-health clinics aimed at obtaining more funds.

At the same time, Cambodian social workers were learning their craft from established American professionals, those specific intellectuals who were often the very source of the biased perceptions, categorization, and stereotyping of what being a Cambodian American should mean. Thus, as bilingual, mediating second-tier professionals, Phauly Sang, Mr. Eam, Peter Thuy, and Sam Ngor were crucial to the human technologies for constituting autonomous subjects, but were also promoting values that they were not entirely in accordance with. In their conversations, they occasionally criticized what they saw as the extreme individualism and selfishness of American culture. Phauly, for instance, who had lost her husband in the war, would not consider marrying a non-Cambodian man despite the interest she had attracted from male coworkers, because she was not convinced that long-resident Americans shared Cambodians' cherishing of human relationships. Even so, all of them felt that they were doing extremely gratifying, if frustrating, work that gave them the chance to provide necessary resources, help, and culturally sensitive comfort to their countrymen, especially to the weak, the confused, and the elderly.

Perhaps it would not be wrong to say that contemporary neoliberal capitalism progressively divests society of its moral obligations by evacuating institutions of moral purpose, and by forcing more and more social institutions such as the family to serve the economy, and not the other way around. In late 1999 Bill Clinton, a Democratic president, cut back on social programs and pushed needy families onto workfare, saying that "Work is more than just a weekly paycheck. It is, at heart, our way of life. Work lends purpose and dignity to our lives, instills in our children the basic values that built our nation."[40] But dignity now demands greater sacrifice, because working people have fewer claims on the state than before, and must turn to their families and community for support to make ends meet. As neither industry nor the state seems invested anymore in the working poor, their acute vulnerability can be shielded only by access to a variety of family and social networks that sustain individuals one paycheck away from being homeless. It is the job of immigrants employed in the helping professions to regulate their compatriots, who may not yet realize their impending loss of entitlements, and move them off welfare.

Work as the centerpiece of an American ideology of respectability takes on new meanings in such circumstances, as institutions formerly endowed with moral purpose—such as the welfare state and the family—are either stripped down or forced to perform as economic ventures. At the same time, the entrepreneurial figures who deploy nepotism to mobilize unpaid or underpaid labor within ethnic enclaves build business chains they can extend to their home countries.

TRANSNATIONAL CAMBODIANS

There is a tiny community of elite Cambodian Americans—aristocrats, professionals, and students, many of whom arrived before the refugee wave—who link their notion of the American way (democracy and market freedom) to the reconstruction of their home country. An estimated six hundred successful Cambodian Americans, who come largely from the Seattle area, have gone back to "strengthen democracy and liberalism in Cambodia."[41] Working people and college students have sought employment with social-service agencies with names like CANDO that aim to teach Cambodians the basics about democracy, elections, voting, and political responsibility.[42] Some of the more prominent returning Cambodian Americans have run for political office, mainly supporting opposition political parties. As mentioned earlier, doughnut king Ngoy returned to Cambodia, while another former doughnut entrepreneur, Noeun Kim Ou, became Prime Minister Hun Sen's defense minister. Some Cambodian Americans ran for office as independents, including a woman from Oakland who closed her restaurant to participate in the elections, but lost. Yu was cynical about Cambodian Americans who returned to engage Cambodian politics: "Why? Because they were in the government before. Also to make money through the government connection. But most lost all their money."

Cambodian Americans who wish to share their notion of American citizenship—representative government, fair elections, and entrepreneurialism—include businessmen who want to build business parks in Phnom Penh, but doing so would entail relocating squatters who not so long ago were war refugees like themselves. Many simply returned to provide economic resources to relatives and the hometown, and perhaps in the process also scout out business opportunities. Yu returned to Cambodia three times with friends to "help the poor," including relatives, and to rebuild a Chinese school in Battambang. He believed that Cambodia would prosper in the future, and then perhaps he would return to set up business there. He had been reluctant to sponsor two surviving brothers to come to America because, he said, the wait for siblings was about ten years. But he may also have been thinking about employing them as local agents for his future transnational business ventures. Like many Cambodian American tourists, Yu had no intention of living in Cambodia, but wanted to maintain kinship, cultural, and economic connections. Indeed, Cambodian Americans are considered no longer "pure"

Khmer, because they are cut off from their Cambodian spiritual home;[43] but even so, many are attracted by the idea of promoting a combination of American democracy and transnational ethnic enterprises.

.   .   .

Despite the street glamour of Southeast Asian gangsters, the majority of Cambodian Americans are employed workers, service providers, and small businessmen. Doughnut entrepreneurship represents the emergence on a small scale of transnational ethnic networks that build on nepotism and labor mobilization among kin and ethnic labor markets. They are modest operations, however, compared to Asian managers and professionals from Taiwan, Hong Kong, and India, who have forged transnational business networks in the high-tech industries and other venues of power. As we turn to these other affluent Asian immigrants in the next chapter, it should become clear that the varied insertions of Cambodian and other Southeast Asian immigrants into the globalized economy have had a splintering effect on the concept of Asian American identity, reflecting their differential positioning along the black–white continuum.

PART IV

Reconfigurations of Citizenship

Chapter 10

Asian Immigrants as the New Westerners?

That common, legendary root goes even deeper—to America itself, to the New World Dream of rebirth and self-realization in a spacious land uncontaminated by memory, tradition, and restraint. California became, as it had to, the New World's New World, its last repository of hope. In California, you come face to face with the Pacific and yourself. There is nowhere else to go.

SHIVA NAIPAUL, *Journey to Nowhere*

California's "New Ethnics" are three parts Hispanics and one part Asians. In one generation here, Asians' incomes have equaled those of Anglos. Over half of all Asians have a college degree: Their rapid economic progress makes Asians the most successful immigrants ever. . . . "the California Dream of the '50s and '60s is dead." . . . But a New California Dream for immigrants has been born. Barring economic calamity, the New Ethnics will build a new society based on American laws, Asian business skills, and Hispanic labor.

PATRICK REDDY, *"Immigrants and the New California"*

The first quote, penned by a Caribbean novelist who had absolutely no intention of lingering in California, is an older interpretation of mainstream American visions of the state, circa 1980.[1] But for new Asian immigrants, California is the Old World's New World, the West of the East, a place where the Pacific ends and a hypermodernity (skipping over the old modernities of Europe and the American eastern seaboard) begins. Asian immigrants are the quintessential American dreamers, seeking, in Naipaul's words, "rebirth and self-realization in a spacious land uncontaminated by memory, tradition, and restraint"—or at least, seeking through hard work and social mobility ways of paying back as well as transforming those entanglements across the Pacific. While the West is a closed frontier for old dreamers, to Asian immigrants it is an ever-expanding frontier of global capitalism that integrates America into Asia ever more closely.[2]

The second quote captures in an optimistic vein the radical demographic changes that have come with immigration and are reconfiguring class in California.[3] But can the ever-widening class structure be so neatly split between Anglos and Asians on the top, and Hispanics on the bottom? And do American laws still ensure that conditions in the wide range of workplaces safeguard our values concerning the conditions of free labor, and thus our moral understanding of American citizenship? This chapter considers the changing ethnic composition of California, showing how theorizing about Asian Americanism has been outdistanced by the new demographics of globalization. As the frontier continues to move eastward across the ocean, the diversity of citizen-subjects skillful at exploiting the ambiguity of borders now raises questions about American citizenship. In what ways can the mobility and agents of neoliberal capitalism produce continuities or discontinuities in the process of racial bipolarism on the one hand, and in the ethical substance of American citizenship on the other?

ASIAN AMERICA: A UNIFIED COMMUNITY OF ADVERSITY?

Southeast Asian immigrants are only one element in the recomposition of the Asian American population, in this hypercapitalist age in which the old model of coming to belong through the shared adversity of an ethnic group has been outstripped by the new demographics of globalization. The rise of the notion of Asian Americanism can be understood within the larger American historical tradition that ethnics can gain equal citizenship only through suffering, having overcome cultural differences through a social death and been reborn as "clean-cut" Americans. In this scheme of citizenship through moral suffering and justice, Native Americans, African Americans, and immigrant ethnics have had to constitute themselves ideologically as communities of adversity and suffering.[4] This ideological structuring of belonging has shaped social concepts about what it means to be particular kinds of American ethnics, and since the Civil Rights Act of 1964, the language of victimization has taken on a whole new dimension, especially for women and for Asian American advocates demanding moral justice.[5]

The forging of an Asian American political identity began in the 1960s, when college students and professors on the West Coast first articulated a shared history of racial exclusion and oppression. Inspired by the African American civil rights movement, Asian American activists pointed to early twentieth-century exclusions of Chinese workers, the exploitation of Asian plantation and railroad workers, and the incarceration of Japanese Americans during World War II, and maintained that Asian Americans, regardless of their background, were constituted as a single race through their experiences in the United States. While African American struggles were their immediate inspiration, these Asian American activists' arguments were situated within the structure of ethnic belonging, shaping a social consciousness of historical injury that constituted social capital to be used as the ground of their moral right to belong. The leading texts in this effort are Ronald Takaki's *Strangers from a Different Shore: A History of Asian Americans* and Sucheng Chan's *Asian Americans: An Interpretive History*. These widely read books have been influential in shaping undergraduates' views about how Asian Americans should see themselves. Takaki justifies attributing homogeneity to the diverse flows from Asia over the past two centuries on the basis of their shared experience of racial exclusion and their convergent labor histories. Because the appearance of Asians and their origins from across the Pacific challenge the old notion of America as a homogeneous nation of European origins, Takaki says, Asian residents and immigrants as a group have not been "allowed to feel at home" but rather treated as "strangers from a different shore."[6]

Chan also points to a common racial oppression, but she is interested in the making of "Asian American culture" since the 1970s, primarily a construction of students, faculty, writers, and artists. These efforts, "molded by one or more Asian traditions," are blended with "selected strands of the Euro-American heritage," and "the legacy born of the struggles of nonwhite people to survive and to carve a place for themselves in a country whose culture is infused with a consciousness of color hierarchy."[7] Thus while Takaki's definition of *Asian American* depends on the common historical experience of discrimination as a race anomalous in European visions of the American nation, Chan's focus is on the contemporary production of a unique identity by elites of diverse Asian backgrounds, mainly on or near Californian campuses.[8] As Chan has noted, Asian American university departments and their selection of books and courses have everything to do with the production of a politically correct Asian American identity. For activists of this generation, the pan-Asian identity was "based on the idea that Asian Americans shared a common history of exclusion in America, that they had been discriminated against, that they had been exploited as cheap labor and then discarded."[9]

A third discourse on Asian Americanism focuses explicitly on political coalitions that form in response to continued racial labeling and discrimination against Asian Americans. As the 1965 change in immigration law allowing family reunification increased the diversity of immigrations from Asia, the claim of uniform racial oppression gave way to a more equivocal formulation of a pan-Asian ethnicity forged through struggles to defend the interests and rights of citizens identified as Asian Americans. This political strategy was inspired by the concept of African American panethnicity that arose in the face of the shared racial discrimination of the distinct and various populations brought to this country as slaves.[10] The continued perception of Asian Americans as "foreigners within"[11] and periodic racial attacks against individuals for being "Asian" compelled activists to organize, through a web of associations, a "pan-Asian ethnicity" that fought against racial stigmatization and struggled to protect common interests.[12] Asian American scholars do not deny the diversity of Asian immigrants or the differences in their historical and cultural experiences, both in their home countries and in the United States.[13] Attention to the heterogeneity and the changing composition of Asian Americans,[14] however, takes a backseat to the construction of a community that has suffered moral injustice, and thus won the moral right to be equal citizens. Thus, on the one hand, the effects of ongoing racial categorization and discrimination impose a racial commonality on rather diverse communities; on the other, the call for a pan-Asian ethnic alliance stresses the production of a panethnic "culture and consciousness" that is born of political exigency, but ends up promoting the concept of a subordinated Asian race in America.[15]

More recently, the pan-Asian category has expanded to include Pacific islanders, creating a whole new ethno-racial entity called Asian Pacific Islander American. Roping in marginalized immigrant communities such as South Asians, Southeast Asians, and Tongans has made possible the claim that the total number of Asian Americans exceeds eleven million at the turn of this century.[16] The hope is that by expanding the Asian American category, opportunities will be enhanced for constructing a sufficiently large voting bloc to win political representation and to combat continuing racism and discrimination. As a postmodern version of the American tradition of interest-group politicking, Asian Americanism is a strategy to seek moral justice and redress for past adversity, even when recent foreign-born newcomers had no part in that history. The point is not that individual Asian Americans may not have been discriminated against, but rather that Asian Americans must be constituted as a community of shared racial oppression in order to gain the moral capital to be considered equal citizens.

Asian Americanism as an idea has been mainly the product of Chinese American or Japanese American academics and activists seeking to forge a racial community that has historically been wronged, but they have great difficulty in reproducing that model in a context of extreme flux and diversity among Asian American populations in the country. This narrative strategy is what Anthony Appiah has called a "politics of compulsion,"[17] the compulsion to self-script an ethnicity- or race-based identity not only to attract political recognition, but also to regulate citizen-subjects who may claim Asian American ancestry.

This struggle for a politics of recognition is reflected in Asian Americans' ambivalent relation to the hegemonic concept of the "model minority." On the one hand, the biases of Asian American scholarship have privileged the experiences of Chinese male railroad workers as the foundational history of Asian America, marginalizing the experiences of women and the other Asian groups involved in the complex making of this diverse community.[18] The category "Asian America" not only subsumes tensions of gender and national origin, but its focus on former Chinese labor contribution to society also becomes an authenticating claim to model-minority status. Thus Asian Americanism is simultaneously open to "Asian values" conservatism and celebrating the model-minority idea and critical of the racial victimization of

Asians in general. On the other hand, when Asian American proponents criticize the model-minority ideal, stressing its regulatory function of keeping the natives' heads down, they point to the way it excludes Southeast Asian refugees as welfare recipients living in poverty, unable to measure up. This process of othering reveals the racial, cultural, and class gaps that exist among the diverse populations that proponents of Asian Americanism would subsume under a single racial category.

The ambivalent links, then, between Asian Americanism and the model-minority concept regulate relations between "more successful" and "less successful" Asian American populations, between the more deserving and the less deserving Asian American citizen-subjects. Such moral judgments pressure questionable newcomers from Asia to shape up. An author writing about the Vietnamese boat people feels compelled to defend their model-minority potential despite their initial lack of language or education skills:

> What came as a surprise was the particular set of values that these refugees brought with them, derived from their Confucian and Buddhist heritage, which proved to be of utmost importance in determining their achievements.
>
> Although non-Western in origin, these values differed very little from what we call middle-class American values—namely, the belief in hard work, achievement, and education, willingness to face new challenges, the delay of immediate gratification for later gain, the importance of family life and respect for the family from the wider community, and finally, a balance of work and play.[19]

Nevertheless, many newcomers from the Asia Pacific and from a variety of classes cannot be easily fitted into an overarching Asian American identity, and their presence has made even more untenable the claims that Asian Americans can be constituted as a single community of adversity and racial oppression.

The issue is one of reclassification of victimhood, not statistics. The Civil Rights Act of 1964, especially its affirmative-action provisions, reduced the space for empowering entire communities, and instead refocused on victimized individuals who have been disadvantaged and discriminated against. *Victim* took on a new connotation as individuals, through affirmative-action–type programs, fought for individual rights as opposed to moral justice for their entire community. One effect of the end of affirmative action has been to increase the number of Asian American students in universities across the nation, which has shifted attention away from the moral status of historical victimization and spotlighted instead the moral status of individualized packaging of achievements. It is an irony that Asian American proponents of the concept of a community of racial exclusion have individually benefited, both professionally and socially, from a variety of multicultural opportunities, along with Asian American professionals in other fields of privilege.

Not surprisingly, there are Americans of Asian ancestry who do not agree with the idea of Asian Americanism as a political project, not least because it is an exclusively race-based notion that neglects the variety of Asian immigrant experiences and is unable to accommodate either contemporary changes or the diverse roles and situations of Asian immigrants in the American economy and society. Debates about whether there is a new sense of race emerging across all groups claiming Asian ancestry have made front-page news. In a letter to *The New York Times,* Judy Kim wrote,

> While encouraged by the inclusion of a front-page special report on Asian-Americans . . . , I disagree with the premise that an Asian-American racial consciousness is burgeoning. It is the very diversity of Asian-Americans that precludes the development of this racial consciousness. As a recent college graduate, I also have trouble accepting the idea that college campuses are molding this special racial consciousness, having witnessed students participate in the vibrant ethnic communities at Yale and the lack of a compelling pan-Asian student organization. . . . While certain ethnic coalitions are desirable to advocate a political agenda that addresses issues like anti-Asian violence, I disagree that these strategic alliances are enough to constitute a separate, distinct, racial identity.[20]

Asian American leaders may invoke the community of adversity, but the real fights are increasingly focused on high-profile instances of racist discrimination. The case of former government scientist Wen Ho Lee (originally from Taiwan)—who was detained in shackles and charged, without evidence, with giving classified nuclear secrets to China—demonstrates that the struggle has shifted from the plight of an entire imagined Asian American community to a focus that is increasingly elite-based.[21] Two major academic organizations called for scientists of Asian ancestry to boycott federal laboratories by not applying for jobs with them. Each year, Asians and Asian Americans account for more than one-quarter of all doctorates awarded by American universities.[22] Even so, Asian American activists maintained that the violation of this individual's civil rights resulted from racial profiling, and have threatened a withdrawal of Asian American professional talents from key industries. Racial profiling and hate crimes have come to replace labor exploitation as the central concern of Asian American advocates.

It would be helpful indeed to distinguish explicitly between political strategies used to fight specific instances of anti-Asian discrimination and the kind of scholarship that can capture the complex, contradictory, and cross-class experiences of diverse Asian American communities.[23] Asian American political strategies in the majority of cases leave out of consideration huge numbers of Americans who can claim Asian and Pacific ancestry. The usual political coalitions have been unable to bridge the ethnic, cultural, and class divides that have only widened as immigration from the Asian continent continues unabated. Asian Americanism's restrictive view does not embrace the diversity of Asian American communities, or the relations among them as they are dispersed across the class and cultural spectra. Political interests are dominated by Chinese American and Japanese American leaders, who have little connection with or understanding of the situations of other Asian American communities. For instance, historical differences among Asian countries have left a legacy of unfamiliarity or estrangement between mainland Chinese and Filipinos, or Vietnamese and Cambodians, in the United States. Asian American elites are not immune to feeling culturally superior to immigrants from other parts of Asia. Rather, age-old cultural rankings and hostilities have become intertwined with the American racializing process, which discriminates along class lines and assessments of biopolitical potential. The different social and class positions of what are in fact a variety of immigrant populations explode any attempt to contain all of them within a single "national community of fate" in the United States.[24] The traditional expectation of ethnic succession—that through the contribution of suffering, a community of adversity can be brought under a single racial rubric—is becoming outdated in a nation in which diverse Asian populations are now represented in novel configurations of the political economy.

Theoretically speaking, the model of Asian America as a community of ethnic exclusion is unable to conceptualize new transnational Asian subjects, except to identify them as "foreign-born" and therefore not Asian American.[25] And despite rhetorical gestures to the contrary, Asian Americanism as a conceptual category has gradually picked up biopolitical criteria; in the practical world of an economy driven by forces of globalization, it operates within the framework of racial bipolarism, sorting out populations in the churning demographic diversity by separating the wheat from the chaff, the wealthy from the poor, the well educated from the less educated, the whitened from the blackened. By ignoring the majority of disadvantaged immigrants, the discourse in effect participates in the racial coding of Asian Americans as elite citizen-subjects rich in wealth and intellectual accomplishments. The Asian America model thus inadvertently excludes in the same way that the model-minority concept initially excluded them. In this sense, it becomes an encoding technique of governmentality—in the interests of economic flexibility.

THE MOVING FRONTIER

Richard Rodriguez has said, "California is becoming a world city—an extraordinary meeting place of Asia and Latin America with white and black America."[26] Mark Baldassare concurs: "We will be inventing a new kind of society, and we don't really have any urban states to use as a model. California of the future may look a lot like Los Angeles today."[27] California is the moving frontier, the land where Ralph Waldo Emerson's notion of self-reliance in the wilderness is tested anew each day by newcomers, especially from Latin America and Asia. In an America being recast by continual waves of immigrants, the geosocial landscape has been transformed, as bridges are built between the cities on the West Coast and cities in Asia. These new production networks spanning the Pacific are an effect of neoliberal laws intended to enhance U.S. access to Asian capital, knowledge workers, and industrial laborers, many of whom are already here as immigrants or university students.

In particular, the progressive incorporation of Asia into the West Coast economy has been crucial to the emergence of the Silicon Valley as the hub of the global information technology (IT) industry. In the 1980s, the decentralization of the microelectronics industry and the IT sector gave birth to interrelated industry segments that depend on local production networks.[28] Asian immigrants have become vital fixtures at both the high end (as engineers, managers, and capitalists) and the low end (as industrial employees and pieceworkers) of the software industry, hardware manufacturing, and related distribution systems, especially the semiconductor industry. The integration of Asian immigrants into this production system is not accidental, but rather the result of neoliberal policies regarding immigration and work conditions.[29] The effect has been an ethnic resegmentation within the restructuring of IT capital.

Expatriate Entrepreneurs and Techno-Migrants

Asian resident-expatriates have become a significant sociocultural force in Northern California because of their centrality to the growth of the computer industry, which has come to dominate the area's economy. In the 1980s, companies hired Taiwanese and Indian citizens already in the country and trained at American universities. Many U.S.-trained Asian engineers, programmers, and venture capitalists have contributed to the growth of the industry as a whole. Santa Clara County, the heart of Silicon Valley, has a total population that is half white and one-quarter each Asian and Hispanic.[30] AnnaLee Saxenian reports that in 1999, one-quarter of the valley's businesses were run by Asian Americans, accounting for some $17 billion in gross revenue each year.[31] By the end of the century, almost a third of the chief executive officers in Silicon Valley were Asian-born.[32] The first Californian Bill Gates may well be a Taiwan-born female CEO of a business-integration software company.[33]

Asian immigrant entrepreneurs, many of whom are U.S.-educated and formerly employed by large corporations, have become a crucial part of the supply chain in the IT industry. Immigrants mainly from Taiwan and Hong Kong operate small companies that constitute the manufacturing base of the area's globally oriented corporations. They run contract manufacturing firms that provide "business and employment services" to the larger corporations. These network-centric production systems have become ethnicity-specific, relying on personal relations of intraethnic solidarity and paternalism to regulate workers (discussed further below). It is estimated that there are three hundred firms managed by Asian entrepreneurs in the valley.[34]

The rise of Asian-run high-tech companies focused on computer and other electronics hardware manufacturing and trade has spawned similar enterprises in the Hsinchu Industrial Park in Taiwan, creating a transpacific economic network. Thousands of expatriate entrepreneurs have returned to Taiwan, but they maintain daily contact with partners in the Silicon Valley, and some visit the States almost monthly.[35] One of them is Pehong Chen, a Taiwanese graduate of Berkeley who is the CEO of Broadvision, a three-billion-dollar e-commerce provider. Chen has two thousand employees, many of whom have become millionaires. Asked about being at the top of the ethnic hierarchy in Silicon Valley, Chen said, "We carry our weight. Why shouldn't we be represented at the top?" He is considered a cyberhero, like Jerry Yang of Yahoo![36]

Indian high-tech immigrants have tended to operate firms specializing in software and business products, and their connections to India, though not as dense, are growing.[37] Nevertheless, Indian entrepreneurs are playing a major role running Internet companies. Together with ethnic Chinese entrepreneurs, they were responsible for almost one-third of the area's start-ups in the recent dot-com boom.[38] The transpacific economic networks formed by these Asian immigrant entrepreneurs not only lead to industrial upgrading on both sides of the ocean, but also become supply chains for the Asian professionals in demand at Silicon Valley firms.

Although a third of the engineering workforce in high-tech firms such as Hewlett-Packard and Intel was already composed of immigrants from Taiwan and India, the demands for high-tech professionals rose even higher in the late 1990s. High-tech companies lobby the U.S. government annually to raise the numbers of skilled contract migrants, especially from Asia, allowed to enter the country. Companies claim that American universities are not producing enough qualified engineers to keep up with the numbers needed to sustain the growth of the technology industry. An Asian American maker of chip circuits explained in 2000 that if the visas for contract high-tech workers were not readily available, businesses like his would fail: "We have been hiring people from Canada, from France and from Yugoslavia. We have engineers from Taiwan and Vietnam. It's like a small United Nations."[39] The computer industry has successfully pressured the federal government to increase the intake of skilled foreign workers to sixty-five thousand. Under the H-1B visa program, high-tech workers are admitted to the country for six years, but now they are free to pursue permanent residency (a green card) while working for an American company. More than half of the H-1B visas issued to foreign employees in the high-tech industry go to workers from India.[40]

So-called body shops have sprung up to form employment chains linking Silicon Valley firms to Bangalore and other centers of software expertise in India. The body-shopping regime is riddled with opportunities for exploiting high-tech workers, from the moment of recruitment to their possible eventual expulsion from the United States. Recruitment practices may include accepting bribes from would-be contract workers in India, who may be able to buy false papers and qualifications. Once contract workers arrive in the United States, many are vulnerable to exploitation by the body shops and corporate firms. Body shops hold their visas and find them employment, often taking a cut of their salaries (between 25 and 50 percent). Furthermore, by keeping the workers' visas and holding out the promise of eventually getting them green cards, the body shops make it risky for the migrant worker to change employers, complain about illegal conditions, or undertake unionizing activities.[41]

Techno-migrants are interested in changing their immigrant status. Especially since the recent economic downturn, contract migrant workers who have lost their jobs have been sent home. An Indian engineer complained that a body shop "threatened to send some [workers] back to India if they did not get contracts [to work with high-tech firms]. These workers were in tears. They were nervous wrecks, ashamed to ask for money or help from their families back home."[42] Those who have remained have formed a group, the Immigration Support Network, to lobby for an extension of contract time beyond the current six years, and the provision of temporary green cards for those awaiting status adjustment. Despite the current slowing of the economy, new body-shop operations have already begun exploring getting techno-migrants from China.[43]

The phenomenal demands of the computer industry have thus shaped a market rationality that has deeply integrated elite Asian immigrants into the economy in California and elsewhere. Asians of different nationalities play specific roles in the Silicon Valley hub of global manufacturing and service chains. As venture capitalists and knowledge workers, these Asian immigrants represent a part of the racially encoded class divisions—ethnic Chinese entrepreneurs versus South Asian techno-migrants—associated with the new capitalism. Besides economic and intellectual capital, these elite Asian immigrants possess the kinds of cultural assets that allow them to mobilize labor and other resources across various spheres of production and distribution.

The High-Tech Sweatshop

The decentralization of the Silicon Valley industry has produced a new regime of production in which the outsourcing of most mass-production processes to places in Southeast Asia[44] has been synchronized with "a gradual but strategically important re-concentration of manufacturing activities in Silicon Valley," leading to the creation of unequal working conditions at both the global and the local levels.[45] This so-called "post-Fordist" reorganization of global production has been called "systematic rationalization," a mode of labor management in highly flexible and segmented regional production networks that stabilizes working conditions and wages below those established under union-represented, Fordist norms.[46] In the Silicon Valley, ethnic cleavages are an effect of this systematic rationalization, as local production networks become highly dependent on immigrant and ethnic labor recruited and regulated by Asian paternalism. While Hispanic workers are very important in a wide range of low-wage industries,[47] Southeast Asian women are overwhelmingly represented in contract manufacturing, often working as electronics assemblers and pieceworkers at their own kitchen tables.

Contract manufacturing services represent the unglamorous but fastest-growing sector of profitability in the electronics industry. Corporate giants such as Intel, Hewlett-Packard, Apple Computer, and Sun Microsystems depend on contract manufacturers to produce cutting-edge products such as personal computers and cellular phones faster and more conveniently than offshore manufacturing can.[48] Solectron Corporation of Milpitas is the largest contract-manufacturing business in Silicon Valley, founded by two IBM engineers originally from Hong Kong to handle the overflow from that company's manufacturing operations.[49] Manufacturing work is contracted out to smaller companies operated by Asian immigrants who, using local ethnic networks, employ mostly nonunionized Southeast Asian women as "temporary workers" hired for ninety days. But after the end of their ninety-day term, they can be hired back immediately at no improvement in wages, contract security, or grievance procedures.[50] Since the early 1980s, home-based assembly work has been farmed out to Southeast Asian communities as contract manufacturers turned to smaller subcontractors and even to their own employees in order to meet stepped-up production schedules. Residual non-automated work is sent out with shop-floor workers to be assembled in their homes, for which they are usually paid a piece rate. These homeworkers are largely invisible, and there are no official statistics on them.

It is estimated that by 1999, 45,000 of the 120,000 Southeast Asian American people in the valley (mostly Vietnamese) were hired for assembling printed wire boards.[51] Most of these homeworkers are women, who often enroll other stay-at-home relatives and even children to assemble circuit boards and other components. The work involves using toxic solvents, fusing components, and wiring boards. Homeworkers make four to five dollars an hour, or forty to fifty dollars per board. The work is sometimes paid by the piece, such as a penny per transistor; even with overtime, workers barely earn the minimum wage. Piecework is not illegal, but it is subject to minimum-wage and overtime laws. In many cases, workers are already employed by the same company at hourly wages, and are paid on a piecework basis for their home assembly work.[52] A mid-1999 exposé by reporters at the *San Jose Mercury News* triggered an investigation by the Department of Labor into contract manufacturers' practice of bending the law by paying Southeast Asian immigrants piece-rate wages for work in the home.[53] In another case, Asian lawyers filed suit against Asian-owned companies for owing back wages and overtime compensation to a Cambodian worker who took home work and assembled components, earning a piece rate of one to five dollars.[54] In many subcontracting take-home arrangements, the labor laws violated included those first established in the 1930s after unions fought to abolish the sweatshop abuse of earlier immigrants. Fifty years later, the global restructuring of capital has brought back piecework in the electronics and garment industries. Almost a third of all American workers are contingent workers such as these contract and temporary workers. In conditions of hypercapitalism, neoliberal policies favoring profits outstrip concerns about human health and well-being.[55]

What is striking now is that local Asian network production systems deploy cultural authority, kinship, personal relations, and language to take advantage of employees working in substandard conditions. Two nonprofit agencies, the Santa Clara Center for Occupational Safety and Health and the United Food and Commercial Workers' Union, are focused on the plight of Southeast Asian workers in Santa Clara County, and they have tried to organize unions among workers in electronics sweatshops and supermarket chains. But they face obstacles because poor immigrants consider Asian employers (even of a different ethnicity) their patrons and protectors from the larger society. A lawyer said, "There's a lot of fear about complaining about employers. [The workers] are very desperate financially, and they're afraid that if they say anything they'll be retaliated against." To reach the workers, the occupational safety center used skits and radio dramas about the hazards of chemicals used in the industries that employ pieceworkers, and about workers' rights against arbitrary dismissal. An organizer from the union said, "In Chinese culture, employers have the same kind of authority as teachers and parents. If that's the case, you can't get workers to challenge them. And I think, partly, confrontation and conflict are not highly valued. I talked to one worker who said, 'We're in a new country. We don't want to start problems.'"[56] The use of personal relationships induces a sense of loyalty among immigrant employees who, because of language and skill deficiencies, fear they have no work opportunities outside the local ethnic networks. So Southeast Asian workers shuttle in and out of the electronics, garment, and food industries depending on volatile market fluctuations, earning below minimum wage at the bottom of the labor commodity chain and invisible to society at large. Subjected to unregulated labor conditions in innumerable hidden venues, these workers vital to the information industry are unprotected as American citizens. The greater capacity of transnational managers to move among different sites of production, and to shift rapidly among different streams of low-skilled workers both here and abroad, has severely degraded work conditions in the United States. Ethno-racial affiliations—once the firm ground for the mobilization and organization of American communities of adversity—are now deployed in ways that control, isolate, and weaken workers, inflicting a symbolic violence that blurs the moral difference between loyalty and exploitation.

The global restructuring of the electronics and IT economy, then, has enrolled Asian immigrants at the top and bottom levels of production networks, each occupation distinctive for being both gendered and ethnicized—as in the male Chinese contract manager, the male Indian engineer, the Southeast Asian female pieceworker. This ethnic ranking is very much like patterning I observed in runaway electronics factories established in Southeast Asia more than a decade ago.[57] It is both eerily familiar and temporally disconcerting that the racially segmented industrial network spawned in Asian developing countries has returned to the United States and become a centerpiece of the IT industry. A demographic reversal has taken place as more and more low-skilled workers are engaged in homework instead of having secure jobs, and are employed by footloose factories that can slither in and out of national spaces of production.

As scholars have noted, American law in the age of hypercapitalism has always opted for undercutting rights in favor of flexibility and profitability.[58] Indeed, the cases of worker abuse exposed by the *San Jose Mercury News* drew mainly angry letters to its Web site. Long-resident Americans argued that the main issue should not be the legality of undercompensated piecework assembly, but rather the opportunities for "entrepreneurship, opportunity, advancement through hard work, individual choice," all at the center of Silicon Valley values.[59] In recent years, the United States has seen backpedaling on union-protected workers' rights and race-based rights, while the narrow space of civil rights that remains is focused on individual freedom, including the freedom to pursue flexible business practices that promise greatest profits. The ends of the global commodity chains have looped back to the center, bringing with them Asian managers, professionals, and workers.

A number of questions are thus raised about how the two streams of new Asian immigrants—low-skilled workers and entrepreneurial actors—are indicative of changing trends in American citizenship. Do the migrations and practices associated with Asian immigrants represent a break in the symbols of American citizenship? What are the implications of the new demographics of entrepreneurship and widespread piece labor for the substance of free labor? What kind of idealism remains in a moral project of citizenship increasingly governed by mobile, flexible, and supranational forms of capitalism?

RACIAL BIPOLARISM IN GLOBALIZED SPACE

Nikolas Rose has used the term *the capitalization of citizenship* to describe the ways in which neoliberal criteria have come to dominate our norms of citizenship.[60] As transnational networks become more integrated, Asian entrepreneurs and workers have become important for making the United States grow by pushing the frontiers of economic space. Do the ethnic stratifications that distribute Asian immigrants across the class and occupation spectra suggest a rupture in the process of racial bipolarism, as I have claimed throughout?

I have suggested that the black–white continuum in American society is fundamentally about degrees of perceived deserving and undeserving citizenship, a kind of racial logic that has persisted from the earliest history of this country. Relative positioning in the national moral order is not state policy, but rather a dynamic of the political unconscious that variously informs official and unofficial thinking, perception, and practice. The intertwining of race and economic performance has shaped the ways that different immigrant groups have attained status and dignity; and in the process of relative positioning, group status competition, and group status envy, ethnic cultures have become race-based traditions. The bipolar racial dynamic has historically been part of a classificatory system for differentiating among successive waves of immigrants, who were assigned different racial stations along the path toward whiteness. White privileges were extended beyond their historical association with an Anglo-Saxon genealogy to powerful members of groups that could maintain economic and political links to the Old World. At the same time, the idealized construct of ethnic succession developed a structure of expectations for how citizenship acquisition ought to work in a just and moral world for less-fortunate immigrants. The succession model was about constructing a racial identity that transcended the component nationalities of immigrants to become, ideally, generic white. As discussed in earlier chapters, this racial classificatory mobility became available to Asian immigrants only in the 1960s, when the gradual attainment of middle-class norms by ethnic Japanese Americans and Chinese Americans earned them the label of model minority.

In the current age of globalized capitalism, the process of earning honorary whiteness continues, and Asians have come to represent ideal citizens who not only embody economic and intellectual capital but also possess the transnational networks and skills crucial to American expansion. As the new figures of moral worthiness, Asian entrepreneurs strive not so much to be accepted as whites as to participate more fully in the national space by combining nepotism and globalism to produce wealth and power in the decentralized systems of capitalism. Thus the notion of citizenship as tied to work and earnings gains a further dimension as humanity is increasingly measured against mobile capital. Regardless of whether they are foreign born, resident aliens, permanent residents, or citizens, high-tech managers and knowledge workers are now enrolled in a form of transnational citizenship, one in which high levels of education, capital accumulation, hypermobility, and flexibility are the passports to wealth production as well as to the power to rule over others. The recent prominence of Asian capitalists and professionals in the Silicon Valley, and their capacity to transfer value transpacifically, have transformed American thinking about Asians. Contrary to the rhetoric of Asian American advocates, transnational skills, not intranational adversity, have become the moral capital used to claim a communal identity. In this sense, elite Asian Americans are like homosexuals in that their claims to moral citizenship rest not so much on suffering (though that continues as they are targeted by hate crimes) but on the revelation of their important and diverse roles in a more complex American nation. We can thus say that in recent decades, Asian Americans and gays have become honorary whites because they embody middle-class norms, but perhaps even more because of their cosmopolitan flair. Thus, as the kinds of capital, norms, and actors used as criteria for an ideal American citizenship have changed, the process of achieving honorary whiteness has, through the assimilation of new figures like gay intellectuals, East Asian capitalists, or South Asian techno-migrants, become a force in the emergence of global racial bipolarism.

The current valuation of entrepreneurialism goes beyond individual value-adding activities to celebrate efforts that define value across diverse domains. As David Stark has argued, entrepreneurial figures are valorized for their ability to produce and transfer values across different spheres of worth, by sustaining relations of trust and exploiting the ambiguity of borders.[61] I have already mentioned the links between ethnic Chinese industrial companies in the Silicon Valley and Taiwanese venture capitalists. Their embedded ethnic networks have also allowed ethnic Chinese former employees of the American aerospace industry to set up small companies to supply components, using venture capital from Taiwan. In Los Angeles, immigrant Chinese accounting firms have been crucial in "baby-sitting" new Asian capital through the regulatory channels of the American system.[62]

Intraethnic ideas and practices that can bridge transnational zones and be reproduced in new spaces constitute a hidden force in economic territorialization. In many cases, multinational companies operating in the Asia Pacific depend on Asian managers as much as Asian workers to translate across political, social, and cultural lines. Ethnic Chinese communities can be found all over the Asia Pacific, and over time they have developed different cultural templates for doing business in various places. We should not forget the centrality of bilingualism or multilingualism to these maneuvers and border crossings. Many ethnic Chinese activities are conducted entirely in Mandarin or Cantonese, or in local native languages such as Malay, Tagalog, or Vietnamese, with English used as a language of technology and a medium for communicating with mainstream Americans. In these ways, Asians come to personify the new entrepreneurial figures not simply for their intellectual or financial capital, but also for their capacity to keep in play multiple orders of worth in heterogeneous spheres of production, and for extending their strategies into ever more remote Asian market landscapes.[63]

Together with Silicon Valley corporate leaders, the Asian managerial elite is setting the direction of state action in determining conditions of citizenship that promote the free flow of capital, skilled workers, and labor, as well as the exploitation of flexible workers in California. In this, they have been backed by American political leaders. An internationally circulating corporate and managerial class now influences the economic decisions of governments, shaping labor and immigrant policies in different countries. Asian managers have emerged as ideal citizens for the high-tech era for their skills, accumulation orientation, and transnational-network capital, all of which facilitate operations in multiple arenas of production and distribution. The fusion of neoliberal enterprise values with so-called Confucian values thus racializes the mobile Asian figure who pushes the horizon of American capitalism by linking economies, cultures, and continents.

While many Silicon Valley managers and knowledge workers are currently from Taiwan and India, as time goes on, many of these figures of the technological frontier will come from the Chinese mainland itself. As China emerges as an economic giant, once-despised East Asian groups—including mainland Chinese, whether permanent residents or citizens—are the new darlings in American professional circles, universities, and think tanks. For many mainland Chinese, America is the frontier, the intellectual and economic destination for wealth- and status-making. There are tens of thousands of mainland Chinese students in American universities. To American institutions, they are potential citizens who can provide access to China's markets, knowledge, and power. Since Tiananmen, Chinese immigrants in trouble with their home government have become the poster children of the American human-rights campaign against China. The mistreatment of Chinese expatriates who have become American citizens or permanent residents is front-page news in mainstream newspapers, and it is used symbolically in negotiations of U.S.-Chinese relations. There is a clear trend among American institutions of making intellectual, economic, and political investments in expatriate Chinese subjects. They seem to be paradigmatic figures of the new economy, and have come to embody a continuum of race privilege across the Pacific. These new ideal citizens may not yet have internalized the values of the Constitution, liberty, and equality, but what seems paramount is their embodiment of border-spanning knowledge, skill, and capital.

As human beings are more and more measured in terms of mobile capital, therefore, many economists—such as George J. Borjas—recommend more-restrictive immigration policies against poor (Hispanic) immigrants, while lay-ing out the welcome mat for the possessors of "human capital."[64] In a number of advanced liberal democracies, immigration laws have been adjusted to facilitate the flow of favored professionals and "investor-immigrants."[65]

Does this hypercapitalization of citizenship change the moral meanings of American liberal heroism? When Emerson celebrated American self-reliance, in some pastoral frontier of the land and the spirit,[66] he did not have in mind the capital-enriched figure who easily transcends national boundaries, displaying a reflexive economic cosmopolitanism. He did see a place for Chinese immigrants in the social order that has produced white cultural supremacy in America: Christopher Newfield quotes Maurice Gonnaud, who reported, "Invited to speak during an 1868 reception for the Chinese ambassador, Emerson heralded the influx of Asian immigrants on the West Coast with wholehearted acclaim, saying that 'their power to continuous labor, their versatility in adapting themselves to new conditions, their stoical economy, are unlooked-for virtues' sure to benefit the entire community." Newfield argues that Emerson did not see the Chinese laborers as equal partners with their employers but as engaging "in a corporate union in which racial or cultural differences had already been neutralized even as they were used to assign social station" (here, the Chinese as flexible laborer).[67]

More than a century later, Emersonian liberalism continues to influence what Newfield calls corporate individualism—a political sensibility that, besides stressing individual merit and performance, rejects state control over the "unmodifiable law" of market practices. The current celebration of the new professionals and "symbolic analysts,"[68] Newfield argues, also betrays the Emerson effect; it also valorizes the liberal self whose freedom rejects any form of private or public control. Corporate individualism would replace political sovereignty, which in a democracy ensures social equality, with economic governance, which operates as a separate source of power.[69]

While Newfield discusses Emersonian liberalism in relation to white, male, heterosexual subjects, I argue that there is now a conjunction between the transcendentalist promise of American neoliberalism and the identity categories of elite Asian men. This is the beginning of a deeper ideological process of whitening that goes beneath the skin (that is to say, beyond earlier reservations about the metaphorical whiff of sweat exuded by Asian American nouveaux riches), because these are agents of economic governance over a large part of the Asia Pacific. The new Westerner is an Asian figure who submits more readily to the governmentality of fraternally based network capitalism than to the political sovereignty of a democratic nation.[70] This is a political subject, who is produced through structures devoted to accumulating a movable economic—not spiritual—bank account. The political sensibility produced from overseas Chinese entrepreneurialism has now intersected with the liberal individualism of American managerial and professional classes. The two groups are different but similar kinds of relatively disembedded symbolic analysts who handle money, ideas, and knowledge and who have learned to overcome adversity through the combination of wealth, expertise, and risk taking,[71] while relying on the servitude of many disadvantaged peoples, at home and abroad. The paradigm of citizenship in contemporary America—the self-reliant, flexible, and capital-accumulating individual—has now incorporated the Asian American elite.

Thus, regardless of their racial origins, peoples from different parts of Asia can be consigned either to the whiter or to the blacker end of the continuum of worthiness. In this sense, newcomers experience a reconstitution of their racial identity, even as class differentiations widen dramatically within that race category. When the term *Asian* is invoked on the West Coast, we have the image of a well-educated, competitive, usually male Asian professional, not the Southeast Asian woman seated at her sewing machine.[72]

RUPTURING ETHNIC SUCCESSION

The unruly conditions produced by global markets in the 1930s compelled new forms of welfare-oriented states to assert social control over the apparently natural laws of economic forces.[73] But today, as neoliberal policy scales back the welfare state in advanced liberal democracies, society retreats to a restricted space for protecting individual rights, instead of protecting society in general. In the United States, the country in which capitalism has found its purest expression, the primacy of individual rights cannot dispel the illusory quality of citizenship as experienced by multitudes of working-class citizens. The discursive citizen-subject of government is based on a rights-based notion of citizenship, a juridically protected status that promises that hard work and personal initiative will in time yield social and economic equality. But this progressivism, with its echoes of T. H. Marshall's abstract model of citizenship in the welfare state, does not take into account the state's role in shaping employment structures, or the radically unstable dynamics of the market and demographics. Leftist scholars criticized the Marshallian model for ignoring the role of class struggles in enforcing social rights,[74] but I maintain that the state, through its policy decisions about welfare, taxes, and other fiscal issues, retains a major role in shaping the conditions of class struggles and the distribution of social rights.

In the early 1980s, Reaganite politics—corporate tax reductions, welfare cutbacks, deregulation, and anti-inflationary policies—weakened labor unions. Workers sacrificed wages for job security, and business profits remained high in a time of high inflation.[75] At the same time, fiscal solvency was threatened by an aging American population that increased the ratio of claimants on retirement funds to taxpayers. These two pressures—for high profits and for generational income—made it fiscally feasible to allow high rates of immigration in order to furnish a supply of cheap workers.[76] Gosta Esping-

Anderson argues persuasively that the liberal welfare regime in the United States shapes the postindustrial employment structure. Welfare expenditures have shifted from supporting the poor to education, creating a bifurcated employment structure with managerial, professional, scientific, and technical jobs with a high human-capital content on the one hand, and menial, routine "junk or fun" jobs on the other.[77] As social programs such as affirmative action and the Equal Opportunity Act improved the job-market chances of many women and African Americans, the junk jobs were increasingly filled by the ever-growing influx of poor immigrants, who form a pool of abundant, cheap, self-disciplining labor with hardly any fringe benefits.[78]

Decentralized, dispersed, and flexible forms of capitalism have thus ruptured the process of ethnic succession, which is more a sociological model than empirical reality for many. The continuity of intergenerational and ethno-racial class struggles, which formerly made the sufferings of past generations visible or available to be used by future generations as a basis for citizenship claims, has been broken by the blurring of borders between nations, production sites, and industrial labor histories.

The contemporary working poor do not have the material base to fight for and sustain older and better labor norms when their bosses enjoy greater flexibility to hire them as temporary, underpaid, and replaceable workers. The reversal in the demographics of labor distribution, forcing a growing number of people to do piecework and in-home work, has strengthened the power of corporations to erase or evade the civil-rights gains of the past century. The opportunities found in older factory regimes for making substantial improvements in the quality of work conditions have become less available as labor sites have moved offshore. Floating factories, combined with endless streams of migrant labor, provide a dual means to undermine or simply evade any constructive pressures brought by workers. Forms of labor exploitation, coercion, and denigration that had disappeared from most work venues have reemerged, and the state apparatus comes to be experienced even more as a system of containment and restriction. There no longer exists the material capacity or the symbolic coin to be produced out of advancing the well-being of others, either one's own ethno-racial group or society as a whole. The loss of potential to achieve any substantive accomplishment through organized means that call for communal efforts that can be typed as racial or ethnic means that communal contributions to larger social norms for the well-being of all working peoples are no longer a structure of ethnic succession.

Indeed, in many cases, migrants of the same nationality are the worst abusers of their countrymen. Peter Kwong has studied the extensive human smuggling networks linking Fuzhounese to the New York City Chinatown. Debt-peonage forces migrants to work under slavelike conditions in the warrens of Chinese garment, food, and service industries, places that American labor inspectors and unions have failed to penetrate.[79] American unions have been severely weakened in their fight to sustain decent working conditions in all industries, but especially in those dominated by immigrants of color. For this reason, some Asian American leaders have expressed the desire to reject the transnational linkages and claims increasingly shaped by global capitalism in favor of community-based politics.[80] Few of these activists have linked up with the Asian workers, however, who are embedded in the webs of high-tech production yet disembedded from the social protection of the state. The forms of labor reproduction are now changed in and through the structure of transnational capitalism, so they are no longer directly responsive to long-term gains in labor norms and laws governing the well-being and dignity of free labor as the right of citizenship.

Furthermore, the ethical meaning of citizenship, of Emersonian self-reliance, is now reduced to an extreme form of market individualism in which all that remains is for individuals to try to fight off particular instances of personal discrimination and injustice in a globalized wilderness. Any claim to making a contribution to the good of society becomes empty, since workers cannot put in moral borders to protect the next generation because they have become totally replaceable by the constant influx of even poorer and more exploitable immigrants. So workers do not or cannot aim for higher moral laws for working standards. The symbolics of suffering continue, but the evidence of it and of accomplishments against it are difficult, if not impossible, to fix and make available for claiming by future generations of workers. In addition, the denigration of the old idealism in citizenship—that basic working conditions for the poor must be upheld, and that capitalists will pay society back through taxes—makes entrepreneurial figures, whether local or foreign-born, feel no need to pay taxes or to protect the less fortunate. The only moral obligation they feel is to get rich by maximizing advantages of transnational mobility, links, and opportunities for tax evasion. In this regard, the Enron scandal can be said to be an emblematic rather than a deviant form of corporate capitalism today.

.   .   .

Global flows of Asian corporations and labor have thus transformed the political ground of minority struggles, contributing to the splintering of dominant ethno-racial categories into many newly racialized class positions structured by transnational production systems. Asian American activists have taken their inspiration from the civil-rights struggles of African Americans, stressing the centrality of labor exploitation and struggles in the constitution of an Asian American identity. But the currents of Asian entrepreneurial and labor migrants have greatly complicated this picture, as Asians come to be situated at both the top and the bottom socioeconomic levels. Economic and intellectual capital have come to define the status of Asian Americans, while the hidden servitude of other Asian migrants has fallen off the horizon of most Asian American advocates, whose struggle against racism is more focused on individual cases of hate crimes and racist discrimination.

For African American communities, which have suffered since slavery and have been at the forefront of fighting workplace abuses to establish decent working conditions in the land, the extranational circulation of populations, labor, finance, and social-moral capital is seen as a key feature of their daily oppression. Robert Gooding-Williams has argued that the dynamic of immigrant mobility is dialectically linked to the politics of immobility for older American working communities. To African Americans in the ghetto, the empirical and psychological sense of being localized, stuck in place, or even of having lost ground when it comes to civil-rights achievements, has intensified the danger of the failure to achieve a multiracial democracy in the nation.[81]

Thus high-tech warriors with high citizenship worth work alongside those deemed to have none, regardless of their technical citizenship status. The transnational movement of value has undone the meaning of work in America, erasing the established morality of labor dignity as labor values float down to the lowest level of labor extraction and denigration. The neoliberal logic of exploiting the ambiguities of economic and social borders has erased many hard-won battles for labor rights and promoted tolerance of historically inferior American working conditions for people judged to be socially, morally, or economically inferior—namely, minorities and the latest wave of immigrant workers.

The emergence of an Asian immigrant elite has actually oriented recent Asian American intellectual leaders toward a focus on market individualism, with its stress on the private citizenship travails of elite individuals like Wen Ho Lee. There has been very little interest in the indentured servitude of Southeast Asian migrants and smuggled Chinese workers, whose sufferings recall the earlier decades of Asian labor exploitation in the United States. These hidden workers, along with many Hispanic migrants, face a double bind: on the one hand, they are exploited; on the other, they have few material or political resources to appeal to the state to protect their worth and dignity as American workers. Indeed, by the late 1990s, "a majority of congressional politicians supported a citizenship ideal that relied primarily on an individual's status as a taxpayer, worker, and member of a nuclear family and remained relatively distant from the nation state."[82] In the aftermath of the terrorist attacks on September 11, 2001, how receptive will the American public be to the ethical claims of this new form of indentured immigrant servitude engaged in flexible production?

Afterword

Assemblages of Human Needs

The figure of the entrepreneurial citizen appears to be dominant at this moment in history, even in this time of national crisis occasioned by terrorist attacks on the World Trade Center and the Pentagon. There is much deserved celebration of the heroism and sacrifice of firefighters, policemen, and other rescue workers. Almost immediately after the attacks, the trader subject was hailed as having a key role in saving the national economy, in rallying the stock market as the heart of American capitalist might against the threats of a faceless, borderless enemy. A print advertisement taken out by the securities company Goldman Sachs captured this dual image of heroism. After expressing sorrow over those who had died and gratitude to surviving rescue workers, the message pledged "commitment to those who keep markets open and stable around the world."[1] There was a sense of urgency that the kind of capitalism built around risk taking, instantaneous decision making, and free movement be restored before the "terrorism tax" sapped "the nation's entrepreneurial spirit."[2]

But the aftermath of the disastrous attacks on American soil also represents an opportunity for rethinking the ethical norms of citizenship. Should the citizen ideal of self-reliance and entrepreneurialism continue to be set up for emulation, or has the territorialized basis of citizenship claims shifted, along with the transnationalization of economic networks? As processes of deterritorialization lateralize conditions of living and working, of power and of oppression, across national borders, what is the basis on which claims of solidarity can be made?

TECHNIQUES OF GOVERNMENT, ETHICS OF CITIZENSHIP

We have seen how a group of Asian refugees learned techniques that would shape them into autonomous, self-reliant citizen-subjects of freedom in a nation at the very center of globalization. I thus explored citizenship as less a legal category than a set of self-constituting practices in different settings of power. Following Foucault, I have considered power as a social technology that derives unity not from a process of homogenization or totalization, but from transversality—from passing through individuals, inducing both being-made and self-making. This operational notion of citizenship looks at microstrategies of power relations that traverse domains—the refugee camp, the public hospital, the welfare state, the court, the church, the marketplace, the labor market—converging to constitute newcomers in a new way. In America, human techniques—the diverse microstrategies that allocate, classify, formalize, normalize—seek to govern through freedom, or to adjust citizen-subjects to key values of autonomy and self-definition. There have been unexpected continuities with earlier technologies of governing, and improbable conjunctions between forms of regulation and resistance.

I showed poor Cambodian newcomers interacting with a variety of professional service providers who brokered relations and provided authorized accounts ("truths") of who the clients were, what was wrong with them, what was to be done, and how to go about doing it in order to succeed in America. Cambodians, thus constituted as an American ethnic minority, struggled with these techniques and norms, seeking to recast and resituate their own values within the institutional space, and to challenge the ethical and political dimensions of American citizenship across the wider social field. While there have been structural continuities of policy and practice toward successive generations of urban minorities, I argue that practical citizenship as produced in these everyday domains can be highly unstable and open to modification. Power existed in a dynamic continuum, and the political stakes in meaning and conduct were mutually constituted in interactions between refugees and professional experts. By discussing how service workers and their clients enacted these everyday instances of discipline and deflection, rules and ruses, conformity and chaos, my analysis shows that such fluid power relations produced not only ongoing norms but also their perpetual undoing, and created possibilities for alternative expressions, conduct, and notions of what it means to be human, not merely citizen.

In part I, the suffering and travails of Cambodian refugees captured the rupture of Buddhist-based notions of subjecthood as Khmer-Buddhist values were put into abeyance by people struggling to survive under the Pol Pot regime, which celebrated the revolutionary figure in a posttraditional utopian society. In the border camps, refugees experienced other breaks: in their sense of Cambodian cultural autonomy, in gender relations, in learning institutional dependency on Western institutions that provided the basic necessities of daily life. In the bureaucratic environment of refugee camps, people became defined as refugees, and learned the importance of correct labeling and registration as strategies for gaining access to resources. Women emerged as clever actors in managing these patronage relationships in order to direct resources and power to their families. Indeed, while scholars have argued that refugees are the antithesis of citizens, in the case of refugees from the Indochina conflicts an elaborate refugee support system prepared them to be citizens, to acquire the lessons that would enable them to become particular kinds of citizen-subjects, who would submit to the work discipline of American flexible labor markets.

In part II, we saw how Cambodian refugees encountered different technologies of government—in public health, welfare offices, and the legal system—that stressed the centrality of American values of freedom, self-reliance, individualism, and the necessity for transforming disadvantaged newcomers into low-wage workers. In contrast to the earlier welcome extended to refugees from communist countries, Cambodians and other Southeast Asian refugees arrived in the United States at a time of compassion fatigue. Economic recession fueled fears of another underclass in the making, and there was widespread talk about weeding out "welfare cheats" among the poor newcomers. There was remarkable continuity in perception, policy, and practices in relation to the Southeast Asian refugees and other categories of minorities—African Americans, Puerto Ricans, Hispanics—who generations earlier were the dominant urban migrant class in American cities. Converging rationalities of racial bipolarism, civilization, and market behavior came to shape the identity of ethnic minorities and reinforce social biases and inequalities at the same time that welfare sought to reduce material inequalities. Doctors, nurses, and social workers often viewed Southeast Asian immigrants through the prism of folkloric images of immigrant ancestors, but they believed that the refugees must be helped to become modern rather quickly. Just as policymakers educate social workers about ethnic differences, so social workers see themselves as having an educative, judgmental, and corrective relationship with poor people. I found remarkable continuity in policy and practices in attempts by the helping professions to cleanse newcomers of the supposedly backward or immoral aspects of their antiquated culture, to govern their everyday behavior, and to make them individually responsible subjects of a neoliberal market society.

For instance, in chapter 4, the community clinic was the first site of dynamic citizenship-making for both newcomers and long-term residents, for "clueless" refugees as well as for professional experts. Through their medical encounters, poor immigrants learned the links between their medicalized bodies and the making of political claims; these encounters contributed to their constitution as subordinated subjects, while doctors and nurses found that their sense of themselves as good caregivers was defined in part by their unwitting role as socializing agents of the state. In this sense, refugee medicine—besides restoring the well-being of refugee bodies—is a mediated process for transforming postcrisis subjects into self-scrutinizing sovereign subjects. Health workers found themselves as much caught up in the regulatory processes of biomedicine and refugee care as were the refugees themselves.

Discourses about poverty, work, and what constitutes a worthy citizen came into conflict with welfare ideas about the deserving poor and claims on the state. For Cambodian refugees, the welfare state was the key institutional space within which they acquired but also undermined techniques for constituting self-reliant citizen-subjects, as they were expected too quickly to make the leap from the category of economically precarious, war-traumatized people to the lower-middle class. Most households came to be headed by women—widows or divorcees or wives of unemployable men. They were constrained by welfare policies that discouraged long working hours, and by housing policies that permitted only nuclear families to occupy their subsidized housing units, discouraging apartment-sharing. Nevertheless, they devised strategies for pooling income generated from a variety of sources, including the concealment of family members' wages or sharing resources with family members who had different addresses. Welfare procedures and practices strengthened the position of women vis-à-vis men in caring for and planning the family, and promoted the feminization of patronage systems linked to different helping professions. Women's newfound voices—stories that fitted controlling narratives about being a refugee, welfare recipient, or victim of domestic violence—did not preclude efforts on their part to deflect and question American values.

There was also continuity in feminist-inspired interventions that sought to reorder gender relations by defining and resolving domestic disputes that had implications beyond the family circle. Different authorities—social workers, the police, the courts—intervened in cases of domestic abuse, tending to support women and children while marginalizing men. The agents and authorities were quick to depict wife and child abuse as failings inherent to Cambodian culture, and sought to socialize the newcomers to middle-class norms of conjugal relations and parenting. Indeed, it appeared that the self-image of social workers involved in such cases depended on their work of "empowering" and "liberating" refugee women, even when they also felt sympathy for the men. By having the right to intervene in domestic disputes and to set new norms of gender behavior, service workers morally redefined refugee ethnicity—a process that also legitimized their professional regulation of impoverished and racialized Americans. At the same time, it was clear that Cambodian female clients countered by protecting their own interests, and that they sought to bend the rules and the law to their own agendas and purposes as newly liberated subjects.

Intervention in domestic conflicts also provided opportunities for introducing lessons about individual autonomy and self-invention for the next generation. Social workers and therapists sought to resolve domestic conflict by disseminating middle-class norms of parenting along with messages that amounted to cultural cleansing, as Asian patriarchy was contrasted to the necessity of acquiring American forms of interpersonal negotiation. Interventionist strategies in the domestic sphere focused on young people were aimed at fostering self-actualization through the internalization of dominant codes and the pursuit of personal projects. Like women, children learned to navigate the rules and play off different sources of authority (patriarchal, psychiatric, legal) in pursuit of their own interests. One lesson of ethnic clientship was that the assertion of individual independence seemed most effective when the law could be invoked, with the help of teachers, social workers, and the police. In these various domains, then, the human technologies made concrete social norms of appropriate conduct, to produce self-disciplinary, autonomous citizen-subjects.

In part III, I examined the projects of remaking one's interior self and of redefining one's relation to self and others in the religious context—a process that occurred in parallel to the refugees' interactions with the wider society. The idea of freedom in America—in the sense of release from Cambodian family rules—has made the church an indispensable structure of power providing the means to attain upward mobility and a kind of citizen dignity. Buddha may be obscured, but young Cambodian Americans did not cease to wrestle with Khmer-Buddhist values as they engaged in an inward search for the true self. Many insisted that they remained Cambodian and drew on their roots in Khmer-Buddhist traditions when they interpreted Mormon doctrines, and claimed that they sought to reconcile or to bridge the two religions. In following Mormon prescriptions for reinventing oneself, young immigrant women integrated themselves into structures of social, class, and symbolic mobility through mechanisms that included raced hypergamy in order to move closer to one version of white middle-class respectability.

In the marketplace, poor Southeast Asian immigrants found themselves working in a fluid, low-wage economy. As neither industry nor the state seems invested anymore in the working poor, their acute vulnerability could only be shielded by access to a variety of family and social strategies that included petty crime, gangsterism, and wage work in unregulated labor markets. As earlier urban migrants have been, Cambodian youths were drawn into gangster networks and engaged in criminal activities as a way to make pocket money or even a living. For many boys, however, gangster practices could not be differentiated from the forging of a subversive American masculinity, one that was based on African American styles of rap and fashion. At the same time, in what appeared to be a classic American tradition, a few Cambodian Americans were able to deploy manpower and economic resources to establish economic stability through owning and operating doughnut shops. But what at first appeared to be a multiplicity of independent family-owned businesses revealed itself as a series of franchise chains that depended on nepotism and kinship networks in ethnic enclave markets.

In the final chapter, I studied the implications of local ethnic labor structures and the ways that their conjunction created opportunities and shaped transnational Asian networks in the post-Fordist production systems serving Silicon Valley firms. The corporate and labor markets of American high-tech industries have come to depend on a broad spectrum of Asian immigrants. Asian managers and professionals now employ Southeast Asian immigrants as temporary or piecework laborers, forming part of a flexible, transnational labor market that can be shifted in and out of North America. In this way, the space-making technologies of neoliberalism have lateralized corporate and labor values, elevating the social status and power of the honorary-white Asian managerial elite on the one hand, while undercutting ethnic-succession opportunities for the Asian flexible worker on the other. The range of Asian American class identities in the globalized economy—from the Chinese cyberhero in his sleek office to the Cambodian woman assembling microchips at her kitchen table—thus challenges the image of Asian America that is based exclusively on labor victimhood. Indeed, as mobile capital and talents become the measure of ideal citizenship and indentured servitude becomes the invisible labor form, the substance of American citizenship—formerly based on the dignity of free labor—has been evacuated. Having submitted willy-nilly to techniques that governed through freedom, poor Asian immigrants have finally arrived, but only perhaps to miss benefiting from a central ethical premise of American citizenship.

While earlier generations of poor immigrants were prodded to become self-reliant by displaying the classic American ethic of hard work and candoism, it is no longer clear that low-paid jobs are but a stepping stone to better ones within a person's lifetime. We therefore need to qualify Judith Shklar's claim that work, or earning, is the basis of American citizenship, since it is based on the assumption that the classic American story of ethnic succession continues to be plausible for people starting out at the bottom. It is no longer certain that self-discipline will be germane in a world of hypercapitalism that valorizes flexibility and short-term employment, the kind of job-hopping agility in temporary low-wage markets that in fact undercuts the cumulative gains of the work ethic. In the era of the high-tech revolution, many poor immigrants, including Southeast Asian refugees, are socially invisible. They are employed under conditions that resemble those in developing countries, and actually compete with workers in those countries as yet one more local production team in a global agglomeration of networks. They are closer to the black end of the bipolar racial order, mixed in with other poor immigrants of color whose citizenship worthiness is contingently assessed. Lessons in self-reliance, individualism, and initiative cannot guarantee that low-skilled workers will eventually attain the economic security that eludes the grasp of many, nor can they dispel the image of these workers as "savages" in the eyes of middle-class suburban America.[3] Poor immigrants may learn to become self-disciplining Americans, but as members of a post-modern racialized lumpen proletariat, they daily struggled to survive by hewing to the family ethos of immigrants, pooling income and working around the kitchen table. While for many young Cambodian Americans Buddhism seemed irrelevant to their lives, their parents' Khmer-Buddhist norms ensured that family care and protection were provided for individuals who might be unemployed, underemployed, or underpaid. Such conditions of class exploitation and the hidden forms of welfarism within working-class households produced conditions of citizenship that had more in common with those of low-wage workers overseas than they did with Asian managers, the new emblems of the Asian American success story.

This study, therefore, has considered how the human being as a citizen-subject or ethical object was constituted and contested in various domains of American life. The strategies to normalize refugees as ethnicized, self-reliant, flexible laboring subjects came into conflict with alternative sets of ethical values. Cambodian-Buddhist notions of personhood, gender, and communalism clashed with lessons about individualism, health management, the nuclear family, gender relations, law enforcement, white respectability, market operations, and working conditions. Mormonism, which has been called the third wave of the intersection of religion and individualistic capitalism,[4] furnished poor newcomers with lessons in an inner asceticism devoted to saving and accumulation. As Cambodian Americans struggled to master or evade the nuclear-family form and market individualism, the Khmer-Buddhist ethos seemed to have become irrelevant; for the young especially, Buddha appeared to be in hiding. The growing incongruity between techniques of normalization as self-reliant individuals on the one hand, and the unraveling of norms of American free labor in the shifting terrain of a globalized market society on the other, presents an ethical dilemma over how to conduct oneself. It is no longer clear whether the self-reliant, territorially based citizen can be meaningfully sustained any longer as an ideal figure.

LATITUDES OF CITIZENSHIP

Global economic forces have reconfigured the terrain of citizenship in the United States. The Silicon Valley is the foremost example of how urban, commercial, and industrial centers in the country become the hubs of supply chains that link multiple sites of production across the world. Migrations increasingly shaped and dominated by the forces of neoliberal capitalism have the effect of disembedding local rationalities from their milieus—of "deterritorialization"[5]—and embedding them in the new economic spaces. People who are technically citizens or noncitizens of America become intertwined in these tangled movements, yet they experience divergent rights and privileges. The processes that distribute disparate forms of legal and labor conditions across new geographies of production constitute in effect "latitudes of citizenship." *Latitude* suggests transverse flows that cut into the vertical entities of nation-states and the intersection of global forces in strategic economic spaces such as the Silicon Valley. Because the space of production shaped by transnational networks is distinct from the space of administration, this partial disembeddedness from the nation-state allows a variety of forms to govern social relations. Latitudes of citizenship thus also imply freedom from narrow limits (of nation-states and legal regimes) as well as the scope and flexibility to combine disparate combinations of rights, privileges, and labor conditions in a geography of production. Such ensembles of unequal life chances are shaped by processes at once transborder and highly specific that constitute particular positions of subjection.

By thus lateralizing and devaluing labor in production along with the flow of network capital, the techniques of neoliberalism are splintering citizenship claims. Lines of differentiation according to skill and occupation that are continuous across national borders assign people different political fates— as managers, techno-migrants, or low-paid migrant workers—depending on their specific location in geographies of production and of administration. This layering of the prerequisites for achieving citizenship and the ability to make citizenship claims underlies the stratificatory processes that structure ethno-racial differentiation. When placed alongside preexisting ethno-racial forms, this lateralization of corporate and labor values across national borders raises questions about what is at stake for Americans as citizens, in the global ethical sense that transcends the most immediate differences of culture, race, and nation.

Being a worker in the American national space is no protection against a progressive degradation of labor and civil rights. The relentless manipulation and crossing of borders by capital and people enable the transfer of multiple forms of value across economic zones, thus enriching individuals and companies in the American nation. But the same transfer of values has also undone the meaning of work in America, erasing the established morality of labor dignity and reducing the value of labor to the lowest level of labor extraction and denigration. The neoliberal logic of exploiting the ambiguities of economic and social orders has erased hard-won battles for labor rights and has created tolerance for historically inferior working conditions for people in America judged to be socially, morally, and economically inferior— namely, minorities and the latest wave of immigrant workers. Mobile Asians are honorary whites not merely because of their value-adding activities but because of their space-defying agility in juggling various regimes of worth in an ever-expanding American economy. Such flexible citizenship and leapfrogging of capital markets have ruptured the American structure of belief in the succession model, in the right of workers to make a living with dignity, and in the expectation that political representation will improve the working conditions of ordinary people in the nation. As mentioned above, the ethical claims of migrant workers may be mobilized to oppose further immigration—an outcome that I do not support. Nor do I believe that immigration will be diminished, because intensifying migrations of people have become an irreducible force of globalization.

The old meaning of citizenship—which was based on free labor and the succession model of social mobility—first began to erode with the deindustrialization of America[6] and has now evaporated in the post-Fordist era, as temporary, piecework, and sweatshop workers have proliferated in the shadow of a dominant service economy. Citizenship based on income, the dignity of work, and representation is now mainly achievable only in the service sector, among those workers—in office buildings, hotels, and other major institutions—who have secure jobs to fight for. But for the low-wage, part-time workers in high-tech manufacturing, as well as in the apparel and cannery industries, the expectation of building on the struggles of earlier generations of workers has become less sustainable. Governing rationalities become disembedded as neoliberal forces create assemblages, circulations, and multiplicities of trade and production that breach national borders.[7] A worker who is technically an American citizen may not enjoy basic rights because her conditions of existence are determined by work status and location rather than formal citizenship status. By the same token, transnational entrepreneurs often enjoy rights and privileges regardless of their formal citizenship status. The lateralization of economic frontiers has raised questions about the territorial basis of citizenship, when different assemblages of individuals enjoy such radically different conditions of citizenship within the same national space.

In the aftermath of the terrorist attacks of September 11, 2001, there is a grave likelihood that public sentiment against immigrants has hardened. While the country must take strong measures to protect its borders and to investigate potential crimes against "homeland security," there is increased surveillance of entire migrant populations and of individuals suspected of having the potential to be terrorists. Hundreds of Middle Eastern and South Asian nationals have been detained without criminal charges (often in shackles) and prevented from contacting their families. By violating the human rights of these detainees, the INS has violated its own standards and those of international law.[8] Simultaneously, asylum seekers arriving without proper papers have been detained in degrading conditions, and local police officers are now helping to enforce INS rules in some states along the U.S.–Mexican border.[9] We can expect more crackdowns on the migrant poor and less sympathy from the American public for the ethical demands of immigrant labor. Meanwhile, political mechanisms to secure the borders of the homeland against terrorist suspects do not interrupt the ongoing lateralization of economic relations, which continue to depend on mobile businessmen, professionals, and migrant labor, who enjoy diverse sets of rights and privileges. On what basis can poor migrant working populations make claims for protection under these circumstances?

ASSEMBLAGES OF HUMAN NEEDS

Transnational corporate networks, and the latitudes of citizenship they have generated, thus present a formidable challenge to the advanced liberal state to develop a new ethical model of citizenship, one that is not territorially delimited. Global flows of corporate and labor power make improbable linkages of disparate citizenship conditions in particular sites. Such intersections, however, also define specific assemblages of human needs, raising the question of how claims are to be made, and to which authorities and centers of power. Since the space-making processes of neoliberalism have created these assemblages of human needs that are partially disembedded from political space, what can we suggest to substitute for civic responsibility and sociality?

Chantal Mouffe has asserted that a rights-based citizenship requires the liberal democratic state to have a commitment to defending its central political values and key institutions, to preserving the "unresolvable tension between the principles of equality and liberty."[10] Liberal democratic states are the main guarantors of civil rights, and have—especially though not exclusively through the welfare state—sought to divide up democracy as a social good. But as I have argued, the discontinuity in the heretofore cumulative gains of American labor- and civil-rights laws has implications for how we think about rights-based notions of citizenship, and about appropriate strategies for democratic struggles in the proliferating production sites of political disembeddedness situated both within and outside of the United States. It is hard to imagine how American labor laws and civil rights can be renewed and recast to sustain the moral substance of American citizenship against the proliferation of indecent working conditions that comes with the new geographies of production and trade.

One possible domestic strategy would be to broaden the basis of solidarity from the service sector to include workers in the garment industry, high-tech manufacturing, and other temporary, piecework enterprises. In the past decades, some of labor's most vibrant achievements have come in the service sector, among office cleaners and the lower ranks of white-collar workers. For instance, Justice for Janitors—from its start in a struggle against a single cleaning contractor in Los Angeles—has grown rapidly through the Service Employees International Union into sixteen American cities to secure for janitors living wages, health insurance, and full-time work. The recent support of Ivy League students and faculty for low-paid janitors brought the movement into the national spotlight. Their success goes to show that there are various possibilities for workers to fight for and defend the substance of free labor. More and more, service and skilled employees—in casinos, commerce, finance, media, entertainment, telecommunications, business services, postal and allied services, and tourism, to name a few areas—are the ones for whom the American dream is still attainable by means of labor organization. If American service workers can expand their organizing efforts to claim rights for temporary and piece workers (primarily new immigrants), they will strengthen the ideal of free labor as a measure of American democracy.

Nevertheless, I suggest that rights-based citizenship and related notions of welfare are inadequate in the present environment of dispersed, transnational networks of production. As my ethnography has shown, civil rights, with its sedimentation in codified protocols of particular countries, have proved to be easily evaded because of the deregulation of labor conditions, especially in flexible production sites. The legal framework of interactions can be removed from labor relations, to be replaced by nepotistic or specifically ethnic forms of control that enjoy a continuum of power across political borders.

More than ever, there is a need for governments, corporations, and nonprofit agencies to mobilize resources to attend to the specific substantive needs of populations in various sites and protect against the ravages of globalization. What we have, then, paradoxically, is a broadened notion of sovereignty—if this is taken to mean the kind of state power that "is the crucial agency of distributive justice; it guards the boundaries within which every social good is distributed and deployed."[11] By supplementing a notion of citizenship rights with a concept of a moral economy, state authorities can make a greater commitment to the exchanges of rights and obligations among political leaders, corporate figures, and laboring subjects in specific locations.[12] A moral-economy approach recognizes various clusters of social goods, the variety of actors who can interconnect in spheres of reciprocity, and the range of agents involved in distributive activity. Because it is based on substantive reciprocity in face-to-face situations, rather than on abstract notions of individual rights, *moral economy* implies that the terms of interaction remain mobile and flexible, providing the capacity for local authorities to respond to situated working and social conditions. In this way, moral-economy obligations and constraints can create a sphere for the equitable distribution of social goods and social justice within what are fundamentally assemblages of unequal power relations, in which an ethic of reciprocity requires responses to human needs. Furthermore, the notion of differentiated social goods—that workers need good wages, decent health coverage, and retirement benefits; that corporations need good workers and earnings; and that both parties need each other to sustain themselves—means that a rough parity or, in

Michael Walzer's term, "complex equality" can be achieved.[13] In assemblages of human needs, a variety of agents—the state, the corporation, the local authorities—can distribute different kinds of social goods in a complementary fashion that secures overlapping webs of support and sustenance.

The United States is a problem space directly involved in the reconfiguration of markets that cut across national borders and that depend on different kinds of population flows I call latitudes of citizenship. As citizenship rights become partially disembedded from the nation, and the regulation of labor conditions gives way to the deregulation of transborder flows, the spatial and moral coordinates of American citizenship have changed, and we need to rethink how basic human needs should be protected against economic injustice. Whether we rely on the routine rationalization of substantive needs (as in the welfare state), or on labor struggles to secure workers' rights and the grounds of democracy, or on a noncodified transnational moral economy of corporate reciprocity, we can no longer assume an even spread of civil rights within the nation's boundaries, or the creation of a homogeneous civil society, or that citizenship is entirely embedded in political space. By working with even some degree of coordination, governments, corporations, aid organizations, and the marginalized themselves can secure some human protection in various sites, their differentiated technologies of care sustaining a transnational moral economy. Attempts can be made to synchronize the dispersed geographies of production with a dispersed geography of administration, so that different assemblages of human needs become incorporated more fully into the global operations of transnational networks. The recovery of ethics under neoliberalism requires a multiplicity of actors—not just governments—who can create overlapping spheres of justice to achieve a complex equality for the laboring poor in America and elsewhere. The question remains whether the political sphere continues to be a vital force in the struggle for democratic rights beyond the human needs of hidden, exploited refugee and immigrant workers.

NOTES

PROLOGUE

1. Aihwa Ong, *Flexible Citizenship: The Cultural Logics of Transnationality* (Durham, N.C.: Duke University Press, 1999).
2. I use *Cambodian* to refer to all refugees from Cambodia. The majority of Cambodians are ethnic Khmer, but there are important ethnic minorities, such as the Muslim Cham and Sino-Cambodians. *Khmer* is thus used to refer to the ethnic Khmer majority and to the Khmer language.
3. Refugees who settled in other camps, those controlled by the Khmer Rouge in the border region, were considered illegal immigrants by the Thai government and were not eligible for refugee status and resettlement abroad.
4. In my sample of sixty households, seventeen were headed by women. The real figure was actually much larger, because kinship relations were often distributed among two or more apartments, so that some apartments composed of childless young couples were attached to and dependent on the bride's mother's household. Another study conducted in nearby Santa Clara County found that 25 percent of 278 Khmer families were headed by widows. See Kenneth Minehardt, S. Tom, P. Tse, and C. Yu, "Asian Health Assessment Project," *Amerasia* 13.2 (1986).
5. A term used by Judith Stacey to describe a similar style of research in the same general area: see her *Brave New Families: Stories of Domestic Upheavals in Late Twentieth Century America* (New York: Basic Books, 1990).
6. Soul loss is a Hmong concept that accounts for the onset of mysterious illnesses. This notion is at the heart of Anne Fadiman's book about a Hmong family's encounter with the welfare state and the medical profession, *The Spirit Catches You and You Fall Down* (New York: The Noonday Press, 1997).

INTRODUCTION

1. Alejandro Portes and Ruben G. Rumbaut, *Immigrant America: A Portrait* (Berkeley: University of California Press, 1990), pp. 44–46.

2. According to the 2000 Census, the number of Asian Americans in the Bay Area rose to more than 1 million (close to 4 million statewide). The largest ethnic category was Chinese, followed by Filipinos, Vietnamese, and Koreans. The number of Indians doubled in a decade to more than 300,000. *San Francisco Chronicle,* "Bay's Tech Boom a Magnet for Asians," May 24, 2001.

3. Ibid.

4. William Rogers Brubaker, "Introduction," in his *Immigration and the Politics of Citizenship in Europe and North America* (Lanham, Md.: University of America Press, 1989), pp. 4–5.

5. See, e.g., Will Kymlicka, *Multicultural Citizenship: A Liberal Theory of Minority Rights* (Oxford: Oxford University Press).

6. Alexis de Tocqueville, *Democracy in America,* trans. George Lawrence, ed. J. P. Mayer (Garden City, N.Y.: Anchor, 1969).

7. Max Weber, *The Protestant Ethic and the Spirit of Capitalism,* 2d ed. (Los Angeles: Roxbury, 1998). Drawing together such insights about the authoritarianism of majority rule or of capitalism, Christopher Newfield argues that Emersonian self-reliance is not about radical individualism but about submission to the sociability of a corporate administration: see *The Emerson Effect: Individualism and Submission in America* (Chicago: University of Chicago Press, 1996), p. 39.

8. By *race,* I mean a sociopolitical construction, in specific historical and cultural contexts, of human difference and identity that draws on selected phenotypical and other biological features. Reginald Horsman, *Race and Manifest Destiny: The Origins of American Racial Anglo-Saxonism* (Cambridge, Mass.: Harvard University Press, 1981).

9. Judith Shklar, *American Citizenship: The Quest for Inclusion* (Cambridge, Mass.: Harvard University Press, 1991), pp. 28–29.

10. See, e.g., Michael Katz, ed., *The "Underclass" Debate: Views from History* (Princeton, N.J.: Princeton University Press, 1993).

11. Nancy Fraser and Linda Gordon, "Contract versus Charity: Why Is There No Social Citizenship in the United States?" *Socialist Review* (Feb. 1993): 45–81.

12. See, e.g., David A. Novak, *The Wheel of Servitude: Black Forced Labor after Slavery* (Lexington: University Press of Kentucky, 1978); and Ruth Milkman, *Women, Work, and Protest: A Century of U.S. Women's Labor History* (Boston: Routledge and Kegan Paul, 1985).

13. Brackette Williams, "The Symbolics of Ethnic Historical Traditions and 'Suffering': Some Implications for the Doctrine of Equal Citizenship in the United States," paper presented at the University of California at Berkeley, October 1995.

14. Thomas Sowell rated the most "successful" ethnic groups—Jews and Japanese Americans—as models of such middle-class values as discipline, obedience, hard work, thrift, self-reliance, and politeness: see his *Ethnic America: A History* (New York: Basic Books, 1981).

15. Portes and Rumbaut, *Immigrant America,* p. 26.

16. Thomas J. Archdeacon, *Becoming American: An Ethnic History* (New York: The Free Press, 1983).

17. Charles Taylor, "The Politics of Recognition," in *Multiculturalism,* ed. Amy Gutmann (Princeton, N.J.: Princeton University Press, 1994), pp. 56–57.

18. Renato Rosaldo, "Cultural Citizenship, Inequality, and Multiculturalism," in

NOTES TO PAGES 5–10

Latino Cultural Citizenship: Claiming Identity, Space and Politics, ed. William V. Flores and Rina Benmayor (Boston: Beacon Press, 1997), pp. 27–38.

19. Constance Perin, *Belonging in America: Reading between the Lines* (Madison: University of Wisconsin Press, 1988).

20. Weber, *The Protestant Ethic;* and "Protestant Sects and the Spirit of Capitalism," in *From Max Weber: Essays in Sociology,* ed. H. H. Gerth and C. Wright Mills (New York: Oxford University Press, 1967), pp. 302–322.

21. For Michel Foucault's analytics of power, see his *Discipline and Punish: The Birth of the Prison,* trans. Alan Sheridan (New York: Vintage, 1979); *History of Sexuality,* vol. 1: *An Introduction,* trans. Robert Hurley (New York: Vintage, 1980), p. 90; and *Power/Knowledge: Selected Interviews and Other Writings, 1972–1977* (New York: Pantheon, 1980).

22. See Nikolas Rose, "Governing the Enterprising Self," in *The Values of the Enterprise Culture: The Moral Debate,* ed. Paul Heelas and Paul Morris (London: Routledge, 1992), p. 147.

23. Arthur O. Lovejoy, *The Great Chain of Being: The History of an Idea* (New York: Harper & Row, 1960 [orig. 1936]).

24. Joseph R. Levenson, *The Problem of Monarchical Decay,* vol. 2: *Confucian China and Its Modern Fate: A Trilogy* (Berkeley: University of California Press, 1968).

25. George Coedes, *The Indianized States of Southeast Asia,* trans. Susan Brown Cowing, ed. Walter F. Vella (Honolulu: East-West Center Press, 1968).

26. Dumont, *Essays on Individualism,* p. 72.

27. Karl Marx, "The Jewish Question," in *The Marx-Engels Reader,* ed. Robert C. Tucker, 2d ed. (New York: W. W. Norton, 1978), pp. 33–34.

28. Marx, "The Jewish Question," pp. 42, 46.

29. Jean-Jacques Rousseau, *The Social Contract and the First and Second Discourses,* ed. Susan Dunn (New Haven, Conn.: Yale University Press, 2002); see also Jürgen Habermas, *The Structural Transformation of the Public Sphere,* trans. Thomas Burger (Cambridge, Mass.: MIT Press, 1989).

30. I am grateful to Pheng Cheah for discussing the formation of modern concepts of citizenship with me.

31. Weber, *The Protestant Ethic;* idem, "Protestant Sects."

32. Michel Foucault, "On Governmentality," in *The Foucault Effect: Studies in Governmentality,* ed. Graham Burchell, Colin Gordon, and Peter Miller (Chicago: University of Chicago Press, 1991), pp. 87–104.

33. Foucault, "On Governmentality."

34. Foucault, *History of Sexuality,* vol. 1 (New York: Vintage, 1978), pp. 130–141.

35. Michel Foucault, *Ethics: Subjectivity and Truth,* ed. Paul Rabinow, vol. 1 of *Essential Works of Foucault, 1954–1984* (New York: The New Press, 1997), pp. 74–75.

36. Colin Gordon, "Governmental Rationality: An Introduction," in *The Foucault Effect: Studies in Governmentality,* ed. Graham Burchell, Colin Gordon, and Peter Miller (Chicago: University of Chicago Press, 1991), pp. 1–51; and Rose, "Governing the Enterprising Self," p. 142.

37. See Aihwa Ong, *Flexible Citizenship: The Cultural Logics of Transnationality* (Durham, N.C.: Duke University Press, 1999).

38. Rose, "Governing the Enterprising Self," p. 147.

39. Gilles Deleuze introduced the notion of concrete assemblages to capture the di-

verse things—actors, knowledge, practices—that translate programs and procedures into technologies of government; see his *Foucault*, trans. Sean Hand (Minneapolis: University of Minnesota Press, 1988), pp. 37–38; and Gilles Deleuze and Felix Guattari, *A Thousand Plateaus: Capitalism and Schizophrenia* (Minneapolis: University of Minnesota Press, 1987), pp. 503–504.

40. Barbara Cruikshank has argued that citizen-subjects are not separate, but are entangled processes in technologies of citizenship that are both "voluntary and coercive"; see *The Will to Empower: Democratic Citizens and Other Subjects* (Ithaca, N.Y.: Cornell University Press, 1999), p. 4.

41. Shklar, *American Citizenship*, p. 1.

42. Horsman, *Race and Manifest Destiny;* Michael Omi and Howard Winant, *Racial Formation in the United States: From the 1960s to the 1990s* (New York: Routledge and Kegan Paul, 1986); and Steven Gregory and Roger Sanjek, eds., *Race* (New Brunswick, N.J.: Rutgers University Press, 1994).

43. Omi and Winant, *Racial Formation in the United States,* pp. 66–68.

44. Brackette Williams, private communication.

45. Lewis C. Copeland, "The Negro as a Contrast Conception," in *Race Relations and the Race Problem: A Definition and an Analysis,* ed. Edgar T. Thompson (Durham, N.C.: Duke University Press, 1993), pp. 152–179.

46. David R. Roediger, *The Wages of Whiteness: Race and the Making of the American Working Class* (London: Verso, 1991); Ronald Takaki, *Iron Cages: Race and Culture in 19th-Century America* (New York: Oxford University Press, 1990 [orig. 1979]).

47. Karen Sacks, "How Did Jews Become White Folks?" in *Race,* ed. Steven Gregory and Roger Sanjek (New Brunswick, N.J.: Rutgers University Press, 1994), pp. 78–102.

48. This theory was popularized by Nobel Prize–winning economist Gary C. Becker. See, e.g., his "A Theory of the Allocation of Time," *The Economic Journal* 75 (1965): 493–517.

49. *Underclass* was a term coined by Gunnar Myrdal in *An American Dilemma: The Negro Problem and Modern Democracy* (New York: Harper & Row, 1944). *Model minority* originated with William Petersen, "Success Story: Japanese American Style," *The New York Times Magazine,* Jan. 6, 1966, pp. 20ff. For the spread of the concept in the media, see Ronald Takaki, *Strangers from a Different Shore: A History of Asian Americans* (Boston: Little, Brown, 1989), pp. 474–483.

50. See Brackette F. Williams, "A Class Act: Anthropology and the Race across Ethnic Terrain," *Annual Review of Anthropology* 18 (1989): 401–444.

51. As interpreted by Gordon, "Governmental Rationality," pp. 43–45.

52. W. E. B. Du Bois, *Black Reconstruction in America: 1860–1880* (New York: Harcourt, Brace, 1935); and Hortense Powdermaker, *After Freedom: A Cultural Study in the Deep South* (Madison: University of Wisconsin Press, 1993 [orig. 1939]).

53. Gail Bederman, "Civilization, the Decline of Middle-Class Manliness, and Ida B. Wells's Anti-Lynching Campaign 1892–94," in *Gender in American History since 1890,* ed. Barbara Melosh (New York: Routledge, 1993), pp. 207–239; and Lewis R. Gordon, "Effeminacy: The Quality of Being Black," in *Bad Faith and Antiblack Racism* (Atlantic Highlands, N.J.: Humanities Press, 1995).

54. Gordon, "Governmental Rationality."

55. Nikolas Rose and Peter Miller, "Political Power beyond the State: Problematics of Government," *British Journal of Sociology* 43.2 (June 1992): 173–205.

56. Foucault, *Discipline and Punish;* idem, *History of Sexuality,* vol. 1, p. 90; and idem, *Power/Knowledge.*

57. Michel Foucault, "The Subject and Power," in *Michel Foucault: Beyond Structuralism and Hermeneutics,* ed. H.–L. Dreyfus and P. Rabinow (Chicago: University of Chicago Press, 1989), pp. 208–228.

58. Foucault, "On Governmentality," pp. 87–104, 212.

59. Foucault, "On Governmentality," p. 225.

60. For a brief discussion of his method on the "genealogy of morals," see Michel Foucault, "Questions of Method," in *The Foucault Effect: Studies in Governmentality,* ed. Graham Burchell, Colin Gordon, and Peter Miller (Chicago: University of Chicago Press, 1991), pp. 73–86.

61. This point is made by Foucault in "The Subject and Power"; see also Rose and Miller, "Political Power beyond the State."

62. Rose, "Governing the Enterprising Self," p. 142.

63. Paul Rabinow, *French Modern: Norms and Forms of the Social Environment* (Cambridge, Mass.: MIT Press, 1989).

64. Bruno Latour, "The Powers of Association," in *Power, Action, and Belief: A New Sociology of Knowledge?* ed. John Law, Sociological Review Monograph 32 (London: Routledge & Kegan Paul, 1986), p. 264.

65. Foucault, "Questions of Method," p. 80; see also idem, "The Subject and Power," p. 223, for the different kinds of power relations involved in subjectification.

66. See Michel Foucault, *The Birth of the Clinic: An Archaeology of Medical Perception,* trans. A. M. Sheridan Smith (New York: Vintage, 1973); and idem, *Discipline and Punish.*

67. Benedict Anderson, *Imagined Communities: Reflections on the Origin and Spread of Nationalism,* rev. ed. (London: Verso, 1991).

68. Penny Edwards, *Cambodge: The Cultivation of a Nation, 1860–1945,* Ph.D. diss., Monash University, 1999.

69. For a discussion of this notion of the knowing subject in relation to oneself and to others, see Foucault, *Ethics,* pp. 200–201.

CHAPTER 1

1. John Marston, "Metaphors of the Khmer Rouge," in *Cambodian Culture since 1975: Homeland and Exile,* ed. May M. Ebihara, Carol A. Mortland, and Judy Ledgerwood (Ithaca, N.Y.: Cornell University Press, 1994), p. 113.

2. To protect the privacy of the subjects, I have used pseudonyms for all personal names in this book, except when stated otherwise.

3. For the definitive treatment of recent Cambodian history, see David P. Chandler, *The Tragedy of Cambodian History: Politics, War, and Revolution since 1945* (New Haven, Conn.: Yale University Press, 1991). For the period leading up to the Khmer Rouge takeover, see William Shawcross, *Sideshow: Nixon, Kissinger, and the Destruction of Cambodia* (New York: Simon and Schuster, 1979).

4. See Liisa H. Malkki, *Purity and Exile: Violence, Memory, and National Cosmology among*

Hutu Refugees in Tanzania (Chicago: University of Chicago Press, 1995); and Nevzat Soguk, *States and Strangers: Refugees and Displacements of Statecraft* (Minneapolis: University of Minnesota Press, 1999).

5. Giorgio Agamben, *Homo Sacre: Sovereign Power and Bare Life*, trans. Daniel Heller-Roazen (Stanford, Calif.: Stanford University Press, 1998), p. 133.

6. The Westphalian model is generally taken to depict the normative trajectory of international law that developed during the eighteenth and nineteenth centuries, when territorial sovereignty, the formal equality of states, and nonintervention in the domestic affairs of other states, among other issues, were developed into the core principles of international society. See David Held, Anthony McGrew, David Goldblatt, and Jonathan Perraton, *Global Transformations: Politics, Economics, and Culture* (Stanford, Calif.: Stanford University Press, 1999), pp. 37–39.

7. Agamben, *Homo Sacre*, p. 132.

8. For instance, the Yale Genocide Project was set up to debrief refugees arriving in America in order to obtain a firsthand picture of the Khmer Rouge regime and its aftermath. Works of scholarship based on witness interviews include David P. Chandler and Ben Kiernan, eds., *Revolution and Its Aftermath in Kampuchea: Eight Essays* (New Haven, Conn.: Yale University Press, 1983); Elizabeth Becker, *When the War Was Over: The Voices of Cambodia's Revolution and Its People* (New York: Simon and Schuster, 1986); and Chandler, *Tragedy of Cambodian History*, pp. 273–302.

9. For the latter, see James M. Freeman, *Hearts of Sorrow: Vietnamese American Lives* (Stanford, Calif.: Stanford University Press, 1989); Usha Welaratna, *Beyond the Killing Fields: Voices of Nine Cambodian Survivors in America* (Stanford, Calif.: Stanford University Press, 1994); Nazli Kibrai, *Family Tightrope: Vietnamese in Philadelphia* (Berkeley: University of California Press, 1993); and Nancy Smith-Hefner, *Khmer American: Identity and Moral Education in a Diasporic Community* (Berkeley: University of California Press, 1999).

10. These include Molyda Szymusiak, *The Stones Cry Out: A Cambodian Childhood 1975–80*, trans. Linda Coverdal (New York: Hill & Wang, 1986); Someth May, *Cambodian Witness: The Autobiography of Someth May* (New York: Faber and Faber, 1986); Pin Yathay, with John Man, *Stay Alive, My Son* (Ithaca, N.Y.: Cornell University Press, 2000 [orig. 1987]); Hiang Ngor, with Roger Warner, *Hiang Ngor: A Cambodian Odyssey* (New York: Macmillan, 1987); Chanrithy Him, *When the Broken Glass Floats: Growing up under the Khmer Rouge; A Memoir* (New York: W. W. Norton, 2000); and Loung Ung, *First They Killed My Father: A Daughter of Cambodia Remembers* (New York: HarperCollins, 2000). Their reports depict varying degrees of suffering and cruelty under the Khmer Rouge, ranging from killings, extended tortures, and starvation in some places to relatively benign experiences, at least for some stretches of time, in others. In this study, I have drawn most heavily from the two accounts by authors who were professionals and adult witnesses to events under the Khmer Rouge: Pin Yathay and Hiang Ngor.

11. See, for instance, E. Valentine Daniel and John C. Knudsen, eds., *Mistrusting Refugees* (Berkeley: University of California Press, 1995); and Ebihara, Mortland, and Ledgerwood, eds., *Cambodian Culture since 1975*.

12. I have drawn on Chandler, *Tragedy of Cambodian History*, and Shawcross, *Sideshow*, for the historical account that follows of recent events in Cambodian history.

13. For a view of American foreign policy that led to this murderous air assault on Cambodia, see Shawcross, *Sideshow.*

14. David P. Chandler, "Revising the Past in Democratic Kampuchea: When Was the Birthday of the Party?" *Pacific Affairs* 56.2 (Summer 1983): 295.

15. Like Saloth Sar (Pol Pot), communist leaders were mainly intellectuals, born in the 1920s and 1930s, who were influenced by the Vietnamese communists and participated in anti-French resistance. See Chandler, *Tragedy of Cambodian History*, p. 5.

16. The latest estimate, from the Yale Genocide Project—based in part on the mapping of prisons, killing, and burial sites—is 1.5 to 1.7 million.

17. Chandler, *Tragedy of Cambodian History*, p. 1.

18. For a theory of the inland states in Southeast Asia, see W. F. Wertheim, "Asia Society: Southeast Asia," in *Encyclopedia of the Social Sciences* (Oxford: Pergamon, 1965). Wertheim rejects arguments made by others, including Chandler, that Marx's model of the despotic hydraulic state is an apt description of these rice-producing but highly fluid and tenuous systems of rule.

19. Like most Southeast Asian kingdoms up to the modern period, surplus land and scarce population dictated the dynamics of power. Slavery and debt bondage were mechanisms for the powerful to mobilize labor. Slavery was abolished by the French in the 1880s, who then introduced ownership of land. Debt servitude continued. See David P. Chandler, *A History of Cambodia*, 3d ed. (Boulder, Colo.: Westview, 2000), pp. 144, 147.

20. Ieng Mouly, "Causes of the Suffering and the Options of a Strategy to Rebuild the Khmer Society," in *Buddhism and the Future of Cambodia* (Rithisen: Khmer Buddhist Research Center, 1986), pp. 37–38.

21. Chandler, *History of Cambodia*, p. 105.

22. Ibid.

23. This concept of the peasant moral economy in Southeast Asia was influenced by James C. Scott, *The Moral Economy of the Peasant* (New Haven, Conn.: Yale University Press, 1976).

24. Chandler, *History of Cambodia*, p. 200.

25. Penny Edwards, *Cambodge: The Cultivation of a Nation, 1860–1945*, Ph.D. diss., Monash University, 1999, pp. 253–254.

26. Edwards, *Cambodge*, p. 385.

27. Edwards, *Cambodge*, pp. 387–388.

28. Chandler, *Tragedy of Cambodian History*, p. 4.

29. See Michael Vickery, *Cambodia 1975–1982* (Boston: South End Press, 1984), pp. 13–17. Some scholars of Cambodia think that Vickery may have exaggerated the negative features of rural society and the peasant client mentality in order to find conditions that supported the Khmer Rouge's project.

30. See May M. Ebihara, "Khmer Village Women in Cambodia," in *Many Sisters: Women in Cross-Cultural Perspective*, ed Carol J. Matthiasson (New York: The Free Press, 1974), pp. 305–347.

31. Smith-Hefner, in *Khmer American*, uses the term *practical Buddhism* to describe the balance of merit-making or karmic individualism and relational ethics in Cambodian culture; pp. 37, 204–205.

32. For a brief overview of the peasant system and peasant uprisings between 1930

and 1970, see Ben Kiernan, "Introduction," in *Peasants and Politics in Kampuchea, 1942–81,* ed. Ben Kiernan and Chanthou Boua (London: Zed Press, 1982), pp. 1–28.

33. See Judy Ledgerwood, Carol A. Mortland, and May M. Ebihara, "Introduction," in *Cambodian Culture since 1975,* pp. 18–21. They also argue that the refugee experience has powerfully shaped American Khmers' notions of Khmer culture.

34. Judy Ledgerwood, e-mail communication.

35. For a cross-cultural discussion of the centrality of agricultural work and matrilocality in underpinning rural women's familial power, see Aihwa Ong, "Center, Periphery, and Hierarchy: Gender in Southeast Asia," in *Gender and Anthropology: Critical Reviews for Research and Teaching,* ed. Sondra Morgen (Arlington, Va.: American Anthropological Association, 1989).

36. Ebihara, "Khmer Village Women."

37. In 1992, Ledgerwood conducted research in two villages in which husbands and wives consulted each other about big decisions such as buying a cow, arranging the marriage of a child, and so on, as they claimed was the practice before the Pol Pot time (e-mail communication). But in this case, Peter was talking about the decision whether to see a prostitute or mistress.

38. Judy Ledgerwood, "Politics and Gender: Negotiating Conceptions of the Idea of Woman in Present-Day Cambodia," *Asia Pacific Viewpoint* 37.2 (August 1996): 143.

39. This imbalance in the awarding of merits seems contrary to the ratio in the mother's favor that has been observed among Theravada Buddhists in Thailand: see Charles Keyes, "Mother or Mistress but Never a Monk: Buddhist Notions of Female Gender in Rural Thailand," *American Ethnologist* 11.2 (1984): 223–241.

40. See Smith-Hefner, *Khmer American,* chap. 4, for a discussion of the socialization of boys and girls and the moral significance of puberty rites.

41. For a discussion of karma among Theravada Buddhists, see Charles Keyes, *The Golden Peninsula: Culture and Adaptation in Mainland Southeast Asia* (New York: Macmillan, 1977), pp. 86–88.

42. Earlier Cambodian culture seems to have been less controlling of sexuality; but the sensual images of divine angels associated with Angkor Wat disappeared from Cambodian culture after the thirteenth century, when invasions, social upheavals, and the growth of Theravada Buddhism replaced Hindu literary and iconographic influences with more austere aesthetics. See Chandler, *Tragedy of Cambodian History.*

43. Judy L. Ledgerwood, *Changing Khmer Conceptions of Gender: Women, Stories, and the Social Order,* Ph.D. diss., Cornell University (Ann Arbor, Mich.: University Microfilms, 1990), chap. 3.

44. Edwards, *Cambodge,* p. 387.

45. Most of the subjects interviewed spent time in border camps between 1979 and 1984.

46. Agamben, *Homo Sacre,* pp. 8–9.

47. Frank Smith, *Interpretive Accounts of the Khmer Rouge Years: Personal Experience in the Cambodian Peasant World View,* Wisconsin Papers on Southeast Asia, Occasional Papers 18 (Madison: University of Wisconsin Press, 1989).

48. Pin, *Stay Alive,* p. 63. Judy Ledgerwood is studying the Budd Damnay (or Puth).

For accounts of the Pol Pot era, see François Ponchaud, *Cambodia Year Zero,* trans. Nancy Amphoux (New York: Holt, Rinehart and Winston, 1978); Vickery, *Cambodia 1975–1982;* and Becker, *When the War Was Over.*

49. Michel Foucault, *Ethics: Subjectivity and Truth,* ed. Paul Rabinow, vol. 1 of *Essential Works of Foucault, 1954–1984* (New York: The New Press, 1997), p. 74.

50. Pin, *Stay Alive,* p. 168.

51. Pin, *Stay Alive,* p. 53.

52. Pin, *Stay Alive,* provides a complex picture of Khmer Rouge leaders, some of whom were true believers, others bloodthirsty individuals, some capable of small acts of kindness, but many oppressive and becoming corrupt over time.

53. Chandler, *History of Cambodia,* pp. 214–216.

54. Chandler, *History of Cambodia,* p. 216.

55. Vickery, *Cambodia 1975–1982,* p. 174.

56. Vickery, *Cambodia 1975–1982,* p. 175.

57. Marston, "Metaphors of the Khmer Rouge," p. 112.

58. Chandler, *History of Cambodia,* p. xiv.

59. Ledgerwood, "Politics and Gender," p. 145.

60. David P. Chandler, *Voices from S-21: Terror and History in Pol Pot's Secret Prison* (Berkeley: University of California Press, 1999).

61. Pin, *Stay Alive,* pp. 170–171.

62. Ledgerwood, "Politics and Gender," p. 146.

63. See the autobiographies by Szymusiak, *The Stones Cry Out;* Him, *When the Broken Glass Floats;* and Ung, *First They Killed My Father.*

64. See Smith, *Interpretive Accounts,* p. 19; also Pin, *Stay Alive,* pp. 144, 157, 219.

65. Marjorie A. Muecke, "Trust, Abuse of Trust, and Mistrust among Cambodian Refugee Women: A Cultural Interpretation," in *Mistrusting Refugees,* ed. Daniel and Knudsen, pp. 41–43.

66. U Sam Oeur, "Only Mothers Will Embrace Sorrows," in his *Sacred: Poetry by U Sam Oeur,* trans. Ken McCullough (Minneapolis: Coffee House Press, 1998), pp. 34–35.

CHAPTER 2

1. She was referring to the camouflage fatigues worn by Thai paratroopers.

2. For a study of Cambodian casualties from land mines, see Lindsay French, "Amputees on the Thai-Cambodian Border: The Political Economy of Injury and Compassion," in *The Body as Existential Ground,* ed. Thomas J. Csordas (Cambridge: Cambridge University Press, 1996).

3. Michael Vickery, "Refugee Politics: The Khmer Camp System in Thailand," in *The Cambodian Agony,* ed. David Ablin and Marlowe Hood (New York: M. E. Sharpe, 1990), p. 303.

4. Nevzat Soguk, *States and Strangers: Refugees and Displacements of Statecraft* (Minneapolis: University of Minnesota Press, 1999), p. 189.

5. Vickery, "Refugee Politics," p. 306.

6. Vickery, "Refugee Politics," p. 310. Vickery claimed that the refugee exodus was partly induced for political purposes. He pointed out that in contrast to the "bourgeois refugees," who chose resettlement abroad when the camps they were in were finally phased out in the early 1980s, the majority of refugees of peasant

or working-class background decided to be repatriated to Cambodia if their safety could be assured (pp. 319–321). But while the camps in time drew people seeking to go abroad, they were leaving a destroyed country that was entering a new phase of civil war, as remnants of the Khmer Rouge were still hunting down people suspected of having connections to the PRK or to the Khmer Serei forces. When the camps were finally closed in 1993, everyone remaining—mostly people from Battambang—was sent back. I thank Judy Ledgerwood for sharing this information with me.

7. Judy Ledgerwood, e-mail communication.
8. Margaret Drabble, *The Gates of Ivory* (New York: Penguin, 1992), p. 124.
9. For relief workers' views about running the camps, see Barry S. Levy and Daniel C. Sussott, eds., *Years of Horror, Days of Hope: Responding to the Cambodian Refugee Crisis* (Millwood, N.Y.: Associated Faculty Press, 1986).
10. Drabble, *Gates of Ivory,* p. 127.
11. Some agencies actually provided aid to Khmer Serei forces fighting the PRK regime, thus creating a situation vulnerable to political manipulation. See Vickery, "Refugee Politics," pp. 295, 323–324.
12. See Michel Foucault, "On Governmentality," in *The Foucault Effect: Studies in Governmentality,* ed. Graham Burchell, Colin Gordon, and Peter Miller (Chicago: University of Chicago Press, 1991), pp. 87–104.
13. Rebecca A. Parks, "At the Border: Late 1984," in Levy and Susott, eds., *Years of Horror, Days of Hope,* pp. 358–359.
14. See also Hiang Ngor, with Roger Warner, *Hiang Ngor: A Cambodian Odyssey* (New York: Macmillan, 1987), p. 419.
15. Frederick C. Cuny, "The Cambodian Border Relief Operation in the Context of Other Relief Operations," in Levy and Susott, eds., *Years of Horror, Days of Hope,* p. 303.
16. Judy L. Ledgerwood, "Changing Khmer Conceptions of Gender: Women, Stories, and the Social Order" (Ph.D. diss., Cornell University, 1990), p. 22.
17. Ngor, *Hiang Ngor,* p. 419.
18. Vickery, "Refugee Politics," p. 327, n. 12.
19. Ibid.
20. Vickery, "Refugee Politics," p. 328, n. 12.
21. Ngor, *Hiang Ngor,* p. 419.
22. Barry S. Levy, "Working at Khao-I-Dang: A Physician's Experience," in Levy and Susott, eds., *Years of Horror, Days of Hope,* p. 109.
23. Barbara Bayers, "Medical Training for Refugees," in Levy and Susott, eds., *Years of Horror, Days of Hope,* p. 242.
24. Bayers, "Medical Training," p. 243.
25. Ngor, *Hiang Ngor,* pp. 240–241.
26. Esmeralda Luciolli, "Kao I Dang: The Early Days," in Levy and Susott, eds., *Years of Horror, Days of Hope,* p. 68.
27. Daniel C. Sussott, "Impressions of a Medical Coordinator at Khao-I-Dang," in Levy and Susott, eds., *Years of Horror, Days of Hope,* p. 77.
28. Surangkana Pitaksuntipan, "Family Planning: The Perspective of a Thai Public-Health Worker," in Levy and Susott, eds., *Years of Horror, Days of Hope,* p. 213.

29. Pheng Eng By, "Family Planning: The Perspective of a Cambodian Public-Health Worker," in Levy and Susott, eds., *Years of Horror, Days of Hope*, p. 214.

30. For a history of medical observation, see Michel Foucault, *The Birth of the Clinic: An Archaeology of Medical Perception*, trans. A. M. Sheridan Smith (New York: Vintage, 1973), p. 196.

31. U.S. Committee for Refugees (USCR), *Cambodians in Thailand: People on the Edge* (Washington, D.C.: American Council for Nationalities Service, 1986), p. 11.

32. Stephen Golub, *Looking for Phantoms: Flaws in the Khmer Rouge Screening Process* (Washington, D.C.: U.S. Committee for Refugees, 1986), pp. 11, 19.

33. Golub, *Looking for Phantoms*, pp. 8–9.

34. The irony in this state of affairs is that at the same time that Khmer Rouge suspects were being rejected for resettlement abroad, the United States was indirectly supporting the remnant Pol Pot forces in Cambodia, in order to destabilize the Soviet- and Vietnamese-backed PRK regime in Phnom Penh.

35. Anne Fadiman, in *The Spirit Catches You and You Fall Down: A Hmong Child, Her American Doctors, and the Collision of Two Cultures* (New York: The Noonday Press, 1997), notes that the Hmongs engaged in similar ruses to get all family members sponsored for resettlement (p. 167).

36. Cuny, "Cambodian Border Relief Operation," p. 320.

37. Parks, "At the Border," pp. 358–359.

38. Carol A. Mortland, "Transforming Refugees in Refugee Camps," *Urban Anthropology* 16.3–4 (fall and winter 1986): 379.

39. Mortland, "Transforming Refugees," pp. 380, 384.

40. Mortland, "Transforming Refugees," p. 391.

41. Cited in Mortland, "Transforming Refugees," p. 385.

42. Ibid.

43. This speaker was quoted in an interview conducted in the PRPC in the late 1980s, when it had grown to a small town of thirteen thousand refugees presided over by more than a thousand teachers and staff members; see Mark Fineman, "School of Hard Knocks: Refugee Center Teaches Cultural Shock 1A for New Americans," *San Francisco Chronicle*, June 26, 1988.

44. For these general views, see E. Valentine Daniel and John C. Knudsen, eds., *Mistrusting Refugees* (Berkeley: University of California Press, 1995); and Sogut, *States and Strangers*, p. 248.

45. Marjorie A. Muecke, "Trust, Abuse of Trust, and Mistrust among Cambodian Refugee Women: A Cultural Interpretation," in *Mistrusting Refugees*, ed. Daniel and Knudsen, pp. 36–55.

46. Muecke, "Trust, Abuse of Trust," pp. 45, 49.

47. Muecke, "Trust, Abuse of Trust," p. 45.

48. See Lindsay French, "Marriage Patterns and Gender Relations in Site II, Thailand: Some Sociological Effects of a Peculiar Economy," paper presented at the annual meeting of the Association for Asian Studies, New Orleans, 1990; and Steven Erlanger, "Cambodian Refugees Think of Home with Hope and Dread," *The New York Times*, Sept. 23, 1990, E3.

49. For an ethnographic description of women's networks in pre-1975 Cambodia, see May M. Ebihara, "Khmer Village Women in Cambodia," in *Many Sisters: Women*

in Cross-Cultural Perspective, ed. Carol J. Matthiasson (New York: Free Press, 1974), pp. 305–347.

50. Ledgerwood, "Khmer Images," p. 22.

CHAPTER 3

1. Reginald Horsman, *Race and Manifest Destiny: The Origins of American Racial Anglo-Saxonism* (Cambridge, Mass.: Harvard University Press, 1981); Michael Omi and Howard Winant, *Racial Formation in the United States: From the 1960s to the 1990s* (New York: Routledge and Kegan Paul, 1986); and Steven Gregory and Roger Sanjek, eds., *Race* (New Brunswick, N.J.: Rutgers University Press, 1994).

2. Patricia Williams, quoted in "America, Seen through the Filter of Race," *The New York Times,* July 2, 2000, op ed.

3. Gail Bederman, "Civilization, the Decline of Middle-Class Manliness, and Ida B. Wells's Anti-Lynching Campaign 1892–94," in *Gender in American History since 1890,* ed. Barbara Melosh (New York: Routledge, 1993), pp. 207–239.

4. W. E. B. Du Bois, *Black Reconstruction in the United States, 1860–1880* (New York: Harcourt Brace, 1977 [orig. 1935]).

5. David R. Roediger, *The Wages of Whiteness: Race and the Making of the American Working Class* (London: Verso, 1991), p. 13.

6. Roediger, *Wages of Whiteness,* pp. 13–14.

7. Lewis C. Copeland, "The Negro as a Contrast Conception," in *Race Relations and the Race Problem: A Definition and an Analysis,* ed. Edgar T. Thompson (Durham, N.C.: Duke University Press, 1993), p. 179. I thank Brackette Williams for discussing these points with me and for supplying the references.

8. Brackette F. Williams, "A Class Act: Anthropology and the Race across Ethnic Terrain," *Annual Review of Anthropology* 18 (1989): 401–444.

9. Horsman, *Race and Manifest Destiny,* p. 3. This is the key book that establishes the broad-ranging processes of racialism in the evolution of American citizenship. For related perspectives, see Thomas J. Archdeacon, *Becoming American: An Ethnic History* (New York: The Free Press, 1983); and Richard Polenberg, *One Nation Divisible: Class, Race, and Ethnicity in the United States since 1938* (New York: Penguin, 1980).

10. Horsman, *Race and Manifest Destiny.*

11. Roediger, *Wages of Whiteness,* p. 14.

12. Karen Sacks, "How Did Jews Become White Folks?" in Gregory and Sanjek, eds., *Race,* p. 81.

13. Sacks, "How Did Jews Become White Folks?"

14. Omi and Winant, *Racial Formation.*

15. Horsman, *Race and Manifest Destiny,* p. 303.

16. Amy Kaplan, "Left Alone with America," in *Cultures of United States Imperialism,* ed. Amy Kaplan and Donald E. Pease (Durham, N.C.: Duke University Press, 1993), p. 16.

17. There are several studies on the exclusions of Chinese and other Asians. See, e.g., Jack Chen, *The Chinese of America: From the Beginnings to the Present* (San Francisco: Harper & Row, 1981); Roger Daniels, *Asian America: Chinese and Japanese in the United States since 1850* (Seattle: University of Washington Press, 1988);

Ronald Takaki, *Iron Cages: Race and Culture in 19th-Century America* (New York: Oxford University Press, 1990 [orig. 1979]); and idem, *Strangers from a Different Shore: A History of Asian Americans* (Boston: Little, Brown, 1989).

18. Takaki, *Iron Cages,* pp. 216–217.

19. Takaki, *Iron Cages,* pp. 219–220.

20. See Stuart C. Miller, *"Benevolent Assimilation": The American Conquest of the Philippines, 1899–1903* (New Haven, Conn.: Yale University Press, 1982); and Vicente L. Rafael, *White Love and Other Events in Filipino History* (Durham, N.C.: Duke University Press, 2000).

21. For a personal and broader account of the variety of processes of ethnic cleansing suffered by Native Americans, see Leonard Peltier, *Prison Writings: My Life Is My Sundance* (New York: Holtzbrinck, 1999).

22. Lucie Cheng Hirata, "Free, Indentured, Enslaved: Chinese Prostitutes in Nineteenth-Century America," *Signs* 5 (1979): 3–29.

23. For a discussion of slaveholders' paternalism, see Eugene Genovese, *Roll, Jordan, Roll: The World the Slaves Made* (New York: Pantheon Books, 1974).

24. Paul E. Peterson, ed., *Classifying by Race* (Princeton, N.J.: Princeton University Press, 1995).

25. Judith Shklar, *American Citizenship: The Quest for Inclusion* (Cambridge, Mass.: Harvard University Press, 1991), p. 3. This formulation of citizenship as social standing reflects the influence of Thomas H. Marshall's conception of the social right of all citizens to state benefits and supports that can help equalize the inequities generated by class and the marketplace; see his *Citizenship and Social Class* (Cambridge: Cambridge University Press, 1950).

26. Shklar, *American Citizenship.*

27. *Citizenship and Social Class.*

28. See Stuart Hall and David Held, "Citizens and Citizenship," in *New Times: The Changing Face of Politics in the 1990s,* ed. Stuart Hall and Martin Jacques (New York: Verso), pp. 173–188; and the fine collection edited by Geoff Andrews, *Citizenship* (London: Lawrence & Wishart, 1991).

29. Craig Calhoun, "Introduction," in *Habermas and the Public Sphere,* ed. Craig Calhoun (Cambridge: MIT Press, 1992), pp. 21–22.

30. Michael B. Katz, ed., *The "Underclass" Debate: Views from History* (Princeton, N.J.: Princeton University Press, 1993). The discussion that follows relies heavily on Katz's work, including his *In the Shadow of the Poorhouse: A Social History of Welfare in America* (New York: Basic Books, 1996).

31. Katz, "The Urban 'Underclass' as a Metaphor," in Katz, ed., *"Underclass" Debate,* pp. 6–7.

32. Katz, "Urban 'Underclass,'" pp. 10–11.

33. Katz, "Urban 'Underclass,'" p. 11.

34. Gunnar Myrdal, *An American Dilemma: The Negro Problem and Modern Democracy* (New York: Harper & Row, 1944).

35. Oscar Lewis, *The Children of Sanchez* (New York: Random House, 1961); and idem, *La Vida: A Puerto Rican Family in the Culture of Poverty, San Juan and New York* (New York: Random House, 1966).

36. See Lee Rainwater and William L. Yancey, *The Moynihan Report and the Politics of Controversy* (Cambridge, Mass.: MIT Press, 1967), pp. 39–125.

37. Charles Murray, *Losing Ground: American Social Policy, 1950–1980* (New York: Basic Books, 1984).
38. William J. Wilson, *The Truly Disadvantaged: The Inner City, the Underclass, and Public Policy* (Chicago: University of Chicago Press, 1987).
39. Katz, *In the Shadow of the Poorhouse*, p. 19. I thank Brackette Williams for bringing this reference and others on the underclass to my attention.
40. Andrew T. Miller, "Social Science, Social Policy, and the Heritage of African-American Families," in Katz, ed., *"Underclass" Debate*, p. 255.
41. William Peterson, "Success Story, Japanese American Style," *The New York Times Magazine,* Jan. 9, 1966, 20.
42. Kathryn M. Neckerman, "The Emergence of 'Underclass' Family Patterns, 1900–1940," in Katz, ed., *"Underclass" Debate*, pp. 194–219; Stanley Lieberson, *A Piece of the Pie: Black and White Immigrants since 1880* (Berkeley: University of California Press, 1980).
43. Miller, "Social Science."
44. Carol Stack, *All Our Kin* (New York: Basic Books, 1974); Charles Valentine, *Black Studies and Anthropology: Scholarly and Political Interests in Afro-American Culture*, A. McCaleb Module in Anthropology (Reading, Mass.: Addison-Wesley, 1972).
45. Katz, "Urban 'Underclass,'" p. 21.
46. See Philippe Bourgois, *In Search of Respect: Selling Crack in El Barrio* (Cambridge: Cambridge University Press, 1995).
47. Alejandro Portes and Ruben G. Rumbaut, *Immigrant America: A Portrait* (Berkeley: University of California Press, 1990), pp. 141–142.
48. For important studies of war refugees, see Liisa Malkki, *Purity and Exile: Violence, Memory, and National Cosmology among Hutu Refugees in Tanzania* (Chicago: University of Chicago Press, 1995); and E. Valentine Daniel, *Charred Lullabies: Chapters in an Anthropology of Violence* (Princeton, N.J.: Princeton University Press, 1996).
49. Nevzat Soguk, *States and Strangers: Refugees and Displacements of Statecraft* (Minneapolis: University of Minnesota Press, 1999), p. 194.
50. Liisa Malkki, "National Geographic: The Rooting of Peoples and the Territorialization of National Identity among Scholars and Refugees," *Cultural Anthropology* 11.3: 377–404.
51. Malkki, *Purity and Exile*, pp. 3–4.
52. E. Valentine Daniel and John C. Knudsen, eds., *Mistrusting Refugees* (Berkeley: University of California Press, 1995); and Soguk, *States and Strangers*.
53. Philip Corrigan and Derek Sayer, *The Great Arch: English State Formation as Cultural Revolution* (London: Basil Blackwell, 1985), pp. 4–5.
54. Gil Loescher and John A. Scanlan, *Calculated Kindness: Refugees and America's Half-Open Door, 1945 to the Present* (New York: The Free Press, 1986), p. 210.
55. John F. Kennedy, *A Nation of Immigrants* (New York: Anti-Defamation League of B'nai B'rith, 1958).
56. Roger Charlton, Lawrence T. Farley, and Ronald Kaye, "Identifying the Mainsprings of U.S. Refugee and Asylum Policy: A Contextual Interpretation," *Journal of Refugee Studies* 1 (3–4), p. 243.
57. Loescher and Scanlan, *Calculated Kindness*, pp. 213–214.
58. Loescher and Scanlan, *Calculated Kindness*.

59. Charlton, Farley, and Kaye, "Identifying the Mainsprings," p. 249.

60. Loescher and Scanlan, *Calculated Kindness,* p. 151.

61. See Alejandro Portes and Alex Stepick, *City on the Edge: The Transformation of Miami* (Berkeley: University of California Press, 1994), pp. 50–58.

62. Loescher and Scanlan, *Calculated Kindness,* p. 217.

63. Paul J. Strand and Woodrow Jones, Jr., *Indochinese Refugees in America: Problems of Adaptation and Assimilation* (Durham, N.C.: Duke University Press, 1985); Loescher and Scanlan, *Calculated Kindness;* and Portes and Rumbaut, *Immigrant America.*

64. Donald A. Ranard and Douglas F. Gilzow, "Comments on James W. Tollefson's *Alien Winds: The Reeducation of America's Indochinese Refugees," The TESOL Quarterly* (1991): 531.

65. J. W. Tollefson, *Alien Winds: The Reeducation of America's Indochinese Refugees* (New York: Praeger, 1989), pp. 546, 549.

66. "Responses by Auerbach and James W. Tollefson," *The TESOL Quarterly* (1991): 546, 549.

67. For studies of Vietnamese Americans in San Jose, see James Freeman, *Hearts of Sorrow* (Stanford, Calif.: Stanford University Press, 1992); and in Philadelphia, see Nazli Kibrai, *Family Tightrope: The Life of Vietnamese-Americans* (Princeton, N.J.: Princeton University Press, 1993).

68. See Michel Foucault, "Social Work, Social Control, and Normalization: Roundtable Discussion with Michel Foucault," in *Reading Foucault for Social Work,* ed. Adrienne S. Chambon, Allan Irving, and Laura Epstein (New York: Columbia University Press, 1999), p. 93.

69. Ruben G. Rumbaut and Kenji Ima, *The Adaptation of Southeast Asian Youth: A Comparative Study,* Final Report to the Office of Refugee Settlement, U.S. Department of Health and Human Services, Family Support Administration (Washington, D.C.: Office of Refugee Resettlement, 1988), p. 73.

70. The texts cited by Rumbaut and Ima include John F. Embree, "Thailand—A Loosely Structured Social System," *American Anthropologist* 52 (1950): 181–193. This anthropological construction of Thai society has itself come under scholarly criticism: see, for example, Jack Potter, *Thai Peasant Social Structure* (Berkeley: University of California Press, 1975).

71. Rumbaut and Ima, *Adaptation,* p. 76.

72. Office of Refugee Resettlement, *Refugee Resettlement Program: Report to Congress* (Washington, D.C.: U.S. Department of Health and Human Services, Social Security Administration, 1982), p. 22.

73. David W. Haines, "Vietnamese Refugee Women in the U.S. Labor Force: Continuity or Change?" in *International Migration: The Female Experience,* ed. Rita J. Simon and Caroline B. Brettell (Totowa, N.J.: Rowman & Allanheld, 1985), pp. 62–75; Rumbaut and Ima, *Adaptation;* and Elizabeth Gong-Guy, *The California Southeast Asian Mental Health Needs Assessment* (Oakland, Calif.: Asian Community Mental Health Services, 1987).

74. See, for instance, Rumbaut and Ima, *Adaptation,* p. 123; Tony Waters and Lawrence E. Cohen, *Laotians in the Criminal Justice System* (Berkeley: California Policy Seminar, University of California, Working Paper Policy Research Program, 1993).

75. Jacqueline Desbarats, "Cambodian and Laotian Refugees: An Underclass," paper presented at the annual meeting of the Population Association of America, San Francisco, April 4, 1986; Isabel Wikerson, "Growth of the Very Poor Is Focus of New Studies," *The New York Times,* Dec. 20, 1987.

76. See Aihwa Ong, *Flexible Citizenship: The Cultural Logics of Transnationality* (Durham, N.C.: Duke University Press, 1999), chap. 5, for a discussion of this construction of Chinese Americans.

77. Jiemin Bao, "Chinese-Thai Transmigrants: Reworking Identities and Gender Relations in Thailand and the United States," *Amerasia Journal* 25.2 (1999): 95–115.

78. Williams, "Class Act."

79. *The New York Times,* April 27, 1987, A10.

80. For another account of Cambodian refugee experiences in California, see Usha Welaratna, *Beyond the Killing Fields: Voices of Nine Cambodian Survivors in America* (Stanford, Calif.: Stanford University Press, 1993).

81. Robert L. Bach, "State Intervention in Southeast Asian Refugee Resettlement in the United States," *Journal of Refugee Studies* 1.1 (1988): 51.

82. United States Catholic Conference, *Working with Refugees: A Guide for Community Involvement* (Washington, D.C., 1983), pp. 6, 4.

83. Joseph Cerquone, *Enriched by Their Presence: America's Southeast Asians* (Washington, D.C.: United States Catholic Conference, 1980), p. 4.

84. Ibid.

85. Cerquone, *Enriched,* p. 14.

86. Cerquone, *Enriched,* pp. 5, 17.

87. Archdeacon, *Becoming American.*

88. Sylvia J. Yanagisako, *Transforming the Past: Tradition and Kinship among Japanese Americans* (Stanford, Calif.: Stanford University Press, 1985), pp. 259–260. See also Karen T. Leonard, *Making Ethnic Choices: California's Punjabi Mexican Americans* (Philadelphia: Temple University Press, 1994).

CHAPTER 4

1. See David P. Chandler, *Voices from S-21: Terror and History in Pol Pot's Secret Prison* (Berkeley: University of California Press, 1999).

2. Michel Foucault, *The Birth of the Clinic: An Archaeology of Medical Perception,* trans. A. M. Sheridan Smith (New York: Vintage, 1973).

3. See Jacques Donzelot, *The Policing of Families: Welfare versus the State,* trans. Robert Hurley (London: Hutchinson, 1980).

4. Martin Hewitt, "Biopolitics and Social Policy: Foucault's Account of Welfare," in *The Body: Social Process and Cultural Theory,* ed. Mike Featherstone, Mike Hepworth, and Bryan S. Turner (London: Sage, 1991), p. 248.

5. Arthur W. Frank, "For a Sociology of the Body: An Analytical Review," in *The Body: Social Process and Cultural Theory,* ed. Mike Featherstone, Mike Hepworth, and Bryan S. Turner (London: Sage, 1991), p. 40.

6. Michel Foucault, *The History of Sexuality,* vol. 1: *An Introduction,* trans. Robert Hurley (New York: Vintage, 1978), p. 168.

7. Frank, "For a Sociology of the Body," pp. 61–68.

8. Carol A. Mortland, "Transforming Refugees in Refugee Camps," *Urban Anthropology* 16.3–4 (1986): 385.

9. Dan Phan Quang, "Health Issues of Concern to the Asian Immigrant Population: Epidemiological Issues," in *The Asian Woman*, Cicatelli Associates, Region II Family Planning Training Center (New York: The Asia Society, 1986), p. 8.

10. Lisa M. Krieger, "S.F. General's 'Ellis Island' Clinic," *San Francisco Examiner*, Feb. 21, 1988, 1, 16.

11. For an account of the tensions between long-resident Americans and refugee communities over other forms of public assistance, see chap. 5.

12. Reginald Horsman, *Race and Manifest Destiny: The Origins of American Racial Anglo-Saxonism* (Cambridge, Mass.: Harvard University Press, 1981); see also Ronald Takaki, *Iron Cages: Race and Culture in 19th-Century America* (New York: Oxford University Press, 1990 [orig. 1979]).

13. Alan M. Kraut, *Silent Travelers: Germs, Genes, and the "Immigrant Menace"* (New York: Basic Books, 1994).

14. See Anne Fadiman, *The Spirit Catches You and You Fall Down: A Hmong Child, Her American Doctors, and the Collision of Two Cultures* (New York: The Noonday Press, 1997), pp. 188–190, for an angry critique of such accounts.

15. *Facts of Life in the United States: Information for Refugees Who Come to the United States* (Oakland, Calif.: Lutheran Immigration and Refugee Services and Migration and Refugee Services / U.S. Catholic Services, 1987), p. 18.

16. Michael Taussig, citing Max Horkheimer and Theodor W. Adorno, in *Mimesis and Alterity: A Particular History of the Senses* (New York: Routledge, 1993), p. 66. The reference is to Horkheimer and Adorno, *The Dialectic of Enlightenment*, trans. John Cumming (New York: Continuum, 1987).

17. I thank Lindsay French for reminding me of this fact.

18. Taussig, *Mimesis and Alterity*, p. 67.

19. Alejandro Portes and Ruben G. Rumbaut, *Immigrant America: A Portrait* (Berkeley: University of California Press, 1990), p. 159.

20. Portes and Rumbaut, *Immigrant America*, pp. 171, 175–177.

21. J. D. Kinzie, R. H. Fredrickson, B. Rath, and J. Fleck, "Post Traumatic Stress Disorder among Survivors of Cambodian Concentration Camps," *American Journal of Psychiatry* 141 (1984): 645–650; and James K. Boehlein, J. D. Kinzie, B. Rath, and J. Fleck, "One-Year Follow-up Study of Post Traumatic Stress Disorder among Survivors of Cambodian Concentration Camps," *American Journal of Psychiatry* 142.8 (1985): 956–959.

22. J. David Kinzie, "Overview of Clinical Issues in the Treatment of Southeast Asian Refugees," in *Southeast Asian Mental Health: Treatment, Prevention, Services, Training, and Research*, ed. T. C. Owen (Washington, D.C.: U.S. Department of Health and Human Services, National Institute of Mental Health, 1985), pp. 126–127.

23. J. D. Kinzie, S. M. Manson, D. T. Vinh, N. T. Tolan, Anh Bo, and T. N. Pho, "Development and Validation of a Vietnamese-Language Depression Rating Scale," *American Journal of Psychiatry* 139 (1982): 1277.

24. Elizabeth Gong-Guy, *The California Southeast Asian Mental Health Needs Assessment* (Oakland, Calif.: Asian Community Mental Health Services, 1987).

25. William H. Sack, R. Angell, J. D. Kinzie, S. Manson, and B. Rath, "The Psychi-

304 NOTES TO PAGES 99–104

atric Effects of Massive Trauma on Cambodian Children, II: The Family and School," *Journal of the American Academy of Child Psychiatry* 25 (1986): 377–383.

26. Marjorie A. Muecke, "Caring for Southeast Asian Refugee Patients in the USA," *American Journal of Public Health* 73.4 (1983): 431–437; and Kinzie, "Overview of Clinical Issues," pp. 123–125.

27. Kinzie, "Overview of Clinical Issues," p. 125.

28. Kinzie, "Overview of Clinical Issues," p. 116.

29. The Hmongs were rated the most seriously impaired. See Kinzie, "Overview of Clinical Issues"; Gong-Guy, *California Southeast Asian Mental Health*, p. 8; and Paul Delay and Shotsy Faust, "Depression in Southeast Asian Refugees," *American Family Physician* 36.4 (1987): 179–184.

30. Gong-Guy, *California Southeast Asian Mental Health*, pp. 2–3; see also Kinzie, "Overview of Clinical Issues," p. 126.

31. Gong-Guy, *California Southeast Asian Mental Health*, p. 9.

32. J. White-Baughan, P. M. Nicassio, and D. M. Baughan, "Educational Drama and Problem-Solving Training for Symptoms of PTSD in Cambodian Refugees," paper presented at the Refugee Information Exchange Conference, Sacramento, Calif., August 22, 1990.

33. Ibid.

34. Brad Abramson, "Exorcising Evil that Haunts Cambodians," *San Diego Tribune*, June 22, 1991, A1, A6.

35. Krich, "Culture Clash," *Mother Jones* (October 1989): 52.

36. Jane Gross, "Clinics Help Asian Immigrants Feel at Home," *The New York Times*, June 28, 1992, 10.

37. Ibid.

38. See also Stephen W. Foster, "The Pragmatics of Culture: The Rhetoric of Difference in Inpatient Psychiatry," paper presented at the annual meeting of the American Anthropological Association, Chicago, 1987.

39. Ronald Frankenberg, "'Your Time or Mine?': An Anthropological View of the Tragic Temporal Contradictions of Biomedical Practice," *International Journal of Health Services* 18.1 (1988): 11–34.

40. Lorna Rhodes, *Emptying Beds: The Work of an Emergency Psychiatric Unit* (Berkeley: University of California Press, 1991).

41. The discussion that follows of the clinic's philosophy is drawn from Delay and Faust, "Depression in Southeast Asian Refugees."

42. Arthur Kleinman, *Patients and Healers in the Context of Culture* (Berkeley: University of California Press, 1980); see also Arthur Kleinman, *The Illness Narratives: Suffering, Healing, and the Human Condition* (New York: Basic Books, 1989).

43. James K. Boehnlein, "Clinical Relevance of Grief and Mourning among Cambodian Refugees," *Social Science and Medicine* 25.7 (1987): 771.

44. Delay and Faust, "Depression in Southeast Asian Refugees," pp. 180–181.

45. Delay and Faust, "Depression in Southeast Asian Refugees," pp. 182–183.

46. For an eloquent discussion of this dynamic, see Michael Taussig, "Reification and the Consciousness of the Patient," *Social Science and Medicine* 14B (1980): 3–13.

47. Quoted in Krich, "Culture Clash," p. 52.

48. See Chou Meng Tarr, *Peasant Women in Northeastern Thailand: A Study of Class and Gender Divisions among the Ethnic Khmer Loeu*, Ph.D. diss., University of Queens-

land, 1985; and Jean-Pierre Hiegel, "Introduction to Khmer Traditional Medicine Based on Experience in Refugee Camps in Thailand," in *The Asian Woman,* Cicatelli Associates, Region II Family Planning Training Center (New York: The Asia Society, 1986), pp. 78–88.

49. See Theresa A. Rando, *Treatment of Complicated Mourning* (Champaign, Ill.: Research Press, 1993).

50. For a critique of such a therapeutic commitment to a singular truth, see Catherine E. Foote and Arthur W. Frank, "Foucault and Therapy: The Disciplining of Grief," in *Reading Foucault for Social Work,* ed. Adrienne S. Chambon, Allan Irving, and Laura Epstein (New York: Columbia University Press, 1999), p. 163.

51. Elizabeth Becker, *When the War Was Over: The Voices of Cambodia's Revolution and Its People* (New York: Simon and Schuster, 1986), p. 204.

52. Michel Foucault, "The Ethic of Care for the Self as a Practice of Freedom," in *The Final Foucault,* ed. James Bernauer and David Rasmussen (Cambridge, Mass.: MIT Press, 1988), pp. 1–20.

53. Cited in Foote and Frank, "Foucault and Therapy," p. 158.

54. Ronald Frankenberg notes that Western biomedicine is overly focused on "lifedeath," that part of life in which death is not yet consciously present, if not denied; see Ronald Frankenburg, "'Your Time or Mine?'" p. 18.

55. John Marcucci, "Sharing the Pain: Critical Values and Behaviors in Khmer Culture," in *Cambodian Culture since 1975: Homeland and Exile,* ed. May M. Ebihara, Carol A. Mortland, and Judy Ledgerwood (Ithaca, N.Y.: Cornell University Press, 1994), pp. 138–139.

56. Foucault, "Ethic of Care for the Self."

57. Anthony Giddens, *Modernity and Self-Identity* (Stanford, Calif.: Stanford University Press, 1991), p. 244. Giddens was talking about general forms of regulation in Western modernity, not about regimes in particular institutions, with their specific and hierarchizing effects on different kinds of subjects.

58. Talcott Parsons, "Illness and the Role of the Physician: A Sociological Perspective," in *Mass Psychogenic Illness: A Social Psychological Analysis,* ed. M. Colligan, J. Pennebaker, and L. Murphy (Hillsdale, N.J.: Lawrence Erlbaun Associates, 1985).

59. Chapter 2. See also Judy Ledgerwood, "Portrait of a Conflict: Exploring Changing Khmer American Social and Political Relationships," *Journal of Refugee Studies* 3.2 (1990): 135–154.

60. See Hiang Ngor, with Roger Warner, *Hiang Ngor: A Cambodian Odyssey* (New York: Macmillan, 1987), pp. 116–117; *The Tenderloin Times,* September 1991, 2.

61. Personal communication. For other aspects of Cambodian experiences with modern medicine, see Lindsay French, "Amputees on the Thai-Cambodian Border: The Political Economy of Injury and Compassion," in *The Body as Existential Ground,* ed. Thomas J. Csordas (Cambridge: Cambridge University Press, 1996).

62. See Chou, *Peasant Women in Northeastern Thailand,* pp. 199–200; and Hiegel, "Introduction to Khmer Traditional Medicine."

63. See Muecke, "Caring for Southeast Asian Refugee Patients," p. 436.

64. Muecke, "Caring for Southeast Asian Refugee Patients," p. 437.

65. Muecke, "Caring for Southeast Asian Refugee Patients," p. 435.

66. Ibid.

67. Jean Dietz, "Rape Turns Refugee Women into 'Silent Sufferers,'" *Boston Globe*, June 8, 1986.
68. Michel Foucault, *Discipline and Punish: The Birth of the Prison*, trans. Alan Sheridan (New York: Vintage, 1979).
69. French, "Amputees on the Thai-Cambodia Border."
70. Becker, *When the War Was Over*, pp. 21–22.
71. Krieger, "S.F. General's 'Ellis Island' Clinic," p. 16.
72. Ibid. In this paragraph, I interweave my own interview with the nurse with her statement about the Russians as reported to the press.
73. All published by Education Program Associates, Campbell, Calif., 1986.
74. See Emily Martin, *The Woman in the Body* (Boston: Beacon Press, 1989). Martin critiques obstetrics as a medical control over women's bodies and the birthing process, so that the doctor, not the mother, "produces" the baby.
75. And the bodies of partners having sexual intercourse must be "cool" or in balance to facilitate conception; see Judith C. Kulig, "Conception and Birth Control Use: Cambodian Women's Beliefs and Practices," *Journal of Community Health Nursing* 5 (1988): 241.
76. Patrick Cooke, "They Cried until They Could Not See," *The New York Times Magazine*, June 23, 1991, 46–47.
77. Cooke, "They Cried," p. 48.
78. Marcucci, "Sharing the Pain," p. 138. For an account of beliefs in ancestral spirits who become angry if neglected by the living, and can cause them harm, see Nancy Smith-Hefner, *Khmer American: Identity and Moral Education in a Diasporic Community* (Berkeley: University of California Press, 1999), pp. 68–72.
79. For the development of new kinds of Khmer-Buddhist therapies in postwar Cambodia and in North America, see Marjorie A. Muecke, "Trust, Abuse of Trust, and Mistrust among Cambodian Refugee Women: A Cultural Interpretation," in *Mistrusting Refugees*, ed. E. Valentine Daniel and John C. Knudsen (Berkeley: University of California Press, 1995), pp. 46–48.
80. Giorgio Agamben, *Homo Sacre: Sovereign Power and Bare Life*, trans. Daniel Heller-Roazen (Stanford, Calif.: Stanford University Press, 1998), pp. 98–99.

CHAPTER 5

1. Robert C. Lieberman, "Race and the Organization of Welfare Policy," in *Classifying by Race*, ed. Paul E. Peterson (Princeton, N.J.: Princeton University Press, 1995), pp. 183, 160.
2. See Scott Lash, "Reflexivity and Its Doubles: Structure, Aesthetics, Community," in *Reflexive Modernization*, ed. Ulrich Beck, Anthony Giddens, and Scott Lash (Stanford, Calif.: Stanford University Press, 1994).
3. Michel Foucault, "Social Work, Social Control, and Normalization: Roundtable Discussion with Michel Foucault," in *Reading Foucault for Social Work*, ed. Adrienne S. Chambon, Allan Irving, and Laura Epstein (New York: Columbia University Press, 1999), p. 92.
4. Jacques Donzelot has used the term *tutelage* to describe the range of strategies philanthropic workers used in early twentieth-century Paris, so that when techniques of normalization failed, they turned to coercive interventions to prevent

what they saw as the development of dangerous classes; see *The Policing of Families: Welfare versus the State,* trans. Robert Hurley (London: Hutchinson, 1980).

5. Robert L. Bach, "State Intervention in Southeast Asian Refugee Resettlement in the United States," *Journal of Refugee Studies* 1.1 (1988): 38–56.

6. Ken Moffatt, "Surveillance and Government of the Welfare Recipient," in *Reading Foucault for Social Work,* ed. Adrienne S. Chambon, Allan Irving, and Laura Epstein (New York: Columbia University Press, 1999), pp. 228–232.

7. Nazli Kibrai, *Family Tightrope: Vietnamese in Philadelphia* (Berkeley: University of California Press, 1993). On the continuing grief and discrimination suffered by Vietnamese Americans, see James M. Freeman, *Hearts of Sorrow: Vietnamese American Lives* (Stanford, Calif.: Stanford University Press, 1989).

8. See Kathryn M. Neckerman, "The Emergence of 'Underclass' Family Patterns, 1900–1940," and Andrew T. Miller, "Social Science, Social Policy, and the Heritage of African-American Families," both in *The "Underclass" Debate: Views from History,* ed. Michael B. Katz (Princeton, N.J.: Princeton University Press, 1993), pp. 194–219 and 254–289, respectively.

9. Mimi Abramovitz, *Regulating the Lives of Women: Social Welfare Policy from Colonial Times to the Present* (Boston: South End Press, 1988).

10. See various chapters in *The "Underclass" Debate: Views from History,* ed. Michael B. Katz (Princeton, N.J.: Princeton University Press, 1993).

11. Moffatt, "Surveillance and Government," p. 223.

12. Gwendolyn Mink, "The Lady and the Tramp: Gender, Race, and the Origins of the American Welfare State," in *Women, the State, and Welfare,* ed. Linda Gordon (Madison: University of Wisconsin Press, 1990), p. 111.

13. Indeed, historical studies of African American migrants throughout the twentieth century show that the contingent and interactive relations between political and economic structures and family forms accounted for the changing patterns, interpretations, and gender conflicts, but also the resilience, of black families. See Neckerman, "Emergence of 'Underclass' Family Patterns"; Miller, "Social Science, Social Policy"; Carol Stack, *All Our Kin* (New York: Basic Books, 1974); and Teresa L. Amott, "Black Women and AFDC: Making Entitlement out of Necessity," in *Women, the State, and Welfare,* ed. Linda Gordon (Madison: University of Wisconsin Press, 1990), pp. 280–298.

14. Mink, "Lady and the Tramp," p. 106.

15. By late 1989, AFDC payments also came with the requirement to enroll in work-training GAIN programs.

16. Kibrai, *Family Tightrope.*

17. Cited in Karen Fisher-Nguyen, "Khmer Proverbs: Images and Rules," in *Cambodian Culture since 1975: Homeland and Exile,* ed. May M. Ebihara, Carol A. Mortland, and Judy Ledgerwood (Ithaca, N.Y.: Cornell University Press, 1994), pp. 100–101.

18. Frank Smith, *Interpretive Accounts of the Khmer Rouge Years: Personal Experience in the Cambodian Peasant World View,* Wisconsin Papers on Southeast Asia, Occasional Papers no. 18 (Madison: University of Wisconsin Press, 1989), pp. 24–25.

19. For a similar racial scapegoating of black welfare recipients, see Miller, "Social Science, Social Policy," p. 267.

20. See Stack, *All Our Kin,* pp. 122–123.

21. Carol-Anne O'Brien, "Contested Sexualities: Sexualities and Social Work," in *Reading Foucault for Social Work,* ed. Adrienne S. Chambon, Allan Irving, and Laura Epstein (New York: Columbia University Press, 1999), p. 140.

22. See Judy L. Ledgerwood, *Changing Khmer Conceptions of Gender: Women, Stories, and the Social Order,* Ph.D. diss., Cornell University (Ann Arbor, Mich.: University Microfilms, 1990), chap. 3.

23. See Nancy Smith-Hefner, *Khmer American: Identity and Moral Education in a Diasporic Community* (Berkeley: University of California Press, 1999), pp. 175–177, for a discussion of Cambodian immigrants in Boston trying to control their daughters according to the strict norms of moral virtue.

24. Barry Glassner, "Monster Mothers," in *Culture of Fear: Why Americans Are Afraid of the Wrong Things* (New York: Basic Books, 1999), pp. 87–105.

25. Nancy Fraser, *Unruly Practices: Power, Discourse, and Gender in Contemporary Social Theory* (Minneapolis: University of Minnesota Press, 1989), pp. 150–156.

CHAPTER 6

1. The Self Help Center was later closed by the city health department, possibly because its alternative approach to mental-health counseling was competing with more traditional mental-health centers for state funds. See Bill Kisliuk, "Self Help Center May Fall to State Budget Ax," *Tenderloin Times,* Sept. 1990.

2. Diana Pearce, "Women, Work, and Welfare: The Feminization of Poverty," *Urban and Social Change Review* (winter–spring 1978): 28–36.

3. Historically, in Western democracies, a unitary (masculine) conception of citizenship has not officially distinguished between the concrete existence of men and women. But women's public participation is routinely undercut by their private status as wives and mothers while laws and policies governing public life reinforce their private status. See Carol Pateman, *The Sexual Contract* (Stanford, Calif.: Stanford University Press, 1988).

4. Gwendolyn Mink, "The Lady and the Tramp: Gender, Race, and the Origins of the American Welfare State," in *Women, the State, and Welfare,* ed. Linda Gordon (Madison: University of Wisconsin Press, 1990), p. 102.

5. Mimi Abramovitz, *Regulating the Lives of Women: Social Welfare Policy from Colonial Times to the Present* (Boston: South End Press, 1988), p. 353.

6. Abramovitz, *Regulating the Lives of Women,* pp. 35–36.

7. Nancy Fraser, *Unruly Practices: Power, Discourse, and Gender in Contemporary Social Theory* (Minneapolis: University of Minnesota Press, 1989), p. 130.

8. Carol Stack, in *All Our Kin* (New York: Basic Books, 1974), yields indirect glimpses of the effects of the welfare system on the family life of inner-city blacks; see also Joan Passaro, *The Unequal Homeless* (New York: Routledge, 1995). Even when the discussion is focused on the racialized effects of welfare practices, conclusions are drawn based on very little ethnographic research; see, e.g., chapters in *Women, the State, and Welfare,* ed. Linda Gordon (Madison: University of Wisconsin Press, 1990). In *Heroes of Their Own Lives: The Politics and History of Family Violence* (New York: Penguin, 1988), Linda Gordon gives a historical analysis of social workers' case studies in late nineteenth- and early twentieth-century Boston, providing rich information on the interactions between service agents

and European immigrants. Encounters between non-European newcomers and state agencies have not been made part of the analysis of their socialization to American society.

9. For the concept of pastoral power, see Michel Foucault, "Omnes et Singulatim: Toward a Critique of Political Reason," in *Power,* ed. James D. Faubion, trans. Robert Hurley et al. (New York: Free Press, 2000).

10. This observation has also been made by Leti Volpp in "Feminism versus Multiculturalism," *Columbia Law Review* 101.5 (June 2001): 1181–1617.

11. Ronald Takaki, *Iron Cages: Race and Culture in 19th-Century America* (New York: Oxford University Press, 1990 [orig. 1979]), p. 119.

12. Eugene Genovese, *Roll, Jordan, Roll: The World the Slaves Made* (New York: Pantheon, 1974).

13. Takaki, *Iron Cages,* p. 269.

14. Vicente L. Rafael, "White Love: Discipline, Surveillance, and Nationalist Resistance in the United States Colonization of the Philippines," in *Cultures of United States Imperialism,* ed. Amy Kaplan and Donald E. Pease (Durham, N.C.: Duke University Press, 1993), pp. 185–218.

15. Arif Dirlik, "The Asia-Pacific in Asian-American Perspective," in his *What Is in a Rim? Critical Perspectives on the Pacific Rim Idea* (Boulder, Colo.: Westview, 1993), p. 321. See also Frank Chin, "Come All Ye Asian American Writers of the Real and the Fake," in *The Big AIIIEEEEE! An Anthology of Chinese American and Japanese Literature,* ed. J. P. Chan, F. Chin, L. F. Inada, and S. Wong (New York: Meridian, 1991), pp. 1–93.

16. There are many African American public figures, accompanied by white "trophy" wives, who both manipulate and magnify their social power as *black* men. Even the short-lived "Black is beautiful" trend could not warrant such a gross generalization.

17. Ben R. Tong, "A Living Death Defended as the Legacy of a Superior Culture," *Amerasia Journal* 2 (fall 1974): 178–202. For a view of the debate over the imputed pathological schizophrenia in Asian American identity, see David Palumbo-Liu, *Asian/American: Historical Crossings of a Racial Frontier* (Stanford, Calif.: Stanford University Press, 1999), pp. 301–304.

18. My notion of refugee love should be distinguished from Gil Loescher and John A. Scanlan's "calculated kindness" (*Calculated Kindness: Refugees and America's Half-Open Door, 1945 to the Present* [New York: The Free Press, 1986]), a term they used to describe American policies toward refugees. They argue that American responses toward refugees have been shaped by political considerations, especially as they affected U.S. foreign-policy objectives regarding communist regimes. From the time of the 1965 immigration amendments, a pattern of double standards operated whereby refugees fleeing communist and communist-dominated lands were singled out for special attention, while policy chose "to ignore the claims of other refugees and to define suffering in rigid ideological terms," p. xviii.

19. Sau-ling Cynthia Wong, "Ethnicizing Gender: An Exploration of Sexuality as Sign in Chinese Immigrant Literature," in *Reading the Literatures of Asian America,* ed. Shirley Geok-lin Lim and Amy Ling (Philadelphia: Temple University Press, 1992), pp. 111–112.

20. See D. N. Kyriacou, D. Anglin, E. Taliaferro, S. Stone, et al., "Risk Factors for In-

jury to Women from Domestic Violence," *New England Journal of Medicine* 341.25 (Dec. 16, 1999): 1892–1898.

21. See Gordon, *Heroes of Their Own Lives*, p. 261. Her survey of social-workers' cases in early twentieth-century Boston reveals a direct link between wife abuse and violence against children among European immigrants. Married women "negotiated living with their husbands not as individuals but as mothers responsible for children," ibid.

22. Gordon, *Heroes of Their Own Lives*, pp. 4, 294–295. For a comparative study of the rise of middle-class social regulation in France in roughly the same era, see Jacques Donzelot, *The Policing of Families: Welfare versus the State* (London: Hutchinson, 1980).

23. Gordon, *Heroes of Their Own Lives*, p. 296.

24. Social workers identified Irish drinking and fighting behavior, along with the Italian father's patriarchal control over family members, as important causes of family violence—assumptions that Gordon minimized in her survey of cross-ethnic cases; see *Heroes of Their Own Lives*, p. 11.

25. Ruben G. Rumbaut and Kenji Ima, *The Adaptation of Southeast Asian Youth: A Comparative Study*, Final Report to the Office of Refugee Resettlement, U.S. Department of Health and Human Services, Family Support Administration (Washington, D.C.: Office of Refugee Resettlement, 1988), pp. 75–76.

26. Ibid.

27. Elizabeth Pleck, *Domestic Tyranny: The Making of American Social Policy against Family Violence, from Colonial Times to the Present* (New York: Oxford University Press, 1987), p. 185.

28. Pleck, *Domestic Tyranny*, pp. 5–10. Pleck notes that through most of the twentieth century, as compared to the late nineteenth, there was little public interest in domestic violence as a persistent social problem, because of the ideological domination of what she calls "the Family Ideal" of domestic privacy, conjugal and parental rights, and family stability. It was only in the seventies, when feminist advocates framed their fight against domestic abuse in terms of public-health concerns and interest in preserving the home, that legislation was passed to protect the rights of women and children in the family context and to provide federal funding for shelters and programs.

29. Asian Women's Shelter brochure, San Francisco.

30. Lois G. Forer, *Unequal Protection: Women, Children, and the Elderly in Court* (New York: W. W. Norton, 1991).

31. Pleck, *Domestic Tyranny*, p. 12.

32. Lenore E. Walker, *The Battered Woman* (New York: Harper & Row, 1979).

33. Carol Brown, "Mothers, Fathers, and Children: From Private to Public Patriarchy," in *Women and Revolution*, ed. L. Sargent (Boston: South End Press, 1981).

34. Gordon, *Heroes of Their Own Lives*, p. 299.

35. Brackette F. Williams, "Introduction: Mannish Women and Gender after the Act," in *Women out of Place: The Gender of Agency and the Race of Nationality* (New York: Routledge, 1996), pp. 19–20.

36. I address this point in Aihwa Ong, "Women out of China: Traveling Tales and Traveling Theories in Postcolonial Feminism," in *Women Writing Culture*, ed. Ruth

NOTES TO PAGES 168–189 *311*

Behar and Deborah Gordon (Berkeley: University of California Press, 1995), pp. 350–372.

CHAPTER 7

1. This point was made by Marjorie A. Muecke, "Trust, Abuse of Trust, and Mistrust among Cambodian Refugee Women: A Cultural Interpretation," in *Mistrusting Refugees,* ed. E. Valentine Daniel and John C. Knudsen (Berkeley: University of California Press, 1995), p. 39.
2. For a discussion of Cambodian American experiences with schools, see Nancy Smith-Hefner, *Khmer American: Identity and Moral Education in a Diasporic Community* (Berkeley: University of California Press, 1999), chap. 5.
3. Smith-Hefner, *Khmer American,* pp. 150–151.
4. Smith-Hefner, *Khmer American,* also identified family breakdown as happening primarily among people of rural origins, pp. 187–207.
5. See, for instance, Margery Wolf, *Women and Family in Taiwan* (Stanford, Calif.: Stanford University Press, 1972).
6. Nigel Parton, "Reconfiguring Child Welfare Practices: Risk, Advanced Liberalism, and the Government of Freedom," in *Reading Foucault for Social Work,* ed. Adrienne S. Chambon, Allan Irving, and Laura Epstein (New York: Columbia University Press, 1999), p. 111.
7. Parton, "Reconfiguring Child Welfare," pp. 122–123.
8. Smith-Hefner, *Khmer American,* pp. 174–177. For a greater elaboration on the subject of anxiety over the decline of "the virtuous woman" in Cambodian American communities, see Judy Ledgerwood, *Changing Khmer Conceptions of Gender: Women, Stories, and the Social Order,* Ph.D. diss., Cornell University (Ann Arbor, Mich.: University Microfilms, 1990).
9. Linda Stone and Nancy P. McKee, *Gender and Culture in America* (Upper Saddle River, N.J.: Prentice Hall, 1998), p. 54.
10. Stone and McKee, *Gender and Culture,* p. 55.
11. Susan Dwyer-Shick, "When May Culture Be a Legal Defense in American Courts?" paper presented at the annual meeting of the Law and Society Association, May 31–June 3, 1990.
12. *The Philadelphia Inquirer,* July 2, 1989.
13. Elizabeth Pleck, *Domestic Tyranny: The Making of American Social Policy against Family Violence, from Colonial Times to the Present* (New York: Oxford University Press, 1987), p. 202.
14. See Jacques Donzelot, *The Policing of Families: Welfare versus the State* (New York: Pantheon, 1979); Linda Gordon, *Heroes of Their Own Lives: The Politics and History of Family Violence* (New York: Penguin, 1988).
15. For a discussion of the clash between Cambodian notions of patron–clientelism and the abstract and practical methods of welfare bureaucracy, see Judy Ledgerwood, "Portrait of a Conflict: Exploring Changing Khmer-American Social and Political Relationships," *Journal of Refugee Studies* 3.2 (1990): 135–154.
16. Maggie Scarf, *Intimate Worlds: Life inside the Family* (New York: Random House, 1995), chap. 7.

17. Adam Savetsky, "Viet Parents, Teens Try to Bridge the Generation Gap," *Tenderloin Times*, Sept. 1990, 11.

CHAPTER 8

1. Although more Mormons are resisting the use of the term *temple* because it may set their sect apart from orthodox Christianity, the term, together with *the Mormon Church*, was commonly used by church members during my fieldwork. Recently, in an attempt to gain wider acceptance for Mormonism as a church within the Christian tradition, leaders of the faith have preferred to replace "the Mormon Church" or "the LDS Church" with "the Church of Jesus Christ" as a shorthand reference. See "Adapting 'Mormon' to Emphasize Christianity," *The New York Times*, February 19, 2001.

2. Although Mormons consider themselves part of Protestantism, other sects—such as Southern Baptist, Presbyterian—maintain that despite similar terms for theological concepts, the Mormons' distinctive beliefs and practices set them apart from Protestants.

3. Harold Bloom, *The American Religion: The Emergence of the Post-Christian Nation* (New York: Simon and Schuster, 1992).

4. Marvin Olasky, *The Tragedy of American Compassion* (Wheaton, Ill.: Crossway Books, 1995).

5. Tamar Gordon, "Staging Authenticities and Modernities at the Polynesian Cultural Center," paper presented at the meeting of the American Anthropological Association, Atlanta, November 30–December 3, 1994. In her provocative analysis of the Polynesian Cultural Center operated by Mormons, Gordon makes a case for viewing the church as "an alternative Western subgaze . . . that has harnessed techniques of modernity to promote a uniquely constructed and sacralized Polynesia."

6. Max Weber, "The Protestant Sects and the Spirit of Capitalism," in *From Max Weber: Essays in Sociology*, ed. H. H. Gerth and C. Wright Mills (New York: Oxford University Press), pp. 305–308.

7. For a modern history of the Mormon Church, see Richard N. Ostling and Joan K. Ostling, *Mormon America: The Power and the Promise* (San Francisco: HarperCollins, 2000).

8. John Hawkins, an anthropologist at Brigham Young University, maintains that the native concept is that wards are to be divided by linguistic preference and geographic location. Thus some wards unavoidably reproduce the racial distribution in space. He argues that in mature areas of Latter-Day Saints' experience, "you will find a relatively well-mixed racial/ethnic congregation, with persons of color in senior leadership" (e-mail to author, April 19, 2001). See also Fletcher Stack, "In Their Own Language: Should Ethnic Mormons Have Their Own Wards?" *Sunstone* (March 1998) (originally published in the *Salt Lake Tribune*, Dec. 6, 1997).

9. "New Prophecy Welcomes Blacks," *San Francisco Chronicle*, April 10, 1996.

10. Deborah Laake, *Secret Ceremonies: A Mormon Woman's Intimate Diary of Marriage and Beyond* (New York: Dell, 1993), pp. 38–39. Laake is estranged from the church, but here she cites a learning manual that is produced by the church. See

also J. Boyce, "Messages from the Manuals—Twelve Years Later," *Dialogue: A Journal of Mormon Thought* 27 (1984): 205–217.

11. Laake, *Secret Ceremonies,* pp. 39–40. Mormons believe in progress toward deification after death.

12. Gordon, "Staging Authenticities and Modernities."

13. Peter Steinfels, "Despite Growth, Mormons Find New Hurdles," *The New York Times,* Sept. 15, 1991, A1.

14. "Newspaper Calls Mormon Church an $8 Billion-Year Enterprise," *San Francisco Chronicle,* July 1, 1991, A5.

15. "Catholic Bishops Blast 'Coercion' of Hispanics by Mormons, Others," *San Francisco Chronicle,* Feb. 28, 1990, A2.

16. Richard Rodriguez, "Catholic Latin America, 'Born Again,'" *San Francisco Chronicle, This World Supplement,* Sept. 10, 1989, 18.

17. Gordon, "Staging Authenticities and Modernities."

18. Rodriguez, "Catholic Latin America."

19. Carol A. Mortland, "Khmer Buddhists in the United States: Ultimate Questions," in *Cambodian Culture since 1975: Homeland and Exile,* ed. May M. Ebihara, Carol A. Mortland, and Judy Ledgerwood (Ithaca, N.Y.: Cornell University Press, 1994), pp. 75–76.

20. Anthropological work has stressed that religious conversion can often be understood as a way to make sense of life experiences; see Peter G. Stromberg, "Ideological Language in the Transformation of Identity," *American Anthropologist* 92 (1990): 42–56.

21. Contemporary American televisual churches stress the acts of listening and speaking as part of the process of conversion; see Susan Harding, "Convicted by the Holy Spirit," *American Ethnologist* 14.1 (1987): 167–185.

22. Edward L. Schieffelin, "Evangelical Rhetoric and the Transformation of Traditional Culture in Papua New Guinea," *Comparative Studies in Society and History* (1981): 150, 154–155.

23. Hirokazu Miyazaki, "Faith and Its Fulfillment: Agency, Exchange, and the Fijian Aesthetics of Completion," *American Ethnologist* 27.1 (2000): 31–51.

24. E-mail communication from John Hawkins dated April 19, 2001. Hawkins maintains that at all other levels, leadership positions are open to qualified minorities, so that there are black bishops in the United States as well as "Hispanics, Asians and Polynesians in the various quorums of the Seventy." Overseas, there are Asian and Hispanic leaders acting as mission presidents and area presidents.

25. See Mary Ryan, *The Cradle of the Middle Class* (Cambridge: Cambridge University Press, 1982).

26. "The Awesome Power of Sex," *American Sociological Review,* 1955–1957.

27. Of course, cross-race dating and marriage also occur outside of Mormon contexts for women in dominated ethnic groups who might be seeking to marry hypergamously.

28. Gordon B. Hinckley, "A Proclamation to the World," message delivered at the meeting of the General Relief Society, The Church of Jesus Christ of Latter-Day Saints, Salt Lake City, Utah, September 23, 1995.

29. Professor Jackie Rainer, a historian at California State University, Sacramento,

was a leader of the oral-history project to gather stories from Southeast Asian immigrants in the Central Valley.

30. Rodriguez, "Catholic Latin America."

31. Weber, "Protestant Sects," pp. 312–313.

32. Robert Bellah, Anne Swidler, et al., *Habits of the Heart* (New York: Harper & Row, 1986).

33. Jill Mulvay Deer, "'Strengthen in Our Union': The Making of Mormon Sisterhood," in *Sisters in Spirit: Mormon Women in Historical and Cultural Perspective,* ed. Maureen U. Beecher and Lavina F. Anderson (Urbana: University of Illinois Press, 1987), pp. 198–199.

CHAPTER 9

1. Navi H. Te, "A Laborer's Story," *The New York Times,* Mar. 19, 1995.

2. See the accompanying letter by Leti Volpp and Laura Ho, "Look Also at Who Profits from Sweatshops," *The New York Times,* Mar. 19, 1995. For a study of Chinese immigrant labor contractors in the American underground economy, see Peter Kwong, *Forbidden Workers: Illegal Chinese Immigrants and American Labor* (New York: The New Press, 1997).

3. Ashley Dunn, "Southeast Asians Highly Dependent on Welfare in the U.S.," *The New York Times,* May 19, 1994, A17.

4. Dunn, "Southeast Asians," A19.

5. Frederick Rose, "Muddled Masses: The Growing Backlash against Immigration Includes Many Myths," *The Wall Street Journal,* April 26, 1995, A1.

6. See, e.g., Peter Brimelow, *Alien Nation: Common Sense about America's Immigration Disaster* (New York: Random House, 1995).

7. Nathan Glazer, "The Immigrants," *The New Republic* (special issue, Dec. 27, 1993): 18.

8. Glazer, "Immigrants," 16.

9. See social-work discourses reported in Linda Gordon, *Heroes of Their Own Lives: The Politics and History of Family Violence, Boston 1880–1960* (New York: Penguin, 1988).

10. See, e.g., Evelyn Nakano Glenn, *Issei, Nisei, War Bride: Three Generations of Japanese American Women in Domestic Service* (Philadelphia: Temple University Press, 1986).

11. See, e.g., Herbert J. Gans, *The Urban Villagers: Group and Class in the Life of Italian-Americans* (New York: The Free Press, 1962); Mirra Komorovsky, *Blue-Collar Marriage* (New York: Vintage, 1967); and Michael Burawoy, *Manufacturing Consent: Changes in the Labor Process under Monopoly Capitalism* (Chicago: University of Chicago Press, 1979).

12. Philippe Bourgois's *In Search of Respect: Selling Crack in El Barrio* (Cambridge: Cambridge University Press, 1996) is an ethnography of poor Puerto Rican immigrants, who often supplemented welfare checks with earnings in the drug trade. As happened with other poor minorities, such activities spawned gangs and violence.

13. See Barry Bluestone and Bennett Harrison, *The Deindustrialization of America* (New York: Basic Books, 1992).

14. Saskia Sassen, "Analytical Borderlands: Race, Gender and Representation in the New City," in *Race, Identity, and Citizenship: A Reader,* ed. Rodolfo D. Torres, Louis F. Miron, and Jonathan Xavier Inda (Malden, Mass.: Blackwell, 1999), pp. 363–364.

15. For other examples of Southeast Asian workers employed in irregular, low-paid work, see Janet E. Benson, "The Effects of Packinghouse Work on Southeast Asian Families," in *Newcomers in the Workplace: Immigrants and the Restructuring of the U.S. Economy,* ed. Louise Lamphere, Alex Stepick, and Guillermo Grenier (Philadelphia: Temple University Press, 1994), pp. 99–126.

16. A new report estimates a housing shortage of about 46,000 homes in Silicon Valley by the year 2010. See "San Jose Mayor Forms Housing Crisis Group," *San Francisco Chronicle,* Sept. 14, 2000.

17. Jason Ma, "BCBG Named in Sweatshop Suit," *AsianWeek,* June 4, 2000.

18. Karen J. Hossfeld, "Hiring Immigrant Women: Silicon Valley's 'Simple Solution,'" in *Women of Color in U.S. Society,* ed. Maxine B. Zinn and B. Thornton Dill (Philadelphia: Temple University Press, 1994), p. 65.

19. Janet Dang, "High Tech's Low Wages," *AsianWeek,* Dec. 23, 1999.

20. For a discussion of "ethnic enclaves" among immigrant Chinese in New York, see Kwong, *Forbidden Workers.*

21. California Penal Code, section 1.86.22[f]; cited in Marcus Hoover, "Where All the Madness Began: A Look at Gang History," May 28, 1999; http://pressenter .com/~dpedersn/ (downloaded July 9, 2001).

22. I thank Brackette Williams for pointing out to me the complex and multifaceted nature of African American gang activities.

23. This control of the drug trade may have resulted from the CIA selling crack cocaine to the Bloods and the Crips in order to support the Contra war in Nicaragua; see the research of Gary Webb of *The San Jose Mercury News,* as recounted on National Public Radio's *Democracy Now!* edition of Sept. 16, 1996.

24. Bill Wallace, "Invaders Part of Flourishing Gang Scene," *San Francisco Chronicle,* Feb. 6, 1996.

25. In the sense of this tendency toward low-grade criminal activity and the emphasis on hanging out with other males, Cambodian American gangs are more like the street-corner society found among Italian working-class immigrants in the 1930s; see William Foote Whyte, *Street Corner Society,* 2d ed. (Chicago: University of Chicago Press, 1955).

26. Donna Rosenthal, "Iggy Chinn's Last Patrol," *San Francisco Examiner, Image Magazine,* Mar. 31, 1991, 12–21.

27. Recently, a multiethnic Asian youth center, based on the old Cambodian New Generation aid organization, began to focus on a mentoring program to reach out to "problem youths." Khmer temples in various cities have also struggled to serve the younger generation. See, e.g., Marvin Howe, "New York's Cambodians Pull Together in Struggle to Adjust to a New Life," *The New York Times,* July 25, 1985.

28. Whyte, *Street Corner Society.*

29. "What Is a Street Gang?" American Street Gangs Web site, http://pressenter .com/~dpedersn/ (downloaded July 9, 2001).

30. Paul Willis, *Common Work* (Boulder, Colo.: Westview, 1990), pp. 15–16, 20.

316 NOTES TO PAGES 241-254

31. Zygmunt Bauman, *Globalization: The Human Consequences* (New York: Columbia University Press, 1998), p. 126.

32. The number of independent doughnut shops operated by Cambodian Americans was estimated to be between 2,450 and 5,000 in California. As a result of the Cambodian American entry into the doughnut business and of competition from fast-food outlets, by the late 1980s the Winchell's chain had shrunk from 450 to 120 shops in the state; see Jonathan Kaufman, "How Cambodians Came to Control California Doughnuts," *The Wall Street Journal*, Feb. 22, 1995.

33. John Flinn, "Success the Old-Fashioned Way," *San Francisco Chronicle*, April 30, 1995.

34. William E. Willmott, *The Chinese in Cambodia* (Vancouver, B.C.: University of British Columbia Publications Center, 1967).

35. Debbi Gardiner, "Donuts Anyone?" *AsianWeek*, June 22, 2000, p. 18.

36. Marilyn Strathern, "New Economic Forms: A Report," in her *Property, Substance and Effect* (London: The Athlone Press, 1999), pp. 89–116.

37. Janet Dang, "A Hand for Vietnamese Americans," *AsianWeek*, Nov. 29, 1999, pp. 13–14.

38. Kaufman, "How Cambodians."

39. Ibid.

40. Jason DeParle, "Bold Effort Leaves Much Unchanged for the Poor," *The New York Times*, Dec. 30, 1999, A1. Inquiries among welfare recipients in Wisconsin revealed that they considered the workfare requirement of a thirty-hour week to be "insulting" for welfare recipients, because women formerly on welfare could make more if they worked full-time at a regular job. The crux of the problem was getting employed in steady jobs and finding child-care support, so that mothers could go out to work.

41. Paula Bock, "Phnom Penh Connections," *The Seattle Times*, July 1, 1999.

42. Kathryn A. Poethig, *Ambivalence Moralities: Cambodian Americans and Dual Citizenship in Phnom Penh*, Ph.D. diss., The Graduate Theological Union, 1997.

43. Poethig, *Ambivalence Moralities*, pp. 174–177, 190–191, 205–206.

CHAPTER 10

1. Shiva Naipaul, "Journey to Nowhere," in *West of the West: Imagining California*, ed. Leonard Michaels, David Reid, and Raquel Scherr (New York: Harper Perennial, 1989), p. 282; excerpted from Shiva Naipaul, *Journey to Nowhere: A New World Tragedy* (New York: Simon & Schuster, 1980).

2. For a discussion of the Pacific Rim as a Euro-American concept of regional domination, see Arif Dirlik, "Introduction: Pacific Contradictions," in his *What Is in a Rim? Critical Perspectives on the Pacific Region Idea*, 2d ed. (Lanham, Md.: Rowman and Littlefield, 1998), pp. 3–14.

3. Patrick Reddy, "Immigrants and the New California," *San Francisco Chronicle*, Nov. 17, 1996, A21. Patrick Reddy is a pollster.

4. Brackette Williams, "The Symbolics of Ethnic Historical Traditions and 'Suffering': Some Implications for the Doctrine of Equal Citizenship in the United States," unpublished paper (October 1995).

5. See Wendy Brown, *States of Injury: Power and Freedom in Late Modernity* (Minneapolis: University of Minnesota Press, 1995).

6. Ronald Takaki, *Strangers from a Different Shore: A History of Asian Americans* (Boston: Little, Brown, 1989), pp. 11–16.

7. Sucheng Chan, *Asian Americans: An Interpretive History* (Boston: Twayne, 1991), p. 181.

8. Takaki's case is best made in his earlier powerful book, *Iron Cages: Race and Culture in 19th-Century America* (New York: Oxford University Press, 1990 [orig. 1979]).

9. Steven A. Chin, "Recalling 25 Years of Fight for Asian Equality," *San Francisco Examiner,* May 1, 1994, B1.

10. Robert Blauner, *Racial Oppression in America* (New York: Harper & Row, 1976); Yen Le Espiritu, *Asian American Panethnicity: Bridging Institutions and Identities* (Philadelphia: Temple University Press, 1992).

11. David Palumbo-Liu, *Asian/American: Historical Crossings of a Racial Frontier* (Stanford, Calif.: Stanford University Press, 1999).

12. Le Espiritu, *Asian American Panethnicity.*

13. For studies of the very specific ways in which later different Asian American communities struggled with their ethnic identity, see Victor G. Nee and Brett de Bary Nee, *Longtime Californ': A Documentary Study of an American Chinatown* (Berkeley: University of California Press, 1972); Sylvia J. Yanagisako, *Transforming the Past: Tradition and Kinship among Japanese Americans* (Stanford, Calif.: Stanford University Press, 1985); and Yasuko I. Takesawa, *Breaking the Silence: Redress and Japanese American Ethnicity* (Ithaca, N.Y.: Cornell University Press, 1995).

14. Lisa Lowe, *Immigrant Acts* (Durham, N.C.: Duke University Press, 1996).

15. Le Espiritu, *Asian American Panethnicity,* p. 164.

16. The number of Asian Americans has increased from 1.5 million in 1970 to just under 11 million in 2000, or about 4 percent of the total population in the country; see "Finding Their Voice," *Far Eastern Economic Review* (Dec. 7, 2000): 88.

17. K. Anthony Appiah, "Identity, Authenticity, Survival: Multicultural Societies and Social Reproduction," in *Multiculturalism: Examining the Politics of Recognition,* ed. Amy Gutmann (Princeton, N.J.: Princeton University Press, 1994), p. 163.

18. For a criticism of this mode of orientalism, see Sylvia J. Yanagisako, "Transforming Orientalism: Gender, Nationality, and Class in Asian American Studies," in *Naturalizing Power,* ed. Sylvia J. Yanagisako and Carol Delaney (Stanford, Calif.: Stanford University Press, 1993).

19. Nathan Caplan, "The Boat People Belong Here," *The New York Times,* July 22, 1989.

20. Judy K. Kim, "New York," *The New York Times,* June 3, 1996.

21. The fact that Dr. Wen Ho Lee is a naturalized citizen means that Asian Americanism has now dropped its previous exclusion of foreign-born Americans.

22. James Glanz, "Asian-American Scholars Call for Boycott of Labs," *The New York Times,* May 31, 2000, A23.

23. See, e.g., Karen T. Leonard, *Making Ethnic Choices: California's Punjabi Mexican Americans* (Philadelphia: Temple University Press, 1995).

24. *National community of fate* denotes a political community that is defined in terms

of the peoples within a delimited territory. See David Held, Anthony McGrew, David Goldblatt, and Jonathan Perraton, *Global Transformations: Politics, Economics, and Culture* (Stanford: Stanford University Press, 1999), p. 29.

25. This was the reaction of Asian American movement leaders during the siegelike atmosphere of the Asian campaign-finance crisis during the Bill Clinton administration. The irony of course is that many of these leaders are themselves foreign-born.

26. Richard Rodriguez, "Immigrants Threaten California's Myth about Itself," *Asian-Week*, Sept. 10, 1993, 4.

27. Mark Baldassare, *California in the New Millennium* (San Francisco: Public Policy Institute of California, 2000), quoted in "New Demographics Changing Everything," *San Francisco Chronicle*, Aug. 31, 2000, 1.

28. Boy Luthje, "Race and Ethnicity in 'Post-Fordist' Production Networks: Silicon Valley and the Global Information Technology Industry," unpublished paper, Dept. of Social Sciences, University of Frankfurt, 1998.

29. Luthje, "Race and Ethnicity." This argument about the political character of much of the new immigration has been made by Hing B. Ong and R. Lee, eds., *The State of Asian Pacific America: Reframing the Immigration Debate* (Los Angeles: LEAP Asian Pacific American Public Policy Institute / UCLA Asian American Studies Center, 1996).

30. Karen Breslau, "Tomorrowland, Today," *Newsweek* (Asian edition, Sept. 18, 2000): 52–53.

31. AnnaLee Saxenian, *Silicon Valley's New Immigrant Entrepreneurs* (San Francisco: Public Policy Institute of California, 1999).

32. This statistic was cited in an article on female CEOs, anticipating a similar future for them; see Patricia Sellers, "The 50 Most Powerful Women in Business," *Fortune* (Oct. 16, 2000): 134.

33. Carol Emert, "Boundless Ambition: JoMei Chang," *San Francisco Chronicle*, Sept. 9, 2001.

34. E. J.-W. Park, "Asians Matter: Asian American Entrepreneurs in the Silicon Valley High Technology Industry," in *State of Asian Pacific America*, ed. Ong and Lee.

35. Saxenian, *Silicon Valley's New Immigrant Entrepreneurs*.

36. Pehong Chen's story is reported in Breslau, "Tomorrowland, Today."

37. Saxenian, *Silicon Valley's New Immigrant Entrepreneurs*.

38. Breslau, "Tomorrowland, Today."

39. "A New California," *San Francisco Examiner*, Feb. 20, 2000.

40. "Ambiguity Remains despite Changes in H-1 Program," *San Francisco Chronicle*, Sept. 21, 2000.

41. Aihwa Ong, "The Techno-Migrants," in *Global America*, ed. Ulrich Beck, Rainer Winter, and Natan Sznaider (Liverpool: University of Liverpool Press, 2003).

42. "Law Shouldn't Allow High-Tech Industry to Indenture Immigrants," *San Francisco Chronicle*, Sept. 9, 2000; and "Question of Fraud: Silicon Valley Pushes for More Foreign Workers despite Federal Probes," *San Francisco Chronicle*, Sept. 21, 2000.

43. AnnaLee Saxenian, personal communication.

44. See Aihwa Ong, *Spirits of Resistance and Capitalist Discipline: Factory Women in Malaysia* (Albany: State University of New York Press, 1987).

45. Luthje, "Race and Ethnicity," p. 13.
46. Luthje, "Race and Ethnicity," pp. 3, 16–18.
47. For an account of Hispanic farm labor, see Leo Chavez, *Shadowed Lives: Undocumented Immigrants in American Society* (Fort Worth, Tex.: Harcourt Brace Jovanovich, 1992).
48. Miranda Ewell and K. Oanh Ha, "Multi-Billion-Dollar Industry at the Heart of Valley Growth," *San Jose Mercury News,* posted July 3, 1999, on www.siliconvalley.com.
49. Solectron has grown into a global manufacturing network—employing more than twenty-five thousand in low-cost sites around the world—that provides a range of services spanning the entire production chain. In 1998, this leading original-equipment manufacturer made $5 billion in sales. Contract manufacturing already accounts for 20 percent of the $500 billion electronics equipment market, and is expected to account for more than 60 percent of the market in the next decade. See Traci Hukill, "When Unions Attempt to Organize Silicon Valley's Growing Vietnamese Workforce, They Find Custom, Language, and History Stand in the Way," *Metro, Silicon Valley's Weekly Newspaper,* Sept. 16–22, 1999.
50. The United States is the only liberal democratic country in which employers need not demonstrate cause to fire an employee; see Ruth Colker, *American Law in the Age of Hypercapitalism* (New York: New York University Press, 1998), p. 184.
51. Hukill, "When Unions Attempt."
52. This description of homework among Vietnamese immigrants is taken from Miranda Ewell and K. Oanh Ha, "Long Nights and Low Wages," and "Agencies Probing Piecework," *San Jose Mercury News,* July 8, 1999.
53. Ewell and Ha, "Agencies Probing Piecework."
54. Janet Dang, "High Tech's Low Wages," *AsianWeek,* Dec. 23, 1999.
55. Colker, *American Law,* pp. xi, 193.
56. Both quotes are from Hukill, "When Unions Attempt."
57. See Ong, *Spirits of Resistance.*
58. Colker, *American Law.*
59. "Letters" following Ewell and Ha, "Agencies Probing Piecework," www.siliconvalley.com (July 8, 1999).
60. Nikolas Rose, "Inventiveness in Politics," *Economy and Society* 28.3 (1999): 467–493. Karl Marx and Friedrich Engels in *The Communist Manifesto* predicted this outcome—that as capital overtakes society around the world, it will play an overwhelming role in determining citizenship.
61. David Stark, "Value, Values, and Valuation: Work and Worth in the New Economy," paper presented at the Social Science Research Council conference on "The New Economy," Emory University, Atlanta, April 13–14, 2001.
62. Yu Zhou and Yen-Fen Tseng, "Regrounding the 'Ungrounded Empires': Geographic Conditions of Transnationalism," *Global Networks* 2 (2001).
63. As China looms large in American economic calculations, Americans are increasingly realizing that many market activities conducted in Mandarin will have to be penetrated with the help of bilingual agents.
64. George J. Borjas, *Heaven's Door: Immigration Policy and the American Economy* (Princeton, N.J.: Princeton University Press, 2000). For a recent critique and an argument that such north–south migrations are an index of the integration of

the Western Hemisphere, see Susanne Jonas and Susie Dod Thomas, eds., *Immigration: A Civil Rights Issue for the Americas* (Wilmington, Del.: Scholarly Resources, 1999).

65. See Aihwa Ong, *Flexible Citizenship: The Cultural Logics of Transnationality* (Durham, N.C.: Duke University Press, 1999), pp. 119–130.

66. Ralph Waldo Emerson, "On Self-Reliance," in *Selected Essays* (Harmondsworth: Penguin, 1985), pp. 175–204.

67. Christopher Newfield, *The Emerson Effect: Individualism and Submission in America* (Chicago: University of Chicago Press, 1996), pp. 199–200.

68. In *The Work of Nations* (New York: Vintage, 1991), Robert Reich develops the idea of a "collective entrepreneurship" that exerts economic governance through professionals he calls symbolic analysts; he rejects the idea that private and state regulation have the capacity to control the dispersed world markets. This view of economic governance excludes the vast majority of workers from having a say in their employment conditions.

69. Newfield, *Emerson Effect*, pp. 4–7. As mentioned earlier, Colker, in *American Law*, made a similar observation about the relative absence in America of state regulation of business interests compared to other capitalist countries, such as Australia and Canada.

70. Ong, *Flexible Citizenship*.

71. Newfield, *Emerson Effect*, makes this point about the liberal sensibility of the American managerial and professional middle classes, pp. 12–13.

72. On the East Coast, subethnic Chinese men from Fuzhou along with immigrant female garment workers are brutally exploited as debt migrants and workers in hidden Asian-run enterprises; see Peter Kwong, *Forbidden Workers: Illegal Chinese Immigrants and American Labor* (New York: The New Press, 1997); and Ko-lin Chin, *Smuggled Chinese* (Philadelphia: Temple University Press, 1999).

73. Karl Polyani, *The Great Transformation: The Political and Economic Origins of Our Time* (Boston: Beacon Press, 1957).

74. See Brian Turner, "Outline of a Theory of Citizenship," in *Dimensions of Radical Democracy*, ed. Chantal Mouffe (New York: Verso, 1995), pp. 33–62.

75. Gosta Esping-Anderson, *The Three Worlds of Welfare Capitalism* (Princeton, N.J.: Princeton University Press, 1990), p. 181.

76. This point was made by Robert Skidelsky in "What Makes the World Go Round?" review of *The Cash Nexus* by Niall Ferguson, in *The New York Review of Books*, Aug. 9, 2001, 46.

77. Esping-Anderson, *Three Worlds*, p. 207.

78. Esping-Anderson, *Three Worlds*, pp. 226, 228.

79. Peter Kwong, "Forbidden Workers and the U.S. Labor Movement: Fuzhounese in New York City," *Critical Asian Studies* 34.1 (2002). See also idem, *Forbidden Workers*.

80. Evelyn Hu-DeHart, "Introduction," in her *Across the Pacific: Asian Americans and Globalization* (Philadelphia: Temple University Press, 1999).

81. Robert Gooding-Williams, "Introduction: On Being Stuck," in his *Reading Rodney King, Reading Urban Uprising* (New York: Routledge, 1993).

82. Dorothee Schneider, "Symbolic Citizenship, Nationalism, and the Distant State:

The United States Congress in the 1996 Debate on Immigration Reform," *Citizenship Studies* 4.3 (2000): 255–273.

AFTERWORD

1. Goldman Sachs advertisement in *The New York Times,* Sept. 17, 2001, B9.

2. Richard W. Stevenson, "Aftermath: The Prospect of a War without a Wartime Boom," *The New York Times,* Sept. 23, 2001.

3. This term has repeatedly been used against immigrants by a member of the California Coalition for Immigration Reform. As Mexican workers spread to the suburbs in places such as Long Island, New York, housewives have called them criminals and rapists. Recently, two people lured by the promise of work were severely beaten up: Al Baker, "An Unlikely Voice in the Immigration Debate," *The New York Times,* July 6, 2001.

4. Max Weber, *The Protestant Ethic and the Spirit of Capitalism,* 2d ed. (Los Angeles: Roxbury, 1998), p. 264.

5. Gilles Deleuze and Felix Guattari, *A Thousand Plateaus: Capitalism and Schizophrenia,* trans. Brian Massumi (Minneapolis: University of Minnesota Press, 1987), pp. 503–504.

6. Barry Bluestone and Bennett Harrison, *The Deindustrialization of America* (New York: Basic Books, 1982).

7. Gilles Deleuze, "Postscript on Societies of Control," *October* 59 (winter 1991): 3–7.

8. See Amnesty International report by William F. Schulz, March 14, 2002: http://www.amnesty-usa.org/news/2002/usa03142002_2.html.

9. "Long Resistant, Police Now Start Embracing Immigration Enforcement," *The New York Times,* March 15, 2002.

10. Chantal Mouffe, "Preface: Democratic Politics Today," in *Dimensions of Radical Democracy,* ed. Chantal Mouffe (London: Verso, 1992), pp. 11–13.

11. Michael Walzer, *Spheres of Justice: A Defense of Pluralism and Equality* (New York: Basic Books, 1983), p. 281.

12. The working concept of moral economy I use here was originally conceived by James C. Scott, *The Moral Economy of the Peasant* (New Haven, Conn.: Yale University Press, 1976).

13. Walzer, *Spheres of Justice.*

INDEX

Aaronic Priesthood, 199
Abramovitz, Mimi, 144
ach tunsiy, 110
adversity, community of, 254–59
AFDC (Aid to Families with Dependent Children), 63, 87, 95, 136, 137; gender dynamics and, 147–53; nuclear family unit and, 144; unwed mothers and, 139–40; working poor and, 125, 128–29, 132–33, 307n15
Afghan refugees, 81, 84, 86, 127
African American gangs, 234–35, 238, 240, 315n22
African Americans, xvii–xviii, 3; Cambodian refugees and, 106, 123; gender fracture and, 136, 137, 307n13, 307n19; Mormonism and, 198, 199–200; racist love and, 146, 309n16; as underclass, 13, 76–77, 84, 86, 128; welfare state and, 308–9n8
African immigrants, 81, 95
Agamben, Giorgio, 27, 40, 121
Agent Orange, 96
agrarian utopia, 18, 41, 44
Aid to Families with Dependent Children. *See* AFDC
Alcoholics Anonymous, 163
Alger, Horatio, 231
All Our Kin (Stack), 308–9n8
American Citizenship (Shklar), 3
American Red Cross (ARC), 54, 56
ancestral spirits, 120, 210, 306n78

Angkar Padevat, 18, 29, 40–41, 46, 54, 58, 91
Angkor Wat, 18, *31*, 31–32, 34, 39, 169, 210, 219
anti-Americanism, 28
anti-communism, 80–81
anti-immigrant sentiments, 4, 81–83, 89, 247
Apple Computer, 263
Aryan Nation, 240
Asian Americanism, 254–59, 317n13, 317n21
Asian Americans, 2, 102, 117; globalization and, 266–70; Mormonism and, 198–200, 312n5, 313n24; racist love and, 146, 309n17
Asian Americans: An Interpretive History (Chan), 254
Asian BoyZ (ABZ), 238
Asian clinics. *See* refugee clinics
Asian GirlZ (AGZ), 237
Asian immigrants, xii, 81, 84–87, 95, 99, 131, 259–68
Asian Street Walkers, 236
authority, male. *See* male authority
authority figures, 112, 115–16
autonomy, 9, 61–64, 144, 146–47, 175, 185; Mormonism and, 218–22

Bach, Robert, 126
Baldassare, Mark, 259
bang, 238

323

premarital sex, 138–40, 173, 178, 224
Preng, Mrs., 151
Presbyterian Church, 219
prescription drugs. *See* drug therapy
preventive medicine, 113–15
primitivity, xvi, 13–14, 73, 96
prostitution, 53, 63, 73, 213
Protestantism, 8, 195–96, 201, 202, 206,
    214–15, 217–20
proxy baptism, 208, 220
pseudonyms, 291n2
psychology, immigrant, 98–99
PTSD (post-traumatic stress disorder), 96,
    99–101, 104, 119, 150
puberty rites, 37–38, 214, 294n40
public assistance. *See* welfare services
public health. *See* medical care
public housing, 123, 137, 139, 151, 185
public/private boundaries, 146–47
Puerto Ricans, 78, 314n12
Puth, 40–41, 294–95n48

Quorum of the Twelve Apostles, 198, 211

Race and Manifest Destiny (Horsman), 71
racial bipolarism, xvii–xviii, 10–14, 71–73,
    298n9; Asian Americanism and, 259;
    globalization and, 266–70, 320n72;
    Mormonism and, 210–14. *See also*
    ethno-racialization
racial profiling, 258
racial subjectivity, 227
racist love, 146
Rafael, Vicente, 146
Rainer, Jackie, 215, 313–14n29
Randy Yu's doughnut shop, *242*, 242–45
rape, 46, 47, 53, 61–62, 113
Reagan administration, 100, 270
Reaganomics, 144, 270
realpolitik, 50–51
reciprocity, xvi, 32, 64, 297n49; Mormonism
    and, 204, 206–7
reclassifications, 43–47, 257
Reddy, Patrick, 253
Refugee Act (1980), 83, 85, 87
refugee camps. *See* border camps
Refugee Cash Assistance (RCA), 87, 131,
    132
refugee clinics, 94–95, 98, 101–3, 108,
    113–15, 118–21, 157, 184–85

Refugee Employment Social Services, 125
refugee exodus, 48–51, 295–96n6
refugee love, 145–47, 165, 309n18
refugee status: in border camps, 53–54,
    58–59, 297n35; in U.S., 69–70, 78–83,
    84; Vietnamese invasion and, 50–51
refugee studies, 26–28, 78–79, 292n8,
    300n48
refugee training, 83–84
Reich, Robert, 320n68
reincarnation, 208–9, 210
relief agencies. *See* volags (voluntary
    agencies)
Relief Society, 199
relief workers, 52–53, 56, 57, 59, 296n9
religion, national, 31, 39–40
Republican Party, 197
resettlement, 58, 83–90, 297n35, 302n80
resistance to biomedicine, 114, 117, 118
respect, parental, 170–71
RESS (Refugee Employment Social Ser-
    vices), 125
Revolutionary Organization. *See* Angkar
    Padevat
risk management in child welfare, 175–78
Rita, 222, 225–26
rites of passage, 60, 217
Rodriguez, Richard, 217, 259
Roediger, David R., 71
Rosaldo, Renato, 5
Rose, Nikolas, 16, 266
Rumbaut, Ruben G., 4, 98
runaway children, 180–90
Russian refugees, 116

Sacks, Karen, 72
Said, Edward, 72
Saloth Sar. *See* Pol Pot
Salvadoran immigrants, 181–82
Samoans, 198
Sang, Phauly, 55, 122, 131, 152, 173, 179,
    246–47
sangha, 30–32, 40
San Jose Mercury News, 264, 265
Santa Clara Center for Occupational Safety
    and Health, 264
sasenaa-jiet, 31
Sassen, Saskia, 231
Sau-ling, Cynthia Wong, 147
"savages," 281, 321n3

Compositor: Integrated Composition Systems, Inc.
Text and display: Baskerville
Printer and binder: Malloy Lithographing, Inc.